Prussia and the
Seven Years' War 1756–1763

FRIEDRICH II

Prussia and the
Seven Years' War 1756-1763

Johann Wilhelm von Archenholz
Translated from the Original German by F. A. Catty

LEONAUR

Prussia and the Seven Years' War 1756-1763
by Johann Wilhelm von Archenholz
Translated from the Original German by F. A. Catty

FIRST EDITION

Leonaur is an imprint of Oakpast Ltd
Copyright in this form © 2016 Oakpast Ltd

ISBN: 978-1-78282-533-3 (hardcover)
ISBN: 978-1-78282-534-0 (softcover)

http://www.leonaur.com

Publisher's Notes

Contents

Chapter 1: Causes of the War

After a long and tedious war the treaty of Aix la Chapelle, 1668, had re-established the tranquillity of Europe. The advantages of peace were beginning to be felt, and the renewal of hostilities appeared improbable for many years to come. Nevertheless the great powers of Europe were never less peaceably inclined than at this time, and never was more zeal displayed, than in the efforts of the different Cabinets to renew the horrors of war. And they succeeded. Alliances were formed, based not upon the principles of good state policy, but dictated by private feeling. The desire of making conquests gave way to the wish of satisfying the passions of revenge and hatred.

Two princesses, who at this time governed in their own right large populations, considered themselves injured by a monarch upon whom all eyes were now turned, who, crowned with laurels, had already terminated two wars, the great powers of whose mind caused universal astonishment, and whose virtues as a monarch made him an example for kings. The deepest plans were laid in order to humiliate this prince or rather to annihilate his political existence; and thus began one of the most extraordinary wars that ever devastated the world; whether it be considered from the numbers of troops of different nations and languages which composed the armies, the astonishing inequality of the powers engaged, the commanders and their deeds, the application of the improved science of war, the bloody battles, the sieges and the naval combats, or by its remarkable occurrences and its extent by land and sea.

The Empress Maria Theresa could ill brook the loss of the territory of the beautiful and populous Silesia, which Frederic the Second, King of Prussia, had conquered immediately after his accession to the throne, and to which he had established his right both at the peace of Breslau and at that of Dresden. She had been forced to resign this province to a conqueror, who from the small extent of his dominions had hitherto not been feared, and whose family had only been for the last two generations admitted into the circle of the crowned heads of Europe; but after Theresa's accession he was the first of her crowned enemies who took up arms against her, had made unexpected demands, and established his right by five different victories.

The value of this loss was first discovered when it was in the hands of Frederic, who knew how to turn to his own advantage its fertility and the industry of its inhabitants. But it appeared an easy matter to obtain possession of it again, by means of a powerful coalition, and Elizabeth, Empress of Russia, who considered herself traduced in her private character by some expressions of Frederic, was the first to join the alliance; Augustus the Third, King of Poland and Elector of Saxony, who had already been driven out of his capital by his powerful neighbour, and who hoped by his defeat to strengthen himself, and acquire fresh territory, followed her example, and renewed the treaty which he had previously made with Austria in 1745. At last Louis the XV., King of France, increased the number of Prussia's powerful enemies, and by means of subsidies induced Sweden to do the same.

The alliance of Austria with France which excited the astonishment of the whole world, and was considered as a master stroke of diplomacy, was in fact the effect of circumstances! For although France was much annoyed at the recent alliance between England and Prussia, and Count Kaunitz the Imperial ambassador in Paris had for some years been paving the way towards an alliance between the courts of Versailles and Vienna, still France was not really anxious to destroy the power of the King of Prussia.

The principal efforts of this court were directed against England, and the desire of gaining possession of Hanover was caused by the wish to carry out deeper plans in America. By this treaty with Austria, France had the privilege of sending troops into Germany, and promised to assist the empress by sending 24,000 auxiliary troops. This number was however increased to 180,000 in consequences of new projects, intrigues and the occurrences of the war.

This extraordinary and powerful coalition of such great powers against a young monarch was not formed from the important considerations of state policy, but by court intrigue; and for some centuries without parallel, was unworthy of an enlightened age. The great alliance formed in the 16th century and known by the name of the league of Cambray, against the then powerful and warlike republic of Venice, could not be compared with this; neither could that of so many of the European Powers against Louis the XIV., and more especially in the latter, in which the alliance was formed against the most powerful empire of the world. The Empress Theresa at the time of her greatest need in her first war had many resources left. In the midst of her enemies and with the loss of whole provinces she placed her reliance upon Hungary with its rich gold mines and courageous people; upon English soldiers, ships and money; rich and powerful resources which did not deceive her hopes.

A pretext for the war was wanting in Vienna, but one was easily found in the trifling dispute which existed between the King of Prussia and the Duke of Mecklenburg-Schwerin, respecting the levying his troops. Frederic availed himself in this quarrel of certain rights of his house, which he made good by means of his power. Austria called this a breach of the treaty of Westphalia, and spoke of rousing up all the powers who had guaranteed it. This was the outward and plausible excuse that was given to the secret treaty of spoliation, by which these mighty powers had determined on the dividing among themselves, the territories of a monarch not so powerful; which induced the wits of the day to say, that the war was undertaken half through precaution and half from speculation.

The overthrow of Frederic would have been unavoidable, had he not gained timely information of the alliance by means of the treachery of a Saxon secretary of the name of Mentzal, who handed over to the Prussian ambassador Malzahn in Dresden, the originals of the secret negotiations that he might take copies of them. The ambassador had false keys made in Berlin for the closets in which these documents were kept. Never was treachery more beneficial to a whole country, blessed as was Prussia with a wise and benevolent king, who, without being in the least aware of it, was on the point of seeing the destruction of his improving dominions.

The nature of his kingdom consisting of widely dispersed and undefended provinces, and his feeling of security, invited the allies to commence a campaign, which promised none of the usual impediments of warfare, but a succession of easy victories. The timely discovery of their political projects diminished greatly the danger of a prince who was prepared for war, in a time of peace, in a manner as yet unheard of in Europe, and who possessing the highest talents as a general, had an army of disciplined and tried soldiers 160,000 strong and a well filled treasury at his disposal.

His great mind knew how to make the most of these advantages, and as the court of Vienna refused to give him assurances of their peaceable intentions in spite of the reiterated representations of his ambassador Klinggräf and his informing them of the discovery of the secret treaty, he determined to be beforehand with his enemies, and to be the first to commence hostilities. Frederic had no other means of safety or of diminishing the threatened danger but by being the first to seek it.

The allies had hardly began their preparations for war; money was wanting and the troops destined for the war were for the most part in their quarters, from the Pyrenees to the Caspian Sea, when the King of Prussia in the month of August 1756 marched forth from his camp like a giant, at the head of 60,000 men, and invaded Saxony. The possession of this country was absolutely necessary to him in order to make a descent upon Bohemia, and by its acquisition he gained an other great advantage, the command of the Elb. All the troops re- treated in haste, and the important towns of Wittenberg, Leipsic and Torgau fell into his power without resistance.

This sudden step was accompanied by a manifesto for his justifica- tion, drawn up by Frederic himself and by a friendly explanation on the part of his ambassador at the court of Saxony, of the necessity of his march through that country into Bohemia. He had no ally but the King of England George the II., who anxious about his electorate of Hanover, had formed an alliance with Frederic, but which promised only to be of advantage at a distant period. The safety of the Prus- sian monarch depended entirely on the rapidity and the impression made by his operations. The march upon Saxony was masterly, not only from the discipline observed throughout, but also from the skil- ful direction of the troops. The army marched in three columns under the command of the king, the Duke Ferdinand of Brunswick and the Duke of Bevern, with orders to concentrate in the neighbourhood of Dresden.

As soon as the first intelligence of the march of the army reached the court of Saxony, the greatest excitement prevailed and secret councils were held, at which Count Brühl presided. This minister, whose greatness did not consist so much in being a deep politician as in the art of leading his king and living in kingly style, possessed the talent of governing to such an extent, that he is perhaps the only instance in history of a man being the favourite of two kings, father and son, of opposite characters and opinions.

In addition to this, he had the all important title of prime minister. He hated the King of Prussia, who, on his accession, had endeavoured to gain him over to his interests, but in vain, and had wished to procure for him the dignity of prince from the Emperor Charles VII., which the minister would have been glad to obtain by any other means, but would not accept, offered through the intervention of Frederic. This mutual hatred continued to grow, fostered on one side by rancour and the want of power of injuring, and on the other by power, talent and an advancing and victorious army.

They were so little prepared for war in Saxony, that Brühl had not even thought of bringing up the regiments which were in Poland. He had also a short time previously reduced the army in order to supply means for his own luxuries. The magazines were empty, and there was a deficiency of all the necessaries for an army. In this dangerous position of affairs the most unwise plan was pursued. The Saxon troops were drawn together in the greatest haste, forming an army of 17,000 men, and encamped on the Bohemian frontier, not far from Pirna. The camp was supported by the Elb which at this place rushes with impetuosity between rocky banks, and makes a bend near the fortress of Königstein and Fort Sonnenstein, and was almost entirely encompassed by hills and a range of steep rocks. Nature had made this position remarkably strong, and art did what was required to make it impregnable.

The position would have been well chosen, had the intention been to prevent the Austrians from entering Saxony, but against the Prussians it was useless and Dresden and the whole electorate fell into their hands m consequence of this step. The extent of the camp was too great for the Saxon Army, and they were forced to increase the defences by outworks, redoubts and palisades, for which the woods on the neighbouring hills provided the materials. But they thought only of defending themselves from the attacks of the Prussians, and forgot a far more dreadful enemy, one who had attacked and dispersed so many armies, had neutralised the effects of victories, and put a stop to the most tedious wars.

Hunger, with the dreadful import of its name, and its fearful consequences, must have been unknown to a minister, accustomed to live in Asiatic luxury and profusion, who never thinking of scarcity made no preparation for the supply of his brave troops, and in the midst of this distress, kept the most sumptuous table. In the meanwhile the army had only provision for a fortnight in the camp. There was ample supply of palisades, but no bread, and no confidence was placed but in the imperial troops, which were assembling in the greatest haste under the command of Field-Marshal Count Brown, in Bohemia.

Frederic was now in Saxony, and had entered into a correspondence with the King of Poland, who with his two eldest sons, the princes Xavier and Charles, and his minister Brühl had taken refuge in the camp at Pirna. Augustus in his letters always talked of neutrality, and Frederic required convincing proofs of his sincerity, which Augustus and Brühl had no intention of giving. The King of Prussia who knew the value of these offers of neutrality, made every preparation for making himself master of Saxony, under the assurance that he only took it in trust as security; a new discovery this in state politics, in order to prevent the taking possession of a neighbouring state from being called an invasion, but to which the opponents generally gave its right name.

Large supplies of forage, corn and provisions were exacted for the Prussian Army. The town of Torgau was fortified, and mounted with cannon, which had been found in the different towns of Saxony. Some thousands of citizens and peasantry were forced to work at these fortifications, and in the beginning were paid for their labour. In this town the head quarters of the commissariat and the military chest were placed, and here likewise were all the contributions of the country brought in.

On the 10th of September the King of Prussia entered Dresden which had been deserted by the troops, and took possession of the town and the Palace. The conduct of the king and his soldiers on this occasion are characteristic of the spirit of the time, by the display of refined and courtly manners, even during war and its distressing and horrid scenes. Frederic fixed his head quarters in a garden in the suburb, in the neighbourhood of which, his army was encamped. Every means were taken to diminish the fearful aspect of war in the eyes of the Saxons, and to place the conduct of their new ruler in the most amiable light. He wished to be looked upon as a friend, as a future ally and as a guest, and to make this impression, nothing was wanting in his amiable demeanour. The foreign ambassadors were received, and almost all persons of any rank in Dresden, as well as the magistrature of the town paid their court, and met with a gracious reception. The king, contrary to his custom, attended church, and made the clergyman a present of Champagne. He dined in public, and crowds of Saxons came as spectators.

He paid his compliments to the queen and the rest of the royal family through Field-Marshal Keith; and the court, not to be behind hand, invited him to dinner and offered him chamberlains for his service, both of which he declined. Notwithstanding these acts of politeness, the treasury in Dresden was placed under seals, the Collegiate Halls closed, the mint seized, some of the most important of the civil officers dismissed, all the artillery and ammunition from the arsenal removed to Magdeburg, the Swiss guard of the palace disarmed, and the revenues of the electorate were appropriated.

All communication between Dresden and the camp was broken off, excepting for the passage of some carriages, laden with supplies for the table of the King of Poland, and the couriers of the two kings. The camp at Pirna was invested by an army of 32,000 Prussians, whilst an army of observation of nearly the same number under the command of Keith was posted on the frontiers. The Duke Ferdinand of Brunswick entered Bohemia at the head of the advanced guard, and gained the first laurels of this war by dislodging the Austrian general, Wied, who was posted at Nollendorf with 8000 men.

Although the alliance which had been formed for the destruction of the King of Prussia had been betrayed to this monarch, and he had become possessed of copies of most of the papers relative to it, still he was in the dark respecting many points. An exact knowledge of the projects of his enemies was absolutely necessary to his safety; thus it became imperative on him to justify his invasion of Saxony by incontrovertible evidence, and he saw himself under the necessity of seizing the Saxon archives. These state papers were kept in three apartments of the palace, which communicated with a private room of the Queen of Poland, who alone had the key and watched these archives as the most valuable treasure.

The request that they should be delivered up, was flatly refused by the queen, his declared enemy. The Prussian general, Wylich, *commandant* of Dresden, had orders to take possession of them, and to this effect sent Major Wangenheim, who requested to have the key; upon this the queen appeared and declared she would not permit the apartments to be opened; Wangenheim withdrew, and the *commandant* went himself to the queen. All his remonstrances were in vain; she kept firm to her determination, and declared she would protect the door with her own person. Wylich threw himself on his knees, spoke of the necessity of fulfilling his orders, and while he entreated her to give way, gave her to understand that in case of further resistance he must have recourse to force. Upon this the keys were brought, and Frederic received the wished for papers, which were handed over to his privy councillor Count Hertzberg, and amongst others, some remarkable state papers, which fully justified the Prussian monarch in the eyes of all unprejudiced persons.

This disrespectful conduct to a queen, although justified by circumstances, was represented as a most unheard of outrage, and it was enhanced by the dismissal of the Saxon ministers a few hours after by the King of Prussia. The same day the queen called the foreign ambassadors together, and described her melancholy position, in a most pathetic discourse, in which she distinctly stated, that her cause was that of all the crowned heads of Europe. This occurrence, with great exaggeration was reported in the different courts, painting the conduct of Frederic in Saxony, in the blackest colours; and this tended not a little to increase the number of his enemies, and to cool the ardour of many of his friends.

It is well known that the wife of the *dauphin*, mother of Louis the XVIth, who was daughter of the Queen of Poland, threw herself at the feet of Louis the XVth, and implored him with tears, to assist in the deliverance of her parents, and the land of her birth. The court of Versailles was no longer actuated by motives of policy, and France declared herself openly against Frederic, as guarantee of the treaty of Westphalia, which she declared had been broken by the invasion of Saxony.

Thus France took an active part in a war which was so contrary to her interests, and which had been looked on in Paris as a political farce. It now became the fashion in this capital to detract from the merits of the King of Prussia, and on account of its novelty, to praise to the skies, the alliance with Austria. It went so far that the French academy gave as a prize subject, the praise of the treaty in verse, which however was prevented by the government. The French ambassador was recalled from Berlin, and the Prussian ambassador at Versailles received his *congé*. Frederic acted in the same manner towards the French minister at the court of Dresden, Count Broglio, who till now, notwithstanding his arrogant bearing and intrigues, had been allowed to remain.

Nevertheless every effort was made to bring about a peace between the kings of Poland and of Prussia. The English and Dutch ambassadors, Count Stormont and Calkoen, devoted all their energies to this praiseworthy undertaking. Frederic required, that as a proof of the most perfect neutrality, the Saxon troops should be dispersed, and retire to their different quarters; Augustus promised to remain neutral, but refused to enter into any engagements. Shortly after his arrival in the camp, he had harangued the troops, and entreated them to cut their way, with him, through the enemy, in order to reach Bohemia. He said, he was ready to sacrifice his life in the attempt; it was due to his subjects, and for the rest, he trusted to heaven.

The impossibility of success was pointed out to him, and he retired with the princes, his sons, and his minister to the fortress of Königstein. From hence he sent another address to the army, offering them the honour of saving their king, and declaring he was ready to sacrifice the last drop of his blood. The trusty Saxons, whose characteristic is love and obedience to their rulers under all circumstances, declared their willingness to fulfil the expectations of Augustus. But the scarcity was already so great in the camp, that both men and horses were reduced to a third of their rations. Their confidence however increased in consequence of the news of the approach of the Austrian Army, which, although in detached bodies, was already 70,000 strong in Bohemia.

The zeal and activity of the court of Vienna to begin the war was extraordinary. In spite of this the greater part of the cavalry in Bohemia was not mounted, and did not receive their horses until the end of August, in the camp at Kollin, at a time when the Prussians were already in Bohemia; so unprepared were they, that there was a scarcity of horses to convey the artillery and ammunition into Bohemia. Theresa gave her own horses to draw the cannon; and the Austrian and Bohemian nobility were active in following her example. Everyone assisted, and the transport was effected with unexpected rapidity.

The state of affairs, and the loss of so much valuable time, which might have made Frederic master of Bohemia, altered his plans; and as he could no longer depend on the neutrality of the Saxons, so as to have no enemy in his rear, he insisted upon a formal engagement from Augustus, that, if he wished to withdraw his troops from their present position, in case the Prussians were victorious that should be no disadvantage to Saxony, but if, on the other hand, they were unsuccessful, the Saxons should share their fate. Augustus however would hear of no engagement, and in his answer of the 12th of September, he says:

> It would appear that your majesty only looks for security in the destruction of my army, either by the sword or by hunger. With

regard to the latter, as yet there is no fear; and I trust that with the protection of the Almighty, and the fortitude and fidelity of my troops I am far from being in danger of the former.—I am ready to smooth all difficulties for an arrangement upon a point, which your majesty has so much at heart, and to do all that is consistent with my honour.

This determination on the part of a monarch, who by disposition was so easily led, was quite unexpected. Frederic made one more effort; he sent his favourite, General Winterfeld, who was alike remarkable as a soldier and as a courtier, that he might by his eloquence give the necessary force to the written representations of his master, who most ardently desired an alliance with Saxony, "between two neighbouring states", as he expressed himself in his letter to Augustus, "which are necessary to one another, and to whose real advantages it is requisite to be always united". As this effort, however, remained fruitless, and all was to be left to honour and conscience, Frederic wrote on the 15th September:

I much regret that I cannot carry my complaisance farther.

Winterfeld was however again sent to the king, but in vain; although the difficulty of his position was increased by the approach of the day for holding the Diet of Poland, which was fixed for the 4th of October, and he was forced to beg for a safe conduct to Warsaw. Frederic would not give his consent to this before the decision of the fate of Saxony. The request of Augustus became more urgent; the High Chancellor of Poland, Malachowsky, went in person to the Prussian camp, to support the request by the threat, that the Poles would not tamely submit to the forcible detention of their king. But Frederic remained unmoved.

Brown had received orders from his court to venture every thing in order to extricate the Saxons. The junction of the two armies under so skilful a general, considered by Austria as one of her greatest men, would have given another character to the war. Frederic was aware of this, and therefore doubled his precautions in investing the Saxon camp, so as to cut them off from all relief. In order to do this more effectually, Field-Marshal Keith advanced into Bohemia with a strong body of men, to watch the operations of the Austrians.

The Prussian Field-Marshal, Count Schwerin, had already marched from Silesia upon Bohemia, with an army of 30,000 men, and was encamped near Königsgrätz. These two Prussian armies were, according to Frederic's plan, to keep the enemy in check, that they might not he able to assist the Saxons. He himself awaited daily the capitulation of the besieged army, which he considered essential, previous to his march upon Bohemia, as they might become masters of the Elb, and would have been in the rear of the Prussians. The want of waggons and boats to convey provisions, and the fearful defiles, by which the entry into this kingdom is on all sides defended, rendered much preparation necessary.

It was requisite that Brown, in order to succour the Saxons, should cross the Eger; but he had no pontoons. These, and the requisite artillery only arrived in the camp on the 30th of September, and he immediately began his march. Frederic's object was, by a battle to force him to retreat; he gave the command of the besieging army to the Margrave Charles; joined his troops that were at Aussig, and marched with them on the 30th of September, the same day that Brown had passed the Eger. The two armies came in sight of each other at day break the following morning near Lowositz, a small Bohemian town.

The Austrian Army consisted of fifty two battalions, sixty squadrons of horse, and ninety eight pieces of cannon. The Prussians were twenty four battalions strong, sixty squadrons of horse and one hundred and two cannon. The heights of Lobosch and Radostiz, which commanded the position of the Austrians, were unoccupied by Brown, and the fog was so thick, that it was not possible to see any distance. These circumstances induced Frederic to think, that the Austrians had crossed the Elb, and that he had only fallen in with the rear guard. Some thousand men, Croats and Hungarian infantry, posted at the foot of the hill of Lobosch in some vineyards, and who made an ineffectual fire upon the advancing Prussians, strengthened this supposition, as these light troops generally covered a retreat. The Austrian cavalry who exposed themselves to the cannonade of the Prussians, and retained their position, confirmed the mistake. They fought in the fog without seeing one another. In the mean time the king had made himself master of the heights.

As Brown's centre and left wing, from being supported by a morass, and other impassable barriers, were in security from all attacks, he had directed all his attention upon the town of Lowositz, which covered his right wing, and in which he had posted his best infantry and a number of ordnance; in advance of the town, there was also a battery and a redoubt. Towards midday the fog dispersed, and the Prussians made a regular and spirited charge, leapt a wide ditch, overthrew the

Austrians, and pursued them under the fire of the cannon of Lowositz. The heavy fire of the artillery drove them back with great loss. The infantry of the left wing of the enemy could not be attacked by them from being posted on the bank of a deep ditch.

The next attack of the Prussians was to drive the Croats out of the vineyard, who were protected by its hedges and walls. They succeeded, but with difficulty. Brown now endeavoured to take possession of the heights. The Prussians posted there fought like lions, and when they had no more cartridges, attacked the storming party with the butt end of their muskets. This fighting, hand to hand, lasted till the Austrians were driven down the hill, and into Lowositz; the Prussians took advantage of the disorder of the enemy to set fire to the town, and in this confusion drove them out of it, by which means the fate of the day was decided.

Brown made a masterly retreat covered by the infantry of the left wing, which had not been in action, and was the only part of his army, which was not in disorder. He destroyed the bridge over the Elb at Leutmeritz, and also all the bridges on the Eger, that his retreat might be secured. He gave up the field of battle to the king, but did not give up all claim to the victory. This, however, was not doubtful, as the event proved notwithstanding that the Prussian Army had suffered severely, and a number of prisoners had been made on either side. In Vienna for nine days prayers were offered up for those who had fallen in the battle, which was called by the wits, a thanksgiving: "that, it was no worse."

Such were the occurrences of the first battle of this remarkable war, which had lasted from seven in the morning until three in the afternoon, and was a pledge of the future conduct of the Prussians, to the whole world, for the battles that were to succeed. The king was so impressed with the courage of his troops, that, in his letter to Field-Marshall Schwerin, in which he describes the battle, he says:

Never, since I have had the honour of commanding my troops, have they done such wonders of valour.

A valour, which was necessary against the powerful resistance he met with, a resistance, which forced Frederic's troops to exclaim: "These are no longer the old Austrians;" on the other hand the soldiers of the enemy, when they saw their wounds, cried out: "We have got the old Prussians again." The loss of the victorious army, in killed and wounded, was 3,300 men, and the number of prisoners was 700.

The loss of the Austrians was some few hundreds less.

Brown was ill; nevertheless he constantly exposed himself to the severity of the weather, slept in the open air, and suffered day and night all the inconveniences of warfare, so that at last, he one day fell to the ground from exhaustion in the presence of his devoted army. This general was forced to withdraw his troops to the other bank of the Eger, and to abandon entirely his plan of assisting the Saxons. It was determined that this distressed ally should cross the Elb, on the night of the 11th of October at Königstein, in order to attack the Prussians on both sides.

However a stormy and rainy night, and the transport of the heavy copper pontoons by land and with half starved horses, delayed the passage of the river, which it was decided should take place two days later. Frederic employed this valuable time, in strengthening the posts on the Elb, and in fortifying his own position with *barricadoes* and entrenchments. The ground on the right side of the river near Pirna and Königstein is hilly and covered with thick underwood. The deep hollows which separate these lofty hills are nearly impassable, and especially so to an army with a powerful enemy in the neighbourhood, and in possession of the heights. Such was the position of the Saxons; they hoped, when they had passed the Elb, to hear something of the approach of the Austrians; but they saw no traces of their allies, who had been prevented by the difficulties of the ground, and a Prussian corps under general Lestwitz, from advancing; on the other hand the Prussians saw themselves masters of the defiles, which must be passed to reach Bohemia.

The Saxon troops endeavoured to form at the foot of the Lilienstein, which the narrow space would not permit; here they encamped without order and disheartened, full of anxious expectation as to their melancholy fate. The cause of this change of position for the worse, was the want of knowledge, on the part of the Austrians and Saxons, of the nature of the ground, and from this, all their decisions were guided by chance. This was also the cause of the loss of a letter from Field-Marshall Brown to Rutowski. A continued heavy rain had rendered the roads so had, that the advance was most difficult, and the Saxons were forced to leave their cannon on the opposite side of the river.

The abandoned camp of Pirna was immediately seized by the Prussians, who fell upon the rear guard of the Saxons. A tremendous storm prevented the report of the cannonade from being heard, so that the Austrians were not aware of it. All seemed to conspire against the Saxons even to the very elements. After a courageous resistance of four hours, this body of men. were taken prisoners, and the Prussians became masters of the greater part of the artillery and baggage. This, however, could not have reached the army, in consequence of the bridge having broken away.

The King of Poland was not an eye witness of this accumulation of misfortunes: he had removed from his headquarters at Strüppen, a few days previously, with his sons and his minister to Königstein. From this place he issued repeated orders to Field-Marshall Rutowsky for the most impracticable movements, which, had they been fulfilled, could not have led to a junction with the Austrians.

Never was a well disciplined and courageous army in such a melancholy position. It was the counterpart of that of the Romans at Caudinum, and if the passing under the joke was not enforced, as by the Samnites, it was from the change which had taken place in the maxims of warfare in the twenty two centuries, which had intervened between the two occurrences. Hunger raged amongst the Saxon troops, added to this, the cold set in, and they had lost their baggage. Three days and three nights they were under arms, without food and with a scarcity of ammunition. They were encamped without covering, surrounded by high hills and steep rocks, encompassed by a watchful enemy, without hope or means of deliverance. Their fate was completely in the hands of the conquerors, to whom, with the consent of Augustus, they capitulated on the 14th of October, after a blockade of four and thirty days.

This monarch was bowed down by his misfortune. He wrote on this day to Field-Marshall Rutowsky:

> One must submit to the will of Providence. I am a free king, so will I live, so will I die, both with honour. I place the fate of my army in your hands; your council of war must decide, if we are to surrender or die, and whether it shall be by hunger or the sword.

The minister Brühl wished to induce Field-Marshall Brown to maintain his dangerous position for another day, and wrote to him:

> If we capitulate, we will not neglect to insure your Excellency's retreat, so that the whole Prussian army may not fall upon you.

Brown took no notice of this proposition, which betrayed a man, who did not know his opponent, and expected to gain advantages by a capitulation. The terms, under which this was agreed upon, were hard, as well for the Saxon troops as for the king. The whole army 14,000 strong were to lay down their arms; the officers were dismissed, but the non-commissioned officers and soldiers had no choice; they were obliged to take the oath of fidelity to the King of Prussia.

It was a most touching spectacle, 14,000 soldiers threw down their arms, and supplicated for bread. Hunger and despair among high and low, had produced the most distressing scenes in this valley of lamentations, under the eyes of Augustus himself.

The distress had increased to the highest pitch, but the relief was sudden. The soldiers exhausted through deficiency of nourishment and hardships, received supplies for their most pressing wants; to each company twenty six-pound loaves of bread were distributed. The general officers who were prisoners, were invited to the king's table at headquarters at Strüppen.

The misfortune of the Saxons brought no disgrace with it. It was indeed a glorious epoch in their history. They had so long, with their small army, withstood the power of Prussia, and fought courageously against the greatest difficulties, and were now only obliged to submit to the laws of nature and a higher a destiny. Their resistance, however, saved the ill prepared imperial army in Bohemia, and all the provinces of Theresa in Germany, where the troops were dispersed; and especially for Austria, it was attended by the most important effects: it was the greatest service, which this kingdom had received from a foreign power, since the deliverance of Vienna, by the brave king Sobiesky.

This advantage was, however, very reluctantly acknowledged both by the imperial troops and the Court. The soldiers of Brown's army called the army of Pirna, in derision, the Saxon pickets, and in the imperial city this sacrifice of a great prince and his country, was looked upon as a matter of duty.

For more than a century no European monarch had suffered such an humiliation as the King of Poland. He was deprived at once of the whole of his Saxon Army, who were devoted to him, and he remained in Königstein with a small guard and only a few followers. All his endeavours to gain better terms were in vain; Frederic himself dictated the answers to the fourteen articles of capitulation of this treaty of submission. Some of these answers, which related to pressing necessities of the troops, were laconic, and consisted in the monosyllable, Good! But everything betrayed the decisive tone of a conqueror, who thought he granted more than they had a right to expect.

Augustus implored that his own guard, a body of chosen men, might be excepted, and remain with him. Frederic's answer was humiliating in the extreme, and expressed the right of the strongest in the most offensive terms. It ran thus:

They must share the fate of the rest of the army, as he did not wish to have the trouble of taking them again prisoners.

The colours, standards, and drums of the Saxon Army were given up to the King of Poland, and in order that at least one of his many requests might he complied with, the fortress of Königstein was declared neutral during the whole of the war.

Ten Saxon regiments of infantry remained complete with the exception of being new officered from the Prussian army, and being clothed in the uniform of the Prussians. The remainder, and the cavalry were draughted into the different Prussian regiments. In addition to this, Saxony was forced to supply 9284 recruits to complete the regiments, in the course of the next month.

The officers were released on parole, not to serve again, in this war, against the King of Prussia. So great, however, was Theresa's and Augustus' hatred towards Frederic, that this was derided, and they released the officers from their parole, to the disgrace of the army. Blinded by sympathy, they forgot that honour is the bond which keeps European armies together; a phantom, an uncertain and invisible power, upon which the light of truth must not shine too brightly, but which leads men on fearlessly to death.

The act of Frederic by which, as conqueror, he turned to his own use the whole army of an enemy, and made them serve in the war, is without example in history. He had, however, reckoned too much upon the distressed position of Augustus, the impossibility of his supporting an army and on the state of need in which the men were, without allowing for the national love of the Saxons for their prince and their country. This was displayed, much to the astonishment of Frederic; for although desertion was expected, the deliberate and orderly desertion of whole battalions had not been thought of. The most of them went off in marching order, after having dismissed or shot their officers; they took with them the bread and ammunition waggons, the military chest, in short, everything necessary for their march, which was, of part towards Poland, and the remainder to join the French Army.

To reconcile them to his service, Frederic had promoted many of the non-commissioned officers, but this was impolitic, for these patriots became the leaders of the desertion, and the other officers, who would not join them, were forced to get out of the way. The Saxons who remained, were placed in garrison in the towns; but even this failed; at Leipsic they forced open the gates, and marched forth at midday. In Wittemberg, Pirna and in other towns they forced the Prussian officers to allow them to go over to the enemy; and in many battles whole companies deserted, and turned their arms against the Prussians.

Augustus, who awaited his fate upon the rock of Königstein, received passports for himself and his suite, that he might reach Warsaw in safety, for which place he immediately started. Frederic wrote to him a most courtly farewell letter on the 18th of October. He addressed him in this, as in all former letters, by the term of brother, a term of politeness and affection in use in the letters of congratulation and condolence of the crowned heads of Europe, in the 18th century, even in the midst of warfare. The king was treated with the highest marks of respect on his departure, and all the troops were removed from the road by which he was to pass, not to expose to their gaze, the unfortunate monarch in his distressing position.

The correspondence between the kings now ceased. But General Spörken renewed it in Augustus' name with Frederic. The principal subject of these letters was the establishment of a number of stations from Poland, through Silesia into Saxony, in order to facilitate the communication. Frederic appeared at first disposed to enter into the arrangement, but in consequence of the discovery of the repeated attempts of the court of Saxony to give the enemy ail possible information, and to induce the Saxons in the Prussian service to desert, the correspondence with Spörken was suddenly broken off. In his letter of the 2nd of December he writes:

My moderation is abused, and the unfriendly conduct of your court leaves me no alternative but the force of arms; this is the last letter you will receive from me.

No occurrence in the 18th century previous to the French revolution caused such a sensation in Europe as the misfortunes of this royal family, connected, as it was with so many mighty potentates. All the crowned heads felt for them, and even George the Second let it be known at the principal courts, that he did not approve of the conduct of Frederic in Saxony. The political pamphlets, which appeared in Vienna, were dictated by the most deadly hatred, and were of the most abusive character. The King of Prussia was accused of the meanest practices, and described as the instigator of the conspiracy which had been discovered in Sweden against the senate; they went so far as to reproach him with the anger of his father, his punishment in Cüstrin, and the imperial mediation, which they stated, had been the means of saving his life.

This immeasurable hatred was now the leading feature of the court of Vienna, which hitherto had been noted for its pride. But this was so far lost sight of, that the Empress Maria Theresa, who but in this case, never forgot her dignity, and looked on female chastity as the first of virtues, lowered herself so far, as to flatter the mistress of Louis the XV., and to address her as cousin. A correspondence was begun between the empress and the Duchess de Pompadour, which was commenced by the sending a portrait of the former, set with diamonds, to the duchess; who was by this step led to forget her low origin so far, as frequently to make use of the familiar expression of, "my dear queen", in her letters. Still Theresa, impressed from her cradle with the dignity of her rank, the daughter of the proud Charles the Sixth, and granddaughter of Leopold, the most haughty of the emperors, who refused to receive Sobiesky, the preserver of Vienna, from a point of court etiquette, was content to put up with the conduct of the duchess.

This occurred at the time that Frederic had given the king's mistress repeated proofs of his contempt. These were the reasons, that at Versailles state policy was laughed at, against which the Marquis of Belle Isle was the only one to remonstrate. The balance of power in Germany, the object for a hundred years of the greatest French ministers, was derided. The campaign was now at an end; the Austrian Army withdrew further into Bohemia, which was also evacuated by the Prussians, under Field-Marshalls Schwerin and Keith, in order to occupy their winter quarters in Saxony and Silesia. Frederic remained the whole winter in Dresden, and treated Saxony as a conquered province. He worked constantly with the Saxon ministers; gave his orders upon all points respecting the government, and levied troops and money for the war, throughout the country.

Chapter 2: Preparations for the Campaign of 1757

Great were the preparations of the allied powers, for the approaching campaign against Prussia. French and Swedes, Germans from all the provinces of Germany, Hungarians and Transylvanians, Italians, Walloons, Croats, Russians, Cossacks and Calmuks, all were in activity, and these people collected from far and near, were congregated, not so much for conquest, as to plunder, murder and lay waste the country.

These armies required large sums for their equipment, and as most of the courts were in want of money, every nerve was strained to raise it, either by loans, or by inducing capitalists to make advances of supplies on credit. The King of Prussia had a great advantage over all his opponents, in not requiring such assistance. His well filled treasury, and the abundance of the country, of which he had taken possession, enabled the Prussians to open the campaign with a superfluity of every requisite.

Frederic, to make up for the deficiency of light troops, formed seven battalions of volunteers, and in addition to these, increased his army both cavalry and infantry, by 40,000 men. The Saxons of all ranks, who, from similarity of language, manners and ideas were more inclined towards the Prussians, than the Austrians, were anxious, that, as there must be war, their monarch should ally himself with the former. They were not treated with harshness by them, for the only hardships the Saxons had to endure at this time, were finding the supplies for the army, which were not oppressive, moderate war taxes, recruiting stations and other trifling inconveniences. They lived with the Prussians in good fellowship.

In Dresden the theatre was open, balls and masquerades were given, at which the nobility and the citizens attended, and the king gave concerts repeatedly, in which, the mighty monarch himself took part. His tranquillity of mind, strengthened by his philosophy and the knowledge of his power, was, however, disturbed in many instances. During this winter an occurrence took place, the particulars of which are very little known. The king was to have been poisoned.

A lackey, of the name of Glasau, who was a great favourite of the king's, so much so, that he was often required to sleep in the king's bedchamber, had been bribed to take away his life. But few knew of this project, and it was not to be expected any of these would betray it. An accident, at the moment of its perpetration, discovered to the king, that an attempt upon his life was intended. Glasau threw himself at the feet of the monarch, and entreated for mercy, which, however, could not be extended to him. He was seized, judicially interrogated in the presence of the king, and dispatched the following day in chains to Spandau, where he was immured in a dungeon in solitary confinement, and in a short time after ended his days. It appeared so necessary to the king, to keep secret the names of all the persons connected with this crime, that he would not allow him even to be attended by a physician, in his last moments.

The moderation of the King of Prussia at this time in Saxony, was grounded on the slight hopes, which were not quite extinct, of inducing Augustus to come to terms, and to form an alliance with him. But the wound was too deep, the alliance with Austria and Russia too close, and the hopes of the King of Poland of a speedy change of the aspect of affairs for the better, were too great to allow him to listen to the propositions of Prussia. On the other hand, the complaints of his ambassadors, supported by his powerful allies, in Regensburg and in all the courts of Europe, were without bounds.

At the Imperial *Diet* the most unseemly expressions were made use of, both in speaking and by letter; even abuse was not spared. Sympathy got the better of all circumspection, and weakened the discretion and memory of learned men so far, that, in the political pamphlets of the day, Frederic's invasion of Saxony was described as having no example in history. The object was, however, fully attained; all the allied courts redoubled their activity in their preparations for the war.

France displayed so far her earnestness, that, in order to hasten the downfall of the King of Prussia, the court of Versailles offered George the II. to be neutral with regard to Hanover, if he would neither increase nor assemble his German troops, concede his fortresses to the French, and allow them free passage into Prussia. The King of England, although Hanover was of so much importance to him, declined the proposition. This zeal against Prussia, actuated the Marquis of Havrincourt, the French ambassador, in all his endeavours in Sweden, where most of the senators were venal, and where the minds of the higher classes had been much embittered towards the name of Prussia, by the discovery of the conspiracy against the senate, of which the queen had been aware.

The treaty of alliance between Prussia and Sweden, formed in the year 1743, was now at an end, and left the latter at liberty to form fresh alliances; in addition to this, came the promise of France, that in case of taking an active part in the war, Sweden should have as a reward Stettin and the whole of Prussian Pomerania. To all appearance this decided the affair. Nevertheless Frederic made one more attempt. He required the support of Sweden, as responsible for the treaty of Westphalia, that treaty so glorious for her, and so intimately connected with the well being of the Protestant religion, and which they were now so anxious to violate.

These grounds appeared to have some weight with a nation, who since the reformation, had adhered to Lutheranism almost to idolatry; and the danger of the protestant church so far turned the balance with the lawgivers of Sweden, who were obliged to act in consideration of the feelings of the people, that in December 1756, the King of Prussia received assurances of the strictest neutrality; and in fact, when at Regensburg, Frederic's downfall was voted for, the minister for Sweden held back his vote, for Swedish Pomerania, under the excuse that he had no instructions. But the intrigues and the gold of the French minister at Stockholm finally gained the upper hand, and war was determined on, against Frederic in Sweden.

The plan of division, and the intended destruction of the Prussian monarchy, were as extraordinary as the war itself. As Sweden was to have Pomerania, so was Silesia to be given to Austria, the kingdom of Prussia to Russia, the Duchy of Magdeburg with Halberstadt to Saxony, and the Westphalian provinces fell to the lot of France. The electorate of Brandenburg alone was to be reserved for the dethroned king, in case he should submit in proper time; if not, the powers had determined, that it should be given to the next heir. This determination, supported on all sides by strength and vindictive feelings, against so contracted a power, seemed to require no good fortune for its completion, which might indeed be hastened or retarded, but under all circumstances could not fail in its fulfilment.

In no part of Germany was greater activity displayed than in the south. The *Diet* at Regensburg resumed the long abandoned practice of fulminating its thunder against the King of Prussia. He was formally placed under the Ban of the Empire, and forfeited his lands in the Empire, his rank and titles; nine Protestant princes voted for this, and amongst others, the courts of Anspach and Darmstadt, who were related to Frederic, the Duke of Holstein Gottorp and the Princes of Schwartzenburg and of Anhalt. Besides these princes the opponents of Frederic had, in addition to the catholic princes, sixty votes in the princely Senate; however twenty six stood out for an enquiry into the causes of the war, a cessation of hostilities, and the intervention of the Empire in this quarrel. Amongst these last, who were guided by reason and moderation, were all the counts from Weteravia, Franconia and Westphalia.

The imperial cities, however, in whose walls state policy never, and freedom seldom prevailed, and who all more or less, from ignorance, looked upon the emperor as their monarch, showed their usual characteristic upon this occasion; they voted blindly with the imperial party. For the most part the princes of the Empire were drawn to the side of Maria Theresa, through fear or by hope, and forgetting the friendship they owed to Prussia, the many benefits they had received from this house, the bonds of religion and of blood, they justified the opinion of many statesmen, that in case of a war with Austria, no one could depend on the support of these princes against her.

Such terms of abuse were made use of in the manifestoes and other state papers, against the king, that he was forced to address himself to the Empress Theresa, and to remind her, that monarchs might be enemies without degrading themselves by invective; for it was not words, which were unworthy of them, but the sword which must decide their quarrel. This remonstrance remained long unheeded, and it was not until after he had gained some battles that they had any effect.

The princes of the different circles were directed to prevent the king from receiving any assistance from these districts; all the vassals of the Empire, in the army of the Prussians, were recalled, and an imperial order was issued that all booksellers and printers publishing Prussian political pamphlets, should be punished by fine and imprisonment. The impartial said that the emperor was forced to play the despot in the Empire, from family circumstances. Plotho, the Brandenburgian ambassador at the Diet at Regensburg, answered all the anti-Prussian pamphlets, as well as the pedantic discussion upon the sanctity of the archives, with force and justice; and as he found insurmountable difficulties in getting them printed, throughout the south of Germany, he established a printing press for his own use, at Regensburg.

The putting in force the imperial ban, was now set on foot. The attorney general of the Empire commenced proceedings, and prevailed on the imperial Notary, accompanied by two witnesses, to serve a citation on the ambassador, Baron Plotho. This citation required the appearance of the ambassador before the *Diet*, within two months, reckoning from the 22nd of August 1757 to state what he had to say against the imperial edict. Plotho, who knew what his rights were, treated this invitation with the greatest disdain, requested the bearers of it to take it back again, kicked it as far as the door himself, and then ordered his servants to throw it out of the house.

In addition to the determined conduct of this minister, who always acted with discretion, and alarmed his enemies, came the representations of France. The court of Vienna was requested to give up the project of the imperial edict, as no advantage could be gained by it, and it might induce the kings of Prussia and England, and other German princes to withdraw from the German confederation. It was also decided on, to proceed against Frederic without any imperial edict, as an enemy of the Empire, and to take no notice of his declaration, that he had acted as sovereign of Prussia, and not as Elector of Brandenburg, in his aggression on Saxony.

This sentence of these German Amphictyons, was to be supported, in spite of the reclamations of the friends of Prussia and her ambassadors, by an army raised from all parts of Germany under the fearful name of imperial army of execution, in order to give sufficient weight to the decree of the majority. At first 120,000 men were required for this service, but this number was afterwards reduced to half. Thus a new army was added to the numerous troops assembled for the downfall of Frederic, and people now began to fix upon an early day for the ending of the war.

Frederic, who had nothing left to him but to make the best use of his means to meet the coming storm, set actively to work at his finance department in Saxony. He now saw that the long wished for alliance with this country would be disadvantageous, and that the unencumbered possession of an extensive and productive country would be of much more advantage to him. No province could serve so well as a centre for his operations, and for covering his rear, and his flanks. The position of this country, between two powers so different in politics, was a national misfortune for the Saxons. It was only from Saxony that Frederic could carry on his operations in Bohemia, and by seizing on it, secure himself from an invasion from the Austrians.

From the beginning of the war, there was no alternative for the Saxons but to be either the allies of Prussia, or to fall into its power. Frederic now renounced his former plans, and no longer exercised the same moderation. Hitherto the sum of 190,000 dollars had been required for the support of the courts of law; this was reduced to 30,000, and so in other departments. The Queen of Poland required money. Frederic who well knew what use, to his disadvantage, would be made of it, sent her only 7800 dollars; she renewed he request, and stated the sum requisite for the present wants of herself and her family, at 174,000 dollars a month; the answer was, she must apply to her husband.

This reform extended to all departments. The singers, and dancers of the opera were not formally dismissed, but, as they received no pay, they started for Italy, for which country, the celebrated director of music Hasse departed also. The two most important people at the court of Saxony, were the confessor of the queen, and the director of the opera. The first had a salary of 12,000, the latter of 15,000 dollars; but now they were forced to be satisfied with 2000 dollars. In this time of need the Empress Elizabeth came to the assistance of the Queen of Poland, and presented her with 100,000 *rubels*.

The immense quantity of porcelain which was found in Dresden, and in Meissen was now sold for the benefit of the Prussian treasury, as booty. Schimmelman, a Saxon dealer, bought it for 200,000 dollars, and by this means laid the foundation for the immense riches, with which he first visited Berlin, then Hamburg, and lastly Copenhagen. He rose to the rank of a Danish minister of state, and died the richest man, who had ever existed in this northern kingdom.

Frederic, however, left the palace in Dresden untouched. He often visited the celebrated picture gallery, but without appropriating any of the pictures, and always made handsome presents to those in charge of it. But he did not preserve this moderation with regard to the Count de Brühl, whom he looked upon as the prime mover of the alliance, which Saxony had formed with his enemies. This minister had a beautiful residence a few leagues from Dresden; this was, by Frederic's orders, destroyed. A like fate attended his palace in Dresden, as well as his garden, which was an ornament to the town, and was open as a promenade to all. Here, where art and nature had done so much, all was laid waste, and the remains of a pavilion long remained as a monument of a vengeance, hardly to be expected from so wise a king.

Thus in a moment disappeared the invaluable collections of a private individual which were hardly to be equalled in brilliancy, and rarity, by those of any king. Everything, that for beauty of workmanship, and from expense was remarkable, and from its cost could not find purchasers in London, or Paris, was bought to ornament his palace The most choice of these were at Dresden; every room decorated with the most costly ornaments, and clocks of every description. But the most extraordinary was the remarkable wardrobe of this minister; whole apartments were fitted up with closets full of dresses, to each of which, there was a particular watch, sword and snuffbox, and the dresses were painted in miniature, in a book, which was daily laid before him for his selection. Of his forty footmen four alone had charge of this treasure of clothes, which was rarely shown to strangers; but this practice was entirely given up, in consequence of a traveller exclaiming contemptuously: *"Montrez-moi des vertus, et non pas des culottes."*

The Saxon recruits, for the Prussian Army, were now called upon to serve. The Elector of Saxony made the strongest remonstrances against this, but to his representations on this subject, Frederic replied, by requesting him not to trouble himself with such matters. The states general were not more fortunate in their remonstrances, and, as they pleaded the necessity of obedience to their sovereign, Frederic replied:

I am your monarch, so long as I retain possession of Saxony; therefore you are bound to obey me.

Frederic knew but too well that he could expect no assistance from the republic of Poland; but not to neglect any of the forms of state policy, he sent a requisition for the 4,000 men, guaranteed by the treaty of Wehlau, for the protection of the states of Brandenburg, and at the same time, he requested the republic not to allow the Russians to march through their territory, as otherwise, the war would be carried on in Poland. This request was not attended to at Warsaw; for even the nobles, who did not adhere to the king, trembled before the Russians. The Empress Elizabeth kept up this fear by menaces, and the taking possession of Elbing and Thorn, by which she made it to be understood, that she would, with her army, prevent the king from disturbing the tranquillity of Poland.

The Austrians were very desirous of getting possession of Königstein; they therefore determined on taking it by surprise, with the consent of the Saxon *commandant.* Frederic was informed of this plan, and in a letter, reminded the commandant of his duty, which was, not to allow a fortress, which had been confided to him, and declared neutral, to be taken; with the remark, that, as he looked upon the fortress as impregnable, it was not possible that it could be taken unexpectedly by surprise. Should it occur, he would be looked upon as a traitor, and incur the penalty of the loss of honour and life. This admonition had its effect, and the attempt was not made.

Frederic was always on his guard, and learnt every thing that was going on by his watchfulness. The Countess Brühl received a cask of Hungarian wine from Poland; this circumstance, in itself, was of no importance, but occurring to such a person, whose most trifling actions were watched, it was communicated to the king. He ordered the immediate delivery of the wine, and only required to have the cask. The wine was drawn off in the palace, in presence of witnesses, and the cask, which was lined with letters and papers, was brought to the king.

The activity in preparations for war, which were making in all the provinces of Germany, surpassed all example for the last few centuries. In all the previous wars, even under Charles the Fifth, and Gustavus Adolphus, when the people fought with the zeal of religion, the preparations were not so great, as now, that all the people of Germany flew to arms. The fear of the immense power of the enemy diminished every day the party in favour of Prussia. Even the brother in law of Frederic, the Duke of Brunswick, to save his dominions, wished to give them over to France; the Landgraf of Hesse Cassel hesitated, and seemed to have forgotten the friendship of Prussia, and the protection she had hitherto extended to him, together with the subsidies of England. In the south of Germany, the Markgraf of Bayreuth alone, preferred to sacrifice his territory to sending troops against his royal brother in law. Frederic was touched by this instance of heroism, and as he looked upon the states of the *markgraf* as the inheritance of his house, he refused the sacrifice dependant upon his adherence, and gave his consent to the sending the Bayreuth Army contingent, to the army assembled against him.

Thus was the army of the Empire brought together, but it rather placed the honourable and old German confederation in a laughable position. The contingents with the exception of the Bavarians, the Wurtemburgers, and the troops from the Palatinate, and some few others, were a horde of undisciplined men, divided in bands of a motley appearance, and not unlike the armies of the Crusaders. In Swabia and Franconia, there were states of the Empire, who only furnished a few men; many had only to send a lieutenant without men, and he was not infrequently a farming man taken from the plough; others sent only a drummer, and gave him a drum from their old armoury. Many nuns, in the convents, laid aside their rosaries to embroider banners, which by the blessings of the priests, should overcome the heretics. Pig-drivers advanced to the sound of the fife, and old and worn out cart horses were supplied to carry dragoons. The prelates of the Empire, who prided themselves upon being the confederates of so great a monarch made their servants shoulder the musket, and sent them to the army. Arms, accoutrements, baggage, all was incongruous, in this congregated herd of men, to whom the name of soldiers was given, and of whom great things were expected.

The court of the king in Warsaw, found it very hard to bear their present position and one indiscretion followed close on another: Plesman, the accredited Prussian secretary of legation to the Republic of Poland, in consequence of his zeal in the service of his king, had not the favour of the Polish court, who therefore determined on his downfall. He was at this time on a journey in Saxony, and, as he passed by Reichenbach, fifty Austrian hussars fell upon him, and carried him off to Egra, where he was placed in chains, and treated as a felon; ill-treatment, which had such an effect on his health, that for many months he could not speak out loud. He was carried to Vienna, and thrown into prison in a dark cell. His servant, who was taken from him, met with the same fate. This conduct remained for some time concealed from Frederic; when he became aware of it, and insisted upon his being set at liberty, he received for answer, that Plesman was arrested at the instigation of the court of Poland; Frederic, however, soon brought the affair to an end.

As master of Dresden he had an extensive field for reprisals. He contented himself with seizing on the person of one man; the secretary of legation, Just, was thrown into prison. The royal family were in dismay, and the elector made representations to Brühl. For the first time this minister perceived that it would not answer to irritate this determined man any further, and Plesman, after an imprisonment of seven months, was set at liberty.

In the meantime the greatest preparations were made, to be able to open the campaign early, in order to be beforehand with the allies. The most to be feared of these were the Austrians, and against them,

Frederic determined to unite his strength, in order to strike a decisive blow, if possible, before the other troops should come up. The imperial court took an opposite course, and confined themselves to the defensive, in order to fall upon the king on all sides, and annihilate him at once; Brown therefore divided his army into four bodies, in order to cover Bohemia.

Frederic invaded this country in the end of April, in five divisions, after having made other movements to deceive the enemy; and, to act also on the defensive, had fortified positions in the neighbourhood of Dresden, to protect Saxony. The leaders of these five armies were; Field-Marshall Schwerin, who marched from Silesia by Trawtenau, the Duke of Bevern, who advanced by Zittau, Prince Maurice of Anhalt-Dessau by Commotau, Prince Henry of Prussia by Newstädtel, and Frederic himself led the fifth through Peterswald. With such precision was the march directed, and completed with such order and punctuality, that the five *corps d'armé* entered the Bohemian territory on the same day.

They made themselves masters of a very large imperial magazine; and the Duke of Bevern, with 16,000 men, soon fell in with the enemy, 28,000 strong, who were encamped near Reichenberg, under the command of Count Königsegg. His position lay between two thickly wooded hills, and his order of battle resembled a fortification; his infantry represented the bastion, and his cavalry the curtain. The Austrians were immediately attacked, and after fighting for five hours, were driven out of the field with a loss of 1600 men, killed, wounded, or taken prisoners. The Prussians lost 300 men.

After this battle, the duke advanced, and shortly after formed a junction with Field-Marshall Schwerin, who had entered Bohemia over the mountains of Silesia in five columns, and had beaten the rear guard of the imperial army at Alt-Bunzlau, consisting of 1500 men, who were dispersed or taken prisoners, but with the loss of General Wartenberg who commanded on this occasion, and was killed.

Frederic marched over the Bohemian mountain Paskopol without opposition, and crossed the Moldaw in presence of the enemy, who had here collected all their force, and neglected this invaluable opportunity of falling upon the king's small and detached force, and at a time that he would have been taken at a disadvantage. There was now a great spirit of jealousy among the commanders of the imperial troops, which showed itself in many striking instances, and Brown was under the orders of Prince Charles of Lorraine, who acted as commander in chief. These generals expected no invasion of Bohemia, and rather thought that the king would endeavour to defend himself in Saxony. Brown wrote on the 9th of April to Keith, requesting the return of the hostages taken in the preceding year from Bohemia, as without doubt the Prussians would not return. Under Frederic's dictation, Keith wrote, that Brown was in the right, and that the hostages should return to Bohemia.

Early on the morning of the 6th of May, the whole Prussian Army 100,000 men concentrated in the neighbourhood of Prague, and with exception of the troops under Keith, and Prince Maurice, who remained on the other side of the Moldaw, were in the immediate vicinity of this capital. A few hours after commenced one of the most remarkable battles, recorded in the annals of warfare. The Prussian Army, actually in action, was 64,000 strong, and the Austrian 74,000.

The latter were posted on fortified hills; and the approaches were through marshy meadows, ponds partly dried up, of which the bottoms were muddy and covered with grass, dams and small foot bridges over which, the soldiers could only pass in single file. The Austrians remained quiet in this strong position; they were occupied in cooking, and the cavalry were out in search of forage, when Frederic advanced; for notwithstanding the reports brought in from the outposts of his approach, they would not believe that he was actually on the march.

Prince Charles now recalled the foraging parties of cavalry, and met the attack of the Prussian infantry, which was made with the greatest courage and determination, in spite of the disadvantages of the ground. They could only cross the dams in single file, and those who waded through the meadows, often stuck in the clay at every step they took. The regiments of Meierrinck and Treskow sank to their knees in the morass, and were with difficulty extricated. But they all helped and encouraged one another. Several battalions were forced to leave their cannon behind, notwithstanding the need they stood in of them.

About one o'clock the difficulties were overcome, and the Prussians began to form in order of battle. Without waiting to recover from their fatigue, they rushed on the enemy, who received them with a heavy cannonade. Winterfeldt's regiment attacked one of the batteries, but the greater part of his men were killed This did not hinder the grenadier battalion of Wreden from advancing, crying out: "Comrades! let us come on, you have gained glory enough." The king had given orders not to fire, but to charge with fixed bayonets. The fire of the Austrian small arms was so fatal, that the courage of the Prussians was checked by the prospect of certain death, and several Prussian regiments began to give way.

During this time, the cavalry of both armies were engaged; Prince Schöneich who commanded the Prussians, attacked the whole Austrian cavalry with a part of his own, and forced the first rank to retreat; but his flank was turned, and he was driven back by the second rank of the enemy. The Prussian cavalry, however, formed again received reinforcements, and attacked the Austrians again with success. The line of the Austrian cavalry was broken, and they were driven back on their infantry, which they threw into confusion.

The Prussian hussars took advantage of this disorder, to rush in, and complete their defeat. Field-Marshall Schwerin was actively engaged in endeavouring to form the infantry, who had been driven back by the heavy fire of the Austrians, and lead them against the enemy. He placed himself at the head of his regiment, got off his horse, and with the words "Forwards my children!" seized a banner which in his hand led the way to victory. The Prussians followed in his path, but alas! their noble leader fell to the ground, killed by a musket ball, and covered with the banner of his sovereign.

Many Prussian generals followed this example, and led on their troops on foot. Prince Henry of Prussia also leapt from his horse, and stormed a battery at the head of his men. The whole force of the Prussians now rushed on the Austrians, and drove them back to their tents, which had been left standing, that no time might be lost

The Duke Ferdinand of Brunswick, Frederic's greatest support on this occasion, as well as during the whole war, remarked the determination and courage of the enemy, whose left wing still kept their position. He requested the king to allow him to depart from the plan of the battle, as he wished to turn the flank of the Austrians. The answer was, he was to act as he thought advisable. Ferdinand led forward some Prussian regiments, outflanked the enemy, and attacked them in the rear; drove them from hill to hill, and made himself master of seven redoubts, which were defended by Austrian grenadiers, the picked soldiers of the imperial army. The enemy were now in great disorder, and one wing was nearly cut off from the rest of the army; Frederic took advantage of this, and advancing into the space between them, completed the separation.

Unfortunately for the Prussians, their light cavalry was not come up, otherwise the destruction of the imperial army would have been complete. The defeated army now formed two bodies, the smaller of which took to flight, and the other threw themselves into Prague. This place of refuge was chosen on the spur of the moment, without consideration of the consequences of such a step. The difficulties of this position were apparent a few hours after, and the same day, some faint endeavours were made to withdraw from it; but the Prussians had taken possession of ail the outlets from the town, as far as the darkness of night would permit, and drove the Austrians back to the prison they had chosen.

Such were the events of this remarkable battle, which had lasted from nine in the morning till eight in the evening, and which from the number of combatants, the blood spilt, the faults committed by the defeated, the death of one of the leaders at the moment of the greatest disorder, the courage of both armies, the difficulties that were surmounted, the consternation caused by the defeat, might be compared to the Battle of Cannae, where Hannibal gained a victory over the Romans. The defeat of the Romans decided the fate of all Italy, with the exception of Rome, and the defeat of the Austrians would have decided the war, and changed the whole political state of Germany, but for a trifling circumstance, the want of a few pontoons.

The army of Prince Maurice was above Prague, at Branic, on the other side of the Moldaw, over which they wished to form a bridge, to take the enemy in the rear. But the river was swollen, which had not been allowed for, and they had not sufficient pontoons to complete the bridge. These brave Prussians remained spectators of the battle, and all that Prince Maurice could do in this position, was to cannonade the parties of defeated Austrians, who were flying to join the army under General Daun.

The loss of the Prussians on this day was 16,500 killed and wounded, and 1500 were taken prisoners. Many of their most celebrated generals remained on the field of battle; besides Field-Marshall Schwerin, the generals Prince of Holstein, Prince of Anhalt, Goltz, Hautscharmoy; Fouquet and Winterfeld were dangerously wounded. The Austrian's loss upon this occasion was 19,000 killed and wounded; and in this number is included 5000 taken prisoners; 60 pieces of artillery, a number of colours and standards, the military chest, and a considerable quantity of baggage, fell into the hands of the victors. The king wrote from the field of battle to his mother:

I and my brother are both well, the campaign is lost for the

Austrians, and I have 150,000 men in the field. We are masters of a country, that will supply us both with men and money. I shall send a part of my army to pay their respects to the French, and I will follow the Austrians with the rest.

Notwithstanding the decisive character of this battle, the expectations of all Europe were disappointed, with regard to the effects, which ought to have, but did not follow this victory. Everybody imagined that the Austrian Army which was put to flight, would be followed and cut to pieces, and that those who had sought refuge in Prague would be forced to capitulate by want and hunger; but the fate of war frustrated the hopes of the Prussians, shortly afterwards, and gave fresh courage to their enemies. By the Battle of Prague, each of the conflicting parties lost one of their best generals, for Field-Marshall Brown died in consequence of his wounds. Frederic regretted the death of Schwerin, his preceptor in the art of war; he was in the habit of saying, "he would be a perfect general, if he would only allow one to come near him." After the end of the war the king placed a statue on the Wilhelmsplatz in Berlin, in honour of him.

The death of this general has been compared by some to that of Decius. Without wishing to detract from the merit of the Prussian general, the similarity does not appear to us very great. The German general was not, in spite of the danger, which his soldiers shared with him, without hope of surviving the attack; the Roman rushed on to the enemy, to meet a death, which he had no hope of avoiding.

The last moments of Brown were embittered by the fact of the army being shut up in Prague. Suffering from the most dreadful agony, he advised repeatedly, that the troops should rush out, and that the cavalry should cut their way through the enemy in the night. This advice, had it been followed with decision, might have had a successful issue. The Prussians had dearly purchased their victory; they were worn out with the fatigue of the day, and in consequence of the inequality of the ground, were not in the best order of battle. The good advice of the field-marshal was not listened to, and a melancholy fate awaited him; for he was doomed to prolong his existence to be a spectator of the scenes of distress in Prague.

This large city had now within its walls a whole army; besides the garrison there were 50,000 men, and all the principal generals of the army; amongst these the Saxon princes, Prince Frederic of Zweibrücken, the hereditary Prince of Modena, and Prince Charles of Lorrain. Frederic invested the town, which was near ten miles in circumference, and commanded all its approaches by erecting batteries. He summoned the enemy to surrender; the answer was, they would defend themselves to the last.

In the beginning, it was supposed in Vienna that so powerful an army could easily break through the barriers of their prison; but their repeated and fruitless attempts, carried out in despair, were useless; and the Austrians driven back by the fire of the batteries, were forced to return to their rations of horseflesh. This was the food of the army at the end of the first week; the horses of the cavalry and artillery were slaughtered, and the meat sold. Such an extraordinary occurrence, as the whole army being shut up in this city had not been thought of, so that the magazines in the town, were badly provided, the troops were in want of every thing, and the eighty thousand inhabitants were in danger of dying from hunger.

The want of order and regularity of the army in the town, was beyond expression. In order to drive the Prussians out of the Mansfield garden, a vigorous sortie was made under the command of General Buttlar. The party consisted of volunteers, grenadiers and 1000 Croats, who marched in advance. These troops had to scale a wall seven feet high, and they were sent without being provided with ladders; they had doors to break through, and had no axes for the purpose. The Croats, whose activity had been much exercised by the habits of their youth, overcame these difficulties; the walls were scaled, and they fell upon the Prussians.

But the resistance of the latter, and the want of axes, rendered their courage useless; for the other troops were forced to remain on the other side of the wall. These, who were commanded by General Materni, not to be idle, and without regard for their brave companions threw, by his command, a great number of hand grenades, by which several hundred Croats were either killed or wounded, and facilitated the work of the Prussians in driving them out of the gardens.

The remainder fell back upon the grenadiers, who deceived by their blue dress, in the twilight of morning, received them with repeated discharges of musketry; had the Prussians not stopped their pursuit, all the Croats would have been killed. Such was the disorder and confusion in the besieged army, and such ill directed, and ill appointed undertakings could not succeed. In order to excuse their want of success, and to take the blame from the generals, everything that went wrong, was attributed to the feeling, that was said to exist in the town, in favour of the King of Prussia; which in reality neither existed in the army, nor amongst the citizens.

All the princes had their quarters in the Clementinum, a very large Jesuit's College. The position of this building protected its inhabitants from the shells of the enemy; nevertheless the precaution was taken of protecting the windows with boards and straw. The removal of every possible danger, and their well supplied tables, notwithstanding the scarcity in the town, caused ennui to the young princes, who to pass their time entered into different puerile games amongst one another. The hereditary Prince of Modena took no part in these amusements; he was ill, but incessantly occupied in relieving the sufferings of those around him, and he divided his provision of wine among the wounded soldiers. His example was not followed, but rather that of the Prince Charles of Lorrain, whose bigotry was excessive, and who daily attended high-mass.

These religious exercises, and other occupations, diminished the anxiety for the distresses of the army, and the dangers of a town besieged by so powerful an enemy; so much so, that the most simple precautions of defence were neglected. A trifling circumstance, the walk of a monk during the early part of the siege, was the saving of Prague, and the monarchy. This man, whose name was Setzling, perceived a column of dust approaching the northern side of the town. He conceived this to be a body of Prussians, whose object was to take possession of the Belvedere, a height which commanded the Moldaw, and which together with the village of Buben, was not occupied. He assured himself of the fact with his telescope, by ascending the observatory, and hastened to communicate it.

Some thousands of Croats now took possession of the height, and the village, and thus defeated the intention of the Prussians, who would otherwise have fallen upon the portion of Prague, which lies on that side of the river. From this time, the observatory was occupied; not by officers, but by four hussars, who were to watch on all sides with telescopes, and make a report every quarter of an hour.

Prague, although not strongly fortified, was still a strong position for 50,000 men. It was now regularly besieged, and more closely invested. As the principal object was to burn the storehouses, and thereby to increase the existing distress, shells and red hot shot were thrown into the town, which set fire to numbers of houses. Twelve thousand of the inhabitants were driven out of the town, to diminish the consumption of provisions; but the cannonade of the besiegers drove them back into the town. At the end of the third week of the siege, the whole of the new town and the Jews' quarter, were in ashes; also several store-houses with their stores of provisions, were destroyed.

Helpless old men, women and children were killed by the shells, or crushed by the falling houses. The misery was beyond description; the streets were encumbered with carts and horses, the churches were full of the sick and the wounded, and men and animals died off as in time of plague. The clergy, the magistrates and the citizens supplicated for mercy from Prince Charles, which he could not here exercise. He sought for a capitulation, and desired to be allowed to march out of the town; of this Frederic would not hear, and offered conditions which it was not considered right to accept.

During this time the Prussians had to contend, not only against the enemy, but likewise the elements. A dreadful storm, accompa-nied by torrents of rain, tore their tents to pieces, and flooded their camp. The Moldaw became so swollen, that it overflowed its banks, and destroyed the Prussian bridge of boats over the river at Branic. The pontoons were carried away by the stream, whose course carried them to Prague, and the Austrians seized four and twenty of them; the Prussians saved the others from falling into their hands. But the posi-tion of the besieged was not improved; indeed it daily, hourly became worse, and the many generals in Prague who continually held coun-cils of war, knew not what to advise. The hope of cutting their way through the enemy was extinct, and their dependence upon the army of General Daun, which was at Kollin, was very slight.

A most courageous sortie under the command of their best gener-als, and with an army consisting of half the troops in the town, was as fruitless as the former had been. The Austrians fought with despera-tion for five hours, and were driven back. But the most successful at-tack upon the Prussians would have been no avail to the Austrians, without cavalry, or heavy cannon, and what was still worse, worn out by hanger, and without provisions. A continued march with all these wants, in the presence of a watchful and well provided enemy, was impossible. Nothing remained but to submit to their fate.

Such was the critical position of Maria Theresa; all the passes of her kingdom of Bohemia towards Lusatia, Voigtland, Saxony, and Sile-sia, in the hands of the Prussians; the flower of her troops, her most celebrated generals shut up in Prague, the rest of her army beaten, disheartened, and dispersed, in small bodies, so that she was in want of defenders for her own country; the capital of Bohemia reduced to the last extremity by hunger and lire; the army on the point of laying down its arms, and submitting to be made prisoners, and the whole kingdom, even to the provinces adjacent to Austria, ready to fall into the power of the conqueror. All hope of succour from Saxony was cut off, the imperial hereditary lands were exposed to the attacks of the enemy, and even Vienna was not safe from a siege.

The Prussians, who since 1741 had been victorious in eight battles, and had not been once defeated, were looked upon as invincible, and to their king nothing was impossible. The dismay in the imperial city was unbounded they fancied the conqueror was already at its gates, and were consulting upon the means of inducing him to make peace by great sacrifices.

His favourable position was sacrificed by a too hasty determination on the part of Frederic which could only be excused by the pressing danger of his position. The siege of Prague had lasted longer than he expected; and he knew that the Russians, the Swedes, the French, and the troops of the Empire were approaching his dominions from all sides. Every day was of value to him; always victorious; he thought not of the possibility of a defeat; he therefore left the greater part of his army before Prague, and marched with 12,000 men to unite with the Duke of Bevern, and attack General Daun, and thus destroy all the hopes of the besieged.

This general had come from Moravia to join the principal *corps d'armée* of the Austrians, and on the day of the Battle of Prague, he was eight leagues from that city. His proximity saved the Austrians, who had fled from the field of battle. The number of these fugitives was 16,000; these he added to his army, in which he received several small bodies from the states of the Empire. The three battalions in garrison at Vienna joined the army in Bohemia, and this city, the seat of pride, was now left to be defended by a few invalids. With these reinforcements, Daun was encamped upon the hill at Kollin, with 60,000 men, where he had carefully entrenched himself. The circumspection of this general and his contracted capabilities of acting on the offensive, made it most probable, that, notwithstanding the express orders of his court, he would not take any decisive, at any rate not any effectual steps for assisting the besieged; in addition to this, his troops were depressed, and the very name of the Prussians sounded fearfully in their ears.

The Duke of Bevern, who was sent against him with 20,000 Prussians, took advantage of this, and under Daun's eyes, seized upon several well-stored magazines. The light troops of the Austrians were not, however, inactive, and 4000 Croats attacked a number of provision waggons, which under the command of Major Billerbeck, were being escorted to the army. He had only 800 infantry with him, and notwithstanding the inequality of numbers, he defended himself for three hours, and reached the Prussian camp in safety. The king, at the head of his troops, now formed a junction with the Duke of Bevern, and attacked the enemy on the 18th of June. Daun had in the mean time changed his position; one of his lines was formed on the declivity of the hill, the other upon the summit; in advance of him lay villages, hollows, and precipitous heights, in some places inaccessible; and a well placed and numerous artillery rendered him fearless of any attack.

Nevertheless the attack was made on the Austrian right wing under General Hülsen, and carried on with a courage, and decision, which astonished the enemy. Seven times the Prussians renewed the attack against the Austrians in their strong position, driven back by their heavy fire, forming again, to renew it again. Full of warlike ardour they clambered over the bodies of their companions, as over heaps of earth. But accident, and not courage, nor science in the art of war, decided the fate of this day.

The Prussians had already gained great advantages; the right wing of the enemy was beaten, the body of cavalry under the command of General Nadasti, had been driven back as far as Kollin by General Ziethen, so that it was completely separated from the army of Daun, who had already determined on retreating, and the *aides-de-camp* were on their way to each wing with orders for this purpose. The cannon were being removed, and the secret order under Daun's own hand, in pencil, to the generals, was: "The retreat is to Suchdol;" when the fate of the day was changed, and the balance turned most unexpectedly to the disadvantage of Frederic.

The orders and wishes of the king were never so badly executed as on this day. The right wing was to have cooperated with the left, by keeping a certain position, without coming into action. This was not done; Prince Maurice of Dessau, one of his best generals, allowed himself to be guided by the imprudence of General Manstein, who entered into pursuit of a party of Croats. Maurice, instead of steadily advancing with the main body of the army, broke the time by halting to support Manstein. By this means the whole disposition of the army became changed, and fell into disorder; an attack was made, were there should have been none.

The Austrians behaved with the greatest bravery. The Hungarian infantry regiment of Haller, had expended all their ammunition; at the moment it was impossible to get a supply. In this dilemma the Hungarians, who would not fall back, had recourse, not to their bayonets, but shouldering their muskets, to their swords; they rushed on the Prussians, did great execution, but in their turn suffered severity, for the greater part of this regiment was cut to pieces by the Prussian cavalry.

The Prussian battalions, which were much thinned by the fire of the enemy, now formed in small bodies with considerable intervals, of which the cavalry took advantage to charge the enemy, and with great success; but a *cuirassier* regiment following this example, came under the fire of a battery, were completely put to the rout, and threw the infantry regiments in their rear into disorder. The order of battle which had been deranged by many errors, increased the disorder which already existed in the right wing.

Some Saxon regiments of cavalry who were in Daun's army, now fell upon the Prussians without orders from Daun, but by those of Colonel Benkendorf, who took upon himself to take this decisive step. When once the line of infantry is broken by the cavalry, nothing remains for them but to be cut to pieces or taken prisoners; so was it with the Prussians at Kollin, notwithstanding their courage; whole squadrons of horse rushed onwards, but even in this confusion of men and horse, the body guard of the king formed into solid squares, and fired by platoons with the same order and regularity as if they had been on parade; but fresh bodies of Saxon cavalry came up, and taking the Prussians in the rear, forced them to give up this unequal fight.

The Saxon dragoons thirsted for revenge; the defeat they had met with twelve years previously in Silesia, still rankled in their minds, and as they cut down the Prussians they constantly exclaimed: "Take that for Striegau!" All those who came within the reach of these men, were either cut down or made prisoners; the body guard of Frederic, which consisted of a thousand of the finest soldiers, for the most part foreigners, but educated at Potsdam in the military school, were completely cut to pieces. They fought, as if for their country, to the very last, and covered the ground with their bodies; only two hundred and fifty survived this day.

The Austrians remained masters of the field of battle; it was nine in the evening, and the left wing of the Prussians, who were victorious, and knew nothing of the defeat, were going to encamp and celebrate the victory, when news came that the battle was lost, and that they must retreat. Prince Maurice came in person to give this order; the troops formed immediately in line to attack the enemy; the Austrian soldiers seemed to think it was not right to do things by halves, and the right wing, without orders, began to descend the heights, to attack the Prussians; but they were stopped by the command to halt, which ran through the ranks

The leaders of the Austrians remained quiet spectators of the novelty of the Prussians retiring from the field of battle, and thus Frederic was enabled to retreat, without molestation, from this part of the field of battle, which he had retained until late in the night; his retreat was made with the greatest order and military judgment. His loss was 8000 men of his best infantry, but only 16 pieces of cannon, which could not be removed, in consequence of the horses being killed. The Austrians lost 9000 killed and wounded; the loss of the Saxons was also considerable, but to them was attributed the glory of the victory, and they had now, within a twelvemonth, twice rescued the Austrian monarchy, at Pirna and at Kollin.

This defeat dispirited the Prussians; over accustomed to victory, it filled their minds with evil forebodings for the future, and many of the commanders, even of high rank, who had hitherto cared but little for the enemy who was advancing on all sides, from thinking that good fortune had attached itself to Frederic, were now disheartened; they thought of the famous Charles the XII., who for nine years carried every thing before him, until on one unfortunate day the blind goddess deserted and forsook him for ever; this they applied to their own case, and exclaimed: "This is our Pultowa!"

The king collected his scattered forces at Nimburg; like Marius on the ruins of Carthage, Frederic sat deep in thought, without raising his head, and making figures with his stick in the sand; the future was fearful to think of. At last he sprang up, and gave his orders to the soldiers, as they arrived, with cheerfulness. He gathered together the small remains of his bodyguard; all the soldiers of this chosen body were known to him personally; their names, their age, their country. Many had he honoured with his favour, and had determined to push their fortunes; but they were no more; in a few hours they had all fallen; they had fought like heroes, and for him had died. Never upon the occasion of any of the misfortunes of his life, but this, was Frederic known to shed a tear, but now he wept.

The rejoicings at Vienna were beyond all bounds; the most brilliant fetes were given, great presents made, and medals struck in honour of

45

the victory; all the officers who were present, received an addition to their pay; the wounded the same, and the soldiers a gratuity; and in order to render this day for ever memorable to the Austrians, the order of Theresa was instituted, and one of the statutes of the order required, that the 18th of June should be always celebrated to perpetuate the memory of this victory.

Shortly after this battle Frederic wrote a remarkable letter to his friend, the Lord Marshall, which well describes his feelings. In it he says:

> Good fortune, my dear Lord, leads us often to put too much confidence in our powers; three and twenty battalions were not troops sufficient to force sixty thousand men from a strong position; another time the affair shall be better arranged. Fortune has this day turned her back upon me; I should have been prepared for it; She is a woman, and I do not pay my court to the sex; she has declared herself for the ladies, and I am their opponent. What say you to this alliance of the Markgraf of Brandenburg? How astonished the great Frederic William would be to see his grandson hand and glove with the Russians, the Austrians, nearly all Germany and the French! I do not know, whether it would be a disgrace to me to succumb, but I well know it will be no honour to overcome me.

This philosophy under his misfortune diminished the number of his unarmed enemies, and increased the number of his admirers. Frederic's position had, by this one defeat, become fearful; his best expectations had disappeared, and his overthrow seemed unavoidable; as if misfortunes of all kinds were to come on him at once, he received, a few days after the battle, the news of the death of his mother, whom he had always tenderly loved. She had pined away, from anxiety for the future, from the beginning of the war, and the defeat of the Prussians was her death blow.

The Battle of Kollin decided the fate of the besieged in Prague, and the siege was raised on the 20th of June, two days after the battle, and after having lasted forty four days. The retreat of the Prussians was made with the greatest order, and not secretly; they left the trenches with their bands playing, but not without loss. A number of wounded and some cannon fell into the hands of the enemy, who now hurried out of their prison, and fell upon the rear of the retreating army. The dangerous position of these was benefitted by the arrangements of the king, who very wisely divided his force in several separate bodies, and thus deceived the enemy; this facilitated the march through the Bohemian mountains.

In addition to this, the inactivity of the Austrian commanders was taken every advantage of by their watchful and active enemy, which was the cause of the Prussians recovering, most unexpectedly, the greater part of the cannon they had left behind. This was mostly in the village of Tuchomierziz near Prague. Notice of its being there was given to the Austrians, immediately that the siege was raised, but they did not attempt to make themselves masters of this booty, until three days after. It was now too late; the peasants met the troops, sent for this purpose, with complaints, for, in the mean time, the rear guard of the Prussians had not only taken the cannon, but also driven away all the cattle from the village and the neighbourhood.

The eyes of the king were now turned upon the defence of his own provinces, which required protection; for the Battle of Kollin was the signal for the French, Russians, Swedes and troops of the Empire to fall upon the Prussian states. The authorities of the Empire declared the king, in due form, to be the enemy of the Empire; the Russians, with 100,000 men, invaded the kingdom of Prussia, which was defended by 30,000 men, at whose head was Field-Marshall Leywald; the principal body of the French army had taken possession of the whole of Westphalia; an other body of French troops united with the troops of the Empire, to invade Saxony, and the Swedes were embarked on the Baltic to fall on Pomerania.

The Prussian subjects of Frederic, who, notwithstanding these fearful prospects, never despaired of the fortunes of their king, looked upon his ruin as their own, and participated in the fame of his great deeds, determined to he active in his support. Frederic had always governed them with mildness, and by good laws, and at that time, the French system of finance had not been thought of in the Prussian states. They were anxious to display this love to their king, as well as their patriotism, to the world. The states general of Pomerania assembled of their own accord, and determined to raise and keep on foot, at their own expense, 5000 men. The states general of Brandenburg, and also those of Magdeburg and Halberstadt, followed their example, and respectively raised 5000 and 2000 men; these were soldiers who did not belong to the regular army.

These provinces also furnished a number of Hussars, who served during the whole war, and under the command of General Werner, and Belling distinguished themselves greatly. A great difficulty lay in the way of forming these troops; there was a deficiency of officers, but this was soon remedied; men, who had become gray in the service, and lived retired on their estates, joined immediately, and served in different ranks. In Stettin a small fleet was equipped, consisting of two frigates carrying 20 guns, three brigs of 10, and nine other vessels carrying 6 guns each.

This patriotism was displayed throughout the kingdom; in order to save the king's studs, the horses were distributed among the farmers; in the Westphalian provinces Minden, and Ravensberg, which were in the hands of the enemy, their efforts were very much contracted by their position; but they showed their intentions by keeping the revenue from the enemy, wherever it was possible, and sending it to their monarch. This was also done in the other provinces which were in the hands of the enemy, and they would not, throughout Westphalia, permit any deserters to remain in their neighbourhood, although these thought themselves safe under the protection of the French; they were driven out of the country with shame and contempt, and forced to join their regiments again.

The army was in want of horses; the President Blumenthal, afterwards minister of state, induced the inhabitants of Magdeburg, and Halberstadt to give up theirs to the king. The nobility, the clergy, citizens, and farmers, all united to make this sacrifice; people gave up their own comfort, took their horses from their carriages, and sent them, to the number of 4000, to remount the cavalry. Field-Marshall Brown was now dead, and the Austrians were under the command of Prince Charles and General Daun. These generals had increased their strength since the retreat of Frederic, of which they wished to take advantage; they invaded Lusatia which the Prince of Prussia, the eldest brother of the king, defended with a strong body of men, on the Bohemian frontier.

A great mistake was made by the Prussians in their movements, by which the pass of Gabel was lost; General Puttkammer defended it for three days with four battalions against 20,000 Austrians, but was at last obliged to retire, having received no reinforcements. After this the Prussians withdrew from Bohemia, and retired on Lusatia, but not without loss of their baggage, and pontoons, which were destroyed, in the passes of the mountains.

At last the king formed a junction with this corps at Bautzen, highly discontented with what had occurred; he received the generals of his brother's army very coldly, and made use of the expression, that they deserved to lose their heads, always excepting General Winterfeld; with the prince, whose fault was want of decision, he was so displeased, that he immediately left the army, and went to Berlin, where he died the following year.

The army under General Daun besieged the town of Zittau, one of the most flourishing manufacturing towns in Germany, and in which there was a magazine of the Prussians. The impetuosity of the enemy went so far, that in order to gain possession of this unfortified town, which was merely defended by a few battalions, and which actually belonged to an ally, they threw a large number of shells, and red hot shot into it; and the consequence was, that this beautiful, rich and densely populated town was in a few hours reduced to a heap of ashes; an act of barbarity to which they were incited by the Prince Xavier of Saxony, who was present, and who imagined that the inhabitants were not favourable to the cause of the Austrians. Upwards of three hundred citizens were buried under the ruins of the houses, of which only sixty remained standing; and the loss of property by this wanton devastation was enormous, for it was above ten millions of dollars.

The Prussian garrison cut their way through the enemy, and only a small number who could not, in consequence of the flames, join their companions, were taken prisoners. All these misfortunes stimulated the king to fresh exertion, and he wished to attack the enemy in their strong entrenchments; and he advanced for this purpose into the immediate neighbourhood of their camp at Ostritz; some of his generals, however, whose advice he asked, placed the danger, and uselessness of this undertaking, in such a strong light before him, that he gave up his intention.

Laudon, who afterwards became so celebrated, now appeared at the head of 2000 Croats, posted at the foot of the Bohemian mountains, and by his position rendered the road into Saxony unsafe; General Manstein who was covered with wounds at the battle at Kollin, and of which defeat he had been the cause, was attacked by these Croats, as he was on his way into Saxony with an escort of 300 recruits. Laudon attacked and dispersed the escort; Manstein who was in a carriage, rolled up in bandages, sprang out of it, defended himself like a madman, and notwithstanding they were desirous to save his life, he was deaf to all remonstrance, and was cut to pieces; in consequence of this, Laudon was promoted to the rank of general. His commission which was sent to him from Vienna, fell into the hands of some Prussian hussars; the king sent it to him, and at the same time wished him joy of his promotion.

Frederic now attacked the position of Daun, who had formed a very strong encampment on the Neisse, where he was very much annoyed by the Prussian light troops; and the Prussian General Werner, who had so distinguished himself in this war, and was an Hungarian and a protestant, carried on these attacks with zeal. He had left the imperial service, where he was neglected, as more was thought of his religious opinions than of his services; in addition to this was the hatred of General Nadasti, and these causes induced him to enter the Prussian service. Ambition, hatred and revenge united in the bosom of this general to make him anxious to impress upon the minds of his enemies his worth, and their loss. He was especially desirous of making Nadasti prisoner; ever in activity, he followed him on the march, and in quarters, and often in the night he crossed the country, to appear unexpectedly in his rear; he kept him constantly in a state of uncertainty, and was more than once on the point of attaining his much desired object.

Nadasti once escaped with so much difficulty that the whole of his baggage, and the escort, fell into the hands of Werner; in this a number of letters were found, from the Queen of Poland, in which she imparted information to this general. Many such letters had already fallen into the hands of the Prussians written at the time that she was sending her compliments every morning to the king; in which letters she was inciting the Saxon soldiers, in the pay of the Prussians, to revolt or to desert.

Fink, the commandant of Dresden, showed these letters to the queen, and in order to put a stop to the continuation of a correspondence, so disadvantageous to the interest of the king, the most stringent means were adopted; the writer of the letters, Schoenberg, although only acting by the command of his sovereign, was seized and sent to Spandau, where he remained during the whole of the war; he was only released by a separate article of the treaty of peace, and received a handsome reward for his sufferings.

Daun remained quiet in his camp; however anxious the king might be for a battle, the imperial general was equally desirous of not meeting the Prussians in an open field of battle, at any rate now that the allied armies were advancing from all quarters. A French body of troops had already reached Erfurt, and other troops of this nation were advancing from the west; the troops of the Empire advanced from the South, the Russians from the East, and the Swedes who were already in Pomerania, came from the North.

Chapter 3: Campaign of the French in 1757

At the time of these occurrences in Germany, France had taken the most decisive steps towards the prosecution of the war. Here, as in Austria private feeling got the upper hand of state policy; the Duchess of Pompadour, flattered by the Empress Theresa, the minister of war, Argenson, who was always anxious to extend his authority, the *dauphiness*, who always in tears was entreating for assistance, and even King Louis himself, jealous of the greatness of Frederic, all were unanimous in employing the whole power of France, to destroy the Prussian monarchy. The jealousy of Louis was tinged with somewhat of hatred, in consequence of his having heard of some jests made on him by Frederic. In addition to this came the strong contrast of their mode of living, in their respective palaces of Versailles and Sanssouci; and the remonstrances of Cardinal Bernis, who was much beloved, both by the king and his mistress, and, who was not disposed for war, were not listened to, notwithstanding: they were urged with much reason, eloquence and justice.

In vain he insisted upon the most simple truths, upon the maxims, as regarded foreign policy, which had been established from long experience; on the political position of Germany, on the empty state of the treasury, and the want of generals. In opposition to this, they brought forward the power of the allies, and its natural consequence, the rapidity and facility of the victory to be gained; in addition to this the cherished expectation of depriving England of her much valued Hanover, and then by its restitution to destroy the faith of treaties and thus effectually to alienate Great Britain and Prussia.

A large French Army now began its march, under the command of Marshall D'Estrées, grandson of Louvois, the minister of Louis the

XIV, He had distinguished himself by his military talents in the Netherlands, and was reckoned by the Great Maréchal Saxe, as one of the best French generals, and he proved himself not unworthy of this honour. He crossed the Rhine, and the Weser, took possession of the fortress of Wesel, which had been deserted by the Prussians, also the Duchies of Cleves, and East Friesland, overran the whole of Westphalia, made himself master of the territories of Cassel, and laid Hanover under contribution.

Here they were not well prepared for resistance. It is true a corps of observation, consisting of Hanoverians, Hessians, Brunswickers, and a few battalions of other troops together with a few thousand Prussians, had been assembled in the spring, but these, in all, only amounted to 40,000 men, and were too small a body to resist the power of the French Army, which was more than 100,000 strong. What made the position of these troops worse, was the inefficiency of their leader, the Duke of Cumberland, who possessed but little talent in the art of war, though considered a good general in consequence of his victory over the Scotch, at the Battle of Culloden, but whose principal merit consisted in being the son of George the Second. The Hanoverian ministry had formed a very inefficient plan of operations, in consequence of their ignorance in the art of war, and this was approved of by the Duke of Cumberland, but not by Frederic.

It was in vain the King of Prussia sent to the British monarch a plan formed after deep consideration, and which would have been highly advantageous to the interest of all. George the Second, although he had been present at the Battle of Dettingen, knew nothing of warfare, and having to decide between the plan of an experienced general, and that of a minister who had probably never seen a camp, he chose the latter, which was restricted to the defence of the Weser; and he sent back to Germany the Hanoverian and Hessian troops, which had been required by the fears of the ministry, in the beginning of the war, to protect the coast of England. Frederic made a last effort, and sent General Schmettau to Hanover, who, in addition to his military talents, was possessed of great powers of eloquence; but these were thrown away on the Hanoverian ministry. They persisted in their plan, deceived by the promises of France, who had made their inactivity the price of neutrality.

The Duke of Cumberland, closely pressed by the French army, always retreated with his. At last the two armies were engaged at the village of Hastenbeck near Hameln on the 26th of July. The allied army was posted upon heights between the Weser and a thicket. The French attacked them here and, after meeting with a spirited defence, made themselves masters of some batteries and one of the heights. The duke who lost all courage and prudence, left the field of battle, and retired on Hameln, at the very moment, that the hereditary prince of Brunswick had retaken a battery, and that the Hanoverian Colonel Breitenbach had gained such considerable advantage as to remain master of the field of battle till night, when he joined the duke with the cannon and colours he had taken. This commander was now in despair at the blunders he had made, but the list of which was shortly to be increased. His loss consisted in upwards of three hundred killed, nine hundred wounded, and two hundred and twenty prisoners.

For the advantage the French had gained, they were principally indebted to General Chevest, who previous to the commencement of the battle had taken the Marquis Brehault, who commanded under him, by the hand, and with heroic enthusiasm said to him:

Swear by the honour of a brave man, that you will sooner see every one of your men dead on the field of battle than give way.

Brehault swore, and kept his word. He was colonel of a regiment from Picardy. Louis the XV., to reward him for his conduct, offered him a pension of 2000 *livres*. Brehault answered, that be had not acted with the hope of reward, and begged that the pension might be divided amongst the officers who most wanted it. He was required to point out those who had most distinguished themselves; his answer was:

None of us did more than his companions; all fought bravely, and are ready to do it again. I must therefore give in the names as they stand in the regimental list.

The victory was however but trifling and not followed by any consequences of importance, had it not been, that, from anxiety for the archives of Hanover and other valuables, which for security had been removed to Stade, the duke, in spite of all remonstrances of his generals, took the decisive step of marching with his whole army to the North, to defend this town. The consequences of this retreat were soon apparent; Hameln which was well provisioned and provided with ammunition, surrendered on the first summons; Minden offered to capitulate, and the town of Hanover sent commissioners to regulate the contributions.

Frederic now withdrew his troops from the allied army. The astonished Duke of Cumberland was however soon enclosed by the French, cut off from the Elb and, placed in such a position that nothing remained for him but to capitulate. This was done on the 8th of September at Kloster Seeven under the guarantee of the King of Danemark. The principal article of this capitulation was, that the Hessians and the troops from Brunswick, Gotha and Bückeburg should be disbanded, but the Hanoverians should remain in the neighbourhood of Stade.

The Danish ambassador Count Lynar was the author of this extraordinary convention, in which the state policy of the 18th century was nowhere apparent; Count Lynar in fact said, that it was not dictated by such earthly knowledge, but by inspiration from heaven. He, in a well known letter, attributed this masterpiece of diplomacy to divine inspiration, which, to use his own expression, had given him power to stop the French Army, even as power had been given to Joshua to stop the course of the sun.

The Marshal D'Etrées had not the honour of this capitulation, as the command had been taken from him, by the court intrigues of the Prince de Soubise. This prince not only the creature, but also the favourite, of the Duchess de Pompadour, was named by the court to a command of a detached body of the army under the marshal. The disputes of these two commanders soon broke out, and the Marshall D'Etrées was in consequence sacrificed, and nothing but the fear of turning all the marshalls against her, prevented the powerful mistress from nominating her beloved Soubise to the rank of commander in chief. She allowed herself, to be persuaded to give it to the Duke de Richelieu, notwithstanding her hatred of him, but who in order to gain her over, had promised to allow her to nominate all the commissaries of the army; an offer which produced its effect. This general found every thing ready for his triumph in the army, and nothing could be easier than to enjoy the honours already prepared for him.

In the short space of eleven months, this was the second army of well disciplined and courageous soldiers, who had been forced to capitulate; but they were disposed of in a very different manner, in these two different instances. Frederic allowed the Saxon Army to remain intact, that they might fight for him; Richelieu, who now commanded in the place of D'Estrées, did the same with the Hanoverians and Brunswickers, but without any intentions as to their future destination. They were not treated as prisoners of war, neither dismissed, disarmed, nor disbanded; the order of their march was regulated, but their future destination was not fixed. The French commander thought, that these troops, who hated the French, would merely by his orders, remain in a state of inactivity; in addition to this error, Richelieu treated the convention as an uncertain political negotiation, whereas he had the right to look upon it, as a fixed military convention.

All the western provinces and towns of the King of Prussia were in the possession of his enemies, with the exception of Geldern. The French under the command of Count Beausobre, blockaded the fortress; in consequence of the river and the ditch, the siege was attended with great difficulties; they were therefore anxious to take it by surprise, for which the most extraordinary preparations were made; a number of French soldiers practised swimming and diving every day, and they were required to jump into the water with order and activity. The plan was that these swimmers should conduct boats, full of soldiers, to the walls of the fortifications. In the town were a number of French and Austrian deserters, and other discontented soldiers, and the burghers were dissatisfied with the duration of the blockade; pardon was offered to the first, and promises to the latter, that they might create disturbances. The Prussian commandant had now been besieged for fifteen weeks, with treachery within his walls, and was at last forced to capitulate; the garrison, which was 800 strong, marched out with the honours of war, and the fortress was taken possession of by the French.

By the convention with the Duke of Cumberland, Frederic lost the assistance of the army, which had kept the French in check, and who could now turn their whole power against him. Frederic, who was hard pressed by the consequences of the Battle of Kollin, was so moved by this circumstance, that he made bitter reproaches to the King of England upon his neutrality. He said in his letters:

> Never would I have given up my alliance with France, had it not been for the great promises of your majesty. I do not regret the treaty, but, Sire, do not from pusillanimity give me up, a prey to my enemies, after having brought all Europe against me.

This letter remained unanswered, but George sent him subsidies; Frederic refused the gold, but requested to have English soldiers, to which the English ministry could not as yet make up their minds.

Hanover was now in possession of the French as well as the Duchy of Cleves, the civil administration of which, however, was made over to the Austrians, and this country was treated, as if it had been abandoned by its masters. According to the plan of operations, the Duke of Orleans, with an army of 24,000 men, was to besiege Cassel, and overrun the Hessian territory; upon receiving information that the country would be occupied without resistance, he thought the enterprise unworthy of his fame, and gave up the command to General Contadis. This general took possession of the country, and gave the Hessian ministry to understand, that, the only way of their obtaining favour and mercy, was by implicit obedience to the orders of his monarch. The city of Cassel was formally given up to the French on the 15th of July, who here formed a magazine and hospital for the army; but the Hessians gained nothing by their submission, for they were treated as enemies, and heavy contributions were immediately laid on them. The commissary General Foulon had charge of these levies, and governed in Cassel like a *grand vizier*, the *landgraf*, not to be a witness to the tyranny of this man, left Cassel, and retired to Hamburg, where he remained during the war.

The conduct of the French had been just and moderate, so long as the Marshall D'Estrées was in command; he displayed under all circumstances his generosity as well as his talents as a general, and he promised his protection to the university of Goettingen, in a letter as honourable to him as to the university to which it was addressed. His disgrace caused some anxiety to the court, who feared the indignation of the country at his being recalled, without cause, in the midst of his successful career; it became therefore desirable that he should leave the army of his own accord. The king wrote to him from Versailles, removing him from the command, which he was to give up to Richelieu, but at the same time stating, that it would be agreeable to the king, that he should still remain with the army; D'Estrées obeyed the kings orders, but did not comply with the wish that he should remain with the army.

As soon as his successor arrived he departed for Aix la Chapelle, under the excuse of using the baths; he made no complaints, and his conduct under these circumstances was so noble, that every one, even Richelieu was touched by it; and he wrote to the king, that D'Estrées had given up the command like a hero, but had imparted his plans and projects as a friend and a gentleman.

Richelieu availed himself of the dispositions of his predecessor, so that he forced the allies to the capitulation already mentioned. But never was a piece of good fortune in war made less use of; the affair of Pirna decided the fate of Saxony, during the whole of the war, even as that of Saratoga had given freedom to the north-eastern states of America; the convention of Kloster Seeven, which was dictated by the stronger to the weaker party, had alarmed the cabinets of London and Berlin, and had reduced the ministers in Hanover, Cassel and Brunswick to despair, had produced no effects of importance, excepting its immediate consequences.

One of the first steps of Richelieu after this, was to take possession of Hanover and Brunswick, and as the French occupied the towns of Brunswick and Wolfenbüttel, the town of Blankenburg was declared neutral as the residence of the duke, to which place he retired with his family, having first recommended his subjects to treat the French as friends. Richelieu entered Hanover, as in triumph; and from here he sent many of his best troops to join the army of the Prince of Soubise, who now, in conjunction with the troops of the Empire, was attacking Saxony.

The prince, at the commencement of his march, had a disagreement with the Swiss regiments under his command; they hesitated to cross the Rhine, especially the regiment of General Lochmann; upon this general being asked by Soubise, why they served; "to cover your retreat," answered the Swiss; at last the Swiss cantons gave their consent to the march of their troops into Germany. Richelieu himself fell upon the Prussian provinces, and besieged Magdeburg; but Frederic foreseeing the fate of the army under the Duke of Cumberland, had withdrawn his troops from it, and strengthened the garrison of this town with them.

The war had now lasted for a year, and notwithstanding the different nations and people of which the armies were formed, no acts of great cruelty or barbarity had been, as yet, committed. Richelieu was the first to set the example; he either plundered or devastated the towns and villages, or else, in order to raise contributions from the inhabitants, threatened them with fire and sword.

The excesses of the French, no longer restrained, were nearly equal to those of the Cossacks; the rich were forced to pay contributions for their fellow citizens, and women and girls were alike subject to the brutality of the soldiery. Nothing was more common than for these troops to hang people as spies, without a shadow of evidence against them, and several hundred Germans, without regard to rank, age or position, met with this fate during the war. The watch word of this new French commander was "contribution," not so much for the service of his king as for his own; protected by the mistress of the king, he committed the most ignoble acts, and not infrequently, carried on the operations of the war to his own private advantage. No general, during the whole of this war, enriched himself so much as he did; and there was so little concealment about it, that the Parisians called a palace which he built, "*Le Pavilion d'Hanovre.*"

A new enemy now came forward against the king, to whom he could not be indifferent; this was the Duke of Würtemberg, who governed a warlike people Not content with sending his contingent of soldiers to the army of the Empire, he placed all his troops in the French pay to fight for the Austrians. These soldiers, who had always, as Protestants, looked on the King of Prussia, as the protector of their religion, expressed the greatest discontent at this arrangement of the duke's, and it at last broke out in open mutiny, on the occasion of 4000 men being mustered at Stuttgart, before the French commissary in the month of June; they exclaimed, that they had been sold, fired on the officers who wished to restrain them, and left their quarters in mid day; only 1000 men remained. The duke, who was at this time with the Austrian Army, went immediately to Stuttgart, raised fresh troops, quieted the old by promising to command them in person, and joined the imperial army, in August, at the head of 6000 men. This increase, from all sides, of the army of the enemy, occurred at a time that the Prussians had been much thinned by the different battles, in which they had been engaged.

Frederic now divided his army into several bodies, in order to check the advance of the different forces upon Saxony and his own dominions. As he destined his principal army, under the Duke of Bevern, to defend Silesia, he only retained 18,000 men under his own command, and this small body was so weakened by different detachments, that when in face of the French at Erfurt, he had only 10,000 men. In order to conceal this weakness from the enemy he did not encamp his troops, but quartered them in the villages, often changing them; by which means, the names of the regiments were always different, in order to deceive the spies; he did not confine himself to acting on the defensive, but carried on his operations vigorously, wherever he could do so with advantage.

Colonel Mayer had been sent, shortly after the Battle of Prague into Franconia, with 2000 men, not only to subdue the states of the Empire, but also to retard the advance of the troops out of the south of Germany, and to display to the recruits in Regensburg, the enterprising spirit of the Prussians. He attacked the Bishopric of Bamberg, raised contributions, went through the circle of Franconia, and overran the upper Palatinate. These unexpected operations had such an effect upon the assembly at Regensburg, that many of the delegates, who had declared themselves in the most decided manner against Prussia, sought safety in flight.

The Elector of Bavaria and also other princes of the Empire became anxious, at the success of Prussia, and declared, they did not make war against the king, and wished to enter into negotiation with Frederic. There were serious thoughts of doing away with the alliance with Maria Theresa; but the defeat of Kollin changed the face of affairs. In the mean time, Mayer threatened Nürnberg, and the town addressed itself for protection to the assembled states of the circle; the Franconian Areopagus showed their wisdom under these circumstances; they required that Mayer should show authority for his invasion in Franconia, and make good all damage.

The Prussian commander, who was better supplied with powder and ball than with parchment, and was accompanied by soldiers thirsting after booty, showed the deputation his body of men, and asked, with a smile, if they wished for better authority than that. He required the neutrality of the town, which was agreed to; indeed the whole circle would have declared itself neutral, had his body of men been stronger; they however only acted on the defensive, and with the intention of cutting off the retreat of the Prussians, troops were assembled on all sides, unexpected by Mayer.

But he, having gained his point, marched back on his return, destroyed the bridges he crossed, cut his way through a body of Würzburg and Bamberg troops, and at last reached Bohemia; in his retreat from Franconia he brought with him hostages, and amongst others two patricians from Nürnberg. The court at Vienna took advantage of these circumstances to recommend to the imperial states more activity in their operations; the imperial exhortation, however, was not attended to. Mayer was looked on as a villain, and his soldiers as a band of vagrant robbers, who were public enemies, and deserved the punishment of murderers.

The Austrians took advantage of the separated position of the different Prussian armies, and General Haddick marched to the gates of Berlin at the head of 4000 men. This capital without fortifications and in part without a wall, and only defended by palisades, was garrisoned by 2000 militia, a few recruits and a few hundred regular soldiers. The royal family, on the news of the approach of the enemy had retired to

Spandau; but there was nothing to fear for the capital from so small a body of men, who were always in danger of being cut off from the main army. Haddick summoned the town, and took possession at the same time of the Silesian and Cottbüsser gates.

The palisades near the first were broken down, and the Austrians rushed into the suburb; the inhabitants showed themselves worthy of the Brandenburgian name, and the trades were anxious to unite and to drive out the enemy; but the want of experience and pusillanimity of the commander, who was hooted and laughed at by the women, would allow of no attempt of the kind. There was only a skirmish between some Prussian troops and the Austrians in the Cöpenicker suburb, but which produced nothing decisive.

The news of the approach of Prince Maurice of Anhalt alarmed the enemy in Berlin. Haddick who knew the danger of his position, was moderate in his demands, and these were at last granted, not so much from fear, as to put an end to the disquiet. The sum which at first had been required was 600,000 dollars, but this was reduced to 200,000. Haddick in consideration of this, received a present of 12,000 dollars, his *aide-de-camp* 3000 in money, besides presents of jewels; on the other hand, Haddick gave an assurance, that the city of Berlin should not again be visited in this way by the Austrians. After this Haddick requested the magistrates to give him two dozen of ladies gloves, stamped with the arms of the town, to send as a present to the empress; he received these and the money, and marched off in the greatest haste. He had but little time to spare for a few hours after General Seydlitz entered Berlin at the head of 3000 men, and the following day, the whole force of the Prince of Anhalt. The king had also began his march to cut off his retreat, but he was fortunate enough, by forced marches, and avoiding the high roads, to escape from the enemy.

In the meanwhile the war was carried on in Prussia, by the Russians, in a fearful manner. Notwithstanding the good will of the Russian ministry towards the court of England and especially of the High Chancellor Bestuchef, who had been won over by English gold, the determination of the Empress Elizabeth, injured as a woman, but determined to revenge herself as a monarch, prevented the endeavours of the court of England, from causing a separation between Austria and Russia. The humiliation of Frederic, and the conquest of Prussia were the foundation of the present Russian system, and it was irrevocably determined on, in the cabinet of St. Petersburg, to follow it up in the most energetic manner. In consequence of this, the Russians marched into Prussia 100,000 strong under the command of Field-Marshall Apraxin, and Memel was taken after a bombardment of five days. The garrison capitulated, with liberty to withdraw from the town; but the faith of this military compact was broken, and the greater part of the Prussian soldiers were either forced to enter the Russian service, or to emigrate to Russia. A number of peaceable Prussian subjects, who were inhabitants of this town, shared the fate of the latter, and were driven forth by the Russians, with their wives and children; their tears and lamentations were of no avail, and these unhappy people were forced to leave their native land, to people the desolate provinces of a nation of barbarians.

These acts of cruelty were accompanied by the issuing of manifestoes, full of moderation; in these they justified the hostilities, by the friendship existing between the two empresses; one of these manifestoes contained a formal invitation to all the inhabitants of the kingdom, without distinction either of rank or of religion, to emigrate to Russia, where the greatest advantages were promised them. The king in a counter-manifesto, explained how contrary this conduct was, to the rights and to the customs of European nations in time of war; he described the mild government of Prussia, in contradistinction to the tyrannical conduct of the Russian, who for the slightest offences, was in the habit of punishing by lacerating the body, and by banishment to wastes and deserts; he then put it to his people, if for such rewards, they would become traitors to their country.

The light troops of the Russians 12,000 strong, Cossacks, Tartars and Calmucks, devastated the country with fire and sword in a manner unknown in Europe, since the time of the Huns. These wretches murdered or mangled unarmed and defenceless people; they hanged them on trees, or cut off their noses or ears; others were hacked in pieces in the most cruel and disgusting manner. They set villages on fire, from wanton cruelty, and that the inhabitants might be burnt alive in them, they often formed a circle round the devoted village, previous to setting fire to it. The graves were disturbed, and the bones thrown about; people of rank and the clergy lacerated with hooks, and placed naked on red hot coals; children were torn from their parents or murdered before their eyes; women and girls dishonoured, and many destroyed themselves, to escape the brutality of these wretches; some sought refuge in Dantzick to which place the archives of the kingdom were conveyed from Königsberg.

Frederic received the accounts of these distressing occurrences at a time, when every day was burthened with misfortunes. However much his sword was required against his enemies, he still made use of his pen; for the most remarkable peculiarities of this extraordinary war, were the constant occurrence of scenes of murder and the issue of numerous manifestoes, and not only the powers of the body, but also those of the mind were brought into the field. Never were so many battles fought in any war, nor at the same time so many manifestoes sent forth as in these calamitous times. By them, great monarchs wished to justify their proceedings, in order to preserve the respect of those countries, whose approbation they could well do without. This was a triumph of public opinion, and rendered necessary by the diffusion of that knowledge, which had already began to spread its light, and has since shone so brilliantly over all Europe.

Field-Marshall Leywald, who commanded in Prussia and to whom Frederic had given full powers to act, could only bring 24,000 men into the field, against the enemy. But with these he attacked them in their entrenchments, at Grossjägersdorf, on the 30th of August. At first the fortune of the day was quite in favour of the small army, who this time did not fight to satisfy the ambition of their monarch, but to defend their homes and their families from a horde of barbarians. The Prussians fought like lions; the dragoons and the hussars stormed the batteries of the enemy, and emulated the infantry who, in spite of the unfavourable nature of the ground, carried everything before them. These brave troops had already taken several pieces of cannon, repulsed the cavalry of the enemy, beaten a grenadier regiment, and routed one wing of the army, when they were deprived of victory.

The Russians had set fire to some villages on the field of battle, and the smoke deceived the Prussians; they fell into disorder, and were now out flanked by the enemy, who were more than treble their number, and were marching back under cover of the dragoons and hussars. The second line of the Prussians, deceived by the smoke, fired on the first, and now the disorder was extreme. Leywald had the same good fortune as Frederic at Kollin, and was allowed to withdraw without molestation. His loss, in this battle, which had lasted for ten hours, was in all, killed, wounded and prisoners, only 1400 men and 13 pieces of cannon; on the other hand the Russians lost 7000 men. Their victory was of no advantage to them, for they could not hope to find support for their large army in Prussia, which they had laid waste, and in addition to this, Apraxin was forced, by his orders from St. Petersburg, to fall back.

Notwithstanding the impediments, which the Great Chancellor of Russia, Bestuchef, placed in the way of a closer alliance, between Austria and his own court, and that he was completely in the interests of the English, this minister was not an unwilling spectator of the war against the king, whom he hated from his having made a jest of him; a characteristic of this monarch, who ever gave a free course to his wit and his satire, and spared not the ministers of the different courts; let it be a Henry or a Choiseul, a Bestuchef or a Brühl who might be the object of his contempt and his jests.

But English gold got the better of the hatred of the High Chancellor, and Apraxin was forced to leave Prussia; he only left a garrison of 10,000 men in Memel, and a few days after the battle marched with the remainder of his army. This retreat was like a flight, and was so hurried, that 15,000 wounded and sick, and 80 pieces of cannon, with many implements of war were left behind. The army marched in two columns, and the route of each was marked by fires, plunder and every species of cruelty; every town and village, through which they passed, was burned to the ground, and the roads were covered with the dead bodies of men and horses. The peasantry reduced to the greatest despair armed themselves, but only made their misfortunes the greater; the Prussians who had been beaten, but not dispersed, followed the Russian Army to the frontiers of Frederic's states.

During this invasion an extraordinary occurrence took place; the king was assisted by an ally of whom he had never thought, and who relieved him of many thousand Calmucks; this active ally was the smallpox. These people, who in their own country were in ignorance of this disease, now saw it for the first time with astonishment and horror; it attacked numbers of them, who fell a sacrifice to it. Their leaders became its victims, and it was now no longer possible to restrain them, and the greater part of this body of half savages went back to their own country without having entered Germany. The Russian general allowed them to go; not sorry to be rid of these people, who were worse than the Cossacks, and could not be kept within bounds; only a few thousand Calmucks, whose love of plunder got the better of all other considerations, remained with the Russian Army, and entered Germany.

This people, who were for the first time brought into the field against the Germans, were the most savage of Frederic's enemies, and quite unfit to be the ally of a disciplined army; as they were unable, from their arms, to assist them in victory, they could only inconvenience them, and force them to share in the disgrace of the devastation and cruelties inflicted by these barbarians. They are a free people but living under the protection of the Russians, on the Caspian Sea and the banks of the Volga, and when required must come into the field; they receive no pay, but only one *rubel* yearly and a sheepskin.

They are a wandering people, and have neither towns nor villages, but live under tents, and wander to the different spots, where they can find food for their cattle, in which their whole riches consist. They are extremely ugly, and so alike, that it is difficult to tell one from another; their face is flat and nearly square; the eyes small and deeply sunk in the head; the nose broad and spreading; the mouth and the ears enormously large, and the latter standing out from the head. Their arms are the bow and arrow, with which they shoot a great distance, and with certain aim.

The Cossacks are very different from the Calmucks. Their numbers are reckoned 700,000 capable of bearing arms; they are in fact a frontier militia, for the defence of the southern part of the Russian empire against the attacks of the Tartars. Their dress is Polish, but generally tattered, and their arms a sabre, a rifle, a pair of pistols, and a lance of from ten to twelve feet long, pointed with iron. Their language and religion is the same as the Russian; they have only one rank in society, and are consequently all equal; they make a separate state, and enjoy certain rights which form a remarkable contrast with the slavery of the Russians, and would even in Europe be entitled to consideration; they inhabit large villages, cultivate small portions of land, but more especially breed cattle and horses; the latter are small, but strong, well trained and swift. Each Cossack has two horses when on service. They have a high sense of military honour, and will not submit to be beaten with a stick; they however allow themselves to be flogged, as a punishment compatible with honour.

The Cossacks were governed by the Empress Elizabeth, a woman who divided her time between love and devotion, and gave up the management of the state entirely to her ministers. By her incessant sacrifices at the shrine of Venus, her heart was full of compassion and philanthropy; she was therefore not fond of war, and nothing but pride and the desire of revenge could have induced her to declare war to the King of Prussia. The ministers, who had been won over by France and Austria, prevailed on her weakness of character on religious grounds, and impressed on her as a duty to assist the King of Poland. With this, they assured her, that the war would be carried on by the Russians without spilling much blood, that it could not last long, as the King of Prussia, attacked on all sides, must soon give in. Thus spoke Count Schuwalof, the favoured lover of the empress; and Bestuchef, notwithstanding his being devoted to the English, had many reasons for supposing that they were not very sincere in their alliance with Frederic; he therefore, in the first instance, gave way to his hatred against Prussia, and thus was the die cast against this unfortunate kingdom.

In addition to the English gold, which had induced the retreat of the Russians, Bestuchef was actuated by another motive. Frederic had a powerful friend in St. Petersburg; this was the Grand Duke Peter, the heir apparent to the throne, who respected the King of Prussia, hated the Danes, and was an unwilling spectator of the war. He feared lest the hard pressed hero should form an alliance with these enemies, and promised him all possible assistance, if he would enter into no treaty with this power; Frederic promised this, and Peter gained over the High Chancellor, who, in order to obtain the favour of the future monarch, by whom he was hated, drew out the plan of operations for Apraxin. The retreat of the Russians from Prussia was thus explained, and the ambassadors of France and Austria discovered the partial conduct of Bestuchef, who was despoiled of all his honours by the enraged Elizabeth; Apraxin also lost his post, as commander in chief of the army, and was brought as a prisoner to Narva.

Frederic who thought the Russians had retired from Prussia not to return, recalled Field-Marshall Leywald with orders to march against the Swedes. This nation had at last thrown away the mask. Troops had been, from time to time, sent to Stralsund; and when the Prussian ambassador at Stockholm, Count Solms, made representations on this subject, evasive answers were given, and these were backed by the assurance, that not a single man should march against Prussia. But no sooner was the whole army in Germany, than they crossed the Peene, a small river which separates Prussian Pomerania from the Swedish portion, on the 13th of September, and took possession of Anclam, Demmin, Pasewalk and other towns which were not garrisoned; their principal aim was Stettin, an important town, but slightly garrisoned, and which promised an easy conquest.

The Swedes now gave out manifestoes, in which, as conquerors of Pomerania, they released the subjects of the King of Prussia from their oath of allegiance, and invited them to join their army; to which they added, that as guarantee of the treaty of Westphalia, they had been forced to take part in the war.

This ally of the French was 22000 strong, and of this number 4000 were cavalry. The war was undertaken quite in opposition to the constitution of Sweden, as it was only on occasion of the meeting of the Diet, that war could be declared; but the French ambassador, Havrincourt, played the elevated part of a monarch of Sweden, and guided the senate according to his wishes. Hostilities had now commenced, and the respective ambassadors had left Berlin and Stockholm. In spite of this, the Swedish senate wished to retain a political agent in the capital of Prussia, in order to gain, with more facility, information to guide their operations; an almost incredible piece of political effrontery.

It was intended to employ the secretary of legation, Baron Nolken, in this post; however, Frederic, who was very averse to this attempt, wrote to the secretary, that he must depart, as, after the commencement of hostilities, he could not allow a spy to remain in his capital Nolken refused to go, referred to the orders from his court, and was so firm in his determination to remain in Berlin, that it was found necessary to send him over the frontier, under an escort of soldiers. This happened in the same month, that the convention at Kloster Seeven was made; so that Frederic, at the moment that he lost an ally, found a fresh enemy in Sweden.

The warlike courage of this people made them a fearful enemy to Prussia. But never was the honour of a crown, or the reputation of brave troops placed in such danger from the bad preparations with which they came into the field; for their appearance and position was a satire on the new art of war. Well drilled and courageous soldiers were in the ranks, full of ardour for battle; but every thing else was wanting; no commissariat, no magazines or stores; no pontoons, no light troops, and worst of all, no subordination. Their leaders, although experienced men, were tied down, in every movement, by the orders from the Swedish council, and the generals, who did not agree with one another, were threatened with responsibility for the consequences of every step they took. This will account for the fact, that these soldiers, after five campaigns, returned to their homes without laurels, and a mark of derision to their countrymen, and yet without loss of that valour, which had caused this people more than once to have decided the fate of Germany, and who at the treaty of Westphalia had dictated to all Europe.

The want of light troops was the cause of the Swedes being often obliged to give up the best formed projects, and the Prussians harassed them on all sides with a few men, and cut off all their supplies. They could not penetrate far into the interior of Prussia from want of magazines; and so many difficulties lay in the way of their forming a junction either with the French or the Austrians, that it was not once attempted; their operations were therefore confined to a small portion of the north of Germany. These troops remained in the neighbourhood of the frontiers of Pomerania, without undertaking any expedition of any consequence, and this state of partial inactivity was preserved by them during the whole war; they, however, did much evil.

Their first expedition was an invasion into Ukermark, a miserable province, containing only six towns and 180 villages, but from which, in six weeks, the Swedes required contributions to the amount of 200,000 dollars; this was the double of the sum that Frederic drew from this province in the whole year. These contributions were to have been continued, but chance freed this country from the enemy. As a party of a few hundred Swedes, who were sent from Prenzlow in search of forage, were marching through a wood, they were fired upon by five Prussians dressed as hussars, and some of them were wounded. The enemy thought that a whole regiment of hussars were advancing; they hurried back to Prenzlow, and the next day the Swedes left the province.

Shortly after Leywald drove them under the cannon of Stralsund, but even here they did not think themselves in safety, but sought refuge in the island of Rügen. A severe frost, which froze the arm of the sea which separates it from the main land, invited the Prussians to undertake an expedition, the success of which could not have been doubtful; but Leywald, who was eighty years of age, was unwilling to undertake such an adventure, and contented himself with the advantages he had already gained, and the taking of 3000 prisoners, who had fallen into his hands in the course of a few weeks.

In the meantime the Duke de Richelieu laid waste the Hessian states and Hanover. His extortions had neither bounds nor rules, and were guided only by despotism, and without taking into consideration the capabilities, or the productions of the country. The Hessian provinces alone were required to furnish 100,000 sacks of corn. This irregular manner of proceeding, and disregard of all remonstrance from the local authorities, drew upon him the displeasure of the court of Versailles, which even his friend, the minister of state Duverney, could not restrain; they were especially dissatisfied at the slowness of his operations, as they had expected a rapid succession of victories from the protector of Genoa, and conqueror of Minorca. Richelieu's excuse was the empty state of the store-houses, and wrote on the 23rd of August:

We have plenty of ovens but no bread to bake in them.

In addition to this, he stated his expectations, that the King of Prussia would attack the French Army. The well known correspondence between the minister and this general show, that the idea of the weak army of Frederic, as compared with that of Austria, was matter of ridicule, and they had already fixed on the month of May of the following year for the siege of Magdeburg.

It distressed Frederic to be at enmity with the French, to whom he was so much attached. This feeling was perhaps stronger in him, than his anxiety to conquer them. He was therefore very desirous of peace with this country, and on the 6th of September he wrote as follows to the Duke de Richelieu:

I can well conceive, My Lord Duke, that your grace has not taken up your present position, at the head of an army, to enter into negotiations. At the same time, I am quite sure, that the nephew of that great man, the Cardinal Richelieu, is quite as capable of making treaties as of winning battles. I address myself to you from the high consideration, which I, although not personally known to you, have for your grace. My object in writing is only to speak of a mere trifle, the concluding a peace, if both parties are inclined for it. I am not aware of your instructions, but have no doubt, that his majesty, in order to insure the rapidity of your progress, has given you full powers; and in order to lose no time in working for the peace of Germany, I send to you Baron von Elchetet, in whom you may fully confide. Although what has occurred, during this year, can hardly allow me to expect a favourable feeling in my interests, yet I can with difficulty persuade myself, that a friendly alliance which had lasted sixteen years, can have passed away, without leaving some traces of good feeling towards me. Perhaps I am led to judge of the sentiments of others from my own feelings. Let that be as it may, I would rather trust my interests to the king, your master, than to anyone else. In case you have no instructions for negotiating, may I beg of you to request them from your court, and to inform me when you are empowered to treat.

To him who, notwithstanding almost insurmountable difficulties, made himself master of Minorca, and who is now on the point of subduing Lower Saxony, nothing can he more glorious than to be the medium of giving peace to all Europe; it will certainly be the most durable of your laurels. Work at it with that activity which has marked your advance, and be assured that none will feel themselves more indebted to you, than your sincere friend, Frederic.

Richelieu answered this letter with similar compliments, and as he was not empowered to treat, he immediately sent a courier to Versailles for instructions. But as they had no thoughts of negotiation at this court, the proposition of Frederic remained unanswered.

As the king now gave up all thoughts of a favourable treaty, he determined to make an impression by his deeds; he therefore advanced against the united armies of the French and that of the Empire, in order to bring them to a battle. His position was indeed fearful; far and near he had enemies, who were always on the increase. It was in vain that he gained victories, that the blood of his courageous soldiers was spilt; the immense power of his opponents was ever growing greater, and cared not for defeat. It was hydra-headed; when he had beaten one army, he was then attacked by two. An imperial edict had declared him an enemy of the German Empire, and that he must be annihilated; the determination and the power to overthrow him, were greater than ever, and his hopes were never less. In spite of this, the liveliness of his disposition was such, even at this time, that he made his will in French verse.

However great his apprehensions might be, of being forced to succumb to the crowd, he still took every precaution to get the better of them; but his army, weakened by so many battles, was now only 22,000 strong, and with an enemy of sixty thousand men to oppose him. The Prussians had given proof of their activity in the middle of September at Gotha; the whole staff of the French generals, with Soubise at their head, had chosen this town as a place of recreation, to be clear of the annoyances of warfare.

Great preparations were made at the court for the reception of the high military guests; it was just the hour of dinner, the tables were covered, and the French were sitting down with the best appetite, when General Seydlitz appeared at the gates of Gotha with 1500 Prussian cavalry. The garrison of 8000 French never thought of resisting; they left the smoking dishes, and hurried out of the town. Seydlitz, who had no thoughts of pursuing them now seated himself with his officers at the ducal table; a singular instance of a court dinner being began by the generals of one party, and finished by those of their opponents.

There were only a few French soldiers taken, but a number of servants, cooks, hairdressers, mistresses and actors, who always formed part of the train of a French Army. The baggage of several generals fell into the hands of the Prussians, with a number of cases of perfumery and luxuries of the toilet, which Seydlitz made over to his hussars; but he sent back the mistresses without ransom. The French were as pleased, as if they had gained a victory, when they again found themselves in possession of these requisites to their comfort. Prince Soubise was furious for revenge, especially when he heard that Seydlitz had accomplished his undertaking with only two regiments.

The Prince of Hildburghausen, who had joined the French as Field-Marshall of the Empire, determined to drive the Prussians from Gotha. For this expedition the picked soldiers of both armies were chosen, grenadiers and light troops; and to these were added Laudon with his Croats and the Austrian cavalry. But this advancing army found to their dismay that Seydlitz was posted in order of battle, and his position was so scientific, that the enemy thought they had the whole Prussian Army before them, an in consequence retreated, without making any attack.

There never was a war in which the name of ally was so little respected, and in which not the slightest regard was paid to the miseries of their confederates whose very misfortunes were made a mockery of. The French treated the Saxons as if they were in the country of the enemy, and forced them to supply forage, provisions, repasts for the soldiery, and even money to the generals, with the threat, that in case of non-compliance, towns and villages should be devastated. And this did not fail to occur; whole districts were plundered; amongst others, twenty villages, in the neighbourhood of Freyberg, met with this fate.

In one of these, Banderode, the house of the principal person in the neighbourhood, whose name was Bose, was plundered as by Cossacks. The valuable furniture, which was too heavy to be moved, was broken to pieces; the casks of wine stove in, and papers and letters torn, from sheer wickedness. The churches were not even respected; altars, pulpits were destroyed, and the metal chalices, which had no value in the eyes of these robbers, were battered and destroyed; in many villages the fields were covered with the feathers from the beds of the peasants As the French could not consume or drive away ail the cattle they found, they cut them in pieces before they were dead, and left them for the birds of prey.

These atrocities were committed by an enlightened people, in the 18th century, and the sufferers were their declared allies. They occurred in Saxony towards the end of October, a few weeks before the Battle of Rossbach, and the regiments most conspicuous in these acts of barbarity, amongst the French, were those of Piedmont, Beauvoisis, Fitzjames and Deuxponts; the Croats and some Swiss regiments also acted in the same manner.

As soon as Frederic left his position by Erfurt to go towards Saxony, Prince Soubise crossed the Saale, and approached Leipsic, with the declaration that he intended to free Saxony of the Prussians. Frederic advanced to meet the enemy, who were so badly posted, that the Prussian hussars penetrated into the French camp, brought away horses, dragged the soldiers out of their tents, and drove them before them. Although these acts of audacity showed they had not a timid enemy to contend with, still was the desire of battle great in the French; they had only one cause of anxiety, the fear that the king might escape them.

Some of his marches and positions strengthened this expectation, and they had already heard of his rapidity of movement, his manoeuvres and his science in the art of war, but this had made so little impression on them, that they were anxious to engage him, where he could have full opportunity of displaying all his knowledge of military tactics. They hoped, not only to defeat him, but to destroy his whole army, and went so far as to make it a question in the French camp, whether it would be honourable, in so large an army, to engage in battle with so small a force? Never was self-confidence more ridiculous or more deservedly punished.

It was on the 5th of November, near the village of Rossbach in Saxony, and two leagues from Lützen, where Gustaphus Adolphus had fought and fallen for the freedom of Germany, that one of the most remarkable battles was decided. The French Army, with the troops of the Empire, were 60,000 strong; the Prussians only 22,000; but the king drew the French from their advantageous position, by a retreating movement. They thought he was anxious to escape from their hands, and therefore endeavoured to take him in the rear; this march was accompanied by military music in victorious strains. The Prussians delighted in this, and wished for nothing better, than to attack

71

them; but at this moment, it answered better to oppose the French vivacity with German phlegm.

During the time that a portion of the French Army remained in front of the Prussian camp, the other parts of the enemy endeavoured to outflank the king in the right wing. Frederic, who had again taken up his position, relied upon the rapidity with which his troops could fall into order of battle; he was therefore a quiet spectator of the movements of the enemy, and did not allow his troops to advance. The Prussians remained in their position, and as it was the dinner hour the soldiers set about preparing their food; the French, who saw this from a distance, could hardly believe their eyes; they thought they had given themselves up to despair. It was two o'clock before the Prussians broke up their encampment, and began their march with the cavalry in the advance, under General Seidlitz. The expectations of the French, which were so quickly, and to them incomprehensibly deceived, were the cause of their trifling resistance and the panic of the army, which rendered this day so memorable.

The great General Seidlitz, who had drilled his cavalry to execute their manoeuvres with the greatest precision, and had brought his men to be almost a part of their horses, showed, in this battle, the great advantage of his knowledge and evolutions. After he had turned the right wing of the French, under cover of a hill, which had concealed this manoeuvre, he came suddenly upon them with the Prussian cavalry, and before they had time to form, dashed in among the enemy.

The light cavalry attacked the heavy cavalry, and put them to the rout; the Hussars were hardy enough to attack, with their light horses, the French *gens d'armes*, and neither the courage of this noble troop nor their powerful horses could withstand this unexpected shock, and they were dispersed. Two regiments of Austrian cavalry endeavoured to make a stand, but they were also driven back; Soubise ordered up the corps de reserve, but they hardly came into action, before they were defeated and driven back. At this moment, the Prussian infantry, which till now had remained passive, advanced in order of battle, and received the French with volleys of musketry; this fire was kept up as regularly as if they had been on parade.

The French infantry now found themselves deserted by their cavalry, and, by a sudden movement of the Prussians, they were attacked on their right flank. Thus pressed, they only received three volleys from the Prussians, and then retreated on their left wing with impetuosity, when these were in the greatest disorder; in the midst of this chaos several Prussian cavalry regiments fell upon them, and cut them down in great numbers. These men, who were for the most part from the marches of Brandenburg, had been told the day before, that the French had determined to take up their winter quarters in Brandenburg; this gave rise to the following mistake, as the idea of such a visitation was uppermost in. their minds; when the French, as they fled during the battle from the cavalry and cried out for "Quarter", and this with the German pronunciation, the Prussians mistook the begging for their lives for a word in derision, and attributed it to the intended winter quarters in their native land; they therefore, with every blow of their swords, cried out: "Yes, we will give you quarters." Many lost their lives by this misunderstanding, until others, who knew German, and saw what was occurring, made use of the word "pardon," which produced its effect upon the soldiers.

It was now six in the evening, and already quite dark; this saved the rest of this mass of men, who would otherwise have been cut to pieces. In vain Soubise tried new French experiments which were based upon false theory. His columns were easily broken, and nothing remained but one general flight; the French, as well as the troops of the Empire, threw their muskets away in order to escape with more facility; a few Swiss regiments, who still continued to light, where the last who left, the field.

On this remarkable day the French artillery, at all times so much feared, had remained in a state of inactivity; notwithstanding that their commanders, the celebrated Count D'Aumale and Colonel Briol, were both present. They had a hundred officers and more than a thousand artillery men with them, and had promised to do wonders, as they prided themselves on the power of regaining the victory even if the army should be beaten. But the battle was so suddenly decided, that the defeated never thought of trying for the honour of a determined resistance, but excused themselves by saying, it was caused by a panic; not forgetting, at the same time, to throw the whole blame of the defeat on the troops of the Empire.

Only seven battalions of the Prussians were in action. The Duke Ferdinand of Brunswick, who commanded the right wing with ten battalions was never engaged; for the troops of the Empire who were opposed to him, took to their heels at the report of the first shot that was fired; by this disgraceful flight, they got out of the way of the battle, and gave up to the French, who even without counting their numbers, were double those of the Prussians, the honour or dishonour of the day. The battle only lasted an hour and a half, and in it the French lost 10,000 men; of these 7000 were taken prisoners on the field of battle; several thousands more were either taken prisoners, or cut down by the Prussians in the course of their flight, and many sprang into the river to save themselves from the pursuit of the Hussars. The panic was so great that crowds gave themselves up as prisoners to a few horsemen, and in one instance two dragoons took upwards of a hundred men of the troops of the Empire. The French cavalry threw away their cuirasses and large boots, with which they left traces of their flight towards Erfurt. The French court, who had taken the command from the Marshall D'Estrées after his victory at Hastenbeck, completed the farce by giving the staff of field-marshal to the Prince Soubise for his defeat at Rossbach.

Schwerin died a few months too soon to enjoy this triumph of the Prussians; in his often expressed opinion, it was only a victory over the French that could complete the military fame of this nation. There were many occurrences which rendered this day extraordinary; the king found on the field of battle, a French grenadier who was defending himself with fury against three Prussian horsemen, and refused to give in; Frederic put a stop to this unequal combat, and asked the soldier if he thought himself invincible; "Yes, Sire!" answered he, "if led on by you."

The king went over the field of battle, to see that assistance was given to the wounded French officers, inquiring of many their names. He paid the highest compliments to their country, saying at the same time:

I cannot accustom myself to look upon the French as my enemies.

Nothing could be more soothing to the feelings of the unfortunate soldiers, who, tranquillized by this condescension, looked on him as the most generous of conquerors, who not content with making himself master of their persons, had also gained their hearts. The booty, which fell into the hands of the Prussians, was very great, and amongst other things a number of the crosses of St. Louis, with which the Prussian Hussars decorated themselves. Sixty three pieces of cannon, and two and twenty standards and colours were taken.

The united armies had 3560 men killed and wounded, but the loss of the Prussians was only 91 killed and 274 wounded; among the latter were Prince Henry of Prussia and General Seidlitz, who never failed to expose himself to danger, and whose example had such an effect, that even the chaplain of his regiment went into the midst of the battle. So easy and so complete a victory against a warlike people was without example in modern history; the shortness of the days at this season of the year, saved the flying army from entire destruction; for it was not a retreat but a flight, and that in the greatest disorder.

This victory against the French gave universal satisfaction to all people in Germany, without regard to party, or private feeling, and all looked upon it as a national triumph. The differences in the forms of government, laws and manners, the numerous peculiarities, so opposite in these neighbouring people, and the hatred caused by long continued war, were not the only causes of this general feeling, which was participated in, more or less by most European nations. But the Germans had other grounds than these, to incite them to this feeling of national hatred.

The French in those days were in the habit of despising and treating with contempt the very name of German, the German language, genius and merit. The infatuation of many German princes, both great and small, had allowed their courts to be surrounded by a number of ignorant French flatterers, who often penetrated into their councils, became their advisers, and generally the scourge of the country; this had sown, during some generations, the seeds of hatred, which, even in the minds of those of the most noble and meekest dispositions, takes deep root, and is of rapid growth.

Nothing was more common, than for German statesmen of every rank to be displaced, in order to make way for Frenchmen, who were ignorant of the language of the country, and who after enriching themselves, and laughing at the Germans, returned to their own country; if scientific men of merit presented the products of their labour to the German princes, they, if Germans, were coldly thanked, or at most received a trifling present, but were generally dismissed without reward. If, on the other hand, they were French, they received handsome sums of money, even were their works of less value; French mountebanks were rewarded with diamonds for the exhibition of their juggleries; and in this, even miserly princes were spendthrifts.

The German people, unacquainted with the merit of the French, only took into the account this preference of their rulers, the difference of manners, and the complaints of all the provinces of Germany. From this, there naturally arose feelings of contempt, and hatred; amongst the educated Germans in every station, accordingly as they were educated, this contempt was not to be found; on the contrary a high feeling of respect for the civilization of this people; but so much the more deeply was the annoyance felt, of being depreciated by them; and this was, more than any thing else, the source of their hatred.

Thus thought high and low throughout Germany, with the exception of a number of court sycophants, notwithstanding these were generally the buts of the French wits. This feeling of the people showed itself on all sides, and often got the better of other considerations. An extraordinary example of this occurred at Rossbach on the field of battle; a Prussian soldier, on the point of taking a Frenchman prisoner, perceived, as he laid his hand on him, that an Austrian *cuirassier* was, with uplifted sword, ready to cut him down; "Brother German!" cried out the Prussian, "let me have the Frenchman!"

"Take him," answered the Austrian, and rode off.

One of the most serious affairs in human life is a battle, in which men meet death by thousands; and it has ever been the custom among civilized nations, to treat, even the defeated, with respect; for no general however brave, however clever he may be, can at all times be safe from the misfortunes of war. This was not the case in this instance; for both by friend and foe, and even by the French themselves, the battle of Rossbach was treated with derision. Soubise, whom the court of Versailles were anxious to justify at the expense of his troops, received a letter of condolence from the king, but in spite of this was openly laughed at, and lampooned in Paris. Fortunately for this unfortunate general, other occurrences soon occupied the wit and love of novelty of the Parisians, and the defeat was gradually forgotten. Not so in Germany, and the word Rossbach was used as a term of annoyance to all Frenchmen, from the Baltic to the Alps, for many years after.

The great partiality of Frederic for the French which was so apparent at this time, could not put a stop to the national animosity. Some hundred officers had been taken prisoners; these were required to reside in Berlin, and it was therefore expected they should go to court; but few of these had been admitted to the court of Versailles, and they therefore found themselves in quite a new region and in consequence of the annoyances they met with, they forgot Rossbach, and that they were prisoners, and behaved with such want of decorum in this capital, that it was found necessary to remove them to Magdeburg.

To give an idea of their conduct: a Prussian *dame d'honneur* who was conversing with a French colonel in the apartment of the queen, asked him what he thought of Berlin; he replied it appeared to him very like a large village; to this unexpected want of courtesy, the lady had the wit to retort:

> You are quite right, sir, since the French peasants have been in Berlin, it has been very much like a village, but previous to that, it was a right good city.

Other French officers, educated and polished men, suffered by this conduct of their countrymen; and their gentle and even noble conduct could not get the better of the unfavourable impression; but still worthy men of this country met with consideration from the Prussians. Frederic gave a fine example of this, and visited General Custine, who was severely wounded, as he passed through Leipsic; he comforted and condoled with him in so gentle and soothing a manner, that Custine, who was almost dying, raised himself in his bed, and cried out:

> Sire, you are greater than Alexander; he reproached his prisoners, but you pour oil into their wounds.

The news of the Battle of Rossbach fell heavily upon the Queen of Poland, in whose breast the strongest passions raged, and increased her grief to the highest point. It broke her heart, and a few days after she was found dead in her bed; she had been ill for some time, but not so seriously as to cause fear for her life, and had dismissed her attendants the previous evening, overpowered with grief; when they went to her apartment the next morning, she was dead. In her, Frederic lost an irreconcilable and bitter enemy, who, guided by false religious feelings, was in no slight degree the promoter of this war, which was the cause of so much unhappiness and misery to her subjects, and who would willingly have sacrificed every thing to her bigotry.

No traces of the defeated army of the French and troops of the Empire were to be found in Saxony or the adjacent provinces, excepting a number of prisoners, brought in by the Thuringian peasants. They destroyed all the bridges, not to be followed, and dispersed in so many different parties, that some did not dare to stop until they reached the Rhine. They always fancied that the king was at their heels; but he was forced to hurry, with nineteen battalions and eight and twenty squadrons, into Silesia, in consequence of the successes of the Austrians in that country. True he left the French Army, under Richelieu, on the frontier of his dominions, but with the hope of restraining the operations of the French by means of an army, which had began to be formed in an unexpected manner.

Pitt, one of the most extraordinary men, who ever presided at the councils of a nation, had just taken office in the British cabinet, where he, as well as in the House of Commons, ruled every one by the capabilities of his powerful mind. He looked on the convention of Kloster Seeven as a stain upon the British nation, which mast he obliterated. He advised that the treaty between King George and the King of Prussia should be fulfilled to the letter, that an army should be sent to Germany, to be commanded by a general appointed by Frederic, and that this monarch should also be assisted by subsidies; all this was done.

The French themselves gave George the Second the greatest facilities for breaking this famous convention, which as yet, had been ratified, neither by him, nor the King of France. It was now stated that, having been determined on, without the knowledge or participation of the English cabinet, it could not be looked on as an act of the government. It had been expected that, by this treaty, a species of neutrality would have been preserved with respect to Hanover; but these expectations were not fulfilled. This province was treated as a conquered country, and indeed so styled in the French edicts. They were not content with the contributions and supplies raised by Richelieu for his troops, with immense sums for himself, but a farmer general was actually sent from Paris, to farm the whole of the Electorate in the French manner, and to plunder it in the most methodical style.

This farmer general was also appointed to the other German states, which might hereafter be conquered, and in consequence of an ordonnance of the King of the 18th of October 1757, the farmer general Gautier established himself in Hanover. All these occurrences drove the Hanoverians almost to despair. George was fonder of his Hanoverian possessions than of his kingdom, and the generosity of the British parliament came to his assistance, and the most decisive measures were determined on.

In England everyone had looked on the convention as broken, and the battle at Rossbach finished the affair. The hitherto dispersed Hanoverian troops were drawn together, and the Landgraf of Hessen, who had so long remained undecided, was at last induced to allow his army to join them, in consequence of the oppressive treatment he had received at the hands of the French. At first he was anxious to remain faithful to the convention, and recalled his troops; their route was prepared when Richelieu's demands changed his determination; he required that they should be disarmed, and refused to allow their departure, but under these conditions. In vain the *landgraf* expostulated and represented that they were not to be treated as prisoners of war, from whom they might at any time take their arms; but that his soldiers were free, and had a right to remain armed.

The Duke of Cumberland also wrote to the French commander, and the Count Lynar, through whose medium this convention had been made, went to the French head quarters. He proposed that the Hessian troops should, to quiet the anxiety of the French court, withdraw to Holstein, as being a neutral country; the *landgraf* was satisfied with this, and Richelieu sent the proposition to Versailles. But the French ministry refused to comply with this arrangement, and insisted on the troops being disarmed.

The English court put an end to this dispute, by the declaration that, in the case of the *landgraf* not putting himself entirely at the disposal of the King of England, they should consider themselves exonerated from further support of the Hessian troops.. The French ended all difficulties in this business, by declaring that the convention was broken by the refusal to disarm the Hessian troops. They ordered contributions to be levied in the Hessian provinces, took an inventory of all property, even to the furniture of the *landgraf*, required an account of his income, and the Duke of Ayen, as French commanding officer, gave it to be understood, that they would not in future be guided by any treaty, but that the right of the strongest would be made use of. The French had long practised this right, and General Count Vauban who commanded in Marburg, carried his scorn so far as to say in a declaration he published on the 22nd of August:

> The Hessians have reason to be satisfied with the manner in which we are good enough to treat them.

The most humble representations from the Hessian government enraged this general so much, that he said he must look upon the minister in Cassel as a rebel to his king; and because he sent no letter of congratulation on the fete of St. Louis, declared him, in his official papers, as extremely culpable.

The *landgraf* now hesitated no longer, but placed his 12,000 Hessians at the disposal of King George, and by this act he laid himself quite open to the rage of the French. A courier was sent from the French headquarters with the most fearful threats, which were to be immediately put in force, if the troops were not withdrawn; the palace at Cassel was to he blown into the air, the town burnt to the ground, and the whole country so laid waste, that it would remain a desert for a century to come. The *landgraf*, who despised these threats, removed from Cassel, and now began the oppressive levies. The French were extremely dissatisfied that an Austrian commissary came to share in the contributions, raised by them, and an order was issued that every person was to give up all the coined gold and silver in their possession within twenty four hours. The storehouses were cleared out, and all the trophies of war, which the Hessians had gained in their many battles, were burnt to ashes.

The convention of Kloster Seeven which had only lasted ten weeks, was now declared null and void. In the meanwhile the troops of the new allies were gathering together, and in addition to the Hanoverians and Hessians, some of the Brunswick regiments had joined them, In consequence of the numbers of the cavalry not being in due proportion with the infantry, the former were augmented by some regiments of Prussian cavalry. Frederic could not spare many soldiers for this army, but he placed at their head a leader, who was in himself a host. This was Duke Ferdinand of Brunswick, one of those extraordinary men, whose exalted talents, greatness of mind and nobleness of heart, render them an honour to mankind. He arrived in Stade, towards the end of November, and found every thing in the greatest disorder.

The army was small and was in want of many of the requisites for war; the spirits of the soldiers were depressed, the Hessians dispersed, and the Brunswickers on the point of going over to the French. This was the wish of the reigning duke, who anxious for the safety of his dominions, had given his consent in the first instance to the troops being disarmed, and afterwards, from his increased fears, wished for an alliance with France. The support of the duke was therefore very uncertain, for he had already given orders for the withdrawing his troops; but the soldiers had no great wish to obey or at the least the hereditary prince, to whom it was equally distressing to be recalled from the path of glory, or to have to fight for the French; he excused himself to his highly exasperated father, who required the return both of his son and his troops.

His two generals, Imhof and Behr, who feared the displeasure of the duke, and had serious thoughts of marching back with the Brunswickers, were placed under arrest. The duke was at last appeased, and the victory of Frederic tended not a little to this, as the 7000 French, who were in the territory of Brunswick, were now recalled.

The reappearance of this army, which had been all but annihilated, was quite unexpected by the French. The quiet, which had hitherto reigned, now suddenly ceased; it was in vain that Richelieu threatened to reduce the whole of Hanover to a heap of ashes, and to devastate the royal palaces, at the slightest inimical demonstration on the part of the Hanoverians; Ferdinand answered him laconically, that he would take the consequences, and give him farther explanations at the head of his army. Now commenced the operations of the allied army; some French corps were driven back, Luneburg taken possession of, and Harburg seized after some hard fighting. Richelieu became furious, ordered the town of Zelle to be given up to pillage, and the suburbs to be set on fire. It was in vain they entreated, that the orphan asylum might be spared; it was reduced to ashes. The severity of the season at last forced both parties to retire into winter quarters.

During these occurrences, Frederic had hurried into Silesia. The Duke of Bevern endeavoured with 50,000 men to protect this province, but was unable to withstand the whole power of the Austrians, who had concentrated all their forces to conquer this country. A Prussian corps, which under the command of General Winterfeld, was posted near Görlitz and not far from the army of the Duke of Bevern, in order to keep the communication open between Saxony and Silesia, was forced to abandon its position, and retreat after a very severe contest with a superior force under General Nadasti.

The occasion of this engagement was the arrival of the Austrian minister of state, Count Kaunitz, at the headquarters of the Austrian Army encamped at Aussig, for the purpose of deciding upon the future plans of operation with the Prince Charles of Lorrain and General Daun. General Nadasti, in order to show his activity to the minister, took advantage of the absence of Winterfeld, who at the time was at the camp of the Duke of Bevern, a league distant, and attacked the Prussian post with a superior force. Winterfeld hurried to the assistance of his men, who were defending themselves in despair, and were at last forced to retire with a loss of 1200 men.

What increased this misfortune was Winterfeld's being mortally wounded; he was Frederic's greatest favourite, and a man of great talent. When he last parted from him, the king sprang from his horse, and embracing him said:

I had almost forgotten to give him his instructions. But I can give him none other than to preserve himself for my sake.

Winterfeld had a noble heart which made him disregard all the envious crowd, who could not forgive the high favour he enjoyed in the estimation of Frederic. The king, the army and in fact all Prussia mourned his loss, and looked on his death as a national calamity; it was so in reality, especially in the present critical state of affairs. The Duke of Bevern who was dispirited and neglected the most advantageous positions for the protection of Silesia, weakened his army 15,000 men, with which he garrisoned different places, and then drew continually back, more than once in danger of being fallen on by the enemy at a great disadvantage; he was enabled, however, to cross the Oder without loss. The Austrians followed in the footsteps of the Prussians with their whole force through Saxony, and Silesia as far as the gates of Breslau, in the neighbourhood of which city the Prussian general encamped.

General Nadasti, who was at the head of the Bavarian and Würtembergian troops in the pay of Theresa, now advanced to the attack of Schweidnitz, as it was impossible for the Imperial troops to take up their winter quarters in Silesia without being in possession of a fortress. Schweidnitz, which was defended by no troops in its neighbourhood promised an easy conquest, and it was taken by Nadasti, the Duke of Bevern not coming to its relief, after a siege of sixteen days; and after the outworks had been stormed, and in part fallen into the hand of the enemy, the commandant offered to capitulate; the garrison which consisted in near six thousand men and four general officers were taken prisoner, a number of cannon and other implements of war fell into the hands of the Imperial troops, as well as between three and four thousand florins belonging to the military chest. The possession of this fortress, which was now garrisoned with 8000 men, facilitated the communication of the Austrians with Bohemia, and General Nadasti now joined the main body of the army near Breslau.

The Prussians were encamped at this place, and the Austrians considered it advisable to attack them before the arrival of the king, who was advancing with his victorious army; the battle took place on the 22nd of November. The entrenched camp of the Prussians was cannonaded with heavy artillery, which had been taken at Schweidnitz, and attacked on five different points at the same time; both sides fought with great bravery, but night coming on, the fate of the day was undecided. The duke, who since the death of Winterfeld had shown great indecision, and who crowded mistake upon mistake, was in a state of great anxiety.

He rejected the advice to fall upon the enemy during the night, notwithstanding it would have been probably successful, as the Austrians were in great disorder which in the night could not be remedied; on the other hand the Prussians who thought not of defeat, were in the greatest order and anxious to renew the battle; but the duke, although not pusillanimous was disheartened, as he expected a fresh attack at daybreak, for the result of which he had the most serious apprehensions, in consequence of the superior force of the enemy. He therefore passed through Breslau in the night, and quite unexpectedly, left Prince Charles of Lorrain in possession of the field of battle; the Imperial Army under the command of this general was 80,000 strong on the day of the battle. The Prussian Army only consisted of 25,000 men; they lost 6,200 killed and wounded, and the Austrians 18,000. The Prussians had also 3,600 taken prisoner and, lost 80 pieces of cannon. Two days after the Duke of Bevern was taken prisoner when reconnoitring; he had no escort with him, and it was strongly suspected, that he gave himself up to this fate, in order to avoid meeting the responsibility of the forgone occurrences.

The Austrians regretted more than any other who had fallen in this battle, Colonel Veltez, a man of great genius; his death was the occasion of General Daun's showing a noble feeling which was proof of a great mind. On receiving the news of his death this general exclaimed, in great distress:

> We have lost a man, who was worthy of leading an army, and I am not ashamed to say, that at the Battle of Kollin, he gave me advice which with his assistance was the cause of my victory.

General Kyau now took the command of the Prussians, and led the remains of the defeated army to join the king; the result of this retreat was the taking of Breslau. The commandant, General Lestwitz, now looked upon everything as lost, and considered a favourable capitulation as a piece of good fortune; the town was given up, without having been at all defended, and the garrison, consisting of 3,000 Prussians, were allowed to withdraw with the honours of war; but most of these soldiers entered the Imperial service; Frederic was highly displeased with the conduct of the commandant, who had hitherto shown himself to be a courageous officer, and sent him a prisoner to a fortress. The Imperial Army got a large supply of provisions, firearms and ammunition, for the store-houses and magazines were completely filled, and the quantity had not seen much diminished by the short stay of the Duke of Bevern's army in this neighbourhood.

Silesia now appeared to be all but lost to the King of Prussia; never, in any campaign against this nation had Austria's good fortune reached such a point. They considered themselves justified in the greatest expectations; they had gained a battle, taken two fortified places, were in possession of the capital, and had a large army to keep these conquests, and therefore the best prospects of shortly ending this war, with the fulfilment of all their wishes. Such was the fortunate position of the Austrians at the end of November, when the approach of winter was to ail appearance to put a stop to the operations of the Prussians, and winter quarters were seriously thought of, when, to the astonishment of all Europe, the scene was at once changed. The advance of Frederic with his small army was looked on by the Imperial troops as the last attempt of a despairing enemy; the Silesians, who were in favour of the Prussians were without hope and those in favour of the Austrians without anxiety.

Of those who were of the latter party, the Prince Schafgotch, Bishop of Breslau, was a remarkable example. Frederic had raised this priest to the rank of prince, nominated him a bishop, and loaded him with favours. He had often been a companion of the king in Potsdam, and had received the order of the Black Eagle, of which the king was during the whole of his reign, anything but lavish. But this ungrateful man forgot all this, and looking upon his benefactor as lost, endeavoured to make friends with his enemies. He lost sight of all ideas of propriety, and even of common sense. He abused the king, tore off the decoration of the Black Eagle, and trampled it under foot; conduct which offended even the Imperial general, and drew upon him the most contemptuous reproofs.

Shortly after he sought refuge in the Bohemian mountains, to conceal his shame. Afterwards he went to Vienna, where he was treated with contempt by the nobility, and the Emperor Francis and the Empress, who both disapproved of his conduct, did not admit him to an audience. In Rome, where he was hated for the freedom of his manner of living, he found neither protection nor commiseration, and he dragged on the remainder of his melancholy days, as an outlaw in Bohemia where he shortly after died.

The Jesuits were more clever, and they appeared to think better of Frederic's prospects; for the Prussians, wounded in the battle, found useful friends in them. They received them in their immense college, and tended them with care; a course of proceeding dictated by policy, but which was here practised under the garb of philanthropy. Frederic duly appreciated the value and true motives of this generosity, and was therefore but little affected by it.

The conquerors had already began to make arrangements for the government of the country. The Silesians who were in the Prussian service and had been taken prisoners, were allowed to go to their homes; and a number of officials had already taken the oath of allegiance to the Empress Theresa, when the Prussian army, so much despised by the Austrians, approached the capital of Silesia.

The increasing cold in the beginning of the month of December pointed out the pressing necessity of going into winter quarters. Any general, but the conqueror at the Battle of Rossbach would, during the severity of the season, and satisfied with the expectations of the approaching campaign, have contented himself with being master of the right bank of the Oder, with protecting Glogau and covering the frontier of Saxony. Frederic's plans were however far different; he was determined to free Silesia without delay. He had marched in twelve days from Leipsic to the Oder, and had added to his own army the troops of the dispersed army of the Duke of Bevern; they now came every day nearer to the enemy, who had entrenched themselves near Breslau. Determined to attack them had they been even encamped on the crest of the highest hills, the king called the general officers and the staff together, and addressed them in a short but impressive speech.

He pointed out to them his unfortunate position, and recalled to their minds, the valour of their ancestors, the blood of their fallen warriors, which they must revenge, and the fame of the Prussian name; he expressed his perfect confidence in their courage, their zeal and their love of their country, and that they would now attack the enemy, and deprive them of the advantages they had gained. His address raised the spirit of his soldiers to a state of enthusiasm; some burst into tears, all were moved; the most celebrated generals answered in the name of the troops, and promised to conquer or to die. This feeling soon spread itself through the whole Prussian army, and hearing that the Austrians, looking upon their intended attack as an act of despair, had left their advantageous position, and were advancing to attack them, considered the enemy as already vanquished.

This step on the part of the Austrians had been determined on in a council of war. Daun and Serbelloni considered it still more necessary than ever to act with caution, in order to keep the advantages they had already gained; they considered, that the safety of a strong encampment near a well fortified city, which could only be attacked by a weakened army, was an advantage which should not be given up, to run the risk of an uncertain battle in the open country; and in fact there was no necessity for a battle. The pride of the other generals got the better of the wisdom of this advice;

It is beneath the dignity of our victorious arms to remain stationary.

The flatterers added their weight to this advice by impressing on the Prince of Lorrain, that it only depended on him, by a victory, of which there could be no doubt, to put an end to the war at once. This opinion, which was held by Luchesi, one of their best officers, was adopted by most of the generals; and so sure of victory was the prince, that the camp ovens instead of following in the rear of the army, as was customary, were sent forward to the town of Neumarkt, and in fact to meet the advance of the king. Frederic, who had already attacked, and dispersed the small body of men under General Gersdorf at Parchwitz, was astonished, on his arrival at Neumarkt, at meeting this advanced guard of baking apparatus. In order to lose no time, the dragoons and hussars who were in advance dismounted, stormed the town, of which they soon made themselves masters, and took 800 prisoners; Frederic now continued his advance.

On the 5th of December the two armies met near the village of Leuthen. There was no similarity between them; that under Frederic was 33,000 strong, that of the Austrians under the Prince of Lorrain 90,000. The latter full of confidence from their own power and that of their allies, and the possession of the half conquered Silesia; the former trusting in their military tactics and the greatness of their leader. In the one army, in consequence of their stores in Breslau, and their unimpeded communication with Bohemia, abundance reigned; in the other there was a scarcity of many necessaries. The one had enjoyed repose for some time; the other was worn out from forced marches in bad weather. But the Austrians were not inspired by the enthusiasm which led on the Prussians.

Frederic could not have wished for a better field of battle, than the extensive plain on which the armies engaged. The Austrians, who now for the first time, had chosen the open country for the display of their forces, were spread out in immense lines, and could hardly believe their senses, when they saw the small army of the Prussians advance to the attack. But it was now that Frederic displayed his great genius; he chose the oblique order of battle, which had gained for the Greeks so many victories, and by means of which, Epaminondas overcame the Spartans; an arrangement which has been considered a master-piece in the art of war, and is founded on the principle of keeping the greater part of the troops on the opposite side in a state of inactivity, and in being in a position to bring more troops on the principal point of attack than the enemy, and thus to gain the victory.

Frederic made several movements against the right wing of the enemy which were only intended as feints, as his main object was to attack the left. He ordered a part of his line to make a peculiar manoeuvre which has been imitated by other troops, but never accomplished with the same rapidity and precision as by the Prussians. The nature of this evolution consists in dividing a line into several bodies, and crowding these bodies on one another, and then advancing the condensed mass of men. This was invented by Frederic, and was not dissimilar to the Macedonian *Phalanx* from the closed ranks, their depth, the manner in which the troops were advanced, and which had long been considered as invincible, until the sword of the Roman legions dispersed them, and nothing remained of them but their name. A body of soldiers in this position occupy but a very small space, and at a distance, from the different uniforms and columns, appears like a mass of men in the greatest disorder; but it required only the orders of the general to deploy this heap of men in the greatest order and rapidity.

It was thus that Frederic attacked the left wing of the Austrians, and at the moment that the Imperial generals, unacquainted with this manoeuvre of the Prussians, mistook it for a retreat, and that Daun said to the Prince of Lorrain: "They are marching away, let us allow them to draw off their forces."

Several regiments of Austrians disencumbered themselves of their accoutrements and their knapsacks, and laid them in heaps together, in order to free themselves of what appeared to them for the time, an unnecessary charge; but they were soon undeceived, and saw with dismay the scientific approach of the Prussians, who threatened both wings at the same time. Luchesi, who commanded the Imperial cavalry of the right wing, became alarmed in spite of his boasting in the council of war. He thought that the principal attack would be made on this point, and entreated to have reinforcements sent to him. Daun was anxious not to send these before they were required, and it was not until Luchesi said, he would throw off all responsibility, in case the day turned against them, that he sent the greater part of the cavalry of the left wing to his assistance at full trot, and hurried himself with the corps de reserve to his support.

Nadasti, the most experienced general of the army, and who commanded the left wing of the Austrians, soon saw that his wing was the intended point of attack, and that the movements against the right were only to deceive them; more than ten officers were sent to Prince Charles to inform him of the apparent danger. He found himself in the greatest dilemma, from the reports sent in by his two best generals being diametrically opposite. He decided to believe those of Luchesi, who was shortly after killed on the field of battle, and Nadasti was not listened to, until it was too late.

The attack of the Prussians was made with such impetuosity, that the whole of the left wing of the Austrians were completely driven back; fresh regiments came to their support, but they were not allowed to form; they hardly came up, before they were driven back. One Austrian regiment fell back upon another, the line was broken, and they were thrown into disorder. The Imperial cuirassiers formed in line of battle, but a Prussian field battery broke their ranks, and a cavalry regiment falling on them they were driven out of the field. Many thousands of the imperial troops could not come into action, and were carried away by the stream. The greatest resistance was made at the village of Leuthen, which was defended by a great number of Imperial troops and artillery; to this place came crowds of the fugitives, who filled the houses, gardens and every corner of the village, and defended themselves with determination, but they were at last forced to give way.

Notwithstanding the fearful state of disorder of the defeated army, their best troops endeavoured still to make a stand, but the Prussian artillery soon put them to flight, and the cavalry, who fell on them from all sides, took an immense number of prisoners; the Bayreuth regiment of dragoons took two whole regiments of infantry with officers, colours and cannon, at one time. The Austrian infantry made one more effort to form on a height, but the Prussian General Wedel took them in the flank and the rear, and now all resistance was at an end. Nothing but the approach of night, and the good position taken up by Nadasti, which covered the retreat of the left wing, prevented the Prussians from becoming masters of the bridge over the Schweidnitz waters, and completing the destruction of the rest of the army.

On the field of battle 21,500 prisoners were taken; of these 307 were officers; the Prussians took 134 pieces of cannon and 59 stand of colours; the Austrians had 6500 killed and wounded, and 6000 deserted to the victorious army. The loss of the Prussians was 2660 killed and wounded.

There were some features in the events of this day which pointed out the feeling of the Prussians, and which were not unworthy of the so much admired heroism of the Greeks and Romans. The Bavarian General Count Kreit, at that time a volunteer in the Imperial Army, came suddenly upon a Prussian grenadier, who lay on the ground with both his feet shot off, and although weltering in his blood and alone, was quietly smoking his pipe. The astonished general cried out to him: "Comrade! how is it possible, that in your dreadful position you can quietly sit there and smoke! you are at the point of death!"

The grenadier took his pipe out of his mouth, and answered calmly: "What matters it! I die for my king!"

Another grenadier had his leg shot off as they were advancing; he crawled away, supported himself on his musket, and getting to a place by which the column passed, cried out to the soldiers. "Brothers fight like brave Prussians! conquer or die for your king!"

The immediate consequence of this battle was the siege of Breslau, which hard pressed by the victorious army, was left to its fate. Gallows were erected, to hang those who should even speak of submission; but this overwrought feeling of courage soon passed away; for fourteen days after, this town surrendered at the time that the Prussians had made every preparation for taking it by storm; the garrison consisting of 18,000 men, 13 generals, and 700 officers laid down their arms. The Prussians became masters of well filled magazines, and besides the artillery which belonged to the fortifications, 80 pieces of cannon and mortars which had been brought by the Austrians, a number of provision waggons and horses, and a well filled military chest.

The Generals Ziethen and Fouquet, who followed the enemy into Bohemia, took 2000 more prisoners and 3000 waggons; so that the Austrians in the short space of a fortnight lost 60,000 men, and the remainder of their army was now become a body of fugitives, who without cannon, colours or baggage, pressed with want, and perishing from cold, were hurrying over the Bohemian mountains to their country; when they were assembled together again, their numbers were only 17,000.

The king soon heard of the jest of the Austrians upon his small army. He laughed and said: "I can willingly forgive them the foolish things they have said, in consideration of the great follies they have committed."

He was himself astonished at the greatness of his victory, and asked the Imperial General Beck, whom he much esteemed, and who was shortly after the battle taken prisoner, how it was that the Austrians were so completely beaten? Beck answered: "Sire, it was a punishment for our sins, for wanting to prevent your majesty from taking up your winter quarters in your own country."

But when the king required in earnest the real cause, the general then said: "We had expected the principal attack to be made on the right wing, and had made due preparation for this."

"How could that be," answered the king, "a patrol sent out against my left wing, would soon have discovered my intentions."

Nadasti was indeed aware of these intentions, and was the only general, who, on this day, displayed any talent, and saved the remnant of the army; but in consequence of the mean jealousy of the Prince Charles was so badly rewarded by the court, that his name was not mentioned in the official account of the battle; they were, on the contrary, anxious, if possible, to save the reputation of the prince. False accounts of the battle were laid before the empress, and then spread among the public; from this originated the confident assertion, which was strengthened by those about the court, that the prince had twice offered to renew the battle with the king, who would not consent. The emperor met his brother on his return at Vienna, and it was also given to be understood, that any one who should speak disrespectfully of the prince, would be severely punished.

Notwithstanding this, caricatures and lampoons against this prince were stuck on the walls of the public buildings, and even on the Imperial palace. But this expression of public opinion did not reach to the ears of misinformed Theresa, who, in spite of the wishes of her husband, was anxious again to confide the safety of her dominion and the chief command of all her armies to this prince. But he, aware of the hatred and contempt of the people, was juster to himself than was his monarch, and started for Bruxelles. Nadasti did justice to himself, and this general, who was an object of aversion to the empress left the army to, whom he was beloved, and never again revisited the court, where he was hated, but retired into Hungary.

The greatest talent of the King of Prussia was the getting the better of the faults that were committed, and making the greatest use of the advantages gained. The conquest of Silesia, which had been all but lost to him, would not have satisfied this restless commander, and stopped him in his career of victory, had it not been for the advanced season of the year, and the heavy snows which put a stop to his undertakings. It was even necessary to put off the siege of Schweidnitz, until the spring; in the mean time it was blockaded. The last operation of this campaign was the retaking of Liegnitz, one of the largest and finest towns of Silesia, which the Austrians had fortified, and was now blockaded by the Prussians; a regular siege with the ground covered with snow and ice, offered great difficulties, and in addition to this, the Prussian troops required rest and relaxation. In consequence of this, the garrison was allowed to withdraw, but large supplies of provisions fell into the hands of the Prussians, together with a number of cannon and a great quantity of ammunition; the works were immediately destroyed, and the town placed in its former state. The town surrendered on the 29th of December, and thus terminated at the end of the year, this eventful campaign.

Frederic had now the satisfaction of seeing almost all his territories cleared of the enemy. The Austrian troops hurried back to the hereditary states of the Emperor, in order to recover from their fearful defeat; the Russians had left Prussia; the French had retired from the frontiers of Brandenburg, and were only in possession of some distant Westphalian provinces; the troops of the Empire had returned to their homes, and the Swedes had been driven out of Prussian Pomerania by General Leywald; Swedish Pomerania was now in the possession of the Prussians who also took possession of Mecklenburg, and were in safe winter quarters in Saxony.

Thus ended this eventful campaign in which seven great battles were fought without reckoning minor engagements which, in a former century, would have been considered actions of importance. Those great generals, Frederic and Ferdinand of Brunswick, who may be reckoned as rare examples of human nature, and who by their deeds have instructed future warriors, had been victoriously engaged in different fields of battle.

Henry, hereditary Prince of Brunswick, and Laudon had now for the first time displayed their talents, and others, although not so great, but still in other times, capable by their talents of founding the warlike reputation of a people; Seidlitz, Keith, Fouquet, D'Estrées, Nadasti, Haddick, Romanzow, Wunsch, Ziethen and Werner had first had occasion to in part show their extraordinary capabilities. Three other generals each distinguished by the laurels he had gained and immortalized by his deeds; Schwerin, Brown and Winterfeld had fallen in this ever memorable campaign. More than 700,000 men had been engaged; not troops of Asiatics, who had offered an easy conquest to those who attacked them; not the swarms of the Crusaders, who spread themselves over whole provinces without order or discipline, and murdered men from religious fanaticism; but warlike people who fought in Germany, many of them equal to the greatest heroes of foregone times, and not unworthy of the eighteenth century.

The extraordinary changes, which had taken place in this campaign, surpassed all that had occurred in any previous one; they appeared to be quite out of the common course of events, and deceived all human knowledge, foresight and experience. In the beginning of the year, the king was triumphant, the power of the Austrians almost annihilated, a large army shut up in a city, and on the point of surrendering; the imperial city itself not free from danger, and the hopes of Theresa almost extinct. But the scale turned suddenly in favour of Austria; her armies were victorious, and made conquests; on the other hand Frederic was beaten, driven out of Bohemia, abandoned by his allies, and surrounded by his enemies; but he suddenly, regained the upper-hand, to triumph more than ever.

The armies of the Russians, Swedes, of the Empire, of the French and the Austrians, were in part driven back, beaten and dispersed; whole armies had been taken prisoners, and Silesia, torn from the hands of a large and victorious army in the middle of winter. The Russians had been victorious in Prussia, but had fled leaving thousands of sick and wounded, followed by the defeated Prussians to the frontiers of Poland. The warlike Swedes had found no enemy in Pomerania; their soldiers were thirsting for conquest, and their leaders for fame, and the fate of Berlin, was in their hands; but these expectations were disappointed, and they were soon forced to seek shelter in the island of Rügen. The French leader was in possession of all the provinces between the Elb and the Weser, with no enemy near them; in a moment the allied army was assembled when least expected. The Hanoverians took up arms, Ferdinand placed himself at their head, and the enemy became alarmed, retreated and retired to a distant part of Germany.

Till now the English had not been willing to enter on a war by land. But the devastation of Hanover, and the deeds of Frederic, who was by none so highly honoured and appreciated as by this people, changed entirely their wishes. The king became the object of their idolatry, his birth day was kept in London and the provinces the same as that of their beloved king; the Parliament voted him subsidies to the amount of 670,000 pounds sterling yearly, and determined on sending troops to Germany. The great Pitt, who was now at the head of affairs, laid it down as an axiom, that America must be conquered through the medium of Germany.

Chapter 4: Preparations for the Campaign of 1758

The same activity which had been displayed in the field by the Prussians, was now directed, during the winter, to the recruiting their thinned army, and to the supplying their manifold wants. Frederic, upon whom fortune appeared now to smile, had the additional satisfaction of receiving many proofs of the fidelity of the Silesians, and the inhabitants of Breslau were not the last, to give him proof of this. But the monks of a monastery forgot themselves so far, at a time that the town was not only in the hands of the Prussians, but with the king actually in it, as to offer up public prayers for the blessing of heaven on the Imperial troops. Upon the magistrature remonstrating with them on their presumption, they referred to an ancient custom which their predecessors had always kept up in the wars of the emperor.

Frederick gave orders that they should not be impeded in the exercise of this old custom, but that the monastery should pay 6000 dollars to the fund for invalids. The money was paid, and the practice discontinued. The fugitive bishop Schafgotsch showed his audacity, which was so great that, deceived in all his plans by the sudden change of fortune in favour of the Prussians, he wrote a letter to Frederic, in which he sought to excuse himself, and spoke of his fidelity, and his having been traduced by his personal enemies. The king answered him on the 15th of February 1758, and his letter terminated with the following words:

> You cannot escape the vengeance of God, or the contempt of men; for however debased the latter may be, they cannot be so degraded, as not to turn with horror from ingratitude and treachery.

Theresa, in the beginning of December 1757 had considered Silesia as already conquered, and the war as ended. The Battle of Leuthen not only destroyed these ill-founded expectations, but increased the difficulties, that had hereto been found almost insurmountable, of keeping the Austrian Army in the field; new armies were now to be raised, and drilled for war, and in consequence of the great loss of baggage and all the implement of war, entirely new equipped. For this purpose, large sums of money were required, and at the very time that quantities of gold were to be sent to St. Petersburg, to induce the Russians a second time to invade Prussia.

The empress was in want of everything, especially money; the prospects of the future were dreary in its results. In this state of affairs, she was anxious for peace; but France, threatened by the powerful navy of England, and the most anxious of all the European powers for the continuance of war, stimulated the courage of Theresa, raised her depressed spirits, and once more led her in the path of ambition, which she would willingly have abandoned.

In this campaign the leaders were almost all changed; Schwerin and Brown were dead, Apraxin in prison; the Prince Charles of Lorrain, Prince of Hildburghausen, the Duke of Cumberland, Marshall d'Estrées, and the Swedish Field-Marshall Rosen had each been deprived of their respective post in the different armies.

England had always been an ally of Austria and had, more than once, saved this monarchy from destruction. But in Vienna all gratitude was now forgotten as well as all political considerations, to give place to feelings of hatred ad revenge. In spite of this, even after the outbreak of hostilities, a species of cold formal friendship was in appearance kept up; but the doing away with the convention of Kloster-Seeven put a stop to this political farce. The Imperial ambassador in London, Count Colloredo, left England without taking leave, and the Austrians gave up the fortresses in the Netherlands, and the ports of Ostend and Nieuport to the French. It was in vain that General Prince Lobkowitz, who had been taken prison by the Prussians but set at liberty, represented to the empress how much the king was inclined to make peace; she had already formed her determination, in spite of the many impediments, which lay in the way of continuing the war.

Each party began the campaign of 1758 with fresh hopes and new projects, and each came into the field with renewed strength. The Russians were the first to appear in the lists; Fermor was placed at the head of their troops, and received orders, in the middle of the winter, to occupy Prussia. Frederic, who had no expectation of this enemy's advance, but who now had his army in the best order, and with a superfluity of every requisite, wished, previous to meeting the Russians, to gain some decided advantages over the Austrians, and for this purpose turned his attention towards Moravia. In Vienna there was no anxiety with regard to this province, but rather for Bohemia, where the troops were not in marching order, and where, in many districts, especially in the circle of Königsgrätz, epidemic diseases were raging. Neither were the Imperial regiments complete in their numbers, and the strength of the armies was not sufficient to cope with an enemy, whose enterprising spirit required every precaution to contend against it.

The few Austrian troops, who were with the French Army, were therefore recalled, and the 10,000 Saxons, who had been intended to join them, were kept back to protect Austria; very small garrisons were left in Tuscany and in the Netherlands, and all other regiments were required to join the principal army without delay. Throughout the whole kingdom orders were issued for raising levies and recruiting, and the anxiety in Vienna was so great, lest the King of Prussia, in spite of the advance of the Russians, should appear before the walls of the Imperial city, that the inhabitants of the districts on the Moravian frontier received orders to fly to arms in case of the further advance of Frederic.

Besides all these precautions, the event of a campaign in Moravia was very uncertain, and attended with very great difficulties; however Frederic chose this plan as preferable. Notwithstanding this determination he began his operations by besieging Schweidnitz, and covering the besiegers by his principal army. The Austrian garrison of this fortified place, which had been blockaded the whole winter, had been reduced to 5200 men. The trenches were opened in the beginning of April in very severe weather, and the besiegers consisted of only 6000 infantry and 4000 cavalry under the command of General Treskow. The small number of men rendered the operations much more difficult, and the Prussians did not shine so much in a siege as they did in a field of battle; in fact Frederic was not partial to this species of warfare, and from this arose his economy towards, and his slight regard for engineers, who had but little reason to expect advancement from this great man, and in sieges as well as in other things, had to give way to the opinion of the most ignorant infantry officer.

In addition to this came the small number of miners employed in his sieges, the few cannon, and the scanty supply of ammunition served out to the artillery men. The colonel of engineers, Balby, who was a French officer in the Prussian service, wrote to the king making the most melancholy complaints; he stated that in order to get the worn out soldiers to do more work they required to be stimulated by additional advantages, and therefore begged that they might daily have beer and meat served out to them. Balby added the words: "For God's sake, Sire, do not look at the expense." In addition to this request he advised that, after the required bounty, the place should be taken by storm. Frederic agreed to his propositions; the place was stormed with but little loss, and a happy result. The principal forts were taken, and the place surrendered to the Prussians, after a siege of sixteen days, the Austrian garrison giving themselves up as prisoners of war.

It was now thought necessary to besiege Olmütz. This fortified town was garrisoned by 8000 men, well supplied with provisions and all necessaries, and giving prospect of standing a long siege, and making a spirited resistance, commanded, as it was, by General Marschall, a man of experience, courage and determination.

The many difficulties inseparable from an invasion of Moravia were increased by the Prussians having no magazine within forty leagues of Olmütz; but in spite of this, all impediments were got the better of. The king made it appear that he intended to go towards Bohemia, deceived the enemy, and advanced into Moravia. The body of the enemy's, troops who endeavoured to stop their progress, was driven back, the best positions taken up by the Prussians; and the siege regularly commenced. The commandant made the best preparations for defence, increased the strength of the fortifications, augmented his store of provisions, drove the useless inhabitants out of the town, and destroyed the suburbs.

Field-Marshall Keith commanded the besieging army. Their first step, however, promised an unfavourable result. Colonel Balby, a French engineer officer, who here as at Schweidnitz directed the operations, made a most remarkable mistake, which caused everything to go on slowly. The first line of circumvallation was 1500 paces from the fortifications, a distance, which rendered their artillery useless. They advanced gradually nearer, in spite of the sorties and heavy fire of the besieged, and then cannonaded the town with eighty pieces of artillery. In consequence of the Prussians not being able to entirely encompass the town, by reason of the River Morava, Daun, who had come up, found means to throw in a reinforcement of 1200 men to the besieged. The king had not expected the arrival of this army so soon, and cried out in astonishment: "It is indeed the Austrians! They are learning to march!"

The requisites to carry on a siege are enormous; in this, one, for the transport of powder and ball alone for each day, 400 waggons were required. The supplies of provisions and other necessaries for the Prussians came regularly in, and were but rarely intercepted; but much more was required, and there was especially a scarcity of ammunition, which had been uselessly wasted in consequence of the fault of opening the trenches at too great a distance. All now therefore depended on the safe arrival of 3000 waggons laden with ammunition and provisions, and which were expected from Silesia by the route of Troppau. The principal object of Daun was to intercept these, as he wished to save Olmütz without coming to a battle with the king. He was induced to this determination by his cautious disposition, which led him rarely to seek a battle, and he therefore secured himself from the danger of any attack by his well chosen and strong positions. He made use of the strength of his army to send out parties in every direction to occupy the roads, and neighbourhood through which the waggons must pass. This gave rise to many skirmishes, in which advantages were gained on either side, but which did not affect the position of affairs.

Frederic made every effort that the carrying on the siege, and the smallness of his army would allow, to procure the safe arrival of these supplies. Colonel Mosel, an experienced officer, commanded the escort, which consisted of 9000 men; and with these he began his march, which, in consequence of the immense length of the train was dreadfully slow and difficult.

In addition to this, the roads were so much cut up by the continued passage of the waggons, and the heavy rains, that they constantly stuck, and the train was stopped and the line broken; it was therefore necessary for Mosel to halt from time to time, and more than a third of the train were left behind. He could not wait for these, but constantly harassed by attacks, he continued his route which passed under the batteries of the enemy. Here he found Laudon was waiting for him, whose Croats, posted in a wood made a furious attack on the Prussians; these however rushed into the wood, drove the enemy back, and took several hundred prisoners.

During this engagement the train had fallen into the greatest confusion. The peasants were so frightened, that at the first discharge of musketry, they left everything behind, and ran away; many unharnessed the horses, and hurried away. A great number were never heard of more, but went to their homes; indeed many waggons were turned round and driven back to Troppau; Mosel made the best of this disorder, and once more began his march. The king sent General Ziethen to meet him, and he was fortunate in joining him. There were now not more than half the waggons which had started, and many of these could not be brought on for want of the drivers who were dispersed; a fresh halt was required.

The Austrians made use of this valuable time to post 25,000 picked troops in the thickets near Dornstädtel; they were commanded by Laudon, Janus and Ziskowitz, all famed generals, and as soon as the train came into the mountain pass, attacked them on every side. They fired cannon at the mass of waggons, shot the horses, blew up the ammunition waggons, and threw everything into the greatest confusion; the Prussians did not lose courage, but defended themselves for two hours in the most disadvantageous position. They were in small bodies, and these far separated in order to protect the long line of waggons, and the enemy had the advantage of being able to remain in large bodies, and attacked in whole column; by this means the Prussians were at length overpowered. Ziethen was cut off with a portion of the escort, and was forced to fail back on Troppau; General Krokow rallied the remaining troops, and with 250 waggons reached the camp in safety. Amongst these were thirty seven waggons loaded with specie, not one of which had fallen into the hands of the enemy.

The courage of the Prussians, in so unequal a fight could be of no avail, as it was not difficult to disperse the escort of a train some miles in length, and with the different bodies of troops necessarily so separated from one another. In this position, the Prussians did all that could be expected from the bravest soldiers; many were recruits of from eighteen to twenty years of age taken from the frontiers of Pomerania, and who had never faced the enemy, but they fought bravely, and of 900 of these, only 65 were taken and a few wounded, the others covering the field of battle with their bodies.

The immediate consequence of this loss was raising the siege of Olmütz, which ought never to have been undertaken. It was the most inexplicable conduct of Frederic, as in case of a favourable result, the advance of the Russians would have rendered it impossible to retain possession of the fortress, and the loss of the garrison left in it, at a distance from the Prussian army, would have been quite unavoidable; the loss of the train was therefore but little regretted, as every one was anxious that the siege should be raised. This was accomplished by Field-Marshall Keith with such skill and caution, that he was enabled to bring away all his cannon, waggons with provisions, and even the sick, only thirty of the weakest being left to the compassion of the enemy; two mortars and a useless cannon were left behind, as a memento that Olmütz had been besieged.

Frederic made his generals aware of his dangerous position, and addressed them in a speech, telling them how confident he felt in the bravery of his troops, of whom he expected that they would drive back the enemy, should they even be posted on the highest hills, or defended by the strongest batteries. Daun endeavoured to cut off the retreat of the king; and the passes of the mountains, the steep hills and ravines through which he had to pass, offered almost insurmountable difficulties, opposed as the army was by a far superior force. It was hardly to be supposed that an army encumbered with a battering train, pontoons and 4000 waggons should be able to make its way through such roads and against such difficulties. Daun made himself master of all the passes which led from Moravia into Silesia, and imagined that he now had the Prussians entirely in his power.

But Frederic, instead of marching towards Silesia, went through Bohemia, and dividing his army into different bodies, and supporting them at the expense of the enemy, overcame all difficulties in the passes of the mountains, and marching through Glatz arrived in Silesia. Laudon had followed him throughout his march, but this general fell into an ambuscade, near Königsgrätz, and lost several of his men. Keith covered the march of the heavy besieging artillery and the waggons; this train was fortunate enough to pass the hills and ravines in spite of the enemy, and not a single waggon was lost. The retreat was without example, and appeared quite inexplicable. The Austrians could set no bounds to their displeasure with Daun, and nothing but the knowing that Moravia and Bohemia were freed from the enemy, quieted and reconciled the grumblers.

The offensive war against the Austrians was now at an end, for the Russians who had invaded the heart of Frederic's dominions, required all his exertions to drive them back. They had already, in the month of January, directed their march towards Prussia, and finding that kingdom destitute of troops, had taken possession of it without striking a single blow.

Fermor, the Russian general, made a triumphant entry into Königsberg; it was celebrated as a festival by the ringing of bells, the blowing of trumpets and the beating of drums. The inhabitants frightened, and having the cruelties of the Russians during the previous year, fresh in their recollection, entreated for the protection of the empress. The answer of the general is remarkable; he said:

It is fortunate for you that her most gracious majesty, my mistress, has taken possession of this kingdom. You can but be happy under her gentle rule, and I will take care to continue in their present state, all such institutions as I shall deem perfect and not capable of improvement.

He immediately sent a courier with the keys of the city to St. Petersburg, and gave audience to the nobility; this was followed up by great dinners. From this time, the Russians treated the kingdom of Prussia as their property which they hoped to keep undisturbed in their possession, even in case of peace; and it must be owned, treated it during the remainder of the war, with exemplary forbearance Notice was given publicly, that whoever had cause of complaint against the Russian soldiers, had only to refer it to the military council at Königsberg, and the most complete reparation would follow.

The public functionaries were forced to take an oath in the church of the palace, that they would neither secretly nor publicly undertake any thing contrary to the interests of the empress; those who were ill were allowed to take the oath in their dwellings. The consistory received orders to give directions, that prayers should be put up, in the different churches for the empress, and a form of prayer was sent with the order; finally the nobility, as well as the citizens, were required to take the oath in the appointed churches, and they were led there by Russian officers, who presided at the ceremony.

Notice was given of the Russian state festivals, that they might be celebrated by service in the churches, and the abstaining from work. All necessary steps were taken to continue commerce, the forwarding of letters, and all public departments for the advantage of the community, in their undisturbed state. This oath of allegiance which was the mark of actual conquest, not the mere taking possession, offended the king so much, that he forced the magistrature of Dresden as well as that of Pirna, Freyberg and other towns to swear allegiance to him.

The Russians got possession, in Königsberg and Pillau, of eighty eight iron cannon, besides a large quantity of balls, shells and many hundred barrels of gunpowder. Never was a country more easily conquered than Prussia, but never did barbarian troops behave with more moderation in the enjoyment of their good fortune. The court of Vienna, to reward this easy conquest, created Fermor a count of the empire, and the Empress of Russia confirmed all his acts and proceedings.

The Prussians seemed to have quite forgotten their king, in consequence of this forbearance, and bore meekly the yoke of his enemy. In Königsberg especially, more was done than was required; on the 21st of February, the birth day of the hereditary" Grand Duke Peter, the town was illuminated, there was a display of fireworks, and the university requested to be allowed to make a speech in praise of the heir to the Russian dominions. Such illuminations and other rejoicings, at the expense of the inhabitants of Königsberg, were now customary on the Russian festivals, and although it might be that policy, and orders from the Russians, more than good will, were the promoters of them, still Frederic could not forget this conduct, and never during his life time returned to the kingdom of Prussia.

Everything now went on smoothly; the different civil departments of the government were carried on without any changes, and the revenues fell into the hands of the conquerors; still several heads of departments found means to give convincing proof of their zeal and fidelity to the monarch; but this remained a secret to the Russians. Fermor at length left Prussia with his army, whose provision was carried away on 30,000 sledges, and marched towards Pomerania. No sooner were these troops over the frontier of Prussia, and no longer restrained by their superiors than their path was marked as in the former year by blood and burning villages in this unfortunate province.

The army under General Dohna, to which was entrusted the defence of Pomerania, had previous to the arrival of the Russians, hard pressed the Swedes, and blockaded Stralsund; but all these advantages were rendered of no avail by the advance of this new enemy from the north. The operations of the Russians were much impeded by the procuring provisions and formation of magazines; it was not enough that they were masters of the Vistula; they required also the Wartha. In consequence of this, they took possession of Posen in Poland they also occupied Elbing and Thorn, and would have seized Dantzick, but the attempt failed.

The inhabitants of this town, who were then much in favour of the Prussians declared themselves formally against the intention of the Russians of taking possession of their outworks, and made preparations to resist by force if necessary. But it did not come to this. The Russians had no time to lose, as their principal object was the interior of the Prussian states, towards which Fermor began his march, and entering Pomerania and New-Mark at the head of 80,000 men, laid siege to Cüstrin.

General Dohna, who had raised the blockade of Stralsund to approach the Russians, could not prevent this siege with his small army. The system of the Russians was, like other barbarians, to lay waste and burn, and this unfortunate town was therefore in the first few days reduced to a heap of ashes. The shells and red hot shot fell in such quantities as to make it appear that fire was raining from heaven.

Houses were falling down on all sides, and burying the inhabitants in their ruin; there was no safety but in the most rapid flight; all those who could crawl away, fled; children at the mothers breast, the sick rolled up in their beds, all fled over the Oder, in tears and anguish, and looked back on the destruction of their property, and the smoke of their dwellings, which was ascending in clouds. Many were burnt in the flames, others were buried in the ruins, or smothered in the cellars, where they had fled for safety. A great many people, who resided in the neighbourhood, and even rich citizens, and noblemen from a distance, had sent their valuables to this fortified town for protection from the rapine of the Cossacks; there was therefore a great quantity of valuable property, which was all destroyed by fire.

An immense magazine was burnt, and the fire raged to that extent, that the cannon in the storehouses were melted, and the cartridges for muskets and cannon, and the shells, together with the stores of gunpowder, were blown into the air. Perhaps such a dreadful scene had no example in any previous war; for on this day, the 15th of August, in a few hours all that was dreadful and fearful passed before the eyes of the inhabitants, many of whom lost their senses, and believed that the last day was come. The object of the enemy was, that none of the property of the poor inhabitants should be saved, and they continued to throw in combustibles so that every part of the town was on fire; at last towards evening this unnecessary bombardment was stopped. Fermor, however, ordered, that during the night, the rest of the grenades which had been prepared, should be thrown into the town, as they would not be again required during this campaign; the cannon balls were to be saved in case of a battle.

The Russians appeared to think less of conquest than of devastation; for it was the town, and not the fortifications, which was so fearfully bombarded by them; and it was not till two days after, that they attacked the latter; and on the fourth day the commandant Colonel

Schack was required to surrender, as it pleased the Russian general to conform to the customs of civilized nations; but even the summoning the fortress betrayed the barbarian. He threatened to storm and to sabre the whole garrison, if they did not surrender immediately. The answer of the commandant was:

> The town is in fact nothing more than a heap of stones; the magazine is burnt, but the fortifications are in good order, and the garrison has not suffered; I will defend myself to the last.

He did indeed defend himself, but without displaying much judgement. When he excused himself to the king the latter replied: "It is my own fault, why did I make him *commandant*."

The threatened storming was not put in execution, for the attention of the Russians was now attracted by the approach of the king. Dohna who had not been able to relieve the town effectually, came indeed to their assistance, before the arrival of Frederic, threw a bridge of boats over the Oder, and opened a communication, by which means the garrison received continued relief.

The king had left Field-Marshal Keith with the greater part of his army at Landshut, in Silesia, in order to protect that province; he therefore took only 14,000 men, the picked troops of his army, and advanced by forced marches. This small army was full of ardour and the desire of revenging themselves on an enemy they had never encountered, but whose cruelties and devastations were known by report, and required to be atoned for by their blood. Their ardour was still more increased by their passing through the devastated provinces, covered with still smoking ruins and so laid waste, as not to be recognised. They now hurried to meet the enemy; all fatigue was disregarded by these soldiers, who bore with everything, and only desired to save their country. In twenty four days Frederic marched near three hundred miles, and arrived at Cüstrin on the 24th of August, strengthened the garrison and joined the army of General Dohna.

The hussars brought him twelve Cossacks, whom they had taken prisoners; who being the first he had seen he considered very attentively, and said to Major Wedel: "Look here, with such rabble, I must look about me." The king had unexpectedly crossed the Oder at the village of Güstebiese; Fermor's plans were therefore rendered useless. The siege of Cüstrin was now raised, the two armies approached, and every one was preparing for the fight, and never was the desire of going into battle greater than in the army of Frederic; the demon of war seemed to have inspired the whole army. Even the king himself, when he saw the devastated country, the heaps of smouldering ruins, and the numbers of wandering fugitives deprived of everything, was moved; forgetting his philosophy, every feeling gave way to that of revenge, and he gave orders that no quarter should be given.

Every precaution was taken to cut off the retreat of the enemy, to drive them into the morasses of the Oder, and there annihilate them; the bridges which might have assisted their flight were therefore burnt. The Russians had heard of this fury of the Prussians, and just at the commencement of the battle, a cry ran through the whole line: "The Prussians give no quarter!"

"Neither do we!" was the fearful reply of the Russians.

The position of Frederic was indeed desperate, and his fate hang upon the issue of a battle. The armies of the enemy were on the point of uniting and cutting him off from the Elb and the Oder; the French and the troops of the Empire were on the march towards Saxony, towards which country Daun with the Austrians was advancing; the Swedes, no longer attacked by the Prussians, had no enemy to oppose them, and were approaching Berlin, and in addition, to this the Russians, whose motto was *devastation*, were in the heart of his kingdom.

The deep laid plan and arrangements of Frederic were not only to gain a victory, but to annihilate the enemy; at the same time, in case of a defeat, his retreat was secured through Cüstrin. The battle was fought on the 25th of August, near Zorndorf; it began at eight in the morning. The Russians were 50,000 strong, and the Prussians 30,000; the latter, as at Leuthen, were placed in oblique order of battle, and commenced the action with a heavy cannonade.

The order of battle of the Russians was that which they employ in their Turkish wars, an immense square in the middle of which was placed their cavalry, their baggage and their *corps de reserve*; this order of battle is one of the worst that can be chosen, from preventing all possibility of activity in attack or in defence, and the fire of the artillery produced dreadful execution upon this ill placed mass of Russian troops. In a regiment of grenadiers, forty-two men were either killed or wounded by a single canon ball. (This fact is recounted by Captain Tielke, well known by his military writings, who then served in the Russian Army, and was at the battle).

There was also great confusion in the baggage train; the horses became unmanageable, and broke through the ranks with the waggons. The left wing of the Prussians advanced with such impetuosity, that they exposed one of their flanks; the Russian cavalry took advantage of this to rush on the infantry, and drove back some battalions. Fermor thought that the victory was his own. He ordered the square to deploy on all sides, to follow the enemy; this was done with loud cries of victory, but they had not advanced far before they fell into great disorder; those who were behind could perceive nothing from the clouds of dust, and fired upon those in advance.

Seidlitz advanced with the Prussian cavalry in three columns, and drove the Russians back upon their own infantry; another body of Prussian cavalry also attacked the infantry, and cut down all they could reach with their swords. Some Prussian dragoon regiments followed the Russians through the burning village of Zorndorf; Seidlitz, who had completely routed the cavalry of the enemy, now attacked, sword in hand, at the head of his cuirassiers, a heavy field battery, took it, and followed after the Russians. The Russian infantry was now attacked in front, in the rear and on both flanks, and was dreadfully cut to pieces; these soldiers presented an appearance which had never yet been seen on any field of battle by the Prussians.

Instead of closing their ranks and forming compact bodies, after having expended their ammunition, they stood alone in their thinned ranks like statues; they did not do this, in endeavouring to keep their position, from bravery, the love of fame, or of their country, for they did not defend themselves at this time; but it was their brute stupidity, to allow themselves to be killed as they had been placed by their orders; they were cut down in rows, and as one rank was dispatched another appeared ready to share their fate.

It was easier to kill them, than to put them to flight, and often a ball through their bodies was not sufficient to bring them to the ground; nearly the whole of the right wing of the Russians was cut to pieces and the remainder driven into the morasses; a number of these fugitives took refuge among the baggage; the suttler's waggons were plundered, and the spirits drank up as by beasts; it was in vain that the officers stove in the casks, the soldiers lay down on the ground, and licked up the beloved beverage as it ran on the earth. Some died drunk, others murdered their officers, and crowds ran about like madmen without attending to the orders or entreaties of their leaders.

This was the fate of the right wing of the Russians; it was midday, and as yet on the left wing not much had occurred. They were now attacked by the Prussians, but the regiments who could have completed the victory, did not show their usual bravery. They forgot the reputation of the Prussian name, their power and the knowledge of military tactics, at the decisive moment, and gave way before the weakened and half beaten Russians, under the eyes of the king himself. The disorder was great, and the heroism of the Prussian left wing was to all appearance rendered useless; but Seidlitz came up with his cavalry, advanced through the openings of the infantry, who were giving way, received a heavy fire of musketry, and not only attacked the cavalry, but also the infantry, which had till now stood firm, and drove the advancing enemy into the morasses.

This evolution of the cavalry was well supported by the picked men in the Prussian infantry, and some grenadier battalions, all troops which the king had brought up with him. These troops, without paying any attention to the giving way of the battalions near them, and by which their flank was endangered, continued to advance, and following up the cavalry charged the Russians with fixed bayonets; this attack was made with such vigour, that in the space of a quarter of an hour the field of battle was given up by the enemy. The firing now slackened on all sides, and there was a scarcity of ammunition; but they continued to fight with the butt end of their muskets, bayonets and sabres. The animosity on either side was beyond all bounds; even severely wounded Prussians forgot their own position, and thought only of the destruction of their enemies. It was the same with the Russians; some of these, mortally wounded, lay on Prussians who were dying, and tore their flesh with their teeth and these had to bear this agony, until their companions came up and dispatched these cannibals.

The regiments Forcade and of the Prince of Prussia came up with the baggage and military chest in their advance, and seized the greater part of these. The slaughter had now lasted twelve hours, and was only put an end to by the approach of night, and the worn out state of the combatants. The Cossacks still hovered about the field of battle, in the rear of the Prussians, to plunder the dead and dispatch the defenceless wounded; but this horrid occupation was put a stop to, as soon as it was perceived; upwards of a thousand of this rabble, who were hard pressed by hussars, abandoned their horses, sought refuge in a large stone building, and refusing to surrender, fired upon their opponents from every opening. The roof of the building, which was filled with hay and straw, caught fire and fell in; by this means nearly all the Cossacks were burned or smothered, and the remainder were cut to pieces by the Prussians.

Both armies remained under arms the whole of the night. The

Russians were in the greatest disorder, and all their troops were mixed up in a chaos of confusion. They would willingly have resigned, undisputed, the honour of the victory to the Prussians, but all means of retreat were cut off from the bridges over the river having been burnt. In this state of perplexity Fermor proposed on the evening of the battle, a cessation of hostilities for two or three days; his excuse was the wish to bury the dead. To this extraordinary request General Dohna replied:

> As the king, my master, has gained the victory, the dead will be buried by his orders, and the wounded will be properly attended to.

He gave him to understand, by this, that a cessation of hostilities after a battle was not a usual occurrence. The following day there was no engagement, but a cannonade was kept up. The king wished to have recommenced the battle, but the scarcity of ammunition for the infantry, and the worn out state of the cavalry who had exhausted their strength in the previous day, necessarily prevented the continuance of the battle, and gave the Russians an opportunity of drawing off their disabled forces, which they did by Landsberg on the Wartha. They lost by this defeat 19,000 killed and wounded, besides 3000 taken prisoners. They also lost 103 cannon, many stand of colours, and their military chest with a considerable portion of their baggage. The Prussians had 10,000 killed and wounded, 1460 taken prisoners or missing; they also lost 26 cannon by the falling back of their right wing.

The small number of cannon, and the few prisoners taken, together with the fact that a part of the Russian Army had passed the night on the field of battle, led them to claim the victory. But General Panin was so just as to say:

> We kept possession of the field of battle, but it was either dead, wounded or drunk.

Notwithstanding Fermor himself had requested a cessation of hostilities, he sent couriers with intelligence of the victory to all the allied courts and armies, and in Vienna, a *Te Deum* was celebrated; the Prussians allowed the defeated to amuse themselves with these false accounts, and in the mean time made good use of the victory. The king who was now master of the field of battle at Zorndorf followed the retreating army to Landsberg; he was so persuaded of their present want of power, that he only left a portion of his troops as an army of observation under General Dohna, sent another portion against the Swedes, and with the remainder, returned to Saxony where his presence was much wanted.

The king was so generous as to acknowledge the extraordinary services of General Seidlitz, and stated openly, that the battle had been gained by this general. Frederic himself had not failed to expose his own person, but had gone into the heat of the action, and one of his *aides de camp*, and his pages were killed or wounded by his side. The English ambassador Mitchell, who accompanied him in all the campaigns of this war, was with him, and exposed himself to great danger; Frederic said to him: "My dear Mitchell, you ought not to be here."

The ambassador answered: "Sire, should you be here! I am sent to your majesty, and wherever you are, there should I be."

The remembrance of the cruelties of the Russians deprived the Prussian soldiers and peasants of all compassion, and on many occasions of all feeling of humanity; and this to such an extent, that many Russians, who were severely wounded and lay helpless on the field of battle, were thrown into pits with the dead, and buried alive. In vain these unhappy wretches endeavoured to crawl from under the dead bodies, fresh corpses were heaped on them, which soon put an end to their feeble efforts. Among the Russian prisoners were the Generals Czernichef, Soltikow, Prince Sulkowski and several others, who were brought before the king after the battle. Frederic could not forget the devastation of his country; he therefore, after having cast contemptuous looks at them, turned away, saying:

I have no Siberia to send you to; you shall be confined in the casemates of Cüstrin; you have prepared good quarters for yourselves, and now you shall occupy them.

This order was fulfilled notwithstanding General Czernichef expressed to the *commandant* his great unwillingness to comply. He asked if casemates were a fit residence for a general officer? His answer was:

You have not left a house standing in the town, where you could have quarters, therefore you must he satisfied with these.

No notice was taken of their displeasure, and the generals were forced to creep into the cellars under the wall of the fortifications; they remained only a few days here for the king allowed them to have lodgings in the suburb of Cüstrin, which had not been burnt.

The Austrians had endeavoured to make good use of the absence of the king. They could now act on the offensive, and the superiority of their armies promised the most fortunate results to their undertakings; but every thing depended on the rapidity of their operations. In Silesia the number of fortified places, and the well defended passes, offered difficulties that would require time to remove; the operations in this province were therefore subordinate to other plans. But Saxony offered an easier conquest, and Daun advanced rapidly on this country, leaving General Harsch with only 20,000 in Silesia, with directions, if possible, to besiege Neisse; this march of the Austrian general left Keith at liberty to advance into Saxony, and to reinforce Prince Henry. The Duke of Zweibrücken had also directed his march on Saxony with the troops of the Empire, and the Prussians were threatened on all sides with the loss of this province, so useful in time of war; Prince Henry, who had hitherto protected this country with a small army, was obliged to fall back upon Dresden.

Daun's intention was to take possession of this capital, to drive the Prussian entirely out of Saxony, and to cut the king off from the Elb; nothing came of this but that the formidable opponent was for some time kept in his own states. Daun warned General Fermor not to allow himself to he led to give battle to this crafty enemy, whom he did not as yet know; he should rather act on the defensive, until Saxony was conquered. The courier who conveyed Fermor's answer to this advice, after the Battle of Zorndorf, fell into the king power, and it contained the following:

You had good reason to warn General Fermor to have a care of a crafty enemy, whom you knew better than he did; for he has faced him, and been beaten.

Prince Henry, who depended on Frederic's activity, stirred himself in the meanwhile to strengthen his positions against his numerous enemies, and it was well that he did so. Sonnenstein was attacked by the troops of the Empire, and taken, as the commandant became alarmed, and surrendered with 1400 men as prisoners of war. Daun now endeavoured to make himself master of Dresden; he approached this city, which was but weakly garrisoned, and but slightly fortified; the prudence and determination of the commandant, Count Schmettau, saved Dresden. He declared that he intended to burn the magnificent suburbs, which consisted of houses of six or seven storeys, and rose far above the ramparts; this determination caused the greatest consternation at the court, and in the town.

The royal family thought that the palace would be in great danger, and the lamentations became universal, when the houses were being filled with combustibles. The inhabitants, the magistrates, the court, all entreated for mercy; the states general also sent deputations with remonstrances and petitions; Schmettau stated to them the necessity he was under, and that his duty required him to defend himself. He explained that the Saxons could expect no respect from him, as an enemy, for the royal residence, when even their allies paid no regard to such things; he therefore advised them to apply to these their allies, and not to him. This was done, but in the first instance without avail. Daun had flattered himself with the prospect of an easy conquest, and was therefore unwilling to give up a plan which promised so many advantages.

Thinking that perhaps the Prussian commandant only wished to frighten them by words, he threatened to revenge the burning of the suburb in the most fearful manner, and not to spare a single Prussian; Schmettau declared that in case of extremity he would defend himself from street to street, make the palace his citadel, and bury himself in its ruins. It was his intention to have a quantity of gunpowder brought into the palace, to collect by force the principal members of the court and the nobility, and then, in the apartment of the princes, and in the midst of the royal family, to await the determination of the enemy; such a threat, however uncertain its fulfilment might be, had been so well imagined, and the preparations so well regulated, that it could not fail in having its effect. Daun gave up his attack upon Dresden, and Schmettau did not destroy the suburb. The combustibles were removed from the houses, and the inhabitants for the present tranquillized.

In the meanwhile Laudon fell on the circle of Cottbus, and raised heavy contributions from this country. The inhabitants were forced, by the most fearful threats, to give up every thing they possessed of any value, even to their plate, shoe buckles and to their wedding rings, and as this, together with all their money, did not make up the required sum, two magistrates were sent away as hostages. It appeared that the Austrians were anxious to follow the example of the Russians in their acts of cruelty; for not only pillage but fire and devastation characterized this invasion. A man of family of the name of Pannewitz was attacked on his estate, and after his house had been plundered, not being able to make up the sum that was required, he was cut with a sabre, and taken from his bed to be tied, naked and bleeding, to the tail of a horse which dragged him at his heels at a gallop.

The enormous superiority in numbers of the Austrians and troops of the Empire in Saxony, incited them to the formation of fresh plans. Prince Henry was to be attacked in front, and in rear, and his army to be entirely destroyed. The different generals had held meetings, and all preparations were made, when the magic words "Frederic is advancing" put a stop to all their projects; he came, and formed a junction with Prince Henry. He was desirous of a battle, that he might drive the Austrians back, and go to the assistance of Silesia, which was but weakly defended, and in great danger. The enemy had laid this province under contribution, and were besieging Neisse; they had also invested Cosel. Fouquet was entrenched with 4000 Prussians at Landshut, and although he might impede the operations of the enemy, he could not prevent them.

Daun carefully avoided a battle, and endeavoured to prevent Frederic's march towards Silesia by bodies of men posted in strong, and well chosen positions. His principal camp at Stolpen was one of the strongest positions in Saxony it was covered by steep heights, ponds, morasses, woods and ravines. Both this general and his men, were courageous, cheerful and devout. The imaginary victory of their allies at Zorndorf was celebrated by songs and firing of cannon; but the most reasonable among them doubted a victory, when the king arrived, and all their plans were laid aside. Different corps of Austrians were driven from their positions, and there were many skirmishes.

The road towards Silesia was open, but Daun remained immovable. Frederic did not give up all hopes of forcing him to retire on Bohemia, by destroying his magazines and cutting off his supplies. He took no note of the troops of the Empire, upon whose retreat he already reckoned as they were suffering from scarcity; he therefore encamped at Bautzen, as his troops, who had been constantly on the march for eight weeks, required repose. The season was already advanced, and it was necessary to build brick huts for the infantry, and stalls of straw work for the cavalry. The situation of the king and his army can be best imagined from a letter he wrote to the Lord-Marshall in the beginning of October.

I must keep in activity until the snow falls. How willingly would I sacrifice half the fame you write of, for a little repose at the present time!

At last both armies changed their positions; Daun encamped himself securely at a small distance from his former position, and the Prussians encamped at Hochkirch. The security of this camp depended on the being masters of the heights called Steinberg, which General Retzow was sent to take possession of, but of which he found the Austrians already masters. The king sent him orders to drive them from this position, thinking it was the rear guard of the enemy; it was in fact the Imperial corps of grenadiers, who were on this hill, and only a short distance from the right wing of the Austrian army; these circumstances rendered the attacking them with only a few battalions impracticable. Frederic was highly displeased with this declaration of the impossibility of the attack, and repeated the order with the additional sentence, that Retzow should answer for the attack with his head. This general had been educated in the military school of Potsdam, and having become gray in the service had a high feeling of military obedience; but he looked upon this as one of those rare cases, in which it was right not to obey. His answer was, he was ready to lay his head at the feet of his king, whose orders were sacred, but his conscience was still more so, and he could not answer to his God and the world for the sacrifice of so many brave men, without the prospect of the slightest advantage. He should not make the attack, and he left the rest to his majesty's pleasure. He was placed in arrest, and his sword taken from him.

Not having possession of these heights made the Prussian camp untenable; but the king, who was aware of Daun's caution, chose to remain in this dangerous position in spite of the enemy. This extraordinary determination ran him into such great danger as was near causing the downfall of the kingdom, and which, as it showed forth his heroism in the greatest splendour, forms one of the most extraordinary scenes of the war. These important heights were carefully entrenched by the Austrians; and in fact the advantage gained by their possession, was so great, that Daun, at all times so cautious, was induced to form the plan of falling on the king in his encampment. The plan was ascribed to General Laudon, and as it was formed with science, so was it carried out with courage and decision.

Everything was favourable to it; the two armies were posted so near to one another, that the right wing of the Prussians was within range of the cannon of the enemy's camp. This was a rare occurrence in the annals of warfare, and the Imperialists looked upon this bold proximity as a mark of contempt and disregard of their forces, which they considered as an insult, and therefore ardently desired a battle.

The principal part of the light troops of the Austrians were sent to attack the Prussians, and as their skirmishing continued day and night, they formed a good cover for the carrying out of deeper plans.

The Prussians, who when led by Frederic, were accustomed to be the first to attack, could hardly dream of the possibility of an attack from the cautious Daun, who thought he could not be too securely encamped when in the vicinity of his much feared enemy. Daun was aware of his spirit of enterprise, to which nothing appeared impossible, and the rapidity with which the Prussians could be placed in order of battle, and led against an enemy. Notwithstanding he took every care in the preparation of his arrangements, his principal hope and confidence lay in the imaginary safety of Frederic and his army.

The disadvantages of his situation were but too well known to Frederic; he, however, looked upon it as disgraceful to withdraw, and in addition to this, having determined to attack the Prince of Baden-Durlach, his present position was favourable for this enterprise. Old Field-Marshall Keith, who had grown gray in the service, was not without feelings of anxiety, and said joking to his royal friend: "if the Austrians leave us quietly in our present position, they deserve to be hanged;" Frederic answered in the same strain: "Let us hope they are more afraid of us than of the gallows." He at last determined to change his position, and move his camp as soon as the army was fresh supplied with provisions. His strength consisted in 30,000 men; the night of the 14th of October was fixed on for this breaking up of the camp, and it was decided to follow it up by an attack upon the forces, under the Prince of Baden, at Reichenbach. The lives of many thousand men depended on the difference of a single day.

On the night of the 13th the different columns of the Austrian army left their camp to fall upon the Prussians. General O'Donnel led the advanced guard, which consisted of four battalions and thirty six squadrons of horse; he was followed by General Sincere with sixteen, and General Forgatsch with eighteen battalions. The corps under General Laudon, who were posted in a wood, and almost in the rear of the Prussians, was reinforced by four battalions and fifteen squadrons of horse, and in addition to this was joined by all the Austrian cavalry of the left wing; the infantry of this wing was led on by Daun himself.

It was intended that the whole of these troops, with the addition of some small bodies of men, should attack the Prussians on the right wing in front and in the rear. The Duke of Aremberg, with twenty three battalions and thirty two squadrons, was to form a corps of observation on the left wing of the Prussians, and was not to attack them until the defeat was complete on every other point. There were also a number of grenadier volunteers, in the advanced guard, who rode behind the *cuirassiers*, but as soon as they came to the camp of the Prussians, jumped from the horses, formed into bodies, and pressed forward.

The tents of the Austrian camp remained standing, and the usual watch-fires were kept up. A number of workmen were employed during the night in felling trees, and with their singing and calling to one another, were to prevent the out-posts of the Prussians from being aware of the march of the troops; but the watchful Prussian hussars discovered the movement of the enemy, and gave intelligence of it to the king. At first, he could hardly be made to believe it, but as the reports continued to come in, he imagined it was for some other purpose, and not for a regular attack. Seidlitz and Ziethen were at this time with the king, and exhausted all their eloquence to remove his doubts at this important moment; they prevailed on him to give orders, that some brigades should be in readiness, and several regiments saddled their horses in consequence; they were however towards morning countermanded, and the soldiers returned to their beds without anxiety.

Day had not yet broken, and the clock in the village of Hochkirch struck five, when the enemy appeared before the camp. Numbers of picked soldiers came over to the Prussian outposts, offering themselves as deserters. Their number increased so rapidly that they soon overpowered the outposts, and the pickets. The Austrian Army, divided in different bodies, followed close in the rear of the advanced guard, and now advanced in column, from every side, into the Prussian camp. Many regiments of the king's army were first awakened by their own cannon; for the advancing enemy, having left the greater part of their artillery behind, made use of the cannon and ammunition they became masters of in the advanced posts of the Prussians, to fire into the camp.

Never was an army of brave troops in such a dreadful position as the Prussians; who, fully depending on the watchfulness of their king, were sleeping free from care, when in a moment they were attacked by a powerful enemy in the midst of their camp, and awakened by the roar of cannon; it was still dark, and the confusion beyond all description. Several hundreds were slaughtered in their tents before they could open their eyes, others rushed half dressed to their arms; they seized the first that came to hand, and formed in the ranks It was here that the advantage of good discipline was shown in the most striking manner; in this fearful state of affairs, where resistance seemed presumption, and the first thought of all soldiers must be to gain safety by flight, in most armies their destruction would have been unavoidable, and the best troops would have found their graves, as courage could be of no avail: it was only discipline that could save them.

The alarm spread itself suddenly through the whole camp, and in spite of the darkness and confusion, the greater part of the cavalry and infantry were soon in order of battle. The nature of the attack forced the regiments to act singly; they rushed on the enemy, and drove them back on some points, but for the most part, they were obliged to give way to the superior force. It was so dark that it was difficult to know friend from foe; the break of day hardly diminished the confusion, from the heavy fog which covered the combatants. The Prussian cavalry led on by Seidlitz rode about in search of an enemy, and the *cuirassier* regiment of Schonaich drove back a whole line of Austrian infantry, and took 800 prisoners.

The village of Hochkirch was in flames, and served to light the field of battle. The fire raged in all the houses, and in every corner of the place, which was bravely defended by the Prussians. Victory appeared to depend on keeping possession of this place, from its position on a height, and there being here a heavy battery; in consequence of this, Daun continued to send up fresh troops to attack it. There were only 600 Prussians to defend this post, and having expended their ammunition they determined to cut their way through their numerous opponents; a small portion succeeded in their attempt, but the greater part were either killed, wounded or taken prisoner.

Whole regiments of Prussians now advanced and drove the enemy again out of the village. The entrance to this was so small, that only seven men could march abreast; it was therefore impossible to form in line in the midst of the flames, and with every outlet crammed with the troops of the Austrians. Every means were however tried, and this became the principal point of the battle. Prince Francis of Brunswick had his head shot off by a cannon ball; Field-Marshall Keith received a ball in his chest, fell to the ground, and expired; Prince Maurice of Dessau and General Geist were struck to the earth, severely wounded. The Prussians, attacked in front and in the rear, were forced to give way, and the Austrian cavalry made dreadful havoc in the bravest regiments of the Prussian infantry.

The king led on fresh troops in person, and drove back the enemy; but this advantage was rendered of no avail by the Austrian cavalry. The village remained in the possession of the Imperialists, but with the loss of many of their grenadiers. The king now ordered that the right wing, which had fallen into confusion, should withdraw, and sent General Saldern with some battalions of old soldiers to cover their retreat. This highly endowed general who was as efficient in the manoeuvring of infantry, as Seidlitz was in that of cavalry, made his arrangements with such discretion, that without firing a single shot, he prevented with his few soldiers, the victorious army from advancing farther.

The fog at last drew off, and the field of battle strewed with dead bodies became apparent to the two armies, which were both in disorder. Notwithstanding the advantage their discipline had been to the Prussians, the darkness and the nature of the ground had prevented their using their military tactics and fighting to an advantageous result. Both sides were now formed in fresh order of battle. Notwithstanding all the advantages he had gained, Daun did not claim a victory over an army, which had disappointed all human expectation, and notwithstanding it had been surprised in the night, had fought for so many hours with the most extraordinary valour, and having lost many of its leaders, was now ready to renew the battle.

This was the intention of Frederic, when the Duke of Aremberg, who under cover of the fog had taken the king in flank, attacked the left wing of the Prussians; several thousand men were driven back, and a large field battery of the Prussians taken. But this was the extent of their victory; the king who now had the enemy in front and rear, drew his courageous troops together, and after fighting for five hours made good his retreat. He was protected by a heavy fire of artillery and by lines of cavalry which were posted in the plain of Belgern, and behind which the infantry formed. The Austrian Army was in too great confusion to attempt to disturb such a retreat; and in addition to this, Daun had already let the world know at Kollin, that it was his principle to build a bridge of gold for a flying enemy; the cavalry made an attempt to follow the Prussians, but were soon driven back by Seidlitz. The army drew off quietly, and took 1000 prisoners with them.

Frederic did not march any distance; he encamped his army a league from the field of battle on the hill called Spitsbergen, having lost the greater part of his artillery and baggage, his men having no covering but their short jackets, and without tents in this severe season; they were also in want of ammunition, so necessary a requisite in European warfare. The position of the king was so advantageous, and his troops, notwithstanding their having been beaten, were so formidable, that Daun would not make a fresh attack. Retzow who had remained under arrest with his small body of men, but who was still looked on as their leader, hurried with them to the assistance of the king, and aided in covering his retreat; he was again taken into favour by Frederic, and died a few weeks after. In this ill-fated day the Prussians lost 101 cannon, besides their baggage, thirty stand of colours and 9000 men; the loss of the Austrians was 8000.

Almost all the Prussian generals who survived this day were wounded; the king himself was slightly so. He had gone into the hottest of the battle; his horse had been killed under him, and two pages had fallen by his side; he was also in great danger of being taken prisoner. The enemy had surrounded him, near the village of Hochkirch, but he was rescued by the bravery of his escort of hussars. Ever in the thickest of the fight, he seemed to take no care of his life. He never showed his genius and his great capabilities in a higher degree than on this night, which instead of taking from his fame, added to his reputation. Several old regiments, who till now had been victorious, and never present at a defeat, had been forced to turn their backs to the enemy. But for this day, which had indeed not tarnished their fame, they would have been invincible.

★★★★★★

The regiment of Forcade, in which the author served, was one of these, and from its formation in 1713 to October 1758 had only heard of battles being lost. The king once said of them, as he passed before their ranks: "When I want to see soldiers, I must come to this regiment!"

★★★★★★

Field-Marshall Prince Maurice of Dessau, who had been dangerously wounded, was attacked on his way to Bautzen by a party of hussars. The prince said to their leader:

I am severely wounded, and give myself up as your prisoner. I request you to conduct me on parole to Bautzen, and your hussars shall have a hundred *ducats* ransom.

The officer was satisfied, and closed round the carriage with his men. Shortly after a strong body of Prussian hussars came up, and were preparing to attack. The captain of the horse told this to the prince, and requested him to use his authority with the Prussians, otherwise he would endanger his own life. The prince did this, and called out to the Prussians that he was a prisoner, and on his parole. Of this they took no notice as they were anxious to set the prince at liberty, and at the same time to do away with his word, and those to whom he had given it. The captain now came to the door of the carriage with a pistol in his hand, and said:

I must shoot your highness if you do not keep your men back, and renew your parole.

The men were at last prevailed on to withdraw, but with difficulty, as the Prussians imagined it was their fault the prince remained a prisoner; the king decided the conflict, and declared the parole of the prince as binding. This courageous general died a short time after, and before he could be ransomed.

Frederic now endeavoured to forget the loss he had sustained at Hochkirch, and to get the better of its evil consequences. He greeted General Goltz when he saw him a few hours after the battle, with the following words: "They awoke us to some purpose, my dear Goltz."

The general answered: "Those who dare not speak to us during the day time, are often in the habit of disturbing us at night."

"You are right," said the king, "but I mean to pay them off by day for their want of courtesy in disturbing us in the night,"

He spoke to the artillery when they were assembled in the same strain; he asked: "What have you done with your cannon?"

One of them answered him: "The devil came and took it away in the night;" Frederic rejoined: "Well then, we must take it from him by daylight."

This victory of the Austrians was gained on the fete day of the Empress Maria Theresa, and as it is the custom of catholic countries to make presents on this day, Daun presented his mistress with the intelligence of the advantage he had gained; she thanked him in a letter full of the most gracious expressions. The Empress of Russia sent him a present of a golden sword; the Magistrates of Vienna raised a column to his honour, and the Austrian States-General made him a donation of 300,000 florins, to enable him to repurchase the estate of Ladendorf, which had passed from his family.

Even Pope Clement the XIII. who had just been raised to the papal dignity, and had given to the Empress of Austria, the title of Apostolic Majesty, took part in this victory. The successors of St. Peter had during the dark ages been in the habit of arming the Christian warriors with consecrated arms, that they might overthrow the Turks and Saracens. Clement thinking that such holy weapons might do good service in Silesia, sent Field-Marshall Daun a consecrated hat and sword, in order that he might more effectually overcome the heretics; conduct quite unworthy of the eighteenth century, if, not of this war, and which brought down many jests upon this general; Frederic called him in his letters, the consecrated man, and the general with the Pope's cap. This conduct on the part of Rome was highly impolitic, as many of the subjects of Frederic were Catholics, and he therefore had many ways of injuring the Pope. It would appear that these presents were not duly appreciated in Vienna, and the customary festivities, on such occasions, were dispensed with.

Thirty years after, when education had advanced, and they became more enlightened in the Austrian dominions, they formed a juster estimate both of the power of the Pope, and also of the so called heretics; and being ashamed of these gifts, the writers in Vienna denied the occurrence altogether, and attributed this well known historical fact to the imagination of Frederic, in consequence of this monarch having, in an idle hour, written a poetical papal bull, which was afterwards, to complete the farce, translated into Latin and printed; an ironical document, which simple people took for the original, and served others as an excuse for denying the whole affair. The same Pope some years after excommunicated the Duke of Parma; one ceremony was worthy of the other, and they are probably the last of the kind which will have to be recorded in history.

Daun expected, that as soon as Frederic should hear of the siege of Neisse he would attack him in despair; he therefore wrote to General Harsch:

Continue steadily to carry on the siege; I have the king in my power. He is cut off from Silesia, and should he attack me, I shall have good news to send you.

This confidence on the part of Daun was the more extraordinary, from his experience of the many resources of the fertile genius of Frederic. The misfortunes and good fortune of this monarch never came singly; after the battle of Kollin, he lost his mother, to whom he was tenderly attached, and on the day of his misfortune at Hochkirch his sister, the Markgräfin of Baireuth, died. He loved her to adoration, and from her high intellectual endowments, he looked on her, to use his own expression, as worthy of being immortalized by altars and temples.

Daun was never more cautious than after he had gained an advantage. He now entrenched himself in an impregnable camp near Cannewitz, and neglected every occasion of annoying the king. What had been said to Hannibal after the Battle of Cannae by a Carthaginian general might have been applied to him with propriety; "You may know how to conquer, but not to take advantage of your victory." Frederic, on the contrary, made the best use of this valuable time, reequipped his army with rapidity, in part from Dresden, and in part from Prince Henry's army, supplied them with provisions and arms, reinforced his army with 6000 men, sent by Prince Henry, and prepared to march towards Silesia. He said: "Daun has allowed us to get out of check, the game is not lost; we will refresh ourselves by a few day's rest, and then start off to the relief of Neisse."

There were however many impediments in his way; there were a great number of sick in the camp, and the Prussians, who had been wounded in the battle, were in Bautzen. It was necessary in the first place to remove these, to protect Saxony, and by forced marches to elude the enemy, who had taken possession of the roads towards Silesia. All these plans were successfully carried out, and on the 95th of October, eleven days after the battle, Frederic was marching with his whole army towards Silesia, and under such advantageous circumstances, that Daun gave up all hopes of preventing his advance; nevertheless he sent troops under the command of Generals Aremberg, Lascy and Laudon to impede the progress of the king. Laudon here displayed his great activity; he either threw light troops into the ravines to impede the Prussians, or cannonaded them from advantageous positions, and at other times attacked them from the cover of the woods, and rushed with impetuosity on the enemy. Every day the fight was renewed, and the opponent continued on the advance. But all these attempts were without result, for they only took a few pontoons and baggage-waggons from the Prussians.

The Austrian General Harsch, tranquillized by Daun's assurance, continued the siege of Neisse, which like all other Prussian fortified towns, was but weakly garrisoned in consequence of the troops being required in the field. At first he had great hopes of taking this town, in consequence of the king's being at so great a distance, and there being no Prussian army near enough to assist it; and after the battle of Hochkirch, all Europe looked upon the fate of Neisse as decided.

The relief of besieged places is generally the consequence of a victory or some other fortunate occurrence, but it was hardly to be expected, that Frederic, after being defeated and surrounded by powerful armies, could come eighty leagues to the assistance of this hard pressed fortress. He arrived, however, after thirteen days marching, on the 5th of November, within six leagues of Neisse.

More was not necessary to complete his object for Harsh raised the siege on this day, notwithstanding he would shortly have received reinforcements, left a large quantity of ammunition and implements of war behind him, and withdrew into Moravia. He had opened the trenches on the 4th of August, and had began to fire on the town on the 5th of October; but all his operations were rendered useless by the courage of the besieged, who made a sortie as the Austrians were retiring, and took 800 prisoners.

It is here necessary to notice the noble conduct of a high German lady, which has not been generally known, and of which it is probable Frederic had never heard. General Treskow had an estate not far from the town of Neisse of which place he was commandant. His wife was residing on this estate at the time the Austrians were besieging the town. They saw from the first that this undertaking would be of long duration, and that it was possible that Frederic, notwithstanding the distance he was at, might find means to overthrow their plans; they therefore thought that the safest and easiest way would be to obtain their object by treachery. Treskow had previously been a prisoner in Austria, and treated with great consideration; in addition to this, his wife, who had joined him in his misfortune, had met with great courtesy on the part of the court of Vienna; the agreeable recollection of the gracious conduct of the empress was fresh in her mind, and upon this a plan was formed. An officer of the Imperial army visited her, and gave her letters of protection from the Austrian general.

★★★★★★

This account was given to the author by the Baron von Eichberg, who was the officer sent on this occasion. He was then captain of horse, and acted as *aide-de-camp* both to Generals Laudon and Harsh; a few years previous to the first publication of this work he was living in Italy, and it was then that he communicated this fact to the author.

★★★★★★

He was received and entertained as a benefactor. As it was evening when he arrived, it was necessary he should remain the night; when at table the subject of conversation was the praise of the empress, to which the noble heart of the lady could set no bounds. There were no witnesses present, and it was now that a proposition was made; to induce her husband to surrender, large sums were offered, rank and titles; a regular attack was to be made that the general's honour should not be tarnished, and the most inviolable Secrecy promised. Madame von Treskow could hardly contain herself until he had concluded his proposition. She got up, and wringing her hands, bewailed the degradation of having such an offer made to her; she exclaimed repeatedly: "It is possible, that such a proposal can be made to me!"

All offers of condolence and consolation on the part of the officer were in vain, and the assurance of considering the offer as if it had not been made, and the promise of secrecy were fruitless in calming this deeply wounded lady. Her intention of remaining on her protected estate during the continuance of the siege was immediately given up; she refused all protection, all advantages, all quiet, to share with the besieged scarcity, want of rest and danger; her village, the only property of her family, and the reward of fifty year's service, was magnanimously sacrificed. She said to the envoy:

We are poor, this is our all; honour forces me to leave it in your hand, and if you wish to revenge yourselves you can do it.

It was in vain that the officer, moved by this noble conduct, threw himself at her feet, and entreated her to give up her resolution; she forgave him the offence, but would not longer consent to remain in the power of the enemies of Prussia; she left her house the same night, but took no provision with her, although aware of the scarcity in the town; the officer accompanied her to the advanced posts, and then quitted her in admiration of her conduct. Kosel, which had also been blockaded by the Austrians, was now relieved, and Silesia' entirely freed from the troops of the enemy. The campaign was at an end in this province, and it was only in Saxony, that Daun, who was still in that country, which was but weakly protected, could hope to gain any advantages before the end of the winter. All Europe was looking forward to the results of the victory of Hochkirch, but as yet none were to be seen; not that projects had been wanting, for Dresden, Leipsic, and Torgau were to be at once, and at the same time, taken from the king, by different bodies of troops, and Daun himself marched on the capital, determined this time not to be baulked of his intention.

There was only a small body of Prussians in Saxony, but they displayed great activity under General Fink who was their actual leader although they were nominally under older generals; for those brave commanders, Hülsen and Itzenplitz, putting aside all feelings of jealousy, only sought the true path of honour in the fame of their country, respected the wishes of their king, and did justice to the talents of the young general. The most effectual measures were adopted against the overpowering force of the enemy, the garrison of Dresden was strengthened, and the commandant, General Schmettau now found himself under the painful necessity of burning the suburb, as the royal family, deceived by vain hopes, kept back from interfering in this time of danger. They thought it was right, in their distressed position to let things take their course.

The states-general remained silent, the magistrates who looked for the greatest advantage from the city falling into the hands of the Austrians, and expected with this to see an end of all the vexations of warfare, shrugged up their shoulders in answer to the overtures of the commandant, and the complaints of their fellow citizens at their fate; so greatly were they deceived, and so much had they changed in their ideas in the course of a single month, that the unhappy residents in the *faubourg* were left to their fate.

This suburb was, from the manner in which it was built, equal to any of the finest towns in Europe. The extensive buildings of which it consisted were either the palaces or summer residences of the great and the rich, or else, manufactories of a number of the different ornamental works in which the Saxon industry is so much displayed; every preparation was made for burning all these to the ground. Schmettau made fresh overtures, and affirmed his determination to have recourse to this fearful extremity on the approach of the enemy; but the court remained indifferent. The enemy did approach, the Prussians withdrew their advanced posts, and on the morning of the 10th of November the fearful signal was given for the work of destruction to commence.

Combustibles were placed in every room and vacant space, in the midst of the most beautiful furniture, works of art and the productions of manufactories; the inhabitants had taken flight, and but few had been able to avail themselves of the time allowed them to take away their properly, from the want of means of conveyance. In a few hours near three hundred buildings were consumed by fire; an old couple were burnt, and in addition to these, three others lost their lives. This dreadful conflagration was described by the enemies of Frederic with numerous additions, which, had they been true, would have been the disgrace of the Prussian name; but Schmettau received an honourable testimony of his conduct from the magistrates of Dresden which fully exonerated him from the charges of cruelly attributed to him.

Daun, who appeared quite astonished and perplexed at this conflagration, sent to the commandant to ask if it was by the orders of his king that he had committed an act as yet unheard of in any Christian land, and threatened to make him answerable for his conduct. Schmettau referred to his duty, which was to defend the town to the last extremity, and also to well known maxims of warfare; he declared again that he would defend himself against his whole force from street to street, and bury himself under the ruins of the palace.

Daun now prepared to lay regular siege to Dresden, but the bad news from Silesia of the raising the siege of Neisse, the retreat of the Imperial army into Moravia, and the approach of Frederic into Saxony rendered his plans useless; he withdrew his forces, but not without making the courtly assurance that it was done entirely out of regard to the royal family. In the official notification of the retreat it is stated that a certain weighty reason rendered it necessary to withdraw the troops; this weighty reason was nothing more nor less than the approach of Frederic. The attacks upon Leipsic, and Torgau met with a similar fate; both these towns were relieved nearly at the same time by Generals Dohna and Wedel; there was now nothing left for the Imperial troops but to march towards Bohemia, and even the fortress of Sonnenstein was abandoned.

The Austrians now withdrew their forces without having gained a foot of land in the country of the enemy, even as the Prince Soubise had withdrawn to the Rhine after the Battle of Lutternberg. Daun's principal object in the disposition of his armies in their winter quarters, was to place them so as to form a continuous line such as had not as yet been seen in Germany or even in Europe. This cordon, consisting of more than 300,000 soldiers, extended from the mountains which separate Bohemia from Silesia to the Alps. It was formed by the Austrians along the frontiers of Silesia and Saxony, and was continued by the troops of the Empire through Thuringia and Franconia, and united to the French army which was posted on the banks of the Main and the Rhine, and commanded the banks of this large river to the frontiers of Switzerland.

The march of the king after the battle of Zorndorf having given the Russians an opportunity of continuing their operations, they determined to besiege Colberg in order to have a principal magazine and a fortified position for their operations in the more central provinces of Prussia; the harbour of this town would have been a great advantage to them from the facility it gave of receiving supplies, at the same time that the weakness of its garrison promised an easy conquest. The fate of Pomerania hung upon the defence of Colberg which was entrusted to 700 men of the militia, a few invalids and fifteen artillerymen under the command of an invalid officer of the name of Heyden. This officer was a man of great courage, knowledge of the art of war, and he displayed this, together with his decision of character, in the preparations he made for defence. General Palmbach besieged the town with 10,000 Russians, made himself master of the harbour, and in five days was in possession of the covered way.

The taking the town seemed now quite certain; but the valour of the *commandant* and the courage of the soldiers, and the brave citizens he had armed and who fought like old soldiers, put a stop to the progress of the besiegers. The besieged laboured under a great disadvantage from the suburbs which were a protection to the Russians. Heyden would not allow the houses to be burnt for the sake of the citizens, upon whose assistance lie had to depend in consequence of the weakness of the garrison; these citizens, who were well practiced in shooting at a mark, remained constantly on the ramparts, and picked off every man they could see, who was within shot. General Palmbach was much irritated at this defence on the part of the citizens; but he became more reconciled to it, when he was informed, that they were each bound by their oath of citizenship to defend the town.

An extraordinary occurrence took place during this siege. On the sixth day after its commencement, Palmbach unexpectedly received orders to raise the siege; he did so, but had not marched more than three leagues from the place before he received fresh orders to return, and to carry on the siege with more rigour than ever. Heyden, who thought this retreat very extraordinary, took the precaution not to be in a hurry to open the gates, in order to destroy the works, as, if they were really gone, there was plenty of time for this work; the consequence was that, when the Russians returned the following day, they found everything as they had left it.

The town was again summoned to surrender; the commandant replied, that there was not the least cause for his doing this, as the fortifications were in the best condition; to this he added that they would gain as little by fire as they had done at Cüstrin, and to make them aware of the state of the fortifications, Heyden gave orders that the Russian officer, who had been sent, should be conducted over the works. He now made the most efficient preparations for defence; being so short of artillerymen, 120 of the militia were exercised night and day in gun practice; they were well attended to, their food was prepared for them, and sent to the batteries. The garrison were all well supplied with provisions; a precaution which did not a little serve to keep up the courage of the soldiers, and preserve them in health and good spirits.

The besiegers were continually receiving reinforcements from the army, and renewed their attacks with fresh troops. On the fifteenth day of the siege the town was summoned, the commandant reminded of the misery he would bring on the inhabitants, if the town were taken by storm, and that he was justified in the sight of God, the king, and the world, having no hopes of relief, by his position, and by his brave defence with so small a garrison: Heyden answered, that as far as in him lay, he would do his utmost so spare blood; but as an officer, he must from regard to his duty, await the worst. The town was, however, not stormed, but the bombardment was carried on with more activity than ever; shells and grenades, and when these failed, stones were thrown into the town; but at last news arrived in the Russian camp of the approach of a body of Prussian troops, and the siege was raised after having continued twenty nine days.

After the failure of this attempt the Russians evacuated Pomerania and Brandenburg, and retired part into Poland, and part into winter quarters in Prussia. This left General Dohna at liberty to march with his army into Saxony, and to go to the relief of Leipsic, which was besieged by the troops of the Empire under the Duke of Zweibrücken, but who on his approach withdrew their forces. The Imperial General Haddick also retired into the states of the Empire after General Wedel, who commanded in Pomerania, had gained considerable advantages over him. The king who, on the raising the siege of Neisse, had returned to Saxony, after giving directions for the destruction of the works of Sonnenstein, went back to Silesia where he placed his army in winter quarters, and took up his own at Breslau.

The operations of the Swedes had been as inconsiderable during this campaign as during the last, notwithstanding they had been reinforced by 5600 infantry, and 2000 cavalry, and that they had received the subsidies promised by France. They contented themselves with plundering, and laying under contribution those Prussian districts which were not protected by troops, and when their means of subsistence failed in these places, they drew large supplies of provisions from Mecklenburg, which, although an ally, was treated as an enemy, and in the first instance they gave promises of paying for the supplies.

The states general of this province did not approve of this mode of proceeding, and directed them to go to the markets, but they were threatened with force, and the supplies were provided; Count Löwenhaut who was at the head of the body of men sent to raise these supplies, required money also for himself and his men under pretext that they were come to protect the country, which was also given. They departed in August, but previously demanded a bond from the states general that they would allow no moneys to be sent from the province to the King of Prussia; the requisition was ridiculous since the revenues of Mecklenburg were regulated by the military power of Prussia, which, although sometimes suspended, was never got the better of; the states general refused to agree to this proposition, and the consequence was that Colonel Drieberg and the Bürgermeister of Rostock were taken as hostages to the Swedish army.

In the month of August, the treaty of alliance between Sweden and Russia terminated, and was renewed without alteration for twelve years. But the operations of the Swedes remained equally inefficient during the whole war, and the inactivity of their soldiers in the field rendered them despicable in the eyes of their allies, their enemy, and even their own countrymen; the real causes of this inactivity, which have been previously explained, were not generally known, and they were equally laughed at in Stockholm, Vienna and Berlin. But although this excited in them gradually a more sincere desire to participate in the war, they had now forfeited the character they had held for centuries, of a generous and courageous enemy, and dishonoured the martial sprit of their country by disgraceful conduct, and as soon as the Prussians were at a little distance, they gave themselves up to pillage, and all imaginable excesses.

With the exception of not murdering helpless and unarmed citizens they nearly equalled the Cossacks in the devastation they committed; they took every thing they could lay their hands on in the towns and villages they passed through, and deprived the inhabitants of their bread, and their property, not sparing even the seed which was in the ground, and which they destroyed. They were not led on to these excesses by any feeling of national enmity, for in the first instance, they were displeased with the line of policy adopted by their statesmen, and inclined to the side of the Prussians; but the love of plunder soon got the better of these feelings, and steeled their hearts against the misery and lamentations of their victims; added to this the force of habit soon lent its assistance, and proved that in warfare, soldiers often lose the feeling of men, and of humanity. These Swedes were seen in daily public prayer to God; the moment they left their devotions hurrying to commit crimes, and as soon as these were completed, returning to their prayers.

The seizing of Berlin was the great aim of the Swedes in consequence of Brandenburg being so little protected by troops, and they were only ten leagues from this capital in October, when General Wedel advanced, and drove them back. The Prussians did not stop till they had forced them to seek protection under the cannon of Stralsund, and Fehrbellin was the only town that they occupied with a strong garrison to cover their retreat; but this place so remarkable to the Swedes for the defeat that the Elector Frederic William had here suffered, a hundred years previous, was taken without delay by the Prussians, who stormed it, and took prisoners those of the garrison who were not cut to pieces.

The campaign was now at an end on all sides, and Frederic, who had been defeated in October, was now master of the Elb and the Oder. In the short space of seven weeks he had marched from Saxony into Silesia, then back into Saxony, and was now again in Silesia, and in addition to this, in these few weeks, Neisse, Cosel, Dresden, Leipsic, Torgau and Colberg had been relieved. What made his marches the more extraordinary was the being encumbered with a large army which presents so many difficulties to rapidity of motion on a long march. Marshall Belleisle who was then French minister, and had been at the head of an army, and accustomed to military operations, would not hear of these movements of the king in forming plans for the war, although they had been foretold to him; he said: "Let the King of Prussia do what he will, his army is not a weaver's shuttle."

The Austrians in Bohemia and Moravia were now making fresh plans for the next campaign; the Russians in Prussia and Poland were filling their magazines; the troops of the Empire were in their winter quarters in the centre of Germany, and the Swedes, who saw their own portion of Pomerania in the hands of the Prussians, had sought safety under the cannon of Stralsund.

Chapter 5: Campaign of the French in 1758

The campaign of the allies of Frederic during the same year was also very remarkable. In the beginning of the year the Duke of Richelieu was recalled, and resigned the command of the French armies to Count Clermont. This newly chosen leader was a churchman, and had never seen an army before, not even at a review; but Madame de Pompadour, the royal mistress' who then managed Louis the XVth and the French Government without any control over her wishes, was taken with his courtly manners and talents; and in order to reward these she elevated him to the rank of general, and sent him into Germany, to assert the honour of France against a great leader. The choice of such a person astonished the whole world, and when Frederic heard of it, he said:

> I hope that the next general they send will be the Archbishop of Paris.

The court of Versailles strove to outdo that of Vienna in its activity and zeal to overthrow Prussia. They appeared to have forgotten their almost annihilated navy, and the threatening progress of the English, that they might turn all their attention to this end, and employ every means that gold, intrigue and state policy could suggest. The French ambassadors at the courts of Vienna, St. Petersburg and Stockholm could in most instances guide these cabinets according to their wishes; and added to this, the Marquis of Montalembert and the Count de Montazet were sent as French envoys, the latter to the Swedish, and afterwards to the Russian Army; and the former to that of the Imperialists, in order that they might, if possible, direct the operations of the allies in accordance with the plans of France.

These men were both officers of great talents and experience, and they studied the capabilities of the armies and the characters of the generals, in order that the French court might attach them to their interest by handsome presents, and by a knowledge of their private feelings and individual tastes; by these means they were often enabled to form the most advantageous plans for the operations of their allies, as was learnt by the betrayal of Montalembert's correspondence. These officers were in constant activity, and they corresponded with the prime minister at Versailles, with the commanders of the French Army, and with the ambassadors of their country at the courts of the different powers engaged in the war. When the armies were no longer in the field, they went in person from one court to another to form, plans, and to overcome difficulties by the most efficient means.

Previous to the departure of Richelieu, Halberstadt was sorely visited by the French. After the Battle of Rossbach, this general had left the town and the whole principality, but not before he had levied contributions from this province, which only contained ten towns and a hundred villages, to the amount of more than a million and a half of dollars; a portion of this was still unpaid, and as there was now a force of 3000 Prussians in the country, the inhabitants of this drained province refused, by order of the king, to pay it to the French. Richelieu determined to punish them for this, and a body of men 12,000 strong, who were stationed in Brunswick, advanced under the command of the Marquis of Voyer in the month of January, upon Halberstadt; their intention was to have seized the Prussian troops, but they were able to withdraw without loss.

The contributions were now levied with greater rigour than ever, and with the threat, that if more than four dollars in money and three bushels of wheat were to be found in any house, it would be pillaged and set fire to; and the tar barrel was ever in readiness to carry this threat into effect. Voyer's answer to the most moving representations was always: "Money and corn or else fire!" What could not be raised, even from the poor, was made up by bills of exchange; after this came the searching the houses by the soldiers which gave rise to constant pillage. The gates of the city were then burnt, the brick work pulled down, and the walls destroyed.

The last requisition of the enemy was that the inhabitants of Halberstadt should promise to pay a fine of 100,000 dollars, in the event of the Prussians again occupying the town; the deputation from the town refused with firmness to comply with this unjust demand, and at last the French withdrew, taking with them six hostages. Quedlinburg where Count Turpin commanded, had a very different fate from Halberstadt; they expected oppressive levies to be made, but this generous commander who had no tyrannical orders to fulfil, or of he had, did not put them in force, said that all that he required was the necessary supplies for his troops, and a number of waggons with which he withdrew, followed by the blessings of the people.

The getting possession of the principal German free towns of the Empire was the great object of the French leaders. In the previous year they had, on their first advance into Germany, seized the city of Cologne, under the pretext that the King of France was guarantee of the treaty of Westphalia. The city of Bremen met with a similar fate in August 1757, under the excuse, that there was in this place a magazine for the necessaries of war belonging to the King of England. They promised not to make any alteration in the government, or in the laws of the town, but in case of resistance they threatened to use force; the inhabitants compelled by necessity, acceded to the request, and the Marquis of Armentieres then took possession of the town.

He took much from the disagreeables of the position of the inhabitants, by the discipline he enforced, and his noble and generous disposition and bearing; the French only remained here a short time, for they left Bremen fourteen days after; they, however, in four months after, and before the opening of the campaign renewed their project of occupying this town in consequence of their hearing of a similar intention on the part of Duke Ferdinand of Brunswick. There appeared some difficulty in its completion, for the people assembled round the town hall, and threatened the magistrates, if they allowed the French to come into the town; the people would hear of no representations, and the French general allowed no delay; he approached with his cannon, and his troops placed their scaling ladders on the walls. A capitulation was now agreed upon with the French general, Duke de Broglio, which was any thing but dishonourable to the town, as he granted every thing that the magistrates required.

The people were much dissatisfied, especially as they learnt that 3000 Hanoverians were approaching; they assembled together, armed themselves with axes, and were anxious to break open the storehouses that they might get arms, and drive the French who were already advancing, out of the town; they actually came to blows and several of the inhabitants were killed or wounded, but this was the end of the affray. With the taking possession of this town terminated the operations under the command of Richelieu, who now returned to Paris to repose upon his laurels.

The new leader Clermont found the army, entrusted to his command in a most miserable state. The French ambassador at the court of Sweden, the Marquis of Havrincourt, expressed himself in the following manner, on this subject, to the Marquis of Montalembert:

Clermont has found the army in a most wretched state of disorder; there is no regularity, no arrangement in the placing the troops in their quarters, no preparations for the supply of the men, and in short a scarcity of everything.

Clermont in consequence of this state of affairs made the following extraordinary report to his king:

I have found your Majesty's army divided into three different bodies; one is above ground, and composed of thieves and marauders dressed in rags; another is under ground, and the third is in the hospital.

He therefore required instructions as to whether he should bring back the first division, or allow them to remain until they joined the other two.

The Duke of Brunswick gave him no time to improve his position. He opened the campaign as early as February, made himself master of the Weser, and advanced on Hanover. Wherever his outposts showed themselves the enemy fled, and in such haste, that the sick, a number of cannon and their baggage remained behind. Even the town of Bremen, which was so important to them from many considerations was evacuated by the French and also Lippstadt, Hamm, Münster and other important places. It was only in Hoya on the Weser that Count Chabot held his ground until the hereditary Prince of Brunswick drove him thence after a spirited resistance, and took 1500 prisoners. These were the first deeds of this young prince, who afterwards proved himself worthy of being considered among the first generals of his time, and was fated to be the avenger of the house of Orange, and to humble the pride of Holland.

The taking of Hoya led to that of Zelle, Hanover and Brunswick; and the light troops, of the allied carried every thing before them. In the consternation into which the French were thrown, they sought to save themselves by flight, and being in the greatest disorder many of them fell victims to the rage they had excited in the bosoms of the

Hanoverian peasantry, by their many acts of oppression; in the space of eight days, Hanover was completely rid of the enemy, who drew off to the Rhine, and left their magazines behind them, those which they had not time to destroy falling into the hands of the enemy. In order to secure this hurried retreat, Clermont sacrificed 4000 men whom he left in Minden, which place was regularly besieged. The *commandant*, the Marquis of Morangiés, required after five days to be allowed to withdraw his troops, and as this was refused to him, he threatened to blow up the bridge over the Weser, to reduce the town to a heap of ashes, and to bury himself with his garrison under its ruins.

But he did not carry his threats into execution, and these were laughed at by the besiegers. Morangiés now altered his determination, and surrendered the following day, by which the garrison which was now 3500 men strong became prisoners of war, and a large magazine fell into the hands of the enemy. In Hessia, Marburg was the only town now in the hands of the French, and the hereditary prince of Brunswick soon drove them out of this, so that the allies had no longer an enemy to oppose them either in Lower Saxony or Westphalia; the French never stopped till they reached Wesel, having on their way lost 11,000 men who had fallen into the hands of the allies. The former established their head quarters in this town, and sent the greater part of their army across the Rhine.

In the army of Ferdinand there was a deficiency in cavalry, for the few regiments of Hanoverian and Hessian horse with some thousands of Prussian dragoons and hussars which were attached to his army, were not sufficient for active service in the field; the British Parliament therefore determined to send English cavalry to Germany, and to strengthen the army by English infantry. Emden was fixed on as the most convenient place for debarkation; but this place was in the hands of the French, who had fortified and garrisoned it with 3800 men, and in consequence of its harbour fixed on it as a place of strength and principal magazine; but they were not able to hold it. Two English ships of war blockaded the entrance to the harbour, the garrison were seized with a panic, as they feared the being attacked both by land and water; nothing remained for them to do, but to evacuate the town, which was immediately done, but not without great loss from the attacks of the English, the Prussians and the Hanoverians.

A great number of the French were killed, and many taken prisoners; a large quantity of baggage, ammunition and provisions fell into the hands of the allies, and the wounded were left to their mercy. The hostages who were in the hands of the French were now set at liberty, and in the hurry of their retreat they forgot to give notice of their departure to the garrison of Vichte, a neighbouring fort, who were in consequence forced to surrender, and give up 100 pieces of cannon.

At the time that these operations were going on, by which before the end of March the whole of Northern Germany was cleared of the hitherto victorious French Army, all the other belligerents, Prussians, Austrians, Russians, Swedes and troops of the Empire, were still in their winter quarters. The only town now in the hands of the French was Wesel, and it was Ferdinand's determination to take this place, and drive them over the Rhine; but in the first instance he placed his troops in winter quarters in Westphalia in order to await the arrival of the British cavalry.

The French nation who had not got over the disgrace of the Battle of Rossbach, were much annoyed and distressed at this new and unexpected discomfiture. That a large army of Frenchmen should be driven to seek safety in flight by a few Germans, assembled together in haste, and deficient in cavalry, this was more than their pride could bear, and it was the more annoying, as it was caused by the same Germans, who driven into a corner of Germany had been forced to make a disgraceful capitulation. They imagined the enterprising Ferdinand had already crossed the Rhine, that he was even in the heart of France, and would shortly be before the gates of Paris.

These occurrences appeared so extraordinary to the adversaries of Prussia that even the courts of Vienna and St. Petersburg fancied there was an understanding between Prance and Prussia, and it required some trouble on the part of France to get the better of this feeling. But they soon showed that they were sincere; for the most active arrangements were made to call together the troops from the different parts of the kingdom, who were dispatched in haste to strengthen the army on the Rhine, and the fortified places on the frontier were put in the best state of defence as speedily as possible. In order to raise the spirits of the people, who wished more for peace than war, a report was spread that a treaty would in all probability shortly follow through the mediation of Spain.

The Marquis of Belleisle who was at the head of affairs in Versailles, now turned his attention to the causes of the abuses in the French army, and issued orders, the necessity for which, especially in time of war, must be matter of astonishment in all well disciplined armies. These were: that half the officers should be with their regiments, and that no officer should leave the army without leave of absence; should they do so, they were to be punished with the loss of their pay; Belleisle also sent a number of officers to the Bastille, and letters to the different French generals, full of threats and strict orders; but the evil was too deeply rooted to be eradicated without entirely remodelling the French Army. There was no discipline, no subordination, and no order on the march, in camp or even on the field of battle. The very subalterns had their mistresses with them, and officers often left their men to accompany them on the march, in their carriages.

Everything that could contribute to the luxury of the officers was to be found in a French camp; shops of every description for the supply of the most simple and useful articles, and those of refinement and ornament followed in their train; at one time there were 12,000 waggons accompanying the army of the Prince of Soubise which belonged to the sutlers and shopkeepers, when the army was not more than 50,000 strong. In the *garde du corps*, the squadron of the Duke de Villeroy, which consisted of 139 horsemen, had 1200 horses in their suite; this immense train rendered the difficulties in supporting the army much greater, increased the disorder in the camps, and on a march, and impeded their progress. Balls were given in the camp, and officers on guard often left their post that they might dance a minuet; they laughed at the orders of their leaders, and only obeyed them when it suited them.

The Count de St. Germain who was afterwards field-marshal in the Danish service, and still later minister of war in France, gave a remarkable instance of this want of subordination; the occurrence, it is true, took place in the following campaign, but may be mentioned here as more to the purpose. St. Germain was Lieutenant General, and commanded a detached body of 10,000 men. Having disagreed with the Marshall Broglio, he threw off all subordination, and left his troops without acquainting his superior officer with his intention, or taking any precautions for the safety of his soldiers, it appearing to him sufficient to acquaint the marshal by letter where he had left the body of men entrusted to his care; but this conduct was not considered as anything extraordinary either by the French Army or by his countrymen. People said in Paris: "He has sent in his resignation."

The feelings of honour, and the duties of high position in society to which this people are in general so sensitive, were in this instance not thought of, and at the court they were content with blaming that which, in the armies of other nations, would have been considered a crime deserving the punishment of death.

This manner of thinking and acting on the part of the French, which contrasted so strongly with the habits and principles of German discipline, excited in the German troops feelings of contempt, which neither the courage, nor the active ambition of the enemy could get the better of, and besides this the different circumstances of the war must be considered. Frederic had only to show himself, and he gained a great victory and in the easiest manner. Ferdinand gathered a few dispersed troops together in the middle of winter, and in a few weeks the French, who thought of nothing but victory, were driven to the Rhine without striking a blow; and in fact the position of these troops, when they reached the Rhine was most melancholy, and illustrated every possible human misery; worn out, starving and straggling in from every direction; everything from the stores of their shopkeepers to the necessaries supplied by the sutlers had fallen into the hands of Ferdinand's light troops; the French had not sufficient bread, and what to them was almost as great a misfortune, there was a scarcity of hair powder; but they were not in bad spirits in spite of all this, for they danced, jumped and amused themselves on their march.

They were allowed to take liberties on the march that would not have been permitted in other armies; they would often stick their bread on the points of their bayonets, and hang their meat on the handles of their swords, and it was not uncommon to see them with paper ruffles; thus there never was more gaiety in any army, which continued by good and evil fortune in the camp or on the march, by day as well as by night. For want of better amusement, they often stripped women of light character to the waist, and made them run the gauntlet in this state; a punishment which served to amuse them, and was the more extraordinary from the French soldiery never, either in this or any other manner, having been the subjects of corporeal punishment.

All this increased the contempt of the Prussians to a degree which has never been surpassed by any people towards a truly brave nation. No pains were taken to conceal it, even under the most unfavourable circumstances. The following is a remarkable specimen of this feeling: A Prussian hussar was taken prisoner by the French, and taken to headquarters. Clermont wished to speak to him in person, for the taking a Prussian was of rare occurrence in this part of Germany, and the conversation between the French general and the hussar who was a prisoner was carried on through the medium of an interpreter. When he was asked, where Ferdinand was encamped? "Where you cannot attack him," was the answer. He was asked how strong the army of his king was? He answered that if they had sufficient courage, they might go in search of it, and count its numbers. Clermont was not offended at this hardihood. He was rather amused with it, and asked the hussar, if his king had many such soldiers as him?

The man with the death's head answered: "if I did not belong to the worst of them I should not now be your prisoner."

To meet with such sentiments in a man who was not a Frenchman was a mystery to them. The hussar was set at liberty, and Clermont gave him a *Louis d'or*; the Prussian took it, but notwithstanding he had been previously deprived of every thing, and had not a farthing in his pocket he gave it to a French soldier in the presence of the general with the observation, that he would not accept of any present from the enemy of his people. He was asked to enter the French service, and a commission was offered to him, but he replied with a smile of contempt, that he was a Prussian.

Such traits mark the character of a people, and of the times they occurred in. The high feelings here exhibited in a common soldier could only be occasioned by the principles and manner of thinking of the nation to which he belonged, and this was the reason they did not excite the admiration they deserved. The facts were known, but the name of the Prussian who so thought and spoke remains a secret.

This soldier belonged to the black hussars; the horsemen of this regiment were dressed in black, and wore on their foreheads that symbol of corruption, a death's head; each was a living *memento mori*; and the very sight of such an emblem of death, with a sharp sabre in the wearer's hand, to give full effect to his appearance, excited feelings of horror; and in truth these black hussars were objects of terror to the bravest of the French regiments. It was generally reported, that in case of resistance they never gave quarter, and the hussars encouraged this belief that they might the more easily vanquish their opponents.

The effect of this was beyond all belief; whole bodies of men fled before a handful of these hussars, and not infrequently a single one would bring a number of prisoners into the camp; they went into battle as to a dance, and never came back without booty. These black hussars distinguished themselves amongst the light Prussian troops as much by their generosity as by their heroic intrepidity, and of this the following traits deserve to be recorded. A hussar took an Austrian officer prisoner who, according to the customs of warfare, handed him his purse, and his watch on the spot. The Prussian gave both back to him, and said: "You are a prisoner, and will require your money, my companion here (striking his sabre) will give me as much any day."

This black regiment was one day posted so as to receive a heavy cannonade which they had to stand without moving. An officer was smoking his pipe quietly, and at the moment that two of his, men fell from their horses killed by a cannon ball, cried out to the others of his troop: "steady, my boys! if a man falls, close up! that is what we remain here for." In another battle an officer who was severely wounded, cried out as he fell from his horse: "Forwards at them! I am not hurt." Such examples must have raised the sense of duty to a high pitch in the survivors, and have diminished the fear of death.

It is the duty of the historian to record the conduct of individuals in such cases; and it is an agreeable one when it brings honour and credit to his nation. But he must likewise not neglect to state the noble conduct of her enemies. The Marquis of Armentieres, who has already been mentioned, took possession of the town of Zelle; the nobility and the citizens sent a deputation to entreat for mercy. Armentieres answered: "I am not come to this place to do good, but be assured that I will do as little evil as possible in my position." He kept his word, and after the end of the war he sent the *Dictionaire Encyclopedique* to the preacher Roques, in Zelle. The book was then considered as taking the place of all other books; and this present was accompanied with the following words:

> You have given me so many opportunities of being useful to your unfortunate fellow-citizens, that I must not fail in expressing my gratitude to you.

The French, under the command of General Mercieres took possession of the town of Bielefeld, in Westphalia, which is so celebrated for its manufacture of linen, and many of the manufactories were pillaged notwithstanding that it was in opposition to this general's wishes. His conscience told him however that he might have taken more decisive steps for its prevention, and three and thirty years after, in 1790, he sent a considerable sum of money to the magistrates with the request that they would divide it amongst those who had been sufferers, and in case they were dead, that they would employ the capital in the manner they should think most useful to the town. In the town of Hanover they were fortunate in having a philanthropist as the leader of their enemy; this was the Duke of Randau, who lost no opportunity of exhibiting forbearance and generosity.

The French General Vaubecourt, who commanded in the Harz showed also by his praiseworthy conduct, that liberality was not incompatible with the operations of war in the country of an enemy. The inhabitants of the town of Clausthal were so impressed with the generosity of his conduct, that to express their gratitude they had a medal struck with his image, and the inscription:

Recto, Modesto Duel Vaubecourt, Civit. Clausthal. 1762.

We must now resume the history of this campaign. As soon as his troops had recovered themselves in their short time of repose in winter quarters, Ferdinand opened the campaign with the daring purpose of carrying the war, if not into France itself, at any rate to the frontiers of that kingdom. But in consequence of the French army being posted on the Rhine, and in many places in advantageous positions, the passage of this large river presented great difficulties, especially as the German general had no means of forming a bridge. These impediments were, in spite of this, got the better of by means of his arrangements, and on the 1st of June the allies crossed the river during the night not far from Cleves, in part over a bridge formed of boats they hired from the Dutch, and the remainder in flat bottomed boats; the injury which was inflicted on some portions of the Dutch territory in consequence of this assistance was made good by the payment of 4000 florins.

Ferdinand was very anxious for a battle, but Clermont avoided it carefully, and had entrenched himself as strongly as possible with his far superior force near Rheinfeld: to attack him in this position would have been madness, and nothing remained but by scientific movements to draw him from his camp. This was done by his clever opponent, and fourteen days after the passage of the Rhine the French army was in the plain of Crefeld, and the armies engaged here on the 23rd of June. On this occasion Ferdinand displayed his high military talents; he ordered three different attacks to be made, but two of these were only feints; a circumstance which remained concealed from the enemy from the scientific arrangements of Ferdinand. The principal attack was on the left wing of the French in a thicket, upon the possession of which the fate of the day depended; General St. Germain commanded this wing, and in the hope of being reinforced, defended himself in the most courageous manner against superior numbers; the whole of the grenadier corps was in fact sent to his assistance, but these troops missed their way.

At last the hereditary prince of Brunswick came up with the infantry, rushed into the wood, and after hard fighting for three hours drove the enemy out of it. The French cavalry lost the best of their soldiers in this battle, and the Prussian dragoons, enraged at some jokes the French had passed on them, took this opportunity for revenge; the allies had only 1500 killed and wounded in this engagement, but the enemy upwards of 7000 men. The French nation experienced a great loss by the death of the Count Gisors the only son of the Duke de Belleisle, a young man of rare talents and great promise; he was mortally wounded and died in the arms of the Hereditary Duke of Brunswick who knew him, and was attached to him. The victor Ferdinand went over the field of battle, and looking upon the bodies of the dead was much moved, and said to his officers who wished him joy:

This is the tenth exhibition of this kind I have seen during my life time; would to God it might be the last!

After the battle, the hereditary prince advanced with a body of men, took possession of Rörmond without opposition, and sent out skirmishing parties to the very gates of Bruxelles. Contributions were levied in Brabant and in the Bishopric of Liege; but the most important consequence of this victory was the siege of Dusseldorf, in which town the French had their principal supply of provisions This place surrendered on the sixteenth day, but not till after a number of houses had been reduced to ashes by the shells which were thrown into the town; the garrison were allowed to withdraw with the honours of war; but the immense supplies of provisions, ammunition, and a large number of cannon, fell into the hands of the conquerors. In France everybody was alarmed at this fresh discomfiture; the Bastille was filled, and Clermont recalled; the *dauphin* was anxious to place himself at the head of the army, but this was not carried into effect.

Fresh steps were however taken to rescue the honour of the French arms; the army received supplies, the vacancies were filled up, new regulations issued, and the Marshall de Contades, an experienced officer, was appointed to the command of the army of the Rhine. In addition to this, the Prince de Soubise received orders to overrun the Hessian provinces at all risks, with his army which had been reinforced by 6300 Würtembergers These provinces appeared an easy conquest in consequence of the absence of Ferdinand, and it would at the same time be a means of drawing the troops of the allies from the Rhine; Soubise now advanced, and notwithstanding his advanced guard was beaten by the Hessian militia, he continued his march with 30,000 men into the heart of the province.

The Hessian general, Prince of Isenburg had only 7000 men to defend himself with; but he took up an advantageous position between Cassel and Minden; he was aware of his incapability, with so small a body of men, and many of these not regular soldiers, of making a resistance to so large an army, and merely wished to gain time to await the result of the operations on the Rhine. In order to follow up this plan, he wished to retreat; but his troops, who now held the French in great contempt, would not hear of it. He was forced to retain his position, and an engagement ensued between his troops and the body sent against him under command of the Duke de Broglio, 12,000 strong, and for the most part composed of German regiments in the pay of the French.

This battle was fought at Sangershausen on the 23rd of July, and was well contested; the Hessians fought with the greatest bravery, and the victory was doubtful for five hours, but they were at last forced to give way to superior numbers; Isenburg left the field of battle with 1500 men killed, wounded, and taken prisoners, and the loss of nearly all his artillery, and three hundred of these brave Hessians were drowned in the Fulda, in endeavouring to escape from being made prisoners, by swimming the river. By this victory the French became masters of the Weser, and could now spread themselves over Hanover and Westphalia. The Hessian provinces which in the former year had been so sorely visited now felt in reality the scourge of war; an attempt was made to come to terms for this unfortunate country, but Contades sent the deputation away with scoffs, and said that he was a soldier, and could not write.

The Battle of Crefeld and the success of Ferdinand on the Rhine made the English anxious to carry on the war by land, notwithstanding they had hitherto only been willing participators in the war by sea, and the government of this empire as well as the people, wished that the most active measures should be taken to attack the French by sea and by land. The great Pitt was still at the head of affairs in England, and by his powerful mind ruled this proud nation according to his wishes, and from the fertility of his imagination, his powerful eloquence, and the greatness of his genius, he was alike unfettered both in the council, and in the Parliament; his principle was, either to give up a project altogether, or to carry it out by every possible means.

The Parliament voted the sending 18,000 men to Germany, and

had this been done sooner, Ferdinand would have been able to make good his position on the banks of the Rhine, and insured the taking of Wesel, which was invested by the allies. The position of this leader was now becoming critical; he had an army of 80,000 men opposed to him, who were led on by an experienced leader; provisions were beginning to be scarce, and a long continued rain and bad weather had rendered the roads almost impassable, and overflowed the banks of the river. In consequence of this the marches were rendered very difficult; the French had also made themselves masters of the Maes, and were endeavouring to cut off the allies from the Rhine; Ferdinand was therefore anxious for a battle, but Contades aware of his advantage, was careful in avoiding one. In the mean time Hanover required immediate assistance, added to this, there was great cause for anxiety for the support of the army, and also for the safety of the English troops, who were to land in the North of Germany, and might easily be cut off.

These considerations forced the German leader to withdraw his troops to the other side of the Rhine. But this was attended with great difficulties, for the river was broad, and with a strong stream, the enemy watchful, and in the neighbourhood with a greatly superior force. The allies had thrown a bridge over the river at Rees, and in this town was a large magazine, a considerable supply of money, and a hospital for the army; General Imhof was posted here with 3000 men, to protect the town as well as the bridge. He was attacked by General Chevert at the head of 10,000 French; everything depended on the keeping possession of this position, the safety or destruction of the allies hung upon the event, and as it was not in the power of Ferdinand to send reinforcements to Imhof, he had to depend entirely on his own bravery and that of his soldiers.

His position was covered by ditches and hedges; the enemy were not aware of the nature of the ground, which Imhof turned to his advantage, and instead of awaiting the attack of the French went forward to meet them; the attack was very spirited, and the more effectual as it was not expected from so small a force. In the space of half an hour the enemy, in spite of their superior numbers, were driven back, and forced to retreat to Wesel having left behind them eleven cannon, a considerable quantity of ammunition and waggons, and lost some hundreds of prisoners. The French fled with such precipitation that many threw away their aims on their retreat, and upwards of 2000 muskets were found on the road to Wesel.

However trifling this engagement might be in so bloody and

eventful a war, it here stood in the stead of the greatest victory, for it decided the possession of the stores in Emmerich and Rees as well as that of the bridge of boats without which it would have been impossible for Ferdinand to cross the Rhine; and this great general and his brave soldiers without provisions, without hope or the means of escape, and surrounded by the enemy, must have fallen a prey to them. But now all doubt as to their being able to pass in safety was at an end: the German leader, however, deceived the French general by false marches and positions in order to conceal his intention.

In consequence of the swollen state of the Rhine it was necessary to break up the bridge at Rees, and to place it at Griethausen; the French made a last attempt to destroy it with four vessels of a peculiar construction, which were sent from Wesel; but these were captured by armed boats, and the allies were enabled to pass the Rhine on the 9th and 10th of July in spite of the enemy and the swollen state of the river without the loss of a single man. Shortly after this, Imhof was sent with a body of men to meet the English troops, which had been landed at Emden, and who formed a junction with the allies at Cosveld without any impediment.

The arrival of these troops was a great source of rejoicing to the Germans; they consisted in 10,000 men, and were the first division of the 18,000 voted by the English Parliament. These soldiers were a fine body of men and as well as their horses were remarkable from their splendid accoutrements; one of the grenadier regiments had caps richly embroidered with gold and silver, with the motto: *Nec timor, nec pavidus*. One cavalry regiment was mounted entirely on roan horses, another on grey, a third on black, and a fourth on bay horses, and all these picked and beautiful animals. Besides these they brought upwards of 1000 baggage waggons with their horses.

Among the British troops who came to Germany were 2000 Highlanders who soon made themselves known to the enemy by their courage and activity. These soldiers now showed in Germany their accustomed bravery in many remarkable acts; among others they surprised a French cavalry regiment near Dillenburg. The troopers were endeavouring to mount, but they were either cut to pieces or taken prisoners; the Highlanders got on their horses, and rode back to the camp with their booty.

Ferdinand now took up an advantageous position on the Lippe by which means he protected Hanover, and gave his troops time for rest. It was now necessary to evacuate Düsseldorf, and the Hanoverian garrison withdrew, after having spiked the cannon, and thrown the powder into the Rhine; Cleves was also evacuated, and the French immediately took possession of both places Isenburg was posted on the Weser, and General Oberg protected the Hessian provinces with 9000 men; Oberg took possession of the strong position near Sandershausen, and did all that he could to induce the French to attack him in his entrenchments; Soubise, who was near him at the head of 30,000 men, would not but, endeavoured to take him in the rear.

The fear of this drove Oberg from his position, and he was attacked on all sides by the superior forces of the enemy on the 10th of October near Lutternberg. The nature of the ground was too extensive for him to defend himself on all points with so small a body of men; the Hessians defended themselves bravely, and drove back the infantry of the enemy, but in the moment of victory the French cavalry fell on them both in flank and rear; the want of cavalry on the side of the Hessians increased this misfortune, and forced Oberg to retreat. The allies lost 1500 men killed, wounded and taken prisoners, and twenty eight cannon.

The Saxons, of whom a body of 10,000 men had joined the French army a short time previously, were in a great measure the cause of this victory; and indeed from this time, the French gained few advantages in which these brave troops did not play a conspicuous part. In spite of this they had to put up with all sorts of humiliation from their allies, and if any thing went wrong it was laid to their charge.

The greater part of these soldiers were deserters from the Prussian army, Saxons by birth, who would not fight against their monarch; they were formed into twelve regiments, and were now in the pay of the French; they had twenty four pieces of cannon, a present from the Dauphiness, and having her name on them; it was a tribute paid by this princess to the distressed land of her birth. Her brother, Prince Xavier, second son of the King of Poland commanded these troops; without any of the requisites or capabilities for war he was a bad general, a bad friend to his country, and his name is recorded in its annals as a bad ruler from his entire mismanagement of the states in Saxony, which will never be forgotten.

He came to the army haughty and imperious, and excited the bad feelings of the Saxon soldiery, who were willing, and thought they deserved better treatment; they were not content with murmuring but went so far as the expression of their feelings in the presence of Prince Xavier, who having been brought up at a court, where Asiatic splendour reigned, and where eastern respect was customary, could hardly believe his senses. He had thoughts of punishing this offence with the most severe inflictions; but a Saxon general gave him the good advice to take no notice of this expression of the feelings of his people but by altering his bearing towards them. He followed this counsel, and his soldiers, although they could not change their opinion of his capabilities as an officer, respected him as the son of their king.

The victory of Lutternberg procured the staff of Marshall for Soubise. He passed through the neighbouring districts, raised large contributions, and advanced to the walls of Hameln. The government of Hanover was in a state of great anxiety, and the archives and other important papers were sent to Stade for safety; but the position of Ferdinand put a stop to the further advance of the French and also to the union of their forces, which, after a fruitless attempt, withdrew into winter quarters; the principal army under Contades between the Maes and the Rhine, but the troops of Prince Soubise along the hanks of the Rhine and the Main. They entirely left the Hessian provinces, and it was here that the Prince of Isenburg took up his winter quarters; Prince Ferdinand distributed his troops in Westphalia, and established his headquarters at Münster.

By the activity of this great general the French were prevented from carrying out the cruel orders of their court, which were more worthy of a barbarous nation than of an enlightened people. It was decided on early in the summer to make the most use of the advantages they had gained without any regard to the feelings of humanity. Louvois, the minister of Louis the XIV. had already, in the previous century, given the fearful example of issuing orders for devastation, which the great Turenne was obliged to carry out in the Palatinate, and this French *experiment*, which they borrowed from the Tartars, and which for centuries had been branded with disgrace by all European nations, the French themselves not excepted, was again resorted to, to the eternal shame of this polished people. The minister of war, Belleisle, wrote to the Marshall Contades:

> I know of no other resource for our pressing necessities but the money we must draw from the enemies' territories. They must likewise supply everything which constitutes provision, and besides this money; hay, straw, oats, bread, corn, cattle, horses and even men to make up the complement of our foreign regiments. Before the end of September 1758, it will be necessary

to lay waste the country in every direction in front of the Cordon which we shall form in winter, so as to render it impossible for the enemy to approach us.

In the next letter to Contades these orders were more peremptory. On the 6th of October he wrote:

> You must make a complete desert of the whole of Westphalia, and in the districts on the Lippe and in Paderborn, as the most fruitful provinces, every thing must be torn up by the roots.

It is true that the French commanders did not follow to the letter these cruel orders, but still they showed on many occasions their good will towards fulfilling them. Raising contributions by force, belong to the customary evils of warfare, even among the most enlightened people, and are not therefore worthy of notice without they are carried to extremes; this was the case in the country of Hanau, which as well as all Hessia, more especially felt the iron rule of the enemy during this war. The Intendant Foulon, who became afterwards so well known during the French revolution, was stationed here, and shut up ninety three persons consisting of the principal people, the nobility, the magistrates, and many of these were sick, aged and infirm, in a single room, on account of a war tax not having been paid up.

These were left for three days and two nights without eating or drinking, and also without sleep, as from the confined space, the greater part were forced to stand; in addition to this cruelty a similar instance of which has never occurred among a Christian people, on the third day, the guard would not allow of the going out of any one from the room even for the most pressing necessities. The prisoners were not allowed even the portion of felons and galley slaves, bread and water; and when the privy counsellors Günderode, Hugo and other persons of consequence, who were thus imprisoned, requested it, and even lowered themselves so far as to beg for it, they were answered by a person of the name of Lasone who wrote to them:

> I will grant your request this evening, and you shall receive bread and water, but do not expect again to receive such a favour.

The character of the previous campaign had been the extraordinary number of battles and important engagements; this one had however been distinguished by the number of sieges which had been raised. In Silesia and Saxony the fortresses of Schweidnitz and Son-

147

nenstein had been regularly besieged and taken, as well as Minden and Düsseldorf in Westphalia; Frederic had on the other hand raised the siege of Olmütz. The Russians had left Cüstrin and Colberg, the Austrians Neisse and Dresden, and the troops of the Empire Torgau and Leipsic. The fortune of war had so turned that in the middle of December there was no enemy to be found either for the Prussians or their allies, in Silesia, Saxony, Brandenburg and Pomerania, or in Hessia or the greater part of Westphalia.

Chapter 6: Advance of the Russians

In France the whole council of the king, and the *dauphin* himself, were in favour of peace; but notwithstanding this, Louis the XV. and his mistress insisted on the continuation of a war so injurious to the interests of the kingdom. Cardinal Bernis finding his representations, so often made both to the king and Madame de Pompadour unheeded, resigned his office of minister for foreign affairs, which he had held but for a short time, but much to his credit. This resignation followed shortly after the death of the minister of war Belleisle, and the Duke de Choiseul was now the leading minister; and he, faithful to his relations with the court of Vienna, set to work with great zeal for the continuation of the war.

His first step was to form a new treaty of alliance between France and Austria; this was completed on the 30th of December 1758, and in order to give an apparent value to this renewed alliance, to which all impartial Frenchmen were averse, in consequence of its certain disadvantages and its impossible advantages, the minister ordered the academy of inscriptions at Paris to have a medal struck to immortalize the treaty. In the same month the fresh arrangement between England and Prussia was concluded, by which Frederic was promised subsidies to the amount of four millions of dollars yearly, and in the fourth article of this agreement they each bound themselves neither to conclude a peace, nor even a cessation of hostilities with the enemy, without the consent of the other party.

France now made use of all her influence, not only in the court of St Petersburg to strengthen the hatred of the Empress against the King of Prussia, but also in Constantinople to induce the Sultan, who had just ascended the throne of the Ottoman Empire, to leave his sword in the scabbard, notwithstanding the termination of the truce with Austria; a treaty was also formed between Russia, Sweden and Danemark to prevent all foreign ships of war from entering the Sound. Danemark gained no advantage by this, and therefore French gold was required to induce the cabinet of Copenhagen to come to this determination. The other two powers were tranquillized by this treaty, as they had hitherto been in constant fear of seeing the British fleet on their coast.

Frederic determined, in the approaching campaign, to act on the defensive. The hope of the assistance of the Turks probably induced him to form this plan, for so early as the month of January he wrote to General Fouquet who was one of the few he confided in:

The Turks are beginning to stir themselves, they will not long remain idle.

Activity was combined with this system of acting on the defensive, for he neglected no opportunity of turning it to the best advantage, and during the winter he had given a proof of his determination. The Polish Prince Sultowsky, without regarding the neutrality of the Republic of Poland, took an active part in the war; he levied troops, and formed magazines for the Russians, and upon the King of Prussia's making representations, he gave the most insolent answers, justifying his conduct by his independence and his position as a magnate, and redoubling his exertions in favour of the Russians. He resided, in the Polish town of Riesen, some distance from the frontier of Silesia, and had in this place soldiers and cannon, In addition to which he thought himself in perfect safety from the position of his free state.

The Prussian name, which was now looked on with respect, even by the most mighty nations, could not be derided with impunity by so petty a prince. Frederic, without regard to political considerations, sent General Wobersnow with a body of men into Poland, and Riesen was taken without resistance, the prince made prisoner, and his soldiers disarmed. The provisions which had been gathered together for the Russians were destroyed, and all the cannon, horses, waggons and implements of war were carried away, and brought into Silesia together with the Polish soldiers who were forced to enlist in the Prussian service, and the prince was sent to the fortress of Glogau, where he remained a prisoner until the end of the war.

Such was the fate of a proud nobleman, who trusting to his position as master of a number of villages, inhabited by wretched peasants, offered himself unasked as the confederate of powerful monarchs, and was anxious to mix himself up in their warfare. Another ally of this species was the editor of a newspaper in Erlangen, who relying upon the political principles of his monarch denounced the Prussians and the war. As calumnies were not spared in his writings, a Prussian officer took the punishment of this hero of the pen upon himself, for he had him well flogged, and then required a regular receipt from the receiver of the stripes.

No war in Europe ever attracted the attention of distant nations, more than the present. It was remarkable in this, that it raised up adherents to Prussia who were induced to declare in her favour, partly from astonishment at the deeds of Frederic, and partly from the natural feelings of man, which lead him, in an unequal combat, to declare for the weaker; and these in countries where, previous to this, people had little cared or thought of this monarchy of whose existence they were only aware The Spaniards, who with all the strength and power of their empire had never brought half the number of troops into the field, that Frederic now led, in spite of the smallness and comparative poverty of his dominion, never took so lively an interest in the quarrels of Germany as they now did.

In Holland satirical medals against the enemies of Frederic were struck; in Naples in consequence of the unexpected termination of each campaign, and indeed the failure of every enterprise against the Prussians, the people were so stunned, that all considerations of the great distance of the seat of war, and even the Alps being between it and them, were forgotten; they thought it not impossible that the war might be carried into Italy, and that perhaps they might see the Prussians in the neighbourhood of Mount Vesuvius; and in consequence of these fears the number of troops in this kingdom was increased, and the guards in the different towns were strengthened.

In Rome, it is true, there was no fear of the war extending so far; nevertheless the fortunes of the many nations, who were engaged in the contest in Germany, excited the greatest interest in the bosoms of the Romans, most of whom were on Frederic's side; and at the very time that the Pope was endeavouring to weaken his chance of success by means of ostentatious masses, and consecrated presents, they were forming vows for his success. In Venice the city was divided into two parties, into Theresiani, and Prussiani who looked on one another with deadly hatred; each had their separate places of resort where they met, and the one party experienced no mercy at the hands of the other. This party feeling had extended even to the monks, and broke forth with great violence in the monastery St. Giovanni e Paolo. Here the monks fought for the honour of Maria Theresa or Frederic, and for arms used the plates, dishes, and drinking cups. The party in favour of the king was however the strongest, and it was a common saying at that time:

Chi non e buon Prussiano, non e buon Veneziano.
(He, who is not for the Prussians is no true Venetian).

A furrier had hung a picture of Frederic in his shop, and in order to show the high respect he had for it, he placed a burning lamp before it; a mark of respect which in Italy, as in other Roman Catholic countries, is only paid to the most sacred and holy objects. In Switzerland they rejoiced at the victories of the Prussians, as if they had been won by the Swiss; in Germany, not only the protestant Würtembergers who were led against Frederic wished success to his arms, but this partiality went so far, that the catholic Bavarians, the soldiers of the Empire from the Palatinate and Mainz, with their rosaries in their pockets, fought against him unwillingly.

Even in France, where the people did not look at this war with the same eyes as the court, the admiration of Frederic reached as high a pitch as in other countries. The estimation of his great talents penetrated into the very palace of the king; this gave rise to the answer of Madame de Pompadour, when the Duke of Belleisle said to her half in joke, half in earnest, that the war must be carried on with decision or else they would shortly have Frederic in Paris at the head of the Prussians; "Well! at any rate I shall see a king," was the answer of the mistress, who was well aware of the feelings of the court and also of her own power over that weak monarch, Louis the XV.

Notwithstanding the deeds of Frederic and his firmness under misfortunes had raised for him partisans and admirers in all countries, still he had in every direction a multitude of private enemies, who sought to injure him in every possible way. The Prussian provinces as well as Saxony were full of spies, and they came to Dresden in the dress of the servants of the court of the Electorate, and having gained the requisite information from the nobility they were dismissed, and sent away. Chance discovered however the most important of these communications, and the Saxon minister, Count Wackerbart, having had a private understanding with the enemies of Frederic which was found out, the minister was sent to the fortress of Cüstrin, but shortly after set at liberty on condition of his retiring to Poland.

In Zerbst there was a French spy, the Marquis Fraigne who was protected by that court, and allowed to reside in the palace of the prince; Frederic laughed at this inconsiderate protection, had him taken from thence, and sent to Magdeburg. Field Marshall Seckendorf, known by his unfortunate campaigns, and also by his equally fruitless negotiations, forgot his dignity, and the repose due to his years so far as, at the age of ninety, to play the part of a spy. He resided in Saxony upon his estate of Meuselwitz where he was treated with forbearance, and even consideration by the orders of the King of Prussia; in spite of this he entered into a correspondence with the enemies of the king, and Frederic, when he heard of this, had him dragged out of church, and sent to Magdeburg. He was shortly after set at liberty, but not until he had entered into a written agreement to have no communication with the enemies of the king so long as the war should last.

The Prussian troops were never more active than during this winter. Prince Henry advanced into Bohemia, in spite of the severity of the season, the high mountains, the almost impassable roads, and having overcome difficulties which would have been insurmountable to other troops forced the passes, and dispersed the troops of the enemy. Hulsen found the Austrian General Reinhardt entrenched on a hill near Kommotau; he attacked him, and his whole corps 2500 strong were made prisoners without allowing one to escape. Hulsen now marched towards Saatz, and Henry towards Budin, and in these places as well as in Lowositz and Leutmeritz they took possession of a large quantity of provisions and forage; so much, that there was bread for an army of 50,000 men for five months, and forage for a month for 25,000 horses; the whole of this immense store was destroyed, also a new bridge, and 150 boats burned on the Elb; the Austrians themselves having set fire to the magazine at Saatz that it might not fall into the hands of the Prussians

Expeditions were also made from Saxony against the troops of the Empire, and Prince Henry advanced into Franconia sending several bodies out in advance of his main army. These drove back on every point the motley assemblage of people from different countries who formed this army of execution, and who from their composition and discipline, to say nothing of their small utility, formed so striking a contrast in this stirring war, to the large German armies upon whom all eyes were turned. Their flight was now directed from all sides towards Nürnberg, where their principal army was posted in an impregnable camp. But they did not reach this place of safety without great loss, and prisoners were taken by the hundred; they also lost a great quantity of baggage, colours and cannon, and the stores of provisions they had laid up in the Bishopric of Bamberg were destroyed, those in the town of Bamberg having been set fire to by the Imperial troops themselves.

Shortly, after the Prussians came up, the town surrendered, and General Knoblauch wished to take possession ot it; but some thousand Austrians, for the most part Croats, had no desire to quit it. This gave rise to fighting in the streets which was accompanied by the most dreadful cries, and the peaceable inhabitants crept into their cellars; no person was to be seen, it was as if all were dead, and in consequence of this some open shops were pillaged; In the course of a few hours the Austrians were driven back, and the disorder was put a stop to. The inhabitants were forced to put up with paying a heavy contribution, and as they could not find sufficient money for it they gave letters of credit for what was unpaid. The emperor exonerated them from this responsibility, but as the inhabitants foresaw the probability of another visit from the enterprising Prussians they wisely paid the bills. Several small bodies of Austrians who were in Franconia were driven back; Erfurt was taken by surprise, and a contribution of 100,000 dollars was levied in this town.

At Kronach General Riedesel was taken prisoner with 2500 men, and Würzburg as well as other towns, confederates of the Empire, where the Prussians came during this campaign, were placed under contribution; everything prospered except the object of Prince Henry, which was to force the army of the Empire to a battle.

Another body of Prussians invaded Mecklenburg, which was also one of Frederic's resources; for the duke, not considering his own weakness, and the power of his neighbour, had been improvident enough to declare himself at the Diet of Regensburg openly against the King of Prussia, whom he hated, and had already affronted previous to the war. He had first given his vote, that he should be treated as an enemy of the Empire, and then without considering the consequences, placed himself at the head of those princes who wished for a proscription of Frederic; he was anxious to show his active participation in a war, in which the success of the mighty confederation did not for a moment appear doubtful, and flattered himself, that by taking the part of the strongest, he should derive the greatest advantages.

But instead of this, he now saw his territory, which was little favoured by nature, laid waste to by the Prussians, and thus the poor Mecklenburgers had to pay severely for the political errors of the duke. No province which was visited by the armies of Prussia was so severely handled as that of Mecklenburg-Schwerin, which was abandoned by the fugitive duke, and from whose towns and villages people fled by hundreds.

Those, who from their property, political position, indecision, and other causes had remained behind, felt the more severely the iron hand of war; for this province was forced during the seven years of the war, to provide 16,000 soldiers, and forty-two millions of dollars besides an immense quantity of provisions and forage; all this was exacted by overpowering strength, and those in authority were taken prisoners, and kept upon bread and water. In Güstrow the church was used as a prison into which the new soldiers were driven, and remained for some weeks until they were led to join the army. The people who had been instigated to hatred towards the Prussians by their duke, had given many proofs of this, and now was the time for revenge; what could not be carried away was destroyed, and even the beds of the unfortunate people were cut to pieces, and the feathers dispersed to the winds. The Princess Charlotte of Mecklenburg-Strelitz wrote a touching letter to the king stating the cruelties that were exercised in her neighbourhood, which caused them to be put a stop to, and was the first step towards the raising the writer to a share of the British throne.

The Prussians had not continued in possession sequence of the town being strongly entrenched, and having a numerous garrison, which would be shortly reinforced by troops which were marching to its relief. The right of the strongest was displayed in this expedition in a very marked manner, for Dohna, without consideration for his being in a neutral territory, required supplies to be sent in to him from Poland without paying for them. They were taken by force, and a number of the inhabitants, subjects of the Republic, were taken as soldiers, and distributed among the different regiments. To justify this a manifesto was issued by the Prussians in which it was stated that necessity had forced them to take these steps.

The scarcity of provisions at last forced the Prussians to fall back on the Oder, and the Russians, who were anxious to levy contributions on their enemies, and in addition wished to form a junction with the Austrians, also advanced towards this river, under the command of Field-Marshall Soltikow who had now taken the post of Fermor, in consequence of his having requested to be allowed to give up the command from the weak state of his health. Fermor still remained with the army, and served under his successor, by which means he gained at his court the reputation of a great patriot, and reassured his soldiers by his presence. He was always the spring of all weighty determinations, and could thus revenge himself on the Austrians who had ill treated him, without being responsible. The Prussians were also placed under a fresh general, for the king, dissatisfied with Dohna for having more than once neglected to attack the Russians under advantageous circumstances, and for having shown unusual inactivity for a Prussian general, had removed him from the command, and sent in his place, General Wedel. This officer brought with him an order from the King to Dohna and the other generals which gave him powers as yet unheard of in a Prussian Army; Frederic wrote:

> So long as his command lasts, he represents my person, and as such must be obeyed. With the troops he is to be considered as a Dictator was by the Romans.

Wedel joined the army on the 22nd of July, and was not acquainted either with the force of his own troops, or that of his enemy, and knew nothing of the nature of the country; but he had orders to attack the Russians without delay, if he could not prevent their junction with the Austrians by any other means, as Laudon was already on the march with 30,000 men for this purpose. The Russians hastened to meet the Austrian general, and as they had already marched on the 23rd of July, the day after Wedel's arrival, the Prussian general did not think it right to defer the attacking them, and the battle took place at the village of Kai, near the Oder, not far from the frontiers of Brandenburg. The two armies were very unequally matched as to strength, and the position of the Russians was very advantageous; the Prussians, on the contrary, were very much impeded in their operations by the morasses which prevented them from extending their front in opposition to the enemy.

The battle lasted from four in the afternoon until sunset; Wedel was defeated, and was forced to withdraw with a loss of 5000 killed, wounded and taken prisoners. This loss was enhanced by the death of General Wobersnow, a man of great activity and talent, and much beloved by the army; he died fighting like a hero in the battle against which he had advised General Wedel. This general retreated over the Oder, and Soltikow advanced as far as Crossen, placing Berlin in the greatest danger. As there was now no further impediment to the junction of the confederate armies, Laudon divided his, and leaving Haddick behind with 12,000 men, joined the Russians, on the 3rd of August, with the troops under him, which were for the most part cavalry. The movements and plans of these two generals to fulfil their intention, and to get the better of the difficulties which lay in their way, were masterly, and the troops of the Empire, who had done so little during the whole period of the war, now played their part in carrying out Laudon's plans. They invaded Saxony, and forced General Fink, who commanded an army of observation on the movements of General Haddick, to lose sight of the latter in order to protect Leipsic, and Torgau. The united armies of the Russians and Austrians 80,000 strong now advanced, and entrenched themselves on the banks of the Oder, not far from Frankfort, and all Wedel's efforts were now directed to prevent the enemy from crossing this river.

The king who had been satisfied with acting on the defensive in Silesia, had remained for a considerable time encamped at Landshut, and Daun, who was in face of him with the principal *corps d'armée*, was awaiting a favourable moment either to advance or give battle. In order to render these hopes futile, and to drive the Austrians back to Bohemia his watchful enemy employed every means to intercept their supplies, and serious thoughts were had in the Imperial camp of changing their position. The advance of the Russians changed the plans of both leaders, for Daun endeavoured to approach these armies, in order to facilitate their undertakings, and Frederic to work so as to oppose the plans of all.

The unfortunate Battle of Kai, and the junction of the two armies which followed it so closely forced the king to go in person to his Brandenburgian states. Time would not permit him now to take any portion of his army with him, and he travelled with only an escort of hussars. Prince Henry was forced to send a large portion of his troops from Saxony in order to strengthen the army on the Oder, and went himself into Silesia to take the command of the army 40,000 strong, which the king had left encamped at Schmuckseifen, two days march from Landshut, and who had Daun opposed to them at the head of 70,000 men. The body under General Fink also received orders to quit Saxony, and march towards the Oder, and by these operations Saxony was now clear of Prussian troops.

Only Dresden, Leipsic, Torgau and Wittenberg were garrisoned, but the king placed great reliance on the known determination of General Schmettau, the *commandant* of Dresden. Frederic's expedition was attended with success; the troops sent to him came up without loss, he fell upon Haddick's body near Guben, took some pieces of cannon, 500 provision waggons and 600 prisoners, and then formed a junction without any impediment with the army of General Wedel.

He now determined to give battle to the enemy without delay, and for this purpose crossed the Oder. The strength of his army was now 40,000 men, but that of the Austrians and Russians 60,000. They were posted on the heights between Frankfort and Kunersdorf in an entrenched camp defended by heavy cannon. The right wing of the Austrians was covered by the Oder, the left by marshes and thickets, and in advance was broken ground. The Russians had also erected a redoubt on their right wing, and the approaches to their camp were *barricadoed* with trees. In spite of all these advantages in their position, the king determined to attack them on the 12th of August; he placed his men in a wood in a body five deep, of which the three first ranks were infantry, and the two rear cavalry.

From this position the Prussians attacked the left wing of the Russians, which was posted on the hill, called Mühlberg, at the same time that Fink fired into the Russian camp from an adjoining height. The king's intention was to attack the Russians in front, in the rear, and on their flank. Unfortunately he was not sufficiently aware of the nature of the ground, and the march was unexpectedly impeded by large ponds, so that the men were obliged to make long detours by which they were fatigued, and much valuable time was lost. The heavy cannon which could not be turned in the woods, were forced to have the horses taken out, to be unlimbered and turned, and then to have the horses again harnessed to them.

At last the Prussians got through the wood, and approached the Russian entrenchments, which were attacked by a heavy fire from three field batteries; the Russians answered this by the fire of a hundred cannon, which they had posted on their left wing. The king now gave orders to storm the batteries of the enemy; the grenadiers ordered on this service cut their way through the *barricadoes*, advanced through a hollow, and reached the heights which were near the Russian entrenchments, and from which a sharp fire was kept up on the Prussians. These were not discouraged, but went on in double quick time, and charged the batteries with fixed bayonets; the redoubt was also taken, and all resistance was now at an end.

The enemy were completely driven from their entrenchments, and the whole of the Russian left wing sought safety in flight towards the church yard of the village of Kunersdorf, and abandoned their cannon.

The battle had commenced at midday and at six in the evening the Prussians were in possession of all the batteries of the left wing, of one hundred and eighty cannon, and some thousands of prisoners. The victory appeared as decisive as those of the enemy at Kollin and Hochkirch, and messengers were already sent from the field of battle with the good news to Berlin and Silesia, when most unexpectedly the fortune of the day was changed.

The Prussian infantry had completed their work, but the victory could not be taken advantage of, as the Prussian cavalry were on the other wing where they kept the Austrians in check, and the cannon could not follow sufficiently fast; the difficulty of this position was rendered the more disadvantageous from the ground being more favourable to the operations of the artillery than to the movements of the infantry. At last some of the cannon came up, but in too small numbers to complete the work of the day, and in the mean time the king advanced with the other wing upon the Russians, supported in this attack by General Fink. This advance was much impeded by the broken ground, and at one time the men had to march through extensive ponds, at another over small bridges; the Russians took advantage of the time this occupied, to draw their forces together and to make the best use of their artillery.

Laudon, who had as yet taken no part with the Austrians in the battle, now advanced at the same time that Frederic had withdrawn Seidlitz from his post of observation, which this general was extremely unwilling to leave as he foresaw the misfortunes which were to occur, and it was not until after fruitless representations on his part, and repeated orders from the king that he obeyed. His cavalry now advanced in the intervals between the ponds, passed under the fire of the cannon of the Russians, and approached the enemy; but the heavy fire of musketry which mowed down whole rows of men and horses threw them into disorder, and forced them to retreat.

As yet the Prussians had not lost ground; on the contrary they still had gained decided advantages. The Russians were congregated on a hill, one above another, forming an irregular mass from 80 to 100 men high; but this body of men, though without order, were protected by fifty cannon, and kept up a continued fire of musketry. The Prussians were exhausted by a long march, the fighting they had gone through, and the heat of a sultry summer's day; still they had as yet gained the battle, and in all probability the Russians whose loss was severe would have retired in the night. They would willingly have given up the honour of the victory, but that they thought themselves in greater safety in their entrenchments than by flying in broad daylight. But Frederic thought nothing was done, so long as any thing remained to be done, and he on this occasion not only thought but avowed his opinion, that it was not sufficient to gain a victory over the Russians, but that their army must be annihilated, to put a stop to their again coming and renewing their devastations.

In opposition to this the Prussian generals only brought forward the exhausted state of the soldiers, and more especially Seidlitz was anxious to impress this on the mind of the king. The representations of this general, of whose courage Frederic was so well aware, appeared to have decided the question, and the king was on the point of giving up his opinion, when Wedel for whom Frederic had great consideration in spite of his bad fortune in war, came up, and the king said, "What does Wedel think of this?" He was a courtier, and as his opinion was quite that of the king, the order was given to march.

The Russians had placed a large battery in the Jews' burying ground, which commanded the whole field of battle; this had been abandoned from panic on the attack of a regiment of cavalry under the Prince of Würtemberg. The Prussian infantry were only 800 paces from this battery, and were now hurrying to take possession of it; nothing appeared likely to prevent their completing their intention. They had advanced to within 150 paces of their object, when Laudon arrived, threw his men into the battery and opened a heavy fire of musketry upon the Prussians. Their endeavours to approach were of no avail, and only threw them into disorder of which Laudon took advantage. The cavalry charged them on both flanks, and cut down great numbers.

The victory now depended on the taking the Spitzberg, a hill which commanded a pasture ground. This pasture was 400 paces long, from 50 to 60 wide, and in a hollow from 10 to 15 feet deep, and very steep on all sides. This was occupied by Laudon's best troops, and the Prussians endeavoured in vain to pass over the bank which surrounded it, those who succeeded being immediately precipitated into the hollow or killed.

At last the fatigue of the Prussians got the better of them, and their courage was of no avail; the Spitzberg was repeatedly attacked, but not taken; the heavy fire of the musketry and cannon of the Russians and Austrians swept away all who went to the attack, and Fink who endeavoured to storm other heights exhausted the strength of his soldiers in vain. Frederic exposed himself to the greatest dangers, his dress was shot through in several places, two horses were killed under him, and he was slightly wounded. A gold case he had in his pocket saved his life, and stopped the ball which was flattened, and remained on the gold.

His life was also endangered when his horse fell from under him, but his *aide-de-camp* Götz saved him, and gave him his horse from which he had dismounted. The king was entreated to leave this dangerous position, but he answered, "Everything must be done to gain the victory and I must do my duty as well as you." The Russians who fought with great animosity fell to the ground as if killed, allowed the Prussians to pass over their bodies, and then rose up, and fired in their rear; every endeavour to drive the Russians and the Austrians from the heights was in vain.

The Prussian cavalry now attempted to attack the heights, but the science of Seidlitz was in this instance of no avail. These troopers, accustomed to disperse the enemy when even double or treble their number, to put the infantry to flight whatever might be their position, to take batteries and get the better of the greatest difficulties in the nature of the ground, were defeated by the position of the cannon of the Russians. Seidlitz, their brave commander, was wounded; Prince Eugene of Würtemberg was also wounded, in making a second attack. He was followed by General Puttkammer who attacked with the White Hussars, was killed on the field of battle, and the two other most celebrated generals of the Prussians, Fink and Hulsen, were also wounded; all the Prussian troops both infantry and cavalry now fell into the greatest disorder.

At this critical moment Laudon advanced with fresh troops on the rear of the right wing, and attacked the worn out Prussians on the flank, and in the rear. This general who had so often seized the moment of a favourable change of affairs during a battle, and turned it to his advantage, now brought up a body of cavalry, which had been' advantageously posted at a distance from the field of battle, and attacked the enemy who were in disorder. The battle was soon decided, for a panic appears to have seized the Prussians who took to flight; the troops fled into the wood, and towards the bridges, and as all wished to cross at the same time, this increased the disorder, and caused the loss of a great number of cannon. In addition to the cannon they had taken, they lost 165 pieces of Prussian artillery.

The king was also near being taken prisoner, as he was one of the last on the field of battle, and having to ride through a ravine, nothing but the courage and presence of mind of the captain of cavalry Prittwitz could have saved him from this misfortune. Frederic himself thought his escape impossible, and cried out several times, "Prittwitz, I am lost!" This courageous officer who had only 100 hussars to oppose to the thousands who surrounded him, answered, "No, Your Majesty, that shall not occur so long as one of us has breath." Instead of merely defending himself, he kept continually attacking, and prevented the enemy from making a regular attack upon his small body, and in this manner the hussars continued to advance, so that Frederic at last was enabled to join the main body. He afterwards rewarded his preserver with kingly presents, and the promotion to high rank in the army.

Never was the firmness of this monarch so shaken as on this unfortunate day, in a few hours he had been precipitated from the glory of an undoubted victory to the distress of a complete defeat. He endeavoured in every way to stop the flight of his infantry, by prayers and entreaties at other times so effectual from the lips of a king, and more especially of this king, but which were now unavailing; and it is even said, that in this distressing position, he wished for death. His active imagination immediately placed before him the consequences of his defeat as so dreadful that he was forced to send from that field of battle, from which he had only a few hours previous dispatched messengers of victory, orders to Berlin for active measures of precaution and safety. He fancied the enemy already in his capital, and saw it pillaged and laid waste, without the means of his preventing it.

His troops were so dispersed, that on the day after the battle he had only 5000 men with him, and he had lost all the cannon he had taken, together with almost all his own artillery. General Wunsch who commanded a small body of Prussians on the other side of the Oder in order to cut off the retreat of the Russians after the hoped for victory, had marched upon Frankfort towards the end of the battle, and had taken the Russian garrison prisoners; but as the loss of the battle rendered this advantage useless, he was placed in danger, and was compelled to leave the town. The coming on of night was favourable to the king, as he withdrew his troops, and gained some heights where the enemy could not attack him.

The orders of the king for the safely of Berlin were in the meantime sent off. He expressed in these that it was not in his power to protect the city, and that therefore it would be advisable that the principal and richest inhabitants should, if possible, leave it with their valuables. The messenger who was the bearer of these orders, was, by good luck, pursued by a party of Cossacks, and did not reach Berlin until four days after; by this time the face of affairs was much altered, and people had recovered from the first effects of their alarm. The authorities now made representations to the king to be allowed to take other steps, which met with the approbation of Frederic, but the royal family were however obliged to leave Berlin, and to take up their residence in Magdeburg, to which place all papers of importance were removed.

This battle had been the most bloody during this war, for the Prussians lost 8000 killed, 15,000 wounded; 3000 were taken prisoners, and almost all their principal and superior officers wounded; and the Russians and Austrian s had 24,000 killed and wounded according to the report Soltikow gave of the battle to the Empress Elizabeth, and which was written immediately after the battle. He wrote as follows:

Your Majesty must not be surprised at the greatness of our loss. You know that the King of Prussia generally sells his defeats dearly.

He also said:

If I were to win another such a victory, I must be the bearer of the intelligence myself.

Frederic slept the night of the battle in his clothes, and on straw, in the village of Oetscher, in the cottage of a peasant which had been pillaged by the Cosacks, and was open to every wind that blew from heaven; his *aides-de-camp* lay round about him on the bare ground, and a few grenadiers watched over this group. The following day the king crossed the Oder, drew the fugitives again under his banner, formed a junction with General Wunsch, recalled General Kleist with 5000 men from Pomerania, had fresh cannon sent to him, and by these means he, who on the night of the battle had only 5000 men remaining, was in the course of a few days at the head of 28,000. The Russians, who feared him, in spite of his defeat, in trenched themselves anew, and Frederic inspired his men with fresh courage by an address he made to them; in a few weeks Berlin was placed in safety, and his army so strengthened and equipped that he was in a position not only to protect the Electorate of Brandenburg, but also to allow Wunsch to withdraw his army, and march into Saxony.

Among the Prussians who fell in the battle of Kunnersdorf was Major Kleist, a noble German, honourable from his character, and immortal by his poems. He was known to the king, but did not receive that admiration from his contemporaries which will be awarded to him in future times. He said in one of his poems:

Perhaps I shall one day fall for the honour of my country.

His forebodings were fulfilled, unfortunately for the republic of German literature, on this bloody day. Kleist led on a battalion against the enemy, and took three batteries; his right hand was shot away by a ball; he took his sword in his left, and advanced with his men, who loved him as a father, to the attack of the fourth battery. A musket ball struck him to the ground, and he was taken from the thick of the battle to be laid in a wet ditch where he was left to his fate. It was indeed a fearful one; the Cosacks who bear the form of men, but in every thing else are like the wild beast of the desert, and to whom rapine, murder and incendiarism are natural, and compassion unknown, fell upon him as he lay weltering in his blood, and tearing every thing off him, even to his shirt stiff with his blood, left him in this pitiable condition.

His state moved even some Russian hussars who were riding past, and they threw an old cloak over him, and gave him some bread and half a florin; but some Cosacks who came up took these from him, and he passed the whole night naked, in the ditch and without having his wounds dressed. Kleist was severely but not mortally wounded, but his dreadful position and exposure caused his death a few days after in Frankfort, to which place he had been conveyed as a prisoner. The Russians gave him an honourable interment, and many officers joined the professors of this town in following his body to the grave. There was no sword on the coffin, but this was remedied by one of the Russian officers placing his own there.

The Russians did not avail themselves of this valuable opportunity of ending the war, for had decided steps been taken immediately after the battle, this would have been certain. Frederic was astonished at their inactivity, and Daun bitterly reproached Soltikow, who did not fail to retort upon him with equal acrimony. He wrote:

I have already won two battles, and now only wait, till I hear of your having gained two victories, in order to make further movements, as it is not fair that the troops of the empress, my mistress, should do everything.

The Marquis of Montalembert represented to him, that if he did not advance he would give up the fruits of his victory to the Austrians; to which he answered:

I am not at all jealous of such an occurrence. From my heart I wish them even more success than I have had; I have already done my part.

These expressions were caused by the ill-feeling which existed among the Russian generals towards the Austrians, but more especially among their leaders; for the court of Vienna, instead of endeavouring to gain the confidence of these generals, and engaging them by means of their personal interest in its favour, had on the contrary expressed itself dissatisfied; in the first instance with Apraxin who died in prison during his trial, and afterwards with Fermor and Butterlin. They made complaints at one time against their want of will, at another time against their capabilities, and were also dissatisfied with Soltikow in Vienna, against whom complaints were addressed to the empress of his inactivity, of a disinclination to support the confederates, and especially of want of zeal for the common cause; this drew reprimands upon him which were participated in by the other generals, and which no one forgave.

The whole army of the Russians were included in these upbraidings; which were retorted on the Austrians on every occasion, and justified by the want of activity of Daun as well as his want of decision, and too great caution. The great distance of the Russian Army from their court rendered its orders in part nugatory, made obedience difficult, and facilitated the finding excuses.

It was discovered in Vienna, but too late, how much mischief had been done by these complaints, and they were now discontinued, that other more efficient means, which had not as yet been thought of, might be resorted to; but the time for their efficacious use was passed, and the dislike which had been excited from personal ill usage, had taken too deep root to be done away with by flattery and presents. The Russian generals did as much as they were forced to do, and no more, only avoiding to incur any responsibility; and they never seriously wished to form a junction with the Austrian Army as they would by that means have been cramped in their operations, and led on to a protraction of the campaign, in addition to which great difficulties would have arisen in the supplying the army.

The rejoicings at the victory were beyond all bounds in St. Petersburg; Soltikow was raised to the rank of field marshal, and a command was given to Prince Galitzin; the lieutenant generals received the order of St. Andrew, and each soldier six months pay as a bounty.

Laudon received a gold sword enriched with diamonds from the Empress Elizabeth, and each regiment of Austrians who had participated in the battle a present of 5000 *rubles*. The court of St. Petersburg who had long felt ashamed of the bragging of their generals after the defeat of Zorndorf, looked upon this as the first and only victory which the Russians had gained against Frederic as a leader, in spite of its having been gained, not by them, but by the Austrians. Elizabeth caused a medal to be struck in commemoration of the day, and sent two waggon loads of them to be distributed among the soldiers.

In spite of the Russians having gained two victories in the course of three weeks, the position of the king was not much injured by these disadvantages. The evil consequences which arose from them were increased by his absence from Saxony and Silesia, which had been taken advantage of by the enemy; he was now cut off from both these provinces, and in addition to this, his fears were excited for Berlin, and he apprehended a junction of the Russian Army with the principal army of the Austrians,' which was in Lusatia. Daun and Soltikow held a conference on this subject, and it was determined that the Russians in the Prussian provinces should remain on the left bank of the Oder, Daun engaging to provide them with bread and forage, and after the taking of Dresden both armies were to march into Silesia, and in case the siege of Neisse, upon which they had determined, should he successful, they were to take up their winter quarters in this province; after coming to this decision the two generals separated.

The Russians awaited quietly the fate of Dresden in their camp of Fürstenwald, and amused themselves by destroying the sluices of the Frederic William canal which joins the Oder with the Spree. These sluices, a memorial of the greatness of the elector who is immortalised in the annals of Brandenburg, were entirely destroyed by these barbarians. It would appear that Daun had not duly considered all the impediments which lay in the way of providing the promised supplies, for the Russians required 42,000 bushels of corn for each month, and the Austrians nearly double this quantity. The Saxon provinces could not, in their exhausted condition, furnish these, large supplies, at any rate not so quickly as was required, and there were no other means of getting them than by taking what was requisite from the magazines in Zittau, Görlitz and Lauban. In order to bring one month's supply for the Russians, 2500 four horse waggons were required, and as Daun could not reckon on the provision waggons of the imperial army which were in constant activity for the supply of the Austrians, he was in consequence forced to get waggons from Bohemia.

By using the greatest activity it was not possible to get these in action for three weeks, and it was four or live before the supplies could be sent in. By this delay the whole plan for the operations of the war had to be changed, for as it was hardly probable that these supplies could all escape the vigilance of the Prussian soldiers, all these circumstances rendered the fulfilment of Daun's promises highly improbable.

The Austrians had in the mean while invaded Silesia, and Fouquet, who defended the passes into this province with a body of Prussians had allowed the imperial General Harsch at the head of a large body of troops to make good his entry through them.

This Austrian general was ill, and the command was taken by General Ville who advanced into the interior, and his light troops penetrated as far as Breslau. Fouquet's operations led to the cutting off of the enemy from Bohemia, and soon altered the plans of the imperial general, who was placed in a great difficulty from scarcity of bread, and as all the high roads were occupied, had no resource but a rapid retreat through difficult passes; he completed this, after twelve days continual fighting, and it was found useless to make any further attempts on Silesia for the present; but the enemy was more fortunate in Saxony which, undefended by the Prussians, was now surrounded by the Austrians and the troops of the Empire.

The latter had never had so good a chance of making a conquest as at this time in the absence of the Prussians. Their first effort was made on Leipsic the commandant of which, General Hausen, not being able to defend an unfortified place, immediately surrendered the town to the Duke of Zweibrücken, and was allowed to withdraw his men. Immediately afterwards General Kleefeld appeared before Torgau, which is only defended by a rampart and walls, but not fortified; he summoned the town, making at the same time the extraordinary threat, that in case of the slightest delay, the Prussian towns of Halle, Halberstadt and Quedlinburg should be given up to pillage for three days, and then be set fire to.

The *commandant*, Colonel Wolfersdorf, answered, that he would defend himself to the last, that he had nothing to do with the threatened towns; but that he would await the king's orders, if they would allow a cessation of hostilities for six days. Kleefeld was satisfied with this proposal, but made a reservation of awaiting the approbation of the Duke of Zweibrücken. The object of the colonel was to gain time, and receive reinforcements, before the decisive answer of the duke which arrived with 6,000 troops and a number of cannon and mortars.

The besiegers who were now commanded by the Prince of Stolberg, and reinforced by some Austrian light troops, endeavoured to make themselves masters of the suburb; but they were driven back by the Prussians who set it on fire. Two storming parties were now sent forward, but they were both driven back. The besiegers then placed a battery on the banks of the Elb, but by a successful sortie they were driven from this position, and the result of these occurrences was that the besiegers offered to negotiate an honourable surrender with the commandant; this was refused, and they now proceeded to storm the town, but without success. They attempted a fourth time to take it by storm with redoubled vigour, but were repulsed, and whilst the greater part of the garrison were occupied with driving hack the besiegers, Wolfersdorf made a sortie with 400 men, came in the rear of the storming party, and forced them to relinquish their undertaking.

Notwithstanding all this they could hardly look for a speedy termination to the siege. They had no hope of relief, and what was worst of all, there was a scarcity of powder. This decided the question; the Prussian honour had been preserved by the courageous defence of Wolfersdorf, and as the Prince Stolberg now offered him advantageous terms, he accepted them; the Prussians were allowed to withdraw their forces with colours flying, and with all their artillery, and it was agreed that no deserters should be received. But the troops were hardly outside the gates where the Croats were drawn up, before the besiegers broke the faith of the convention. As the Prussian battalion Grolman which for the most part consisted of Saxons, came to the place where the generals of the opposite party were stationed as spectators, the *aide-de-camp* of Prince Stolberg, and several other officers cried out with a loud voice:

Let all the brave Saxons who are for the empress, come out of the ranks, and His Highness will protect them.

This intimation had an immediate effect, and almost all the battalion broke from the ranks; some placed themselves behind the Croats who were marching away, others behind the palisades, and some in the ditch of the town.

Wolfersdorf soon put an end to this shameful conduct by his determination. He called out to the fugitives, that if they did not remain in their ranks, he would have them shot; he immediately shot one dead himself, and ordered his officers, hussars and riflemen to follow his example. He commanded the other troops to halt, and prepare for battle. The prince endeavoured to frighten him by threats, but Wolfersdorf, with a pistol in his hand, astonished him by the following words:

> As Your Highness has broken the terms of the capitulation, I am no longer bound by it. I will take you prisoner with the whole of your suite, and return into the town to again defend myself. Ride immediately within the fortifications or I will give orders to fire upon you.

The Prussians were already marching back into the town, and the hussars and riflemen were shooting the deserters like wild beasts; the disorder was very great, and the generals of the troops of the Empire not accustomed to warfare or its usages, knew not what to do in this dilemma; but Luzinsky, the leader of the Croats, came up, and seriously told them that every point of the convention must be held sacred; the deserters were given up, and forced to form in their ranks. Wolfersdorf made use of the advantage his courage had given him, and required that the escort which was to accompany him to Wittenberg should be placed under his orders, and always remain two thousand paces from the Prussians; his requests were all acceded to.

Wittenberg was now besieged; it was garrisoned by three battalions, one of which had been formed out of the Saxon regiments which had been converted into Prussian troops at Pirna, and these Saxons were only waiting for a favourable opportunity to regain their freedom. The third battalion was equally inefficient, as it was made up of deserters and prisoners, and the commandant thinking he could not place any confidence in such a garrison, accepted the terms that were offered him, by which he was allowed to withdraw his forces and artillery from the town, and proceed to Magdeburg. The troops of the Empire had taken possession of the towns of Belgern, Strehlen and Mühlberg, so that they were now masters of the Elb as far as Dresden, and all these occurrences had taken place during the time Frederic was engaged with the Russians.

Everyone now expected to see Saxony freed from the enemy, Berlin taken, and Magdeburg besieged. But of all this nothing was done, and the king who relied upon the known want of determination of the generals opposed to him, and their inactivity in making use of the victories they gained, was already full of confidence, the morning after the Battle of Kunersdorf. He had a few days previous received the intelligence of the victory near Minden from an officer sent by the Duke Ferdinand, and Frederic had ordered him to wait, in the expectation of having equally good news to send back by him. The officer presented himself the morning after the battle; the king said:

> I am very sorry that I cannot give better news as the answer to such pleasing intelligence; but if you can get back again, and Daun is not in Berlin, or Contades in Magdeburg, before you arrive, you may assure the duke from me, that our losses are not great.

In fact nothing could induce Soltikow to undertake any fresh enterprise, and the eloquence of Montalembert, who had orders from his court to use all his powers for the downfall of Frederic, was exerted in vain. In one of this minister's letters he said:

> The Russians must have the prospect of having Berlin, and the whole of Brandenburg given up to them to pillage.

Soltikow would not listen to any proposal, and said, that his weakened army should not undertake any dangerous enterprise; in addition to this, he was much dissatisfied with Daun's inactivity, which in fact astonished all Europe.

Although the Russians derived no advantages from their victory, a succession of misfortunes such as he had never before experienced in any of his wars, now accumulated on the king. His next loss was that of Dresden. The Austrians had always had their principal aim directed towards the taking this capital; they now determined to besiege it in the absence of the king, and formed a junction with the troops of the Empire 30,000 strong for that purpose. Schmettau was prepared to defend himself; he quitted the new town which is separated from the old town by the Elb, and contented himself with defending the latter. The new town was now occupied by the Austrians, and the Imperial General Guasco threatened to bombard the town with eighteen batteries, but Schmettau promised to reply to it with a hundred cannon.

At this time the news of the Battle of Kunersdorf arrived, and the enemy took advantage of the first shock of this intelligence to represent to the commandant his dangerous position, and the impossibility of his being relieved. Schmettau had always shown himself to be a determined, active and courageous general, and in this instance he did not belie his reputation, and ridiculed all the threats which were now heaped upon him. The Duke of Zweibrücken sent word to him, that if the Prussians burnt the suburbs, the whole garrison should be cut to pieces, Halle, which was in the hands of the troops of the Empire, given up to pillage, and burnt to the ground, all the salt works of the place, destroyed, and the whole of the Prussian provinces laid waste; Schmettau's answer to these threats was the immediate setting fire to the suburbs. One messenger now followed another, and the Generals Maquire and Guasco held conferences with the Prussian commandant, and notwithstanding his disadvantageous position the most determined resistance was to be expected; but a letter from Frederic changed the face of affairs.

The king had informed Schmettau of his misfortune immediately after the battle of Kunersdorf, and had expressed his opinion, that, as it would be extremely difficult to relieve Dresden, he had better, in case of necessity, only try to obtain advantageous terms, and above all things to be careful to retain possession of the money in the treasury. Schmettau was somewhat astonished, but now gave up all hopes, and the Duke of Zweibrücken informed him that if he still persisted in defending himself, not a single Prussian should be spared. As regarded the commandant these threats were of no avail, but on the other hand his menaces were most efficacious, for in consequence of his declaration to the court of the Elector, that on the first shot being fired from the new town, this beautiful quarter would be set on fire, no attack was made from this point, and Schmettau was enabled to keep his garrison together, and oppose his whole force to the attack of the enemy on the other side of the old town. He sought to gain time, in hopes of being relieved or at least of receiving intelligence from the king; but he heard nothing, and gradually the belief in the representations of the imperial generals, respecting the complete prostration of Frederic's strength, gained ground in his mind.

He was now cut off from all means of relief, for the town was completely surrounded, and in this position he remained twenty seven days, constantly harassed by the attacks of the enemy, pressed and threatened. His personal courage was useless, and his confidence in his power of keeping his dissatisfied soldiers within bounds, by means of his determination and the power of Prussian discipline, and in inducing them still to defend themselves, were now of no avail; for his whole attention was at this time directed to the saving the immense sums of money, which were placed in the town. In this town, as the principal city of the country, all the revenues were deposited, as well as the military chests for the troops, and in addition to this, other sums of money were brought to what was considered a place of security.

This treasure amounted in all to above five million of dollars, and the necessity of saving so large a sum, especially in Frederic's present position, decided the affair, as Schmettau did not know that a large body of troops were advancing to his relief. The besiegers well aware of their arrival and progress in Saxony and who already looked on Dresden as saved, forgot their threats, and gave way to all the demands of Schmettau. He began to negotiate when they were on the point of bombarding the town, and was allowed by the terms of the capitulation to withdraw his troops with all the honours of war, their baggage, cannon, ammunition and the waggons laden with specie.

It was also agreed to, that all property belonging to Prussian subjects should be allowed to be taken away, and no deserters received into the army of the besiegers. General Maquire gave his word of honour for the "fulfilment of every article according to the import of the words made use of, without the slightest chicane." The provisions were to remain behind, and these which consisted in 30,000 bushel of corn and near thirteen thousand hundred weight of flour, besides other provisions enabled the Austrians, who were already thinking of a retreat towards Bohemia in consequence of a shortness of provisions, to retain their position in Saxony. This convention was hardly concluded and signed by the Duke of Zweibrücken, when Wunsh arrived with his body of men within four leagues of Dresden. The strength of his troops was worn out by forced marches, and added to this, they had twice repulsed General Brentano, who was sent against them with a body of imperial troops. The besiegers had at this time taken possession of one of the gates, for Wunsh could not advance with his fatigued men; and as he knew nothing of the treaty, had therefore determined to storm the new town.

His approach raised the spirits of the Prussians in Dresden, and some officers advised that in despite of the signed capitulation, the Austrians, who were masters of one of the gates, should be driven back. Schmettau, who was most anxious about the treasure which had been so strongly recommended to his care by the king, would hear nothing of this proposition, although it promised success. Colonel Hoffman thought right to attempt it without orders, mounted his horse for the purpose, and ordered the main guard to follow him; the captain of the guard refused to obey him upon which Hoffman treated him as a coward, and fired at him with his pistol, but missed him. Some soldiers of the guard, to revenge their officer, fired upon him, and the brave colonel was killed. All the hopes of the Prussians were now extinct; Wunsch retreated, and Dresden was occupied by the Austrians.

The capitulation which had been guaranteed in so sacred a manner, was broken on almost every point, and the garrison who were at liberty, and had not surrendered as prisoners of war, most shamefully treated. The officers and soldiers of the imperial troops and even the generals joined in this unworthy conduct. The Prussian soldiers were forced from their ranks to enter the Austrian service; the officers were ill treated, abused, struck, wounded, and some were even killed. The Austrian officers forgetful of all the principles of honour and generosity, and what was due to their position, were the instigators and even the actors in this dishonourable affair, for they cried out: "Shoot the dogs, fire on the canaille!"

The generals in command, Maquire and Guasco, were not backward in lending their assistance to this proceeding, and they forgot their pledged word of honour, which should have been held sacred by them; the arms of the Prussians and their pontoons were taken from them by force, and the waggons and boats promised for the transport of their baggage were refused. The time, which by the terms of capitulation, had been granted for their leaving the town was not allowed them, and they were forced to quit it two days earlier. But at last Schmettau was enabled to get the better of all difficulties, and to withdraw from the town with his treasure and his garrison. No commandant of a fortified town could have behaved better than Schmettau in his difficult position, and he deserved in spite of his misfortune more consideration and praise than those who resisting every attack of a place committed to their charge, are still enabled to retain possession of it.

In ignorance of all that was occurring outside the town, and by Frederic's own letter deprived of all hopes of relief, he followed the directions of his monarch, and gave way to the force of circumstances; but Frederic, who could not punish him for his conduct as an officer, showed his displeasure by removing him from the field of operations. As he felt severely the loss of Dresden he would not pardon the commandant for his misfortune, notwithstanding he had brought him the treasure for which he had expressed so much anxiety. The zeal of Schmettau was undoubted, but this was not taken into consideration, as the result was not favourable, and more especially as he had not repaired the error into which the king had fallen.

This error was indeed great; for Wunsh had orders not to march immediately to the relief of the hard pressed city of Dresden, which was so important from its treasure and the stores it contained, but first was to go to Torgau and Wittenberg, where there was nothing to lose and then march to the relief of the capital; had this been done sooner, the town would have been undoubtedly saved. Added to this, no endeavour was made during twenty seven days to convey secret intelligence to the *commandant*.

No army was so badly supplied with spies as the Prussian, in consequence of their being so ill paid by the king, as the few ducats that the bearers of intelligence received were no compensation for the risk of life they had gone through. The want of these spies which was caused by the principle of economy, would have caused the failure of many enterprises of importance, and their assistance would have given rise to other occurrences during these campaigns, had it not been that Frederic often received the most important information not only from his hussar officers, but also from his partisans, who were in constant activity, and who were numerous, from the astonishment raised by his wonderful deeds. There was also a high spirit of emulation amongst his officers, and this replaced in a great measure the scarcity of spies.

Great generals have always acknowledged the necessity of employing such men; but no one ever derived more advantage from them, than Prince Eugene, who paid them munificently, and was therefore well served by them; and he had to thank the secret intelligence received by this means for many great deeds, which he was enabled to achieve with contracted means. Frederic was therefore anxious to avail himself of the services of the famed robber Kasebier, who lay in chains in Stettin, and who was condemned to imprisonment for life. The craft and courage of this German Cartouche led people to expect great things from him, and he was therefore set at liberty in the beginning of the war. But Kasebier, thinking less of the favour which was shown to him than of the punishment he had already received, promised every thing that was asked, but never returned.

Prince Henry had now marched with his large army from Silesia into Saxony. He had, by means of forced marches, fallen upon the Austrian General Wehla, killed 600 of his men, and taken him with 1800 others, prisoner.

This march, which was of twenty leagues through country occupied by the enemy, and lasted fifty six hours, was completed without encamping; and during this time the troops were only allowed twice to repose for three hours; it continued day, and night during the other fifty hours, and completely upset the plans of the Austrians. Prince Henry had in this as well as his other operations a valuable assistant, his aid de camp Captain Kalkreuth, a man of rare talents, and born to be a general. While young he excited astonishment by his deeds, and later in life when a leader, he was adored by his soldiers, and was the inseparable companion of Henry so long as the war lasted.

At this time the Russians and the troops under Daun were in Lusatia. Henry who, in consequence of the dangerous position of the king, could not venture a battle, directed his efforts against the storehouses and magazines of the enemy; he was fortunate, by well formed plans, in destroying the most important of them, and provisions began to fail in the armies of the enemy. The Austrians had great difficulty in providing means for their own support, and therefore begged the Russians, who had drawn near Saxony, to receive money instead of provisions, and to supply themselves. "My soldiers do not eat money," was the answer of Soltikow, who immediately began his march towards Poland through Silesia.

Laudon accompanied him, and used every means to induce him to besiege Glogau; but this plan had to be given up in consequence of the confederate armies finding, to their astonishment, a Prussian camp at Beuthen on the Oder. The king was posted here, determined to venture everything, even a battle under the most disadvantageous circumstances, in order to save this fortress, and as his force consisted only in 24,000 men, and he was in momentary expectation of an attack, his men were all day under arms; the Russians did not venture to attack him, but went over the Oder, and destroyed all the bridges that they might not be followed. They then kept along the banks of the river, and appeared desirous of directing their operations against Breslau; but they found Prussians in every direction, and the passes strongly manned.

The king was still near the Russians, when he was seized with a severe fit of the gout. This was a great source of anxiety to him, for he expected that the Russians would attack him the moment they heard of it, and had the attack been made, Frederic, who was not in a state to take the command, must have awaited in his bed, under the most dreadful torture both of body and of mind, the fate it would have been easy to foretell. But the Russians were never aware of his helpless position, and the king was saved by his good fortune. As he could neither get on horseback nor bear the fatigue of a carriage, he was carried by his soldiers to Koben, a small town on the Oder, and here he assembled his generals, made them aware of the severity of his illness, and gave them the following instructions:

> Assure my brave soldiers, that in spite of the many misfortunes I have experienced this campaign, I shall not be called away until all is set right again. Tell them that I rely on their courage, and that nothing but death shall separate me from my troops.

He then dictated to his secretary, during the most acute suffering, the necessary orders for the army.

The Russians in the meanwhile continued their devastating march, of which Herrnstadt was the extent in Silesia. As this town, though not fortified, but strong in its natural position, and garrisoned only by a few hundred Prussians, would not surrender, it was set fire to by red hot balls, and reduced to a heap of ashes; and after this act the Russians continued their march towards Poland. Laudon asked Soltikow what he was to do with his army under these circumstances; Soltikow answered: "You may do what you please, but I shall march to Posen." Laudon remained some time longer with the Russian Army, but at length left them highly displeased, and withdrew into the Austrian states.

Towards the end of October the whole of Silesia and Brandenburg were clear of the Austrians and Russians, and twelve burning villages with the town of Gurau in flames, and other signs of devastation inseparable from their time of march, marked the retreat of the latter. The estate of Count Cosel on the Oder suffered at their hands, and he complained to the king, who answered him:

> We have to do with barbarians, who are endeavouring to entomb humanity. You see, my dear count, that I am more occupied in getting the better of the evil, than in making complaints, and I would advise my friends to follow my example.

In fact the acrimony of the mighty confederates was so great against the King of Prussia, as to be the disgrace of the era in which he lived. All the cruelties which had been perpetrated by the Austrians, as well as the Russians, during their invasions of Brandenburg and Silesia, received the seal of approbation, and it was the orders of the highest powers, that nothing should be left to the Prussian subjects but "air and the earth;" these extraordinary expressions gave rise to and were reported in the manifesto, which was published by the Prussian Colonel Kleist, at Grab in Bohemia, on the 17th of November 1759. The activity of General Wunsh had exceeded all expectation, as the body of men placed under his command were only 5000 strong, and with these he had entered Saxony in order to take possession of this country which was filled with the enemy. He had no sooner appeared before the gates of Wittenberg than the commandant of the garrison, which was 2000 strong, was anxious to come to terms; Wunsh, who was desirous of losing no time, allowed him to withdraw his forces, and hurried on to Torgau.

Here the general of the Empire, Kleefeld, who was commandant, offered to surrender, but as they could not agree upon the terms, or consent to his demands, the Prussian general took possession of the suburb, drove the Croats out, and prepared to carry the place by storm. The negotiations were renewed, and the town capitulated; the garrison were allowed to withdraw, but they were obliged to leave behind their cannon and their ammunition. Wunsh now started for Dresden, where the besiegers looked upon his body of men, from its being composed of all sorts of troops, as a whole army, and this induced them to give way to the demands of Schmettau, in the before mentioned treaty, so that there now remained nothing for Wunsh to do but to retreat on Torgau, which in the short interval had already been again invested; the garrison consisted in only 500 men, and General St. Andre was now advancing on the town with a large body of Austrians and troops of the Empire.

As soon as Wunsh heard of this, he started with his light troops, with directions for the others to follow and never stopped till he reached, unobserved by the enemy, the town of Torgau. Here he had wine served out to his fatigued soldiers, and then placed them in order of battle. The troops of the Empire at length became aware of the presence of the Prussians, and prepared for battle, and so certain were they of victory, that they never struck their tents. It is true, Wunsh gave them no time, for he fell on them with his cavalry, attacked them in the front and in their flanks, and drove them back, before the Prussian infantry could come within shot.

The whole body was 10,000 strong, among whom were four *cuirassier* regiments and two dragoon regiments, 1200 grenadiers and 2000 Croats; these all fled into the woods and left the camp and all its supplies and necessaries in the hands, of the enemy.

This engagement was as important in its effects as a brilliant victory, as it raised the Prussian arms in the consideration of the world, and by its means the king was, with the exception of Dresden, again master of Saxony. The noble conduct of one of the imperial generals in this combat deserves to be noticed. A Prussian soldier, worked up to a state of enthusiasm, fought like a knight of the olden time; he carried every thing before him, and without attending to his brave companions rushed into the midst of the enemy. Here he continued to cut down those about him, until severely wounded he fell to the ground with his horse which had been killed. The soldiers who were around him wished to cut him to pieces, but St. Andre held them back by saying: "We must save so brave a soldier and one who belongs to so brave a regiment." He directed that he should be taken good care of, and as soon as he was recovered from his wounds he sent him back to his regiment without ransom, but with a present of money, and a letter of recommendation

The king had not expected so rapid a conquest of Saxony by so small a body of men, and had sent, shortly after, a body of men under General Fink, into this province. This general was also too late to save Dresden, but he did not remain inactive, for he formed a junction with Wunsh, and on the 21st of September attacked Haddick, who was at the head of a large Austrian corps, and after a bloody battle, which lasted the whole day, beat him, and took 500 prisoners

It was thus, that to the astonishment of the whole world, the victorious army of the confederates was forced to act on the defensive, and they were now restrained in all their operations by the small, defeated and dispersed army of the Prussians, by whom all their plans had been were overthrown.

Chapter 7: Continuation of the Campaign of 1759

Notwithstanding all the misfortunes of Frederic during the last few months, the seat of war was confined to Saxony, during the remainder of the campaign. Daun used all his endeavours to drive Prince Henry from this province; but these were rendered of no avail, from his superior capabilities and watchfulness, and he was enabled, not only to retain his position, but also to cover Leipsic and Wittenberg. All this induced the Austrian general to form a new plan by which, he wished to cut off the Prussian general from these towns, and to shut him up in his camp. Daun, to carry out this plan, divided his army into different bodies, and the strongest division was placed under the command of the Duke of Aremberg. Henry gained information of the intentions of the enemy, and learned the detail of their plans from the papers of an *aide de camp*, who was taken prisoner.

He immediately dispatched Generals Fink, Wunsh, Wedel and Rebentish in different directions with their armies. They all fell in with the enemy, who retreated. At last, on the 29th of October, the Prussians came up with the large body under Aremberg, at Pretsch near Duben, at the moment they were in great confusion, and on the point of making good their retreat, which was to be covered by a grenadier corps, under the command of General Gemmingen. They were attacked by General Platen, at the head of a body of dragoons and hussars, who charged the Austrian grenadiers at a hand gallop, drove them back, took 1500 prisoners, and dispersed the remainder.

The king, who was still ill, now removed to Glogau, where he remained until he recovered. He dispatched General Hulsen, with the greater part of his army, into Saxony, where the Prussians had gained the upper hand to such an extent, that Daun thought it advisable to take up a strong position at Plauen, in order to protect Dresden, which was the only town remaining in the hands of the Austrians, after all their previous conquests. It was Frederic's determination to get this important place out of their possession so soon as the troops, which were advancing from Silesia, could form a junction with Prince Henry. In order to carry out this plan with more decision, the king left Glogau, although not perfectly recovered, and joined the army on the 13th of November, after an absence of twenty days.

Everything tended to force the army of Daun to retreat towards Bohemia, in spite of the possession of Dresden, and this retreat would have ensued from the force of circumstances, but that the king was anxious to hasten it. Fink was therefore sent to Maxen, which is situated in the mountains, and Colonel Kleist had orders to invade Bohemia with a small body of men, which he did with success; he took prisoners, pillaged and raised contributions, in order to make the enemy pay for the cruelties and oppression they had exercised in Silesia and Brandenburg.

The position General Fink had taken up, threatened to cut off the communication with Bohemia; but at a distance from the king, and surrounded by the whole of the Austrian Army, this general had misgivings respecting his situation. He was therefore bold enough to make representations to the king, previous to commencing his march, but these met with the displeasure of Frederic, who answered in a manner, which had often rendered apparently impossible enterprises, possible:

> He knows I dislike the raising difficulties; he must make such arrangements as will insure success.

Fink now marched on Maxen, and left General Linstadt, with 3000 men, to defend the pass of Dippoldiswald, by which the communication with Freyberg remained open. Frederic was dissatisfied with this arrangement, and wrote peremptorily:

> That it would be best for the whole army to be drawn together, as he would then be in a better position to receive the attack of the enemy. Added to this, the small force at Dippoldiswald could easily be dispersed, as the enemy would be sure to advance with a strong body, if they came at all.

The king's orders were fulfilled, by which means the position of the enemy was improved, and a passage was opened for them to advance and attack Fink. All the letters from this general to the king fell into the hands of the Austrians from this time; and these causes led to the entire loss of this strong body of men.

The 21st of November was a day of misfortunes, which must be ever memorable to Prussian soldiers. Fink, who was posted in a hollow, was attacked by an army 40,000 strong, who had possession of the heights. On one side was Daun with the Austrians, on the other the Duke of Zweibrücken with the troops of the Empire; but in spite of this, the Prussians fought with great bravery. The fire of the enemy was directed entirely on one point, and the village of Maxen, which was in the centre of the Prussian line, was set on fire by the enemy, in consequence of which, they were thrown into disorder; added to this, the baggage waggons were in great confusion, by the shells from the Austrian's howitzers, which were directed on the point where they were placed.

The disorder soon extended to the whole of the infantry, and their retreat was completely cut off. After having kept up their fire during the whole day, they had expended all their cartridges, and there was no more ammunition. They had no hopes of receiving reinforcements from the king, as he could not be aware of their position. In spite of all this Fink, who had always shown himself a general of experience and courage, now determined to cut his way through the enemy. He assembled his officers, and explained to them his determination; but the utter impossibility of forcing their way through the ravines left no alternative, but either to sacrifice the whole of his army, or give his men up as prisoners of war.

Fink, who knew the numbers of Austrian prisoners, who were in the hands of the king, thought he was but little injuring the cause of his monarch, in adopting the latter course, and therefore he followed the suggestions of humanity. Wunsh proposed to make an attempt during the night with the cavalry, and actually succeeded in escaping; the infantry could not follow, and Fink, of whom Frederic had said that he would be another Turenne, was forced to surrender.

Daun would hear of no arrangement but their being prisoners of war, and went so far, as to insist that Wunsh should be recalled, and that he and his men should give themselves up as prisoners. It was in vain that Fink stated, that Wunsh commanded an entirely separate body of men; the Austrian general insisted, and Fink was forced to comply. Wunsh obeyed the order to return, and although he did not sign the convention, he was made prisoner. The principal article of the capitulation. was that the Prussians should retain their baggage; but 71 cannon, 24 standards and 96 pair of colours were given up to the Austrians, and 11,000 men cavalry and infantry laid down their arms, and were made prisoners, as well as nine general officers; only a few hussars escaped, and conveyed this dreadful intelligence to the king.

Frederic imagined, that this misfortune might have been avoided, and after the end of the war, Generals Fink, Rebentish and Gersdorf were tried by a court martial; as they could not make good their defence, they were all three condemned to be imprisoned in a fortress. Rebentish remained some time longer in the service, but the others were degraded from their military rank, and Fink died as commander in chief of the Danish Army, and Rebentish as a general officer in the Portuguese service.

This misfortune was followed shortly after by another; General Dierke was posted on the banks of the Elb, near Meissen, with three thousand men. The king ordered this general to return, and he was forced to cross the Elb, which was full of ice; General Beck, one of the Empress' best officers, took advantage of this circumstance, and advanced with a strong body of men. There were only a few boats ready, and Dierke was forced, after a severe struggle, to lay down his arms and all those, who had not crossed the river, were made prisoners; by this means 1400 Prussians fell into the hands of the Austrians.

Daun, who was generally so cautious, was induced by these advantages to advance towards the weakened army of the king, in the hopes that he would take to flight at his approach. To his surprise, he found him prepared to receive him, and he therefore quietly withdrew his forces. General Maquire thought he had only to show himself, in order to take possession of Freyberg, which was in the hands of the Prussians. He advanced with 16,000 men, accompanied by an immense baggage train, which displayed his expectations. He was however disappointed, for he found the Prussians drawn up in order of battle, and their cannon balls showed him the way to retreat.

The principal sources of Frederic's success were the faults of his enemies; and even at this moment, the expectations of every one were deceived; for Daun instead of taking advantage of his success and advancing, took up a strong position near Plauen, as if he had been defeated. On the other hand, Frederic, who had lost half his army, and with his regiments much weakened by the protracted campaign, did not change his position, although at the head of only 20,000 men, and kept possession of the whole of Saxony, with the exception of the small district round Dresden.

At the same time, he reinforced his army by 12,000 men from the allied army, who joined him under the command of the Hereditary Prince of Brunswick, at the end of December, near Freyberg. Notwithstanding the severity of the season, Frederic advanced with these reinforcements, and drove back all the advanced posts of the enemy. His intention was to attack General Maquire at Dippoldiswald; but the strength of his position, and the nature of the ground, forced the king to give up this enterprise, and he retreated on Freyberg.

The intense cold of this winter, and the manner in which it was passed by the Prussians, swept off a great many men. The army of the king was distributed in the small towns and villages, in the neighbourhood of Dresden, and were so straightened for room, that only a few of the soldiers could be housed. Some regiments lay the whole winter in the villages; the officers occupied the rooms in the cottages, and the soldiers brick huts, which they had built for themselves, and lay day and night round the fire. The cold was intense, and the snow remained for many weeks knee deep. The soldiers had to drag wood from a distance, and this would sometimes occupy the whole day, so that large parties were seen in every direction carrying these loads towards the villages.

As the cold increased and wood became more scarce, the men following the law of nature, which makes self preservation a duty, laid their hands on everything they could find for fuel, and outhouses, fences and even houses were not spared; even as the Spaniards sought for gold in America, so did the Prussians seek for wood. Provisions were not in abundance, so that the soldier was limited to his rations of bread. In consequence of the number of sick, the duty fell very heavily on those who were in health, and the soldiers had but little repose, when not on guard. When they had no wood, nor snow, nor lumps of ice to fetch for cooking, they laid themselves down near the ashes, to warm their thinly clothed bodies, which whilst one side was burnt, the other was frozen.

This was not all; there was a small camp in Wilsdruf, two leagues from Dresden, and the king would not allow it to be broken up. It was therefore held by four battalions, which were relieved every twenty four hours; by this means every foot regiment, in turn, occupied this camp. The tents remained standing, and were frozen, so that the linen was like boards. The Austrians were forced to follow this example, and these armies exhibited, what was unprecedented in the annals of warfare; they were posted but a short distance from each other, and in spite of the severe weather, were almost without covering, awaiting the return of fine weather to put an end to their sufferings.

Although perfection is not to be found in human nature, and it is unworthy of history to exclaim against every fault, caprice, or whim of a great man, still it is justifiable, from the nature of the case, to doubt of the utility of the mode of proceeding on this occasion, which was persevered in, more from caprice, than from any ultimate views, as nothing could be gained, and the men were worn out in this position.

The cold of this severe winter was of long duration, and every day many of the ill clad soldiers were frost bitten.

★★★★★★

The author was at this time, as indeed almost constantly with the army of the king, and was an eye witness of what is here related. His regiment had very poor winter quarters in the village of Costebaude, two leagues from Dresden, and was marched every week, to the camp at Wilsdruf, to relieve guard.

★★★★★★

At the camp there were no huts, and the pickets had only heaps of burning wood which were not at all times to be procured; the officers had wooden huts, built of boards. The common soldiers, to keep their blood in circulation, ran about the camp, or not caring for their food lay around the fires in heaps to keep one another warm. They were alike unfit for attack or defence, and no regiment ever returned from thus camp to their wretched winter quarters, without increasing the number of their sick. Numbers were buried at a time, and this winter campaign cost the king more men than two battles would have done; but this loss was not so perceptible from their places being filled up by fresh recruits. The Austrians had no better fate than their enemies, for they lay in the villages near Plauen, which were protected from the attack of the Prussians by the forest of Tharandt, and a succession of ravines. Daun's cautiousness led him to take still further precautions; entrenchments were formed in every direction, and all the roads, and even footpaths which led to the highest hills, were *barricadoed*; but their wretched cantonments were the grave of many of Theresa's best soldiers.

The levies of the Prussians were carried on with such activity that by the month of February, the king was enabled to send back the reinforcements he had received from the Duke Ferdinand of Brunswick. This raised great astonishment in Vienna, as it proved, that in

184

spite of the severity of the losses of Kunersdorf, Maxen, and the other misfortunes of the preceding campaign, they had all been made good, by means of the powerful resources of Frederic. At this time the Prussian General Czettritz was taken prisoner, and amongst his papers were found the private orders of the king for his generals; these were printed, and made public shortly after by the Austrians.

There was nothing remarkable in this campaign, as regarded the Swedes. In consequence of General Manteufel being forced to join the king, after the Battle of Kunersdorf, the Swedes, under the command of General Lautinghausen, were now unopposed; they took advantage of this to seize some weakly garrisoned towns, and to make themselves masters of eight Prussian ships of war. These ships had been manned in Stettin, and armed to defend the coast, and the mouths of the Oder against the landing of the Swedes. There were eleven of them of different sizes, and were in part named after the principal personages of the royal house, and in part after the gods of the ancient mythology; their advantage was soon apparent, and the poor inhabitants of the coast were no longer a prey to being pillaged by single Swedish ships. The defeat of this fleet was therefore determined on by the Swedes; they attacked them with nine and twenty ships, and gained their end by means of their superior force, for only three of the Prussian ships escaped.

The Swedish Army advanced as far as Prenzlau; but Manteufel drew a small body of men together, drove them out of Anclam and Prenzlau, and forced them to retreat over the Peene. He never allowed them to stop, but drove them, continually fighting, to Greifswalde, took several prisoners, and in Demmin seized the military chest; he was then forced to put an end to his winter campaign by the extreme cold. The Swedes revenged themselves on this active general; for they surprised him in the night time in Anclam, and notwithstanding they were driven back with great loss, Manteufel, who had missed his way in the dark, fell into their hands.

The king had raised another regiment of black hussars, who distinguished themselves, under the command of Colonel Belling, not only in this expedition, but also during all the campaigns against the Swedes in Pomerania, and the Ukermark. They played a conspicuous part in this portion of the seat of war, and there hardly passed a day that they did not bring in a great many Swedish prisoners, the number of which had already reached 3000.

The campaign of the allies of the king had been carried forward with great success. The English now took an active part in the war, and Parliament had voted in addition the sum of 1,900,000 pounds sterling, without reckoning the enormous expenses of sending their troops to Germany. The French had, however, began by striking a clever blow; they surprised Frankfort on the Main in the middle of the winter. This free city had supplied the due contingent of money and men to the Empire, and therefore the inhabitants did not think they had cause for anxiety from the confederates of the Empire. It is true they had allowed the French to march through, but only in single bodies, and the excuse was the crossing the Main.

A similar request was now made, and it was granted under certain conditions. New year's day was fixed for the carrying out of their plan, and a large body of French was assembled before the town; the new year's greetings of the inhabitants were interrupted, and the beating of their drums informed the Prince de Soubise, that his intention was discovered; it was therefore deferred to the next day. The inhabitants of Frankfort were on their guard, and it was determined, that only one regiment of French should be admitted at a time, and that the gates should remain closed until that regiment had passed over the bridge.

The whole garrison was under arms; some troops accompanied the French through the town, and the others were placed at the threatened gate, in order to enforce the orders of the magistrates. All this did not prevent this important city from being taken without the spilling a drop of blood. The French troops came in the rear of the regiment which had permission to march through the town, dispersed the guard at the gate who offered resistance, and caused a panic amongst the other soldiers who were drawn up in line. They now rushed to the ramparts, made themselves masters of the cannon and of the different gates, and during this time different bodies took possession of the principal places and streets.

By this means the city fell into the hands of the French, who treated it during the first few days as a conquered city. The Prince de Soubise their general went to the council, and made known his orders, which were in this moment of astonishment received with the deepest respect; this leader promised in the name of his king, that they should be allowed the free exercise of their religion, and that their freedom and privileges should be respected. The streets were paraded by strong patrols, and large heaps of wood were kept constantly burning in them, in consequence of the severe cold. The inhabitants were not allowed to leave their houses, or even to show themselves at the windows, and the soldiers of the town were disarmed.

Frankfort was now the headquarters of the French, who by this means were in full communication with the Imperial Army and the troops of the Empire, and by its means they could secure all kinds of supplies from the Rhine and the Main; it was therefore Ferdinand's principal object to deprive the French of the advantage they had gained, as soon as the campaign could be opened. This plan was delayed until the month of April, in consequence of the troops of the Empire, as well as a body of Austrians and French having overrun the provinces of Hessia and the neighbourhood, and it was necessary to drive them hence.

This was effected by the Hereditary Prince of Brunswick, who defeated the troops of the Empire in several engagements, took a considerable number of prisoners, and cleared these districts of the enemy. Ferdinand left 12,000 men to protect Hanover and Hessia, and advanced at the head of 30,000 men upon Frankfort. The Duke of Broglio, who now commanded the French army at this place, took up a strong position near the village of Bergen, in the neighbourhood of Frankfort, from which it was necessary that Ferdinand should drive him in order to carry out his plans.

The armies engaged the 13th of April, and the village of Bergen was attacked with vigour; eight battalions of German troops in the pay of the French were posted here, and also several brigades of French infantry, who kept up a heavy fire; the Saxon troops had taken up a position on the heights over the Nidda. The Prince of Isenburg, not aware of the strength of the enemy, and at all times unfortunate in war, made a separate attack with four battalions of grenadiers, and gave the extraordinary order that the surgeons should fall into the ranks, as it was their duty to follow the troops; they refused in the first instance, and it was only at the representations of one of their number, that they obeyed, and were recompensed, some with wounds and others by being killed.

The French, who were in possession of all the advantages the nature of the ground could give them, made use of these against an enemy who were, on the contrary, in a disadvantageous position. In advance of the village were a number of hollows, and through these the Hessians could only pass in small detachments, and they were also forced to climb over hedges and ditches. The Hereditary Prince of Brunswick advanced to their assistance at the head of his division, and took the French in the left flank. The Hessians, stimulated by this, re-

newed the attack with redoubled vigour, and the French were beginning to give way, when the Duke of Broglio, by a clever manoeuvre,
outflanked the allies; the Hessians were repulsed, and the Duke of
Isenburg killed. Some French regiments, which had advanced in pursuit of the enemy, fell into disorder, and were attacked by the cavalry
of the allies, who carried great havoc amongst them, and cut down a
number of Saxons and French.

Everything depended on the possession of the village of Bergen;
within three hours the attack was thrice repeated, but without success. Nothing was left for Ferdinand but to make good his retreat, in
the presence of a superior force. It was not yet midday, and it was only
during the night that he could hope to effect this; under these circumstances he took up a position so as to induce the enemy to think that
he was going to renew the engagement. He divided his infantry into
two divisions, placed his cavalry in the centre with a small column
of infantry in advance of them, and thus he appeared as if he meant
to attack the village of Bergen and also a wood on his left wing. He
cannonaded both these points, until nightfall, and then withdrew his
forces to Windecken; his loss consisted in 2000 men and five pieces
of artillery.

However trifling this loss might be, the result of the battle was a
great disadvantage to the allies. Frankfort, which would have been a
source of great benefit to Ferdinand, had he obtained possession of
it, remained in the hands of the French, who could now renew their
undertakings with every prospect of success. Although Ferdinand was
forced to act on the defensive, he still remained master of the Weser, in
spite of all the efforts of the French to drive him from this river. They
now advanced, took Cassel, and surprised Minden, in consequence of
the commandant having drawn up his forces at a place near the banks
of the Wesel, in expectation that the attack would be made at that
point. This would have been the case had not a peasant provided the
French with a boat, and pointed out a ford for the cavalry.

The French committed the greatest excesses in Minden, in spite
of the endeavours of the Duke of Broglio and the other generals, and
the unfortunate town was pillaged; a large supply of provisions fell
into their hands, and 1400 men were made prisoners. The French
also took Münster after a regular siege, and the garrison, 4000 strong,
were forced to give themselves up as prisoners of war. The Battle of
Bergen, which was celebrated in France by a thanksgiving, and which
was compared by the courtiers to the greatest conquests, gained for

the Duke of Broglio the dignity of Prince of the Empire which was conferred on him by the imperial court. In Paris the poets composed verses in honour of the victory, the Poissardes rejoiced, and the ladies wore head dresses, *à la Bergen*.

It was the intention of the French to invade Hanover, and to cut off the allies from the Weser; but Ferdinand upset all their plans; he surprised the free city of Bremen by artifice, and thus obtained command of the Weser as far as Stade. At this time not only the possession of Hanover, but the fate of the whole campaign, hung upon the event of a battle, and the loss of Minden induced Ferdinand to accelerate this decision. In order to induce the enemy to give battle he sent out two bodies of men to threaten their magazines in their rear; the Hereditary Prince of Brunswick commanded one of these, and advanced to Hervorden, in order to reinforce General Drewes, who attacked Osnabrück, blew up the gates of the town, drove out the garrison, and took possession of the stores and provisions; Ferdinand now established his principal magazine at this place.

The allies were now in a most advantageous position, and the French in danger of being cut off from their supplies; Contades became alarmed, and threw a number of bridges over the Weser in order to facilitate the communication with the forces of Broglio. A council of war was held on the evening of the 31st of July, and at this it was determined to march that very night, and to attack the enemy at break of day. Broglio was now to join his forces to that of the main division of the army. On the part of the French a battle became actually indispensable, whilst Ferdinand only wished for one that he might gain advantages. The superior numbers of the former, and the dispersed position of the different bodies of the allies, appeared to promise the French a good opportunity for a brilliant victory.

On the other hand, in order to be prepared for an unfavourable result, the French general had nineteen bridges placed over a small stream which runs into the Weser, and let it be known throughout the army that these were to make good his retreat. The French marched in nine columns; one of these under the command of Broglio was to attack the division of General Wangenheim, who was in a strong position at the village of Tornhausen, a short distance from the main body, with 10,000 men cavalry and infantry, and two heavy batteries. Ferdinand learnt the enemy's intention at three in the morning by means of a deserter; this was agreeable intelligence to him, who was so anxious for a battle, that he had already determined on making the attack; he now lost no time in advancing.

Broglio now advanced towards the position of Wangenheim, and the success of his undertaking depended on its being carried out with rapidity; but much valuable time was lost by want of decision and unnecessary halts. The French here gave a remarkable instance of how far behind they were in the art of war, notwithstanding their theory, when they had to put their knowledge to the test of practice. Unable to take up a position and form with rapidity, instead of fulfilling their orders, and making the attack at day break, they had in the first instance to draw together their dispersed bodies, and to form in column; in consequence of this it was five o'clock before Broglio had his men in order of battle, and he was still in expectation of further orders from Contades.

By this means Wangenheim had time to place himself on the defensive, and Ferdinand was enabled to come up to his assistance. In consequence of the masterly movements and order of battle of these generals, all the plans of Contades were frustrated, and Wangenheim now left his position to join the main body of the army. The French found themselves in a most dangerous position, surrounded by a morass, the Weser, and the army of the enemy. It was, however, still necessary that the battle should be fought, and Broglio made a spirited attack; but his troops suffered severely from the fire of the allies, which in a short time silenced that of the French.

The order of battle of the French was so arranged that the best of their cavalry was placed in the centre. This ill-judged arrangement, which had already, in 1704, caused their defeat at Hochstadt, insured the victory of the allies. Ferdinand ordered the English and Hanoverian infantry to advance on this point, whilst the Prince of Bevern attacked the left wing of the French. These columns advanced steadily against the cavalry of the enemy, without noticing the heavy fire of artillery, which came in an oblique direction on their flank.

The cavalry would not await their attack, but rushed upon the advancing infantry, who received them with firmness, were not thrown into disorder, and kept up such a continued fire, that the cavalry were forced to take to flight in great disorder. Other bodies of cavalry renewed the attack, but with the same result; this was repeated, but they were always driven back; at last the *cuirassiers* and *gensd'armes* advanced, who broke the English line, but were immediately driven back.

The infantry not only kept their ground, but continued to advance, resisting all the attacks of the cavalry. The Saxons in the French

Army distinguished themselves on this day; in consequence of a spirited attack from them the English were thrown into disorder, but they speedily formed again, and drove the Saxons back. The flight of the French cavalry had broken the line; the brigades of French infantry next to them were without support, and their flank exposed. Broglio endeavoured to advance with his men, who had been repulsed, to the centre where there was nothing but confusion. This was the important moment, when the whole French army might have been annihilated; courage and science had prepared the way for it, and the greatest defeat of the French during this century seemed certain, when the faithlessness of an English general saved them from complete destruction.

The infantry had done everything in their power, and it now only depended on the cavalry to complete their work. Ferdinand sent the necessary orders to Lord Sackviile, who commanded the English and German cavalry. This Englishman, unworthy of his country, but who was neither wanting in talent nor personal bravery, was jealous of Duke Ferdinand; he was the only person in the whole army who was an unwilling spectator of the advantages gained this day, and this because they were in opposition to his secret views; his object was to take from the reputation of Ferdinand, and although possessing no talents in the field, thus to lead the way to gaining the command himself. The love of his country even gave way to his envy.

He pretended that he did not understand the orders of the commander in chief; three *aides-de-camp*, of whom two were English, brought him one after another, the most express orders to advance, but in vain. He remained stationary, till at last, having lost the valuable opportunity, he rode himself in search of the Duke for an explanation, which any subaltern could have given him. Ferdinand astonished and displeased at his orders not being fulfilled, sent the same request to the Marquis of Granby, who was the second in command. The *marquis* came up immediately, and then Sackville placed himself at the head of these troops; but the moment was passed, and Broglio had made the best use of this delay, in order to draw off his men, and he was followed by the rest of the French troops of the left wing.

During this time the right wing of the allies had been hotly engaged; the Prussian, Hanoverian and Hessian cavalry had driven back the French infantry, cut down large numbers of them, and taken many prisoners; the rest sought safety in flight. Broglio covered the retreat of the right wing towards Minden, and the Saxons, who were in tolerable order in spite of their great losses, covered that of the fugitives of the left wing.

The loss of the French in this battle was 8000 killed, wounded and taken prisoners, a number of cannon and many stand of colours; in addition to this, a few days afterwards a great quantity of their baggage, a part of the military chest and many military papers fell into the hands of the allies; the latter also took possession of the magazines of Osnabrück, Minden, Bielefeld and Paderborn, and only lost 1300 killed and wounded. Contades wrote to the duke, immediately after the battle, and, as victor, requested him to take care of the wounded French; a request quite unnecessary to this noble and generous leader.

Ferdinand received the order of the garter inconsequence of this victory, and King George sent him 20,000 pounds; this the generous commander did not appropriate, but distributed a great portion of it amongst his officers and men. One Prussian regiment which had taken four battalions prisoners, and ten pieces of cannon, received several thousand dollars for their share. In addition to this, he thanked the officers and the different regiments for their assistance and their brave conduct during the battle. Ferdinand was too noble minded to express his displeasure at Sackville's conduct on so public an occasion, and contented himself with omitting the name of this general, at a moment when he praised all others.

But he expressed himself in strong terms of admiration at Granby's conduct, and gave it to be understood how much he regretted that this officer, who gave such fair promise, was not at the head of the British cavalry. Sackville was now recalled, and returned to England, where he trembled for his fate, expecting that it might be the same as that of Admiral Bing, who had been shot three years previously. The people threatened to tear him to pieces, he was abandoned by his friends, and the king, George the Second, would not allow his name to be mentioned in his presence. He was deprived of his military rank, and the king with his own hand struck his name from the list of privy councillors.

He was tried by a court martial, and he defended himself on the plea, that Ferdinand was envious of him, and had sent him different and contrary orders, in order to cause his ruin. He was found guilty, dismissed the service, and declared incapable of holding any command in future. The first time his father, the old and grey headed Duke of Dorset, came to court after this affair, and approached the king, oppressed with grief, the king embraced him, and said: "it grieves me, my lord, that you have such a son as Sackville."

This is the same Lord Sackville, who, under the title of Lord St. Germain, was in office during the reign of George the Third, and it was through his orders that General Burgogne and his whole army were sacrificed at Saratoga, which misfortune caused the loss of America to the English.

On the very day of the Battle of Minden, another engagement was fought by the Hereditary Prince of Brunswick at Gohfeld. Ferdinand now acted in a manner which astonished both friend and foe; for when he was on the point of fighting a battle with a force, far superior to his own, he had nevertheless weakened his own by sending the Hereditary Prince with 10,000 men against the Duke of Brissac. In order to take the enemy in the rear, he had to cross the Werra, over which there was only one very narrow bridge; in consequence of this only one portion of his troops could go over the bridge, and the remainder waded through the river in order to lose no time. The plan of attack was so well arranged, that early in the morning, and when they were not at all prepared for battle, the enemy found themselves surrounded, and were forced to seek safety in a hurried flight, after fighting desperately for some time. They lost all their baggage, and the slaughter was so great that 2000 peasants were employed for three days in burying the dead The loss of the allies was only 300 men.

The actions of a general after a battle are the best criterion of his greatness as a soldier, and Ferdinand showed himself, in this instance, worthy of his high reputation; and the consequences of this day, so remarkable by its two victories, were most disadvantageous to the French. Contades was forced to give up his strong position near Minden, to evacuate Hessia, and to cross the Weser; he was followed and constantly harassed by the enemy, in his passage through a country badly supplied with previsions, and was at last forced to give up all the advantages he had gained in the previous part of the campaign. General Armentieres, who had invested the town of Lippstadt, was forced to leave this place to join the main army.

Minden surrendered to the allies, and large supplies of provisions as well as a number of prisoners fell into their hands. In Detmold, the camp hospital of the French fell into the hands of the victorious enemy, as well as the escort 800 strong. The Prince of Holstein took prisoners, at one time, the whole battalion of the king's grenadiers; several engagements now followed in which the advantage was in favour of the allies. The Hereditary Prince attacked a large body, near the small town of Wetter, cut down a great number, and also took many prisoners; only a few saved themselves by flight; another body was attacked by the light troops, under Colonel Lückner, and defeated with considerable loss. Cassel surrendered to the Hanoverian General Freytag, who made himself also master of the baggage of Marshall Contades, the Prince of Centi, the Duke of Brissac and the other principal French generals, not far from Detmold.

Marburg which offered resistance was besieged, and after the trenches had been opened five days, surrendered with its garrison of 900 French; the fortified town of Ziegenhain was also taken.

Amongst the baggage of Marshall Contades was found his writing case, which contained the private letters and secret instructions of his court; these were published by order of the King of England, and contained, among other directions, the order to lay waste those provinces of which they could not retain possession But what was still more extraordinary than these orders, was the French manifesto which followed their publication, in which, it is true, they did not deny the authenticity of these letters, but rather the inference which was drawn from their contents, and although this was any thing but obscure, they wished to make it appear different from what was supposed; an explanation which was more laughable than well judged. In this they said, that many passages, which redounded to the honour of the French ministry, were left out in the publication of the letters, and that one of these was couched in these words:

> To be careful that the country was not devastated that no excesses by pillage, or the raising of contributions should be allowed, and to use the utmost endeavours that everyone should have cause to be satisfied.

This manifesto, which was a mockery upon the understanding of all sensible people, did not explain how it was, that in the midst of the most oppressive acts, which drew tears from thousands day and night, and reduced so many men to despair in these devastated provinces, general advantage and good will was to be obtained.

General Imhof was now sent to Münster; he invested the town for some time, and then proceeded to besiege it regularly; but upon the advance of General Armentieres he was forced to raise the siege. He again invested the town, after receiving reinforcements, and in spite of the advance of the French, the town surrendered six days after the trenches had been opened. The garrison were allowed to withdraw, but were forced to leave their cannon, baggage and provisions in the hands of the enemy. This occurred on the 20th of November, the same day which was so unfortunate for the Prussians at Maxen, and on which the English Admiral Hawke destroyed the French fleet on the coast of France during a dreadful storm; a combat which was the most extraordinary which had ever been fought at sea.

Imhof found the fortifications at Münster in such a dreadful state, that the town appeared to him hardly tenable; nevertheless he garrisoned it with 5000 men, and returned to the main army. Notwithstanding the lateness of the season, the campaign was not yet at an end; the taking by surprise of Fulda followed shortly after, in which place the Duke of Würtemberg was with his troops. The duke had placed 12,000 men in the pay of the French, and they were encamped near to the town. He so little expected an attack that he had invited the ladies of Fulda to a ball, which was on the point of commencing, when the Hereditary Duke of Brunswick appeared at the gates with his dragoons and hussars. He rushed into the town, a number of the enemy were cut down, and those who resisted were dispersed, and 1,200 prisoners were taken. The Duke of Würtemberg escaped, and withdrew with his troops from the neighbourhood of Fulda.

After this the hereditary prince went into Saxony to join the army of the King of Prussia, and in consequence of this, the French formed a plan for attacking the army of the allies in the camp. But the defeat of Minden had caused great disunion between Marshal Contades and the Duke de Broglio, and each was anxious to throw blame on the other. The court of Versailles alarmed at their discomfiture, and anxious about the disunion of their generals, sent the Marshal D'Estrées with full powers, in the name of the king, to put a stop to the dissensions of these generals, and to form the necessary plans for the future operations of the war. D'Estrées was so noble minded, that he explained to Contades, that he was not come to be commander in chief, but to serve under him; that he would give him his advice when he required it, but in all else he would obey him.

The endeavours of the old field-marshal to reconcile the two rivals were, however, in vain, and the court soon put an end to their disputes by recalling Contades; Broglio was created field-marshal, and made commander in chief of the army. The new marshal was anxious by his deeds to show himself worthy of the honours which had been bestowed on him by the king, and determined, in spite of the severity of the season, to endeavour, on the 25th of December, to surprise the enemy. Ferdinand, who had invested Giessen, and placed his troops in cantonments, was on his guard, and was so well prepared to receive the French, that after a heavy cannonade they withdrew. The misfortunes of Maxen, which rendered it necessary to send troops to reinforce the army in Saxony, prevented Ferdinand from reaping the success he had expected from his fortunate campaign.

The allies having been set in activity by the attempt of the French, did the enemy all the injury they possibly could, and their light troops did good service in all these attacks. This was not the case with those of the French army; and it is extraordinary that the French never excelled fn this kind of warfare, for however much they endeavoured to shine in these skirmishing parties, as well as in the field of battle, they were never able to gain any success of importance; and it would appear, from the manner in which their plans were formed by the superiors, or executed by the officers and common soldiers, that this is a kind of warfare not suited to this nation, who cannot, from their natural vivacity, remain in that state of coolness and watchfulness, which is then necessary.

This made the French feel the more harassed by the skirmishing of the enemy, who allowed them no repose, and which was carried on at this time with great activity and success. Parties of French were constantly attacked, their magazines threatened, their provisions intercepted, and a number of prisoners taken, until at last the excessive cold rendered it absolutely necessary to put a stop to these expeditions, and to remain in winter quarters.

Fresh endeavours were now made to procure peace; England had gained much, and Prussia had not sustained any great loss, for Saxony replaced to the latter the provinces which remained in the hands of the enemy, and in spite of ail the misfortunes they had experienced, the Prussians were still as formidable as ever. With the exception of Dresden, Frederic was in possession of all the places and territory which he had had the previous winter, and his position was such as he had reason to rejoice in. The good fortune of his allies had reached a much higher point; setting aside the campaign in Germany, the English had gained great advantages in America, and in India; had almost annihilated the navy of France, and it was to be expected that in the case of the war continuing, they would gain still greater advantages at the expense of the French.

In spite of this, these allied monarchs made proposals for a peace, and the first overtures were made at the Hague. King Stanislaus, who having twice received, and twice lost the crown of Poland, was now living in philosophic retirement, offered his residence of Nancy as the place of meeting, for settling the preliminaries. With this, both Frederic and King George were satisfied, and the former wrote from his headquarters at Freyberg:

> I gladly accept this offer, and receive it with many thanks. Any negotiations which may be carried on, under the auspices of your majesty, must have a happy termination. But it is not every one who is peaceably inclined. The courts of Vienna and St. Petersburg have rejected, in an extraordinary manner, the proposals which the King of England and I have made. It is to be presumed that these courts will induce the King of France to continue the war, from which they hope to ensure the most successful results. But they will have to answer for all the blood which may be shed. Would that all princes, like your majesty, would listen to the voice of humanity, virtue and justice! This world would then no longer offer such spectacles of murder and devastation.

The opponents of the king gave but very indefinite answers to these propositions. Breda was first proposed as a place of meeting, and afterwards Leipsic, but without any favourable result. His enemies hoped every thing from their extensive coalition, and they therefore never even made any demonstration of setting earnestly to work to make peace. On the contrary, they made the best use of the winter, to increase their army, and repair the losses they had sustained during the preceding campaign. Frederic now followed their example, but he had much greater difficulties to contend with; his opponents ruled a population of ninety million of men, and the number of his subjects barely reached five million; the kingdom of Prussia, besides other provinces of his dominions, was in the hands of his enemies, and from these he could not expect to recruit his armies; but Saxony in a great measure replaced these losses, and was a prolific source from which he continually drew money, provisions and soldiers.

The levies of men and the contributions of the products of the land, which were raised in this unfortunate state, and in Thuringia, were enormous, and it was always requisite from policy, to have them in advance. In the year 1760 the town of Erfurt supplied 400 men, 500 horses, and paid 100,000 dollars; Naumburg paid 200,000 dollars, and Merseburg 120,300 dollars, 631 men and upwards of four hundred horses. When they were unable to make up the number of men and horses, they had to pay in money, fifty dollars for a horse, and 150 for a man. Zwickau paid 80,000, Chemnitz 215,000, the towns in Thuringia together had to make up the sum of 930,000, and the circle of Thuringia 1,375,840 dollars. The war tax levied on the town of Leipsic alone was 1,100,000, and the circle of Leipsic 2,000,000 dollars in money, 10,000 recruits, some hundred thousand bushels of wheat, many thousand horses and an immense number of cattle for slaughter. The forests were sold to enterprising capitalists, to defray these expenses.

The forest of Torgau, the finest in Germany, shared this fate, and its position on the banks of the Elb facilitated its destruction, as the wood was all floated to Hamburg. The farmers were obliged to pay their rents, throughout the Electorate, a year in advance, and by these means, there was less scarcity of money felt by the King of Prussia, than of men. The number of deserters was too great from Frederic's army, for his own states and Saxony to entirely replace them, and he was forced, contrary to his inclination, to have recourse to a system of impressment which from its nature and extent is without parallel. Soldiers, who were taken prisoners, were forced to enter the Prussian service; they were not even asked if they would serve; they were driven into the ranks, and forced to take the oath of fidelity, and thus made to fight against their country.

The whole of the German Empire was overrun with Prussian crimps, and the greater part of these were adventurers who made use of every artifice to ensnare men. Colonel Colignon, who was fitted by disposition for such an office, was at their head, and instructed them by his example. He travelled about in every direction, changing his dress, and persuading men by hundreds to enter the Prussian service. He not only promised, but actually gave papers, in which he nominated young students and shopmen, as officers in the army, either in the cavalry, *cuirassiers*, or the hussars; they had only to choose. The fame of the Prussian arms was so great, and so combined with the prospect of great booty, that Colignon was fully employed in giving commissions. He was put to no expense by this, and in fact saved money, for most of his recruits travelled at their own expense.

In Franconia, Swabia, and on the banks of the Rhine, sons robbed their fathers, shopmen their masters, and overseers stole from the cash box in order to seek out the generous Prussian officer, who gave away commissions. They hurried with them to Magdeburg where they were received as recruits and distributed among the different regiments. Resistance was useless, for the stick was used until they obeyed. In this manner, and by other such means Colignon and his underlings procured 60,000 recruits for the king during the war.

The activity of the king and the emulation of his officers, in addition to the sums of money which were at his disposal, enabled him to overcome obstacles, which in Vienna and St. Petersburg were considered insurmountable. In the beginning of the war the prisoners were exchanged on both sides, as between the Prussians and Austrians at Jägersdorf in April 1758, and afterwards between the Russians and the Prussians in October 1759. On these occasions a field-marshal was reckoned as equivalent to 3000 men or 15,000 florins, a colonel as 130 men or 650 florins, and a common soldier at the sum of five florins. But they soon acted on a different principle; convinced that the want of soldiers must put an end to Frederic's operations, these exchanges became in the first instance more difficult, and were at last entirely put a stop to.

In spite of all this, things took their usual course, and at the commencement of every campaign, the Prussian regiments were generally complete. Those regiments whose recruiting stations were not in the power of the enemy, had their full complement of men. No soldier, unless sick or on especial service, was allowed to be absent from the general muster, which usually took place in the spring, previous to leaving winter quarters. The regiments which had been entirely lost at Maxen were replaced by the sick of these very regiments, and those who had been on other service, together with men who had ransomed themselves, and also by fresh recruits. Such were the means by which Frederic made up the complement of his men, and did away with all traces of his previous misfortunes.

It was in the month of August of this year, that Ferdinand the Sixth, King of Spain, died. Charles, King of Naples, now ascended the throne of Spain, and his son Francis the Fourth, who was only eight years old, that of Naples. The house of Austria had strong pretentions to the kingdom of Naples and Sicily, which they had only resigned from necessity; but their claims upon Parma and Placentia were even greater, and there never was a better opportunity of making them available. The king was but a child, the reins of government but loosely held, the statesmen without good principles, the finances at a low ebb and the troops few in number and without discipline.

It was merely requisite to take possession of these dominions, and every thing promised, that at least they would be able to retain them undisturbed for a time. Spain knew as yet nothing of her new monarch, and was not prepared for such a war; France, who was exhausted by the powerful enemies she had to contend with, was quite incapable of sending an army to Italy, and all this led to the serious consideration of such an undertaking among the privy council of the empress. But as state policy was still subservient to private feeling in the court of Vienna, the hopes of recovering Silesia gained the upper-hand, and the certain acquisition of the important kingdoms of Naples and Sicily was neglected, in spite of these states offering such advantages to the empress and her heirs, from their proximity to the other Austrian possessions in Italy; advantages which could not previously have been made available, and which would have insured to them the dominion of Italy for many centuries.

The King of Sardinia had also claims to this valuable inheritance, and Frederic who was anxious to see a war spring up in Italy, sent his *aide-de-camp* Cocceji to Turin to enquire into the sentiments of this monarch; but this king who had formerly been so fond of war, had now exchanged his sword for a rosary. He was old, and had become bigoted, his only ambition being to excel in the exercise of penance; so that this attempt of Frederic as most of his other negotiations to obtain a diversion in his favour fell to the ground. France was anxious to make peace with England, but to the exclusion of the King of Prussia, who sent an envoy to Paris, in the hopes of opening the eyes of the French court to their own advantage, to withdraw her from so disadvantageous an alliance, and to make the French ministry aware how disadvantageous the destruction of Prussia would be to her interests.

But it was in vain; for the Duke of Choiseul, who was in the interest of the empress, and as well as Madame de Pompadour, ruled this court, would not listen to these reasons. The envoy, Baron Edelsheim was at first graciously received, but was afterwards thrown into the Bastille, in order that possession might he obtained of his papers. Frederic also sent a nobleman to St. Petersburg, who was supported by the English ambassador, and was well provided with money; but he was not able to get the better of the hatred of Elizabeth towards the King of Prussia, or of her hopes of retaining possession of the conquest she had made of Prussia. Her favourites and her minister were of the same way of thinking, and all endeavours towards peace were fruitless. In this position of affairs a new ally appeared in the distance as likely to join Frederic.

The King of Danemark feared the proximity of the Russians, as they were now preparing to besiege Colberg, and thus threatened to become masters of the Baltic. These fears, increased by the pretentions of the hereditary grand duke upon Schleswick, and his hatred of Danemark, induced the court of Copenhagen to propose to undertake the defence of Pomerania for the king. But the further consideration of the desperate position of this monarch rendered the Danes, in the first instance undetermined, and at last unwilling to act up to their offer. An excuse was soon found to break off all negotiation; the King of Danemark made proposals and terms, which he was sure would not be acceded to, and this put an end to the affair. Thus was the King of Prussia left with no dependence but his courage, his sword, and his good fortune.

Chapter 8: Campaign of 1760

The plan of operations of the mighty confederation was to drive the King of Prussia to sacrifice either Silesia or Saxony; but this was not adopted by either the court of Vienna or that of St. Petersburg, until after much discussion, as each party was most anxious for its own interests. The French were desirous that the Russians should besiege Stettin, but Soltikow wished to carry on the war in Pomerania. along the sea coast, and insisted, in the first instance, on taking possession of Dantzick: Augustus entreated that Saxony might be restored to him, as quickly as possible, and Austria on the other hand was as solicitous for the conquest of Silesia. In the end, this last was determined on, and Soltikow received orders to invade this province with the Prussian Army, and to besiege Breslau; a plan of operations which was willingly adopted by the court of St. Petersburg, in spite of such an enterprise being rendered almost impossible of success, from the want of the necessaries of war in the Russian Army. To those who are acquainted with the principles of the art of war, it must ever appear extraordinary that it should be proposed to besiege a large town on the Oder, when the cannon for this purpose had to be brought from Bohemia, and the troops from beyond the Vistula.

Frederic undertook to defend Saxony himself, and sent his brother. Henry with a large army of observation, to watch the operations of the Russians, and the Prince of Würtemberg was sent with a small body against the Swedes. This prince had with the Markgraf of Shwedt, been taken prisoner a short time previous to this, by the Cosacks, but had been released by them, much to the dissatisfaction of the court of St. Petersburg. In order to strengthen the army in Saxony, the two regiments of Prussian dragoons were recalled from the army of the allies, and the king informed all his generals, that in this campaign it would more than ever be necessary to make forced marches, in order to constrain the enemy to give battle. He, therefore, ordered them to give their men every encouragement to induce them to bear with firmness and patience the hardships they would have to undergo, and to remind them of the necessity of showing themselves, on every occasion, worthy of the name of Prussians.

In the beginning of this year, Silesia was but weakly provided with defence. The king contented himself by strengthening the different garrisons, and it was on this occasion, that the Pomeranian infantry regiment of Manteufel gave a remarkable instance of its bravery. They marched from their cantonments near Neisse, where they were quartered far from the other troops; Laudon took advantage of this opportunity to advance on them with four cavalry regiments. He sent an officer to offer them to give themselves up as prisoners, and to retain their baggage; but, in case of their refusal to comply with this proposition, he declared his determination to cut them to pieces.

The colonel of the regiment answered, that the officer should hear the reply of the soldiers himself. He led him to the front of the line, and having explained to them in their own dialect the offer of Laudon and his threat, he required their answer; it will not bear repeating but it expressed, at the same time their contempt for their opponents, and their determination to resist rather than comply with their terms; this ran through the ranks, and was repeated by every soldier. Laudon now gave orders to charge them but his men were received with a heavy fire, and the regiment began its march. The attack was repeated several times, but always with the same result, and after continuing during four leagues of their march, the cavalry wearied with their exertions drew off, after having suffered considerable loss.

Laudon now did, what had not as yet been effected by the Austrians, during four campaigns; he opened the present one in the territory of the enemy. The Prussian General Fouquet was encamped, for the protection of Silesia, near Landshut on a number of hills and with entrenchments. In consequence of the increasing strength of the enemy, this position became dangerous, and Fouquet who was anxious to change it, ventured the most earnest representations; but Frederic would not hear of it, in consequence of his following the advice of the Silesian minister Schlaberndorf, not to leave the profitable towns of the mountains without protection, and he sent repeated orders to Fouquet not to quit his position.

Laudon waited until this general was so weakened by different detachments, that his army was only 8000 strong, and then, at the head of 31,000 men, attacked him on five different points. After he had crossed some of the entrenchments, he summoned the Prussian commander, as in a fortified town to surrender. Fouquet answered him by a discharge of artillery, and withdrew from the heights constantly fighting till he collected all his men in the valley.

Here he formed his men into a square, and encouraged them to continue fighting; they defended themselves with the greatest bravery, until completely surrounded, and with their ammunition exhausted, they were forced to surrender, after fighting for eight hours. Fouquet himself was dangerously wounded in the head, and fell to the ground with his horse which was killed. Several of his bravest soldiers drew round him, and fought until they fell at his side. He received two sabre cuts, one in the arm and another in the back, and an Austrian trooper was on the point of giving him his death blow, when he was saved by the fidelity of a common soldier one of his grooms of the name of Trautschke. He threw himself upon his master and received on his body, wounds which were intended for Fouquet; these were not mortal, the man recovered, and his fidelity was well rewarded.

Fouquet would still have fallen a sacrifice had not Trautschke cried out: "Will you kill the general?" upon this Colonel Voit, of the dragoons, rode up and saved him. Everyone, high and low, now paid him every mark of attention, and Colonel Voit had his horse brought for him.

He asked Fouquet to mount, who hesitated and said: "I shall spoil your beautiful saddle with my blood."

Voit answered, "it will become far more valuable from the marks of a hero's blood."

However, one Austrian officer was mean enough to reproach the general with his defeat; this was immediately put a stop to, but Fouquet said: "Do not hinder him from speaking, gentlemen, it is the fate of war; mine today, yours tomorrow."

A small body of Prussians still continued to offer resistance; Colonel Below was at their head, and having formed into a square they resisted all the efforts of the enemy for a considerable time. It was in vain that the cavalry charged them until the Croats came up, to their assistance, and attacking them in the rear, the flanks and in front, forced them to give way and cry out for quarter.

Fouquet was made prisoner with 4000 men for the greater part infantry; 600 Prussians were killed and 1800 were wounded. The cavalry cut their way through the enemy, and a small portion of infantry escaped and reached Breslau, under the escort of the cavalry. The Austrians lost 3000 killed and wounded, and Laudon cast a stain on his victory by the shameful pillage of Landshut. This town which was not fortified, and was prosperous from its linen manufactures, was treated by the Austrians as a town which had been taken by storm, and suffered all the cruelties usual on such an occasion. They were anxious to reward their soldiers in this manner for their bravery, and thus to encourage them to other deeds of valour.

The most important consequence of the battle of Landshut, was the taking of Glatz. This fortified place, which next to Magdeburg, was the most important in the Prussian dominions, and was well provided with stores of provisions and ammunition, had only a garrison of 2400 men, for the most part deserters and foreigners; in addition to this, the commandant was unworthy of his position; an Italian, who had been raised to this rank by chance. All these evils were enhanced by the absence of the king, and it was in this unfortunate position, that the town was besieged in July by General Harsch.

The Austrians had only raised a few batteries, as their chief dependence was upon a communication which they kept up with the Jesuits and monks of the city, who had gained over the Catholic soldiery. The enemy had hardly shown themselves, when the Prussians abandoned the outworks, which were taken possession of by the Croats, and six days after the opening the trenches, the principal works were stormed. The garrison mutinied, whole companies threw down their arms, and in four hours, the whole town and fortifications were in the hands of the Austrians, without any attempt being made to negotiate for terms. The efforts at defence of a few brave soldiers were of no avail, and thus the Austrians became masters of the town, and gained by this conquest, firm footing in Silesia. This province was now undefended by any Prussian army, and Laudon could choose which town he should first besiege.

Frederic, who was not aware of this accumulation of misfortunes, but was in a state of great anxiety with respect to Silesia, wished much to hurry into that province, but at the same time, did not want to leave Daun and his army in Saxony. On the other hand, if he induced the Austrian general to follow him, Frederic feared that the advance of Laudon would place him between two fires; and in addition to this the troops of the Empire were on their march towards Saxony But when the king heard of the investment of Glatz, which Laudon had commenced previous to the battle of Landshut, this dispelled all his doubts, and he crossed the Elb; and having beaten a portion of the Austrians of Lascy's body, advanced to attack the main army of the enemy. Lascy, who did not expect this, retreated in haste and Daun crossed the Elb also. Both armies now began their march towards Silesia, and the heat at this time was so intense, that on one day, the 6th of July, a hundred and five Prussian soldiers fell to the ground, killed by the heat.

All were anxious to procure water, which the soldiers were not permitted to have from the state of perspiration they were in from the weight of their knapsacks. But they no sooner came near a spring, a pond or even a puddle, than thirst got the better of everything, even the fear of punishment, and the men fell out of their ranks. The officers, feeling themselves the same desire, but obliged to obey the orders of their superiors, were forced on this occasion to be more lax in discipline, which at other times was so strict that disobedience was not only punished by blows, but by death.

The army of Daun was always close by the side of the Prussians, and Lascy in the rear with his large army. This induced Frederic, who had just heard of the battle of Landshut, to form the plan of falling upon Lascy with his whole force. He marched back upon Bautzen and directly in the direction of Lascy, who retreated in great haste and finally crossed the Elb and passed through Dresden. The king now determined to besiege this town, for he was convinced that the cautious Daun would not go alone with his army into Silesia, and abandon Lascy to his fate, and his determination in this was strengthened by hearing of the defeat of Fouquet. Daun had continued his march, as he was most anxious to be in Silesia before the king. He imagined, he had gained some marches upon him, when in fact he had lost so much time; and as soon as he heard of the operations of the king, he suspected his design, and retraced his steps.

Dresden was now invested, and the garrison and inhabitants were thrown into the greatest consternation from the place not being strongly fortified; for the old town had no covered way, no ravelin, and but a small ditch, and the new town was only defended by earthen ramparts protected by palisades and without masonry. The Austrians were in a few hours driven out of the royal gardens and the neighbouring suburb; and it is probable, that had the town been stormed at this critical moment, the fate of Dresden would have been soon decided. But the cruelties inseparable from such an attack, especially in a royal residence, probably induced Frederic to abandon such a project, as he hoped by means of negotiations, to become shortly master of this important place. These expectations were frustrated from the

Austrians having opened a communication with the town from the other side of the Elb, by which means they were enabled to throw reinforcements into the town. The answer of the commandant Maquire when he was summoned was, that he would defend himself to the last. The town was now regularly besieged, and this siege formed one of the most remarkable occurrences of the war.

The Prussians began to fire on the town on the 14th of July from both sides of the Elb, and on the same day the garrison set fire to the piles of wood on the banks of the river, that it might not be used to fill up the ditch; the fire extended, and burnt many houses. As the heavy artillery of the Prussians was not yet come up, they in the first instance, made use of the twelve pounders, howitzers and red hot shot. The fire which had considerably extended was now extinguished by the means which were used, and in which the Jews who were residing in the town, were made to do the principle part of the work. In the hope that the fear of burning this capital, which was the residence of an ally whose territory they were anxious to protect, would induce the Austrians to surrender, the fire of the besiegers was in the first instance more directed against the town than against the ramparts.

The *commandant*, who had his instructions from high authority, did not allow them to remain in the dark on this point; he defended himself, supported by the whole Austrian army, which came up a few days after, and passed continually from the new to the old town as if it had not been besieged. They had driven the small body of Prussians under the command of the Prince of Holstein and who had occupied this side of the Elb at a distance from the king, from their position with considerable loss. The advantages gained by this communication being opened would necessarily render abortive all the attempts of the besiegers. Large bodies of Austrians marched into the town and made sorties, while the garrison remained in repose. Frederic, who had protected the towns of Prague and Olmütz, when besieged by him, as much as he possibly could, now determined to try if the certainty of seeing Dresden a heap of ashes in a few days, would not induce the Austrians to retreat.

The heavy artillery now came up from Magdeburg, and shells were constantly thrown into the town. The inhabitants begged for mercy, and knew not where to turn in their distress. In the houses they were in danger of being crushed, burnt, or suffocated, and in the streets, the cannon balls threatened them constantly with death. The suburb near the Wilsdruf gate, which had escaped in the previous siege, was now set fire to, that the enemy might approach nearer the ramparts. The fire raged furiously, both within and without the town, and many of the streets were in flames from one end to the other. Palaces, which would have been an ornament to any city in Europe, became a prey to the flames; lofty houses fell to the ground on every side, and many of the inhabitants were buried in the ruins, while others abandoned everything to save their lives.

What tended to increase the misery of the unfortunate inhabitants of Dresden, was the rapine of the Austrian garrison, which did more mischief than even the flames and the cannon of the enemy. A number of the cellars and warehouses under ground in this city were bomb proof, and to these many hundreds of families brought all their valuables; these stores were secured by all the entrances being either locked or bricked up, and the inhabitants sacrificing the rest of their property, fled for safety into the vineyards or neighbouring towns and villages; but their hopes of again recovering their property, in consequence of these precautions, were deceived; for their allies, the Austrians broke into these places, and took everything they could lay their hands on.

Many of these wretches were hanged, but it was to little purpose; to such an extent did the want of discipline reach and so unrestrained was the conduct of those who were to protect the town. Literature was also a sufferer by their conduct; for some important manuscripts of the famous Rabener fell into the hands of the Croats. Rabener complained bitterly of this loss and could never be persuaded by his friends to again commence the works which were destroyed: "he did not wish," he said, "to deprive the rogues of the satisfaction they had had during the siege of Dresden."

The bombardment of the town was continued, and a number of shells fell upon the Kreutzkirche, one of the oldest and most beautiful churches in Saxony. The strong old tower resisted for a long time, but at last it gave way, destroyed the roof of the church as well as the interior, and also many houses in the neighbourhood; the raging flames completed the work of destruction, which was caused from the Prussians having considered it as a battery, in consequence of some cannon which stood on the tower and was used on fete days, having been fired on the besiegers.

Although only a few shot had been fired, the tower was considered as a battery which must be destroyed; there were now no bounds to the devastation, as no orders were given for the protection of the other churches, which from their height served as a mark for the cannon of the enemy; and the beautiful dome of the church of Our Lady was often fired at, but in consequence of the form of the Cupola, the balls generally glanced off, and did but little damage.

The principal anxiety of the inhabitants was directed towards the protection of their persons, and the numerous reports of whole families being buried under their houses, added to the scarcity, which was beginning to be felt, induced all, whatever their rank in society, to think of moving away. In consequence of the communication having been restored with the new town, and there being, in that quarter, no danger from the shells, the people were there congregated in the houses, in such numbers, that the lofts were full of them; but a very great number left the town entirely. The roads were crowded with people; old men and women borne to the ground by their infirmities, lent upon their staff or on the arm of their sons or daughters, who, loaded with what they could save, had difficulty in getting along; women who from their childhood had been accustomed to every comfort, now went their weary way on foot with their infants at their breasts, and their children in tears; many found comfort in offering up prayers to heaven, which they did aloud, and they mutually offered consolation to each other.

But the burning town, the hunger which distressed them, and the prospect of the increasing misery, was sufficient to destroy all worldly hope. In consequence of the scarcity of horses and means of conveyance, many who had been brought up in luxury, were forced to carry their property on their own shoulders; beautiful and elegant women, of whom there were so many in this city, were seen loaded like packhorses; the weak and sickly were carried on barrows by their friends; all the customs and refinements of high and polite society were at an end in this time of horror and distress.

The besieged had quite a sufficient number of cannon, and these were well served; but they were unable to silence the batteries of the Prussians, in consequence of the latter having placed them behind the heaps of ashes, formed by the houses which had been burnt. On the 19th of August, in one single day, upwards of 1400 shells and balls were thrown into the town; every part of it was on fire, and it was impossible to endeavour to extinguish the flames, in consequence of the pipes for the supply of water having been cut off by the besiegers. The besieged constantly made sorties, many of which were very successful; and from their always receiving fresh reinforcements, they could make vigorous and extended attacks; they drove the Prussians several times as far back as the trenches, spiked the cannon, and brought prisoners back into Dresden.

Frederic, who was annoyed at these disasters, laid the blame of them on the Bernburg regiment, and charged them with not having sufficiently defended themselves, and having given way too soon to the superior numbers of the enemy. The punishment he inflicted was without example in the annals of Prussian warfare; the common soldiers had their side arms taken from them, and the officers and non-commissioned officers had the lace taken off their caps; the soldiers marched the easier for being deprived of this encumbrance, and the officers did not miss the ornament of their caps; but the effects of it were very great on the minds of soldiers anxious to distinguish themselves.

This regiment which had been raised by the celebrated Prince Leopold of Dessau, and had often given the greatest proofs of courage and discipline, were extremely distressed and bowed down by these marks of degradation; and many of the officers, convinced of having done their duty, requested their dismissal, but which in every case was refused. In France, and indeed in most other countries, an officer can retire from the service, when he wishes; on the contrary, in the Prussian army, where all the officers nave so much emulation to distinguish themselves, it was the custom under the command of Frederic that all should be directed by compulsion, which is not always compatible with honour; this phantom, which has so much influence on the actions of men.

One is too much inclined to look upon every action of a great man, as the consequence of deeply considered principles; but it is allowable to class this system of the king's, as one of his faults; as being contrary to the dictates of reason and experience, and which, in the first instance caused by accident, was afterwards acted on as a principle. The life of this monarch is full of such examples, which are unnoticed by his panegyrists, are unwillingly collected by philosophers, and yet hardly come within the province of the historian.

We must now return to the siege of Dresden, which was only continued for the sake of honour. The Austrians were most anxious to see it terminated, and made an attempt, in conjunction with the troops of the Empire, to surprise the army of the king, which protected the besiegers. The headquarters were in a farm house near the village of Gruna, which was but weakly defended by outposts, and at some distance from the camp; this appeared favourable for their scheme, and the enemy flattered themselves with the prospect of taking the king prisoner, and renewing the scene of Hochkirch. The attack was to have been made at day break, but the plan failed in spite of the rapidity of their operations; the light troops of the Austrians advanced, drove back the advanced posts, and the king had only time to mount his horse, and leave the village.

But this was the extent of their progress; for with a celerity, almost incredible, the Prussians were under arms to oppose the enemy; and, in three minutes, several thousand men, who had previously been in complete repose, were now in the greatest activity; they were asleep in their tents, and the whole line were in repose, when at the first gleam of the rising sun, they were aroused by the cry "to arms," and in a moment they were in order of battle. (The author was an eye witness of this scene).

The soldiers rushed out of their tents half dressed, formed in the ranks, and advanced against the enemy who now withdrew in haste, as Daun was not desirous of a general engagement.

The *Uhlans* distinguished themselves highly on this occasion, and deserve to be more especially noticed. They belong to a separate and not numerous people living in Poland, and who, in spite of being surrounded by Christians, preserve not only their customs and their manners, but also their religion; distinguished by their courage and fidelity, they had fought in all the wars of Poland against the Republic, and were now in the pay of Augustus under the command of Major Schiebel, a Saxon officer who had seen much service; they were dressed in the Turkish fashion, and armed with lances; wherever these *Uhlans* were, they harassed the advanced posts and rear guard of the Prussians, and like the Parthians fought as they fled.

This attempt on the part of the Austrians necessitated a change in the position of the army of the king. The camp was moved from the large garden, and in order to strengthen the left flank of this new position a *barricado* was here formed. The magnificent trees, which were so beautiful and invaluable from their age and their rarity, and formed with their branches such delightful walks, were cut down, and this beautiful garden which was always open to the inhabitants, and was an ornament to the city, was in a few hours laid completely waste; the marble statues, which ornamented the garden, had been taken away by the besieged, and the collection of antiques, the most beautiful and valuable on this side of the Alps, were buried in this very garden; the Prussians were not aware of this fact, and these works of art were preserved for the Saxons.

The siege was not carried on with any vigour from the time that the position of the army was changed, and all hopes of taking Dresden were given up. In addition to the many impediments, which lay in the way of success, was added the loss of a considerable supply of ammunition and corn, the cargo of eight vessels, which were coming from Magdeburg, but which fell into the hands of the Austrians; provisions were also beginning to be scarce in the Prussian camp, in consequence of the enemy being masters of the Elb, so that it was difficult for supplies to be brought in.

When Frederic was on the point of raising the siege he heard of the taking of Glatz, which the besieged celebrated by a *feu de joie*; the king learnt this piece of bad news from the Austrian General Nugent, who had been taken prisoner during a sortie. His dismay in the first instance was very great, as from the strength of the place the intelligence was quite unexpected; but he soon recovered himself, and said: "Well! be it so. When peace comes they must give it back again. We must go into Silesia, that all may not be lost." Laudon, with his usual activity, was anxious to make the most of this advantage, and besieged Breslau; this news hastened the departure of the king, and on the 30th of July in a night of storm and rain, the Prussians withdrew from before Dresden. The fire in the trenches was kept up from a few cannon, which gradually diminished, and at last ceased; the king now quitted his camp, and marched towards Meissen.

Thus ended the siege of Dresden, which had cost the Prussians a loss of 1478 killed and wounded, and 261 prisoners; six churches, 416 large houses and public buildings were reduced to ashes, and 115 were damaged, in this city. A number of the inhabitants were killed, others reduced to beggary; many hundreds who had been raised to independence by the industry and care of their parents had now nothing to depend on; relations were forced to separate, the men to seek their bread in a distant land, and girls who had been used to be waited on were forced to seek a livelihood. The ashes have been removed, and houses and palaces are again built; but Dresden is not what it was.

The unsuccessful enterprise against Dresden was the last link of the chain of misfortunes, which had encompassed the king for the last twelve months. As the campaign of 1757 is without example in the annals of warfare, there it no instance, in which a monarch was subject to such a continuance of discomfiture, in so short a time, without being completely driven out of the field. The battle which was lost at Kai in July 1759 against the Russians was the signal for a continued series of misfortunes; it was followed by the defeat of Kunersdorf, and the loss of Dresden; Fink was taken with his army at Maxen, and Dierke with his men at Meissen; then came the winter campaign with its epidemic; the battle of Landshut, and the loss of Glatz; to crown all came the failure of the siege of Dresden.

The king now marched towards Silesia, and Daun who had taken care to throw as many impediments as possible in his way, had sent his light troops to destroy all the bridges over the Röder, Spree, Neisse and Queis, and to render all the roads towards Silesia impassable, by means of *barricadoes*. Frederic surmounted all these difficulties, and continued his march to the relief of Breslau, which was besieged by Laudon. The king, who knew how to select his generals, with the discrimination of genius, very seldom made use of this judgment in the choice of the commandants of his fortresses; he either left it to chance, or the order of their names and rank, whether the place should be under the command of such an officer as the one at Glatz, or under that of a Heyden; unacquainted with each he was equally astounded at the disgraceful conduct of the first, and the noble bearing of the latter, who from being attached to a garrison regiment, was as yet not called into service in the field, and who, from his rank was not eligible to a high command; who not being of an ambitious character would have passed his life unnoticed in a small town, but whose rare courage repeatedly overthrew the plans of the Russians.

At this time fortune was in favour of Frederic; the king's body guard, which had been nearly all cut to pieces at Kollin, was now again completed, and had their headquarters at Breslau; their colonel, General Tauenzien, was consequently commandant of the capital of Silesia. This general, who had been educated in the military school of Potsdam, and grown gray in the service, combined the highest feelings of honour, with the greatest courage, intelligence and talents; and he required all these capabilities to be united in his single person in a position which has perhaps never had its equal. Laudon was before the town with 50,000 Austrians, and in it there were 9000 Austrian prisoners, ready to break loose; to resist this enemy, within and without the walls, Tauenzien had only 3000 men, and of this small garrison, 2000 were deserters or impressed soldiers and invalids; his whole dependence was placed on 1000 men of the body guard, most of whom were foreigners, and many of them served unwillingly from the smallness of their pay, and were only kept in their ranks by the principles of honour and discipline.

Laudon was not without fears that the approaching army of the Prussians might prevent him from the execution of his project, which he wished to effect without the assistance of the Russians. He was unprovided with the necessary battering train and ammunition, and the ditch of the fortifications was filled with water, which prevented all thoughts of taking the town by storm; nothing therefore remained but to negotiate, or force it to surrender by fire. He summoned the town to surrender, and made use of these reasons that:

> Breslau was a commercial town, and not a fortress; it was therefore contrary to the usage of warfare to defend the town against a superior force; that the king was on the other side of the Elb, and Prince Henry near the Wartha; the Russians would appear before the town, in two days, to the number of 75,000, and that he thought they would prefer falling into the hands of the Austrians to those of the Russians; the garrison should have their own terms, but if they resisted the town should be set on fire by shells from five and forty mortars.

Tauenzien answered in a few words that:

> Breslau was a fortified place, and that he would meet the enemy on the ramparts, even if the town were reduced to ashes.

Laudon now endeavoured to incite the citizens against the commandant, and wrote to the president of the magistrates, Conradi; he expressed his sympathy for the innocent inhabitants, and at the same time did not forget the forty-five mortars, or the 75,000 Russians who were on the march; but such a letter could have but little effect in a town, in which Tauenzien was at the head of its defenders, and the letter remained unanswered. Laudon again summoned the town, and increased his threats; he said: "that the child in its mother's womb should not be spared;" Tauenzien answered: "Neither I, nor my soldiers are pregnant;" after this the bombardment began. The commandant took such efficient measures against the enemy, in the town as well as out of it, that their efforts were useless; and as Laudon's head quarters could be reached, by means of loading the culverins with large charges, he let him have no rest, but forced him to withdraw farther off by throwing shot into his sitting room.

Tauenzien, who was aware of his own weakness, and could not be certain of being relieved, now assembled the officers of the king's guard, stated to them his position and the possibility that the enemy might be able to take the town sword in hand before the arrival of the king; that in case of this, he intended to retire to a portion of the fortifications, with the guard, and defend themselves to the last; and thus, as he said, the world would be spared the spectacle of seeing the whole of Frederic's body guard taken prisoners; the officers all agreed to this noble proposition, and determined to die fighting.

Fortunately it did not come to this extremity, for Prince Henry was approaching by forced marches, and Laudon was compelled to beg of Soltikow, who was eighteen leagues distant, to hurry his approach. He nevertheless made one more attempt to induce the commandant to surrender, and offered to agree to any terms he should ask for. The officer who was sent on this mission, Colonel Rouvroi, placed in the strongest light, the position of the king as being at a great distance, and also the vicinity of the devastating Russians; in addition to this the advantages to be derived from being allowed to withdraw his forces, with other military honours which would be granted; all which, he said, would justify the commandant in the eyes of the world and his king. Tauenzien answered:

I have no idea of the honour of a commandant who surrenders a fortified place, before a breach in the walls is made. It is not usual to commence a siege by destroying the property of the inhabitants; the setting fire to the town has not induced me to alter my determination; on the contrary, it has strengthened it.

"If that be the case," answered Rouvroi, "we will now open the trenches."

"I have long been in expectation, that you would do so," said the other, and they then separated.

This last conference put an end to the negotiations; for on the following day Laudon raised the siege, which he, in the opinion even of his friends, ought never to have began, and in which his dependence was principally on his good fortune in war. The siege had only lasted five days, but in this time much damage had been done; to repair this loss, the king made the inhabitants a present of 50,000 dollars.

The rapid march of Prince Henry not only saved Breslau, but also the whole province, as the Russian Army were already in the centre of Silesia, and only two leagues from the capital; the plan of their leader being, to form a junction with the Austrians, and he had reckoned on the taking of Breslau, that he might provide his army with provisions, from its large magazines, during the remainder of the campaign; but these expectations were deceived by the operations of Prince Henry, and Soltikow did not venture to cross the Oder. Time was invaluable to both parties, for Frederic; anxious for the fate of Breslau, was advancing at a rapid pace; he had left Hulsen with a large body in Saxony, and in face of the Austrian army had crossed the Elb, the Spree, the Neisse, the Queis and the Bober, and passed between the armies of Riedesel and Lascy; the last following him at a distance of six leagues, and the main body of the Austrians being always in advance. The king said in his own account:

> A stranger who observed the march of these different bodies, might easily be deceived, and imagine it was only one army. He would take the army of Daun for the advanced guard, that of the king for the main body, and Lascy's troops for the rear guard.

Notwithstanding the king had a train of two thousand provision waggons with him, and that all the bridges had been destroyed, he was still able to march forty leagues in five days, and reached the Silesian frontier without loss. Daun avoided every chance of coming to a battle, and at last formed a junction with the army of Laudon, in order, if possible, to prevent the king from uniting with his brother Henry, and to cut him off from Schweidnitz and Breslau; Frederic and Daun remained near one another, being only separated by a small stream, called the Katzbach.

The immense superiority of the army of the enemy, which was 100,000 strong, in opposition to the king's of 30,000, forced him to change his position very often, in order to force the enemy to give way, and to insure himself, by activity and watchfulness, from any enterprise on their part; in addition to this, he always remained near the enemy, that they might not attack Prince Henry, who was watching the operations of the Russians. Near Goldberg, the Prussian hussars made themselves masters of a great part of the baggage of the enemy, amongst which was all the travelling baggage of Lascy. The king would not allow this to be meddled with, but sent it back, with a flag of truce, as well as a beautiful Tyrolese girl, who belonged to Lascy's suite. The only thing that was retained was a very good chart of all the Austrian operations and camps, during the campaigns of 1758 and 59; when Lascy enquired for this chart, he was answered that it should be returned, as soon as it was copied.

The Russians, who still continued on the other side of the Oder, not far from Breslau, and were much dissatisfied with the cautious conduct of the Austrians, thought, that as they had not hindered the Prussians from crossing the Elb, the Spree and the Bober, that they would allow them to pass the Oder to form a junction with Prince Henry, and thus fall on them with their whole force, "it will cost the king but little trouble, and only one of his usual marches to effect this," said Soltikow; he therefore expressed his determination to withdraw to Poland, so soon as the kind should cross the Oder.

This threat forced Daun to venture a battle, in order to prevent the passage of the Oder, and it was determined to attack the Prussian camp near Liegnitz on the 15th of August; the position of the Prussians was not advantageous, and the plan of attack was well chosen. Frederic was to be attached, on four different points, at day break and, if possible. There was to be a repetition of the scene of Hochkirch; the ultimate view of the enemy was to cut him off from the Oder, and indeed to prevent his retreating on Glogau; in the Austrian camp they were so certain of success, that the soldiers said, that the bag was open in which they were to put the army of the Prussians, and they had only to draw the strings tight. The king received intelligence of this intended surprise the night before it was to be carried into execution, and he also heard of the boast of the enemy; he mentioned it himself at dinner, and added:

The Austrians are not altogether wrong, but I think that I shall make a hole in the bag which they will have some trouble to mend.

He had not been without anxiety as to his position, with the recollection of Hochkirch fresh in his mind, but had delayed leaving his disadvantageous position, in consequence of some plans with respect to provisions for the army. The night of the 14th was fixed for breaking up the camp, and the English ambassador Mitchell, full of anxiety as to the result of the attack, burnt a portion of his papers, but would not consent to leave the army.

As soon as Frederic received intelligence of the intended attack, he prepared himself for battle, and immediately formed his plan of operations. At nightfall he quitted the camp with the army, but left orders to have the fires kept up by peasants, and the hussars went the round of the camp to keep up the night call of the sentinels; the same thing was being done in the Austrian camp, to conceal their attack, and their customary beating of drums at midnight was not omitted;

thus both armies were endeavouring, at the same moment, to deceive one another. Frederic drew his men to the heights near Liegnitz, and placed them in order of battle.

★★★★★★

The author was present at the battle, and can add his testimony to those who are of opinion, that the intention of the king was to await the army of Laudon, determined to come to a battle for which he had made every preparation; for, if the battle was to be looked upon as the effect of chance, why should he have placed the troops in the advantageous position on the heights, and why did he halt, from midnight till morning, with no impediment in his way? By these means all advantage, gained by the discovery of the intentions of the enemy, would have been rendered useless. By this loss of time (and Frederic was not in the habit of wasting time) the enemy would have been enabled to attack the retreating army, or to have impeded the continuance of their march. At daybreak, the whole army was in order of battle; and it was only at the moment that the attack was made, that there was some slight alteration in the position of some of the troops.

★★★★★★

It was a beautiful summer's night; the sky brilliant with stars, and without a cloud or a breath of wind. No one slept; the soldiers lay down with their arms in their hands, in high spirits, and as they were not allowed to sing, they told stories to one another; the officers walked about, and the generals rode round to see that every one was at his post; the king was seated on a drum, thinking of the probable event of the coming battle.

The day was just beginning to dawn, when Laudon approached at the head of his 30,000 men to attack the left wing of the Prussians, which he thought was still at some distance from him. He was however soon aware, to his astonishment, that he was in face of the whole army of the king, of which one portion attacked him at the moment that he received a heavy fire from a field battery, which had come up in the night; the other body of the army had been posted by Frederic as a corps of observation on Daun's army, which was opposite his right wing. Laudon, who depended upon the support of his commander in chief, did not withdraw from the fight, but opposed the Prussians, and led on the bravest of his troops. He charged the Prussian cavalry, but his men were driven back, and forced into a morass from which they had difficulty in extricating themselves;, the Prussian infantry now advanced, and after some hard fighting drove the Austrians out of the field. These made an attempt to enter in column the village of Panten, which lay in front of the Prussian line; but it was set on fire by the grenades from the Prussian howitzers, and the enemy were forced to confine their operations to the attack of their left wing.

Their hopes of receiving assistance were deceived, for it was not until late that Daun heard of the attack of the king, as the principal army of the Austrians did not hear the report of the cannonade, in consequence of the wind not being favourable; and the general on his arrival at the camp, did not know where the enemy was, whom he looked on as already defeated; and when at last he approached the field of battle, he could only attack the body of Prussians who were waiting for him, under great disadvantages from the nature of the ground; he attempted to break their line, but without success. Laudon, who had done everything in his power, now withdrew, and left the field of battle in the hands of the king, having lost 10,000 men, three and twenty stand of colours and eighty two cannon; 6000 Austrians were taken prisoners, 4000 killed or wounded; the Prussians had only 1800 killed and wounded.

It was a beautiful morning; the sun shone on the field of battle strewn with the dead and dying, and it was now that a most pleasing occurrence took place. The Bernburg regiment, who, as already related, had been degraded at Dresden, went into battle determined to regain their tarnished laurels, or die in the attempt; this determination which pervaded the breast of every one, soldier or officer, old or young, caused these men to render themselves well worthy of the Prussian name, and they did not pass unnoticed by the king. After the end of the battle he rode past the regiment; the officers were silent, in full confidence of the justice of their king, but four veterans held him by the bridle, and entreated for his favour, in consideration of their deeds on that day. Frederic was moved, and answered: "Yes, my children, all shall be forgotten," and on the same day the regiment received their arms and the decorations which had been taken from them; Frederic spoke of the manner in which they had distinguished themselves, and made known to the army their complete restoration to his favour.

The Battle of Liegnitz only lasted two hours, and at five in the morning, when but few have left their beds, this important battle had been fought, which had prevented the junction of the Austrians and

Russians, and rendered futile all their plans upon the fortified towns in Silesia. Frederic ordered a *feu de joie* from the whole army, and then continued his march; a march which was astonishing, and as worthy of record as any occurrence of this war; for this army fatigued by the battle, and surrounded by numerous enemies, was forced to continue their advance without loss of time, and to convey with them all the cannon and prisoners they had taken, and also the wounded; the latter were placed on the provision waggons, and all the carriages they could lay their hands on, even that of the king, was used for this purpose.

The led horses of the king and of the general officers were given for the wounded who could sit on horseback, to ride on; the empty waggons were broken to pieces, and the horses harnessed to the cannon that had been taken; the troopers and the soldiers of the baggage train had to carry the muskets that were taken from the enemy; nothing was left behind or forgotten. Not one of the wounded was left, Prussian or Austrian, and at nine o'clock, four hours after the battle, the whole army was in full march with their immense baggage train.

The army continued their march the same day for six leagues, as far as Parchwitz where Czernichef with 20,000 Russians defended the passage of the Oder. In spite of his victory the king found himself in a fearful position; the provision waggons were empty, and on the 16th of August, there was only bread for one day, besides what the soldiers carried with them; if the Russians kept their position, Frederic could not procure supplies from Breslau, and in order to reach Schweidnitz it would be necessary to engage the united armies of the Austrians; he could hardly expect a favourable issue in case of a battle, encumbered as he was by prisoners and wounded, who must necessarily be protected during the action. But the Russians soon put an end to his anxiety, for they withdrew over the Oder, and in justification of this act, the generals stated that having had no news from the Austrian camp for five days, they feared that they would be defeated or be entirely cut off from the main army; thus the communication with Breslau was open.

The Russian General Czernichef was still on this side of the Oder, with a small body of men; but to hasten his departure, the king made use of the following artifice; he wrote to Prince Henry, informing him of his victory over the Austrians, and of his determination to cross the Oder and attack the Russians, and also reminding his brother to put in action the operations already agreed on; this letter was given to a peasant with the necessary directions that he might fall into the hands of the Russians; the plan was successful, for no sooner had Czernichef read the letter, than he hastened to cross the river. This put an end to the difficulties of Frederic's position, which had never, not even before the Battle of Leuthen, been so dangerous; at that time, the Russians had returned to their own country, and the severity of the weather would have thrown many impediments in the way of his enemies; but now, winter was far off and the Russian and Austrian forces both in his neighbourhood. The victory over Laudon removed these dangers, and the king was never in better spirits, as he could now form a junction with his brother. The fortune of war, which had pursued him for so long with such evil consequences, now appeared to favour him again; he had won a victory on a march, and on the very field of battle, where in the year 1241 there had been fought a bloody engagement between the Christians and the Tartars; a letter written a few days after, to the Marquis D'Argens by the king, expresses his feelings on this occasion:

Formerly the battle of the 15th of August, my dear *marquis*, would have been a decisive one; now it has been merely a slight trial of strength, and a great battle is absolutely necessary to decide our fate. To judge by appearances, one will shortly occur, and we shall then have cause to rejoice, if the result be favourable to us. In the mean time, I thank you for the feelings you express on the present occasion. Not much talent was necessary to bring affairs to their present condition; do not speak of danger. I bought the last victory cheap; it only cost me a horse and a coat. I have not received the letter you mention; our correspondence is, as it were, blockaded; for the Russians are on one side of the river, and the Austrians on the other, and it will be requisite to have a slight engagement to enable the *aide-de-camp* Cocceji to pass; but I trust he will be able to reach you with my letter.

During the whole course of my life, I never was in so critical a position as during this campaign, and be assured it will require next to a miracle to overcome all the difficulties which I foresee. I will always do my duty; but, my dear *marquis*, you must always bear in mind, that I cannot lead fortune, and that I am compelled to reckon on chance in my projects as I have not means to insure their success. It is an Herculean task which I have to complete, and this at an age, when I am losing strength, when my health is breaking and, to tell the truth, at a time that hope, the only support of the unfortunate, is beginning to fail. You are not sufficiently aware of every circumstance, to enable me to tell you all the dangers which threaten the state. I know them all, and conceal them. All the anxieties I keep to myself, and only impart to the world my hopes or the trifling agreeable news which reach me. When the blow I now meditate is struck, and with success, then, my dear *marquis*, will be the time to rejoice. I lead the life of a warrior monk at the present time, and the circumstances I am placed in give good occupation to my mind; the remainder of my time I devote to science, which is my consolation; even as it was that of the great Consul, the father of his country and of eloquence.

I know not, if I shall survive this campaign; should I do so, I am determined to pass the remainder of my days far from turmoil and in the bosom of friendship and philosophy. As yet I know not where we shall have our winter quarters; my house in Breslau was burnt to the ground, during the last bombardment; our enemy grudge us the light of day and the very air we breathe; still, they must allow us to be in some spot, and if it is a safe one, I hope to see you there. What will become of the question of peace between England and France? You see, my dear Marquis, that your countrymen are blinder than you thought they were; they put up with the loss of Canada and Pondichery in order to please the Queen of Hungary and the Empress of Russia. Heaven grant that Prince Ferdinand may repay them for their zeal.

The reigning Duke of Würtemberg, who not only sent his contingent to the army of the Empire, but took a part himself in this war, had advanced, at the head of 12,000 of his own troops, into Saxony. In the first instance this prince had always acted in conjunction with the French, but now he wished to try his fortune with the Austrians; not in expectation of receiving pay from them, but satisfied with the prospect of the contributions he should be able to levy in the territories of the enemy; this he did not fail to do, and the Hessian and Prussian provinces into which he came, were very severely handled, and the town of Halle alone had to pay 75,000 dollars.

In August he joined the army of the Empire, which consisted of thirty five battalions of infantry, and seven cavalry regiments, in addition to which were the Austrians under Haddick, with seven infantry and six cavalry regiments together with 2000 Croats. Hülsen, who was posted at Meissen, left this position on the approach of so large an army, and encamped himself with entrenchments near Strehlen; he was here attacked from all sides on the 18th of August, but made good his position, drove back the enemy, and took 1300 prisoners; Hülsen then withdrew to Torgau in order to protect his provisions, encamped and remained six weeks, when he was forced to leave in consequence of a deficiency of supplies. He now made a masterly retreat to Brandenburg; but by this means Saxony was evacuated by the Prussians, even to Torgau and Wittenberg, who however promised, on taking leave, to return shortly.

Such was the state of affairs in Saxony as regarded the Prussians. In Silesia Daun had been forced, by the retreat of the Russians and the operations and measures of the king, to withdraw, after the Battle of Liegnitz, into the mountains, not to be cut off from Bohemia. In consequence of this Frederic made a circuitous march, and in spite of a heavy cannonade, passed with his whole army close by the camp of the enemy. Soltikow had given up all thoughts of forming a junction with the Austrians, and was watched by General Goltz with 12,000 men at Glogau, the rest of his army having joined that of the king.

A number of skirmishes now took place terminating in favour of Frederic, and showing that fortune had once more turned on his side, and at Hohen-Giersdorf, in the mountains, a sharp engagement took place in sight of both armies, in which the Austrians lost 600 grenadiers and fourteen cannon. The battle did not extend farther, as it would have produced no good effects; the soldiers on the outposts were forbidden to fire, so that every thing now gave the appearance of a cessation of hostilities; the sentinels on either side spoke together, the patrols when they met exchanged greetings, and if they lost their way were set right by the opposite party.

This plan of remaining in such immediate vicinity of the enemy, and which Frederic often made use of, generally embarrassed the Austrian generals, altered their plans and rendered them undecided in their operations; for no general since the time of Caesar had made use of such means, and Frederic, who took the great Roman for his example, and constantly made him his study, gained great advantages by his hardihood, as Daun now gave up all his projects for the present, and withdrew with his superior forces into the mountains in order that his troops might be refreshed.

Chapter 9: Battle of Torgau and Defeat of the Austrians

During these occurrences the Russians had not remained in inactivity in Pomerania, but had sent a fleet to the coast of this province, and Colberg was now besieged by a naval force of seven and twenty Russian ships of war, and an army of 15,000 men. In addition to this, the fleet of the Russians was supported by a squadron of six Swedish men of war and two frigates, and General Demidow had brought 8000 Russians by water, who joined the main army to carry on the siege. In four days seven hundred shells were thrown into the town as well as a great number of red hot shot, and every preparation was made for storming the works; but this attempt did not succeed better than the previous one, for Heyden defended himself with the greatest bravery, and the determination of the citizens, who saw their houses burnt to the ground without a murmur, remained unshaken until General Werner came to their relief from Silesia.

He had only 5000 men, and having marched eighty leagues in twelve days arrived at Colberg on the 18th of September, which was the twenty-sixth day of the siege, and immediately attacked the Russians, sword in hand. Confident in their security from the great distance at which the Prussians were, the besiegers had never even dreamt of the garrison receiving succour; and Werner's small body of men excited such alarm, that they not only raised the siege, but retreated in great haste, leaving behind them their cannon, ammunition, tents, baggage and even their provisions in order to escape from the advancing Prussians. Some made their escape on board the ships, others dispersed themselves in the country, and Werner took several hundred prisoners. Fear took such a powerful hold on the minds of the sailors, that they did not think themselves in safety, even on board their ships, from the pursuit of the Prussian hussars, for the fleet slipped their anchors and stood out to sea. A medal was struck on this occasion to commemorate this extraordinary occurrence, with the motto: *Res similis fictae*; and Ramler composed an ode to celebrate the liberation of his native town.

Werner having completed this bold enterprise and having no longer any Russians to oppose him, now turned his attention to the Swedes, attacked them in the suburb of Pasewalk, took eight cannon from them, cut down 300, and made 800 prisoners; he would have taken possession of the town, had not the Swedes threatened to set fire to it, a risk Werner would not run for the sake of the Prussian inhabitants. He now marched into Mecklenburg, and raised contributions, until the movements of the Russians forced him to return into Pomerania.

The summer was now passed, and the approach of the unfavourable season forced both Austrians and Russians to think of winter quarters; but the enemies of Frederic were not a little humiliated with the thoughts of having done so little during the last campaign with their powerful and superior forces; and to complete their annoyance came the position of Daun in the mountains from which he could with difficulty advance, and where the impediments to procuring supplies were so great that nothing was left for him but to retreat on Bohemia. Every endeavour was now made to induce the king to withdraw, and an attack upon Berlin by the Russians appearing to be the most likely means to effect this object, Daun, to induce Soltikow to undertake this enterprise, promised to support it by strong reinforcements.

20,000 Russians under Czernichef, and 15,000 Austrians under Lascy and Brentano, now commenced their march in Brandenburg, covered in the distance by the whole force of Soltikow; and so exciting was the prospect of booty in a royal city that the Austrians, sure of their prey, made forced marches without stopping for rest, and in ten days had traversed eighty leagues. Count Tottleben, one of the Russian generals, but a German, who had long resided in Berlin, was in command of the advanced guard, and as every thing depended on being the first to arrive, he conducted the march with such rapidity that on the 3rd of October, the sixth day from their departure from Beuthen in Silesia, he appeared before the gates of Berlin at the head of 3000 men.

This large city was only occupied by 1900 soldiers, and without ramparts or walls was not in a position to be defended. General Rochow, who had already had a visit three years previous from the Austrians, still commanded the town, but was supported by men of high reputation, Generals Seidlitz and old Field-Marshal Leywald who, as well as General Knoblauch, were at this time in Berlin, and who, from patriotism, defended in person some slight entrenchments thrown up before the gates of the city.

Everyone took arms, even the invalids and the sick, and after the town had been summoned on the day of the arrival of the Russians, grenades and red hot shot were thrown into it, and during the night two of the gates were attempted to be taken by storm; but the enemy were repulsed, the flames which were making rapid progress were extinguished, and the noble example of these old soldiers, crowned with laurels, but who served as subalterns, increased the courage of the combatants, and forced the Russians to relinquish their attack. On the following day Prince Eugene of Würtemberg came to the relief of the city with 5000 men after having marched eighteen leagues in one day, and was received by the inhabitants as a preserver sent by Providence; the citizens immediately supplied the soldiers with food, beer and wine, and as soon as they were refreshed, Prince Eugene led them against the enemy whom he drove hack as far as Cöpenick.

Czernichef at the head of his army had in the meantime approached, but had it not been for the persuasive powers of the French envoy Montalembert, so often brought into the field, he would now have retreated without giving battle; and Tottleben having received considerable reinforcements again advanced, and forced the Prussians to retreat before his superior numbers. Hulsen now reached Berlin with his army from Saxony, and there was sufficient force to defend the gates of the city, which, had this been done for only a few days would have been saved, as Frederic was in full march from Silesia, and the retreat of the two great armies of the Austrians and Russians was already determined on in the council, even before they were in possession of Berlin.

But the Prussian generals thought it too great a risk, especially as they heard that the principal army of the Russians was in the neighbourhood of Frankfort on the Oder, and that General Panin was approaching at the head of seven regiments to strengthen Czernichef, to say nothing of the difficulty of defending an unfortified town of more than four leagues in circumference with 14,000 men, and which was devastated by the continual throwing in of combustibles. A battle was not to be thought of in the open country, as in case of defeat, Berlin would have been given up to pillage, so that the two armies which had advanced to the relief of the city found themselves under the necessity of retiring to Spandau, and leaving Berlin to its fate.

The fate of the city was less fearful than might have been expected, for it capitulated without delay, and surrendered to Tottleben, who finding a number of old friends in the town which recalled to his remembrance other days, began with great moderation, and in a manner strikingly different from the customary behaviour of the Russians. But what had most influence in producing this effect was the conduct of a merchant of Berlin of the name of Gotzkowsky; an extraordinary man, virtuous, clever and courageous, and who seemed born for the advantage of his country. This worthy man, who had been fortunate in gaining riches of which he made a good use, persuaded the magistrates of the town to capitulate to the Russians in preference to the Austrians, as the former were only auxiliary troops, but the latter were the principal enemies of the Prussians, and from whom no mercy was to be expected.

The noble generosity he had displayed in supporting numbers of the Russian officers after the Battle of Zorndorf had not remained a secret in their armies, and had procured him the high consideration of their leaders in Berlin as well as the friendship of Tottleben. He made the best use of the influence he had thus gained for the advantage of the town, and he constantly was making applications, not only in individual cases, but for the general advantage; every one, whether known to him or not, sought protection from him, and refuge in his house, and that he might secure the success of his requests he accompanied them with presents of gold and jewels from his own coffers.

Tottleben required in the first instance a contribution of four millions of dollars, and insisting on this sum, referred to his instructions from General Fermor, that it should be paid not in the base coin in circulation, but in sterling money, at the peril of giving up the city to pillage. The inhabitants were in despair, until the zealous Gotzkowsky, by means of great sacrifices of his own fortune, reduced the required tax to a million and a half of dollars with a present of 200,000 dollars to the soldiers, and all this to be paid in the current coin of the day. He went with this news to the council house where he was received as a preserver by the assembled magistrates; the money for the soldiers as well as half a million of dollars were immediately paid, and letters of credit given for the remainder.

The Russians held communication with no one but Gotzkowsky,

who was day and night in the streets, and brought every injustice that was committed before the eyes of the officers, preventing many misfortunes, and consoling the unfortunate. It was Fermor's orders that all the royal manufactories should be given up to pillage, and then destroyed, and among these the store house for the issuing the cloth for the soldiers as well as the manufactory for gold and silver-work; the 10th of October was fixed for this work of destruction, and it was only during the night that Gotzkowsky heard of it. He hastened to Tottleben, represented to him that the royal manufactories did not in fact belong to the king, that the profits arising from them did not in any way accrue to his advantage, but were applied to the support of the large institution for orphans at Potsdam; he was required to attest this declaration on oath, and the manufactories were spared.

It was thus in the power of Tottleben to do irreparable injury to the King of Prussia, for the beautiful city of Berlin, which from its magnificent streets and buildings rose like another Palmyra from the midst of a sandy desert, was the greatest manufacturing town in Germany, and the centre from which the necessaries of war for the Prussian Army were drawn. In this capital were immense store houses and manufactures for replacing those stores which were constantly being sent to the army, for never was the commerce of Berlin so flourishing as at the present time; as it was here that lived the richest merchants and those who undertook the contracts for the armies, as well as the Jews who regulated the exchanges of all Germany.

Tottleben still retained his post as *commandant* in Berlin when six days after Lascy arrived, and was an unwilling spectator of the gentle rule of the Russians; he drove the Russian guard from the Halle gate, occupied it with his own troops, wishing to participate in every advantage, although he protested openly against the capitulation. Czernichef settled this dispute by ordering that three of the gates should be given up to the Austrians, and that they should receive 50,000 dollars of the money which had been paid for the soldiers.

It was necessary for Tottleben to act with some dissimulation, as during the time that he was in public threatening the inhabitants with severity in private he made them aware of the good intentions which he justified by his deeds. They had been able to evade the cruel orders of Fermor, but this was not enough, for the demands of the other enemies of Frederic, who set no bounds to their wishes and plans for destruction in his capital, were far more exorbitant and barbarous; for amongst other requests, they wished to blow up the new Arsenal, one of the most beautiful buildings in Europe, and the consequences of its destruction, situated, as it was, in the midst of the most populous and splendid parts of the city, would have been fearful. Tottleben was forced to give way, and some Russian soldiers were sent to fetch the necessary powder from a mill not far from Berlin; but these men, not aware of the nature of the service they were on, approached the powder magazine without any precautions, set it on fire, and it was blown into the air. This saved the Arsenal, as at this time there was a scarcity of powder; but its contents were entirely destroyed as well as all the machinery of the mint and the royal manufactories, and the magazines were cleared, as was the treasury of 100,000 dollars.

The newspapers of Berlin had not used much moderation in speaking of the customary cruelties of the Russians, and it was now that the editors were to be punished, as had Fermor's orders been fulfilled, they would have had to run the gauntlet; the day and hour were fixed, and these unfortunate men were already in the guard house awaiting their dreadful fate. Tottleben, who had not been spared in the newspapers, and who for his own safety thought it necessary to revenge the insult to the honour of the Russians, appeared more immovable than usual; but Gotzkowsky, who made this affair his own, never ceased his entreaties until the punishment was remitted, and the editors were merely taken to the place where the soldiers were drawn up for their punishment, and then received a reprimand.

An order which caused much consternation was issued that the inhabitants should deposit all their arms on the Platz before the Palace, and many believed that the intention was to disarm them that they might the more easily be plundered. Gotzkowsky got this order reversed, but for appearance sake, some hundreds of useless muskets were deposited on the Platz, broken to pieces and thrown into the water. Another order of Fermor's was the levying a heavy contribution on the Jews, and the two principal men of this people, Ephraim and Itzig, were to be taken as hostages; but although Gotzkowsky was the means of averting this evil from them, he was rewarded before the year was out by the basest ingratitude on their parts.

It had been agreed on that no soldier should take up his residence in the city, but Lascy, always the bitter enemy of the Prussians, laughed at this convention, and took up his quarters with several regiments in the town, contrary to the expressed wish of the Russians. This gave rise to great excesses, for not content with getting food and drink from the inhabitants, they insisted on extorting money, jewels and clothes, in short every thing they could lay their hands on. All at once Berlin became a scene of confusion; Croats, hussars and Cossacks robbed, and beat people in midday; if any one was in the streets at night they were stripped of their clothes, and a number of houses were broken into and pillaged. The Austrians by far surpassed the Russians in these outrages, for disregardful of all the terms of the capitulation, they only gave way to their national hatred, and to such an extent, that at last Tottleben found it necessary to send troops into the city, and to fire upon them repeatedly.

They went into the royal stables which were guaranteed by the treaty, and protected by four and twenty Russian soldiers, dragged out the horses, destroyed the royal carriages, and then pillaged the residence of Schwerin, the master of the horse. Hospitals, the refuge of the sick and the needy, and which would have been respected by the greatest barbarians, had no better fate; rapine was their watchword, the very churches were desecrated, and this line of conduct would still have been pursued had it not been for the earnest representations of the Dutch ambassador Verelst, who pointed out to the generals the disgrace they were bringing on themselves and their country.

This love of pillage became like an epidemic, and infected the Saxons, who had always been noted for their discipline and humanity of conduct; they were stationed at Charlottenburg, a town two leagues from Berlin, celebrated for its royal palace, and by their conduct rendered themselves unworthy of their country. They forgot that in all probability the King of Prussia would ere long return to Saxony, and take vengeance on them; and breaking into the palace, every thing they could lay their hands on, looking glasses, porcelain, carpets, and even the pictures were destroyed. Those valuables which were not cut to pieces were stolen, and taken away by the officers; the chapel was pillaged and the organ spoilt; but what caused the greatest annoyance to the king was the destruction of some antique statues, which he had procured from the gallery of Cardinal Polignac.

When Frederic saw this scene of devastation after the peace, he exclaimed: "The wretches! but they could not know the value of these treasures, so—they must be forgiven." The inhabitants thought they had purchased safety by the payment of 15,000 dollars; but they soon found out their mistake, as their houses were pillaged, the men ill treated and the women and girls dishonoured.

Schönhausen, a small palace of the Queen's, was treated in a similar manner to this place; for eight Russian hussars came to it, and required the plate to be given up to them; it was in vain that they were told that it had been sent away, and having searched the palace, and found nothing, they stripped the warden and his wife naked, flogged them, and burnt them with red hot irons. A few days after fresh bodies of soldiers came, and treated the palace as that of Charlottenburg; one of the servants was placed upon a burning fire, and another was cut to pieces with their sabres; the unfortunate women were reserved to satisfy their brutal appetites.

The Austrians as well as the Russians had serious thoughts of taking up their winter quarters in Brandenburg; and they both looked upon the war as nearly at an end, as they had each large armies in the centre of the Prussian states, and they had overrun nearly all the provinces; the Swedes were advancing, the troops of the Empire were in Saxony and masters of the Elb, Laudon was in Silesia, and Daun was constantly near the king with a powerful and superior force.

But this expected triumph soon vanished from their minds, for Frederic advancing rapidly from Silesia soon altered the appearance of affairs, and the cry: "The king is advancing," ran through their ranks like an electric shock, and set them all in commotion. The Austrians and Russians immediately left Berlin, and Czernichef and Tottleben made such rapid movements that in two days they were twenty four leagues from this city; Lascy hurried into Saxony to form a junction with Daun, the Swedes retreated, and the principal army of the Russians recrossed the Oder

Tottleben had received orders from Fermor to take with him on his retreat from Berlin, which commenced the 12th of October, three of the principal merchants as hostages; but Gotzkowsky saved these men, and persuaded him to be contented with their head clerks, who were taken by the Russians to Königsberg, and treated as felons. From the sudden retreat of the Russians there necessarily remained many important matters under discussion, and the magistrates entreated Gotzkowsky to undertake to settle these affairs by going to the Russian camp. This friend to his country made every sacrifice, left his family, and his large establishment, in which upwards of fifteen hundred men were employed, and hurried to the Russian camp under an escort of Cossacks.

When he arrived at the headquarters of the Russians where Fermor was, he was ill treated, and in spite of his safe conduct which insured his return to Berlin, he was to have been sent to Königsberg to await the answer of a letter addressed by the town of Berlin to the empress respecting a diminution of the war tax; nothing but a free distribution of presents of jewellery among the favourites of Fermor saved him from this disagreeable journey.

The Russian general was rendered more vindictive against this worthy man by a circumstance of which he was not aware; Frederic, anxious if possible to prevent the payment of the remaining million of the contribution, had sent orders to the magistrates of Berlin not to hurry themselves, and Fermor hearing of this made the most bitter reproaches to Gotzkowsky:

Your king thinks that he is the master of the whole world; I know that he has given orders not to pay the outstanding bills of exchange; but the empress has the means of insuring herself from loss. What manner of merchants are ye? The whole world must have a care of you, and have nothing to do with men who are subjects of a king who can by his orders prevent them from honouring their bills, and who at his pleasure can deprive these of their value.'

Gotzkowsky referred him to the imperative duties of a merchant, and offered him a bill of 150,000 dollars upon Hamburg as part payment of the million of dollars, offering to remain in the camp until a messenger could fetch the money. All this was done, but before he was allowed to depart he was forced to enter into an engagement to return in four weeks, and an escort of fifty Cossacks were to bring him back; these were attacked by mistake by the Prussian hussars in Kyritz, and for the greater part cut to pieces from the negligence of the trumpeter with the flag of truce, before Gotzkowsky could prevent it by explaining the nature of the mission.

All this caused great anxiety in Berlin, as from the uncertainty of the fate of war, the Russians who were still in the neighbourhood might return, and the merchants were much distressed by the order of the king respecting the bills; for the Russians threatened to lay violent hands on all the property of these merchants in Dantsick, Prussia and Curland, and to post their names in all the exchanges of Europe as dishonoured. Upon this Gotzkowsky went to the king who at first would not hear of the payment being made, in consequence of the Würzburg and Bamberg bills not having been paid; but on the nature of the transaction being explained to him, the monarch determined to pay the contribution himself. Gotzkowsky went himself to the Russian headquarters, and after many fruitless attempts to diminish the amount to be paid, and making great presents, the only advantage he could obtain was the permission of free transport for the merchandise of the Prussian merchants through, the provinces in the possession of the Russians. The conduct of this patriot made such an impression on Frederic that he sent him a present of 150,000 dollars; but he, knowing the wish of the king to establish a porcelain manufactory in Berlin, used the money for this purpose; and thus was opened, in the midst of a war, a manufactory which promised to be one of the first of its kind in Europe.

Frederic was on the frontiers of Saxony when he first heard of the conduct of the Saxons in Charlottenburg, and nothing gave him greater pain than their barbarous conduct, which caused rage to get the better of more philosophical feelings. During the whole course of the war none of the royal palaces had been injured, on the contrary they had been carefully preserved; but now Frederic sent a body of men to plunder and destroy the hunting palace of Hubertsburg, which was so completely and rapidly done that in two hours nothing but the bare walls were left. The court of Saxony were not so much dissatisfied with this vengeance as with those outrages which had given rise to it, but the generals excused themselves by saying they could not control the rage of their soldiers. Frederic sent 300,000 dollars to be distributed to the small proprietors who had suffered the most, but with the utter exclusion of the nobility.

In the meantime Laudon had made an attack upon Cosel, and the season of the year not permitting a regular siege he attempted to take it by storm; which failing he, in consequence of the garrison consisting for the most part of deserters and prisoners, endeavoured to gain them over by offers of indiscriminate pardon; but this ignoble conduct met with no success, and was equally useless in its results as was the bombardment of the town which lasted but one night, and only set on fire the store house and a few other buildings. The following day Laudon, who had heard of the advance of the Prussian General Goltz sent his heavy artillery away, and raised the siege.

The occupation of Berlin by the enemy had been very disadvantageous to the king in Saxony, for Hulsen had hardly quitted this province before the Austrians and troops of the Empire recommenced their depredations, and destroying the bridge at Torgau, took this town which was garrisoned with 2000 men, and which did not offer much resistance; they also took possession of a large supply of provisions together with a number of sick in the hospital who fell into their hands.

Wittenberg was now attacked and regularly besieged, and although but badly fortified was defended with the greatest bravery by its *commandant*, General Salenmon. It was bombarded with great spirit, so that in a few days the greater part of the town was reduced to ashes, the magazines destroyed and the garrison were forced to surrender as they had neither provisions nor ammunition.

Frederic was now deprived of all his magazines in Saxony which was in the hands of the enemy, and it was only by means of his sword, with him a never failing resource, that he could hope again to obtain possession of this country. The Duke of Zweibrücken had left, the banks of the Elb with the troops of the Empire, General Wied remaining in the rear posted in a wood with 3600 men, and the advanced guard of the Prussians having fallen in with him drove him back with a loss of 1900 men. Frederic now advanced upon Duben where, after having routed a whole battalion of Croats, he established a magazine which he protected by raising fortifications, and placing a garrison of 5000 men in it; as, intending to attack the Austrians with all his forces, it was necessary to insure himself from an attack on his rear by the troops of the Empire which were encamped near Leipsic.

This important city, one of the finest and richest in Germany, had always been the object of the different armies, and both friend and foe were desirous of gaining possession of it, as it required but little effort and not a regular siege, from the fortifications being only sufficient at most to resist light troops, and as the town could only be protected by an army outside its gates; but if it had but slight fortifications it was possessed of great riches which gave rise to so many enterprises, that no city changed masters so often as this during the war.

This time the troops of the Empire thought seriously of taking up their winter quarters in it, and the inhabitants, weary of the heavy drain which the Prussian levies was to them, were anxious that they should do so; but Frederic informing his plans never lost sight of this mine of riches, and having sent General Hulsen against the city, the troops of the Empire withdrew in haste, and crossed the Pleisse and the Elster; their example was followed by the Duke of Würtemberg, who having had some misunderstanding with the other generals now returned to his own dominions without having gained any laurels. Leipsic was now taken possession of without resistance, and Wittenberg also again fell into the hands of the Prussians.

It was still the object of Daun to be entirely master of Saxony; for Dresden, the largest, strongest and most important city of this country, was in his hands as well as the greater part of the Electorate; nearly the whole of the forces of Austria were assembled in this province, in addition to which winter had began, and the campaign was to all appearance at an end. But Frederic had determined not to let all important Saxony be entirely taken from him, in spite of the many impediments which lay in the way of his plans for possessing it. The Russians were at Landsberg on the Wartha, only awaiting the approach of their confederates to advance into Brandenburg, and then take up their winter quarters together with the Austrians.

By these movements the king would have been cut off from Berlin, Pomerania, Silesia and in short from all his resources, for beyond his magazine and stores at Duben, which were nearly exhausted, he had no supplies. The Prussian Army was in danger of starvation, and the frost which had set in threatened to close the Elb with ice, so that Frederic's position was fearful; he must either conquer or succumb, and as this could only be decided by a battle, for this he was fully prepared. On the other hand, in spite of the superiority of his forces, Daun would not venture this, and as he thought he could fulfil his wishes by merely acting on the defensive, he withdrew into the strong position near Torgau where Prince Henry had been posted the previous year out of reach of the attacks of Daun. Frederic crossed the Elb near Dessau unexpected by the enemy, and having formed a junction with the Prince of Würtemberg and General Hulsen, he then advanced against Daun.

This general now drew all his detached troops together with the exception of those under the command of General Brentano, who were attacked by General Kleist near Belgern, and defeated with the loss of a large number of killed and wounded, and 800 prisoners. As the king was aware that it was hopeless to endeavour to bring his opponent to a battle, he determined to storm the camp of the Austrians, in spite of all the impediments which lay in the way of such an undertaking, but which, although the most difficult to carry out, was the only one which offered a prospect of success. As it must be done, it were well to do it quickly, and he therefore made his determination known to the army on the evening of the 2nd of November as soon as the troops had pitched their tents after a long day's march, and every preparation was made for giving battle on the following day.

Four days previously he had written to the Marquis D'Argens, describing his position and his failing strength in the following expressive words:

You value life as a sybarite whilst I look upon death as a stoic. Nothing shall induce me to make a disgraceful peace; no inducement, no eloquence can bring me to subscribe to my dishonour. I will either be buried under the ruins of my country, or, when my misfortunes are no longer to be borne, I will find means to put an end to them. I am determined to venture everything in this campaign, and either to conquer or die an honourable death.

With such feelings did the king prepare for battle.

It was on the 3rd of November that this celebrated battle was fought, in which every thing was ventured by these two armies, each crowned with laurels from the many victories they had gained, and who fighting with the greatest bravery, and making use of the best military tactics, caused the fate of this all important contest to remain long undecided; until late in the darkness of the night, the Prussians were at length victorious. The king advanced through the forest of Torgau with four columns, and his plan of operations which was masterly, contemplated not only the defeat but the annihilation of the Austrian Army; as cut off from retreating over the Elb, the defeated could only choose either to fall by the sword or to be made prisoners.

Both wings of the Austrians, or rather the extreme points of the half moon which Daun's army formed, were to be attacked at the same time, and driven back upon the centre, and to carry this into execution, the king divided his army, which consisted in 60 battalions and 130 squadrons, into two bodies in order to make two separate attacks at the same time. General Ziethen was sent with one half of the Prussian Army on the road which leads towards Eulenburg, in order to attack the heights of Siptitz near Torgau, and if the king defeated the enemy with the other half of his army, the Austrians must be utterly destroyed, and the name of Torgau become for ever memorable in history.

But many impediments lay in the way of completing this undertaking, for Daun was posted in a most advantageous position with the best troops of the empress, his left wing supported by the Elb, his right protected by heights and numerous artillery, and with woods, ditches, ponds and morasses in advance of him; Lascy, who was only a short distance from the main army, was also in a strong position and protected by a succession of ponds on each side. It was intended that Ziethen's first operation should be to attack this body, and then to hasten to Siptitz; the dividing of the Prussian Army was to remain a secret to the enemy, and not to occur until the army was in full march, and only when they came to the Leipsic road. Frederic now advanced with his columns across the heath of Domit which was occupied by the enemy's grenadiers, Croats, dragoons and hussars, who fell back in the greatest haste upon the main body. Soon after they came up with an Austrian regiment of dragoons who were in ignorance of the advance of the Prussians, and thus were placed between the columns of the king's forces; the outlets of the wood were occupied by the infantry, and the cavalry surrounded this regiment, so that those who were not cut to pieces were made prisoners.

The king now continued his advance, drew his advanced guard round the right wing of the enemy and although the rest of his troops, infantry, cavalry and artillery were not yet come up, attacked the Austrians without loss of time with this small force, which only consisted in ten battalions of grenadiers; an example which Charles the XII. had given at Narva, and had had used with success against the Russians; a cannonade, which was heard in the distance, but which was merely an attack upon some Croats led the king to suppose that Ziethen was already engaged with the enemy, and justified his rash determination. Never was time more valuable, it was already two o'clock and only a few hours of daylight remained, which would in all probability not only decide the fate of Frederic but also that of the Prussian monarchy.

Daun received the Prussians with a heavy cannonade, so destructive that the oldest soldiers declared they had never seen it equalled, and the king himself said more than once to his *aide-de-camp*: "What a dreadful cannonade! have you ever heard its equal?" Its effects were such that in half an hour 5500 grenadiers were stretched on the ground, killed or wounded in attempting to pass the entrenchments, and almost before they could fire their muskets; only 600 of them were fit for duty the following day. What increased the difficulty of the attack was the hilly nature of the ground, which also impeded the operations of the Austrians, so that their second line was not more than three hundred paces in rear of the first. The king was much distressed at the destruction of his grenadiers, and as their leader, Count Anhalt to whom he was much attached fell to the ground, he turned to his brother, one of his *aide-de-camp* and said; "Everything goes wrong to day, my friends are deserting me, and I have just heard of the death of your brother."

It had rained in torrents but the heavy cannonade appeared to have an effect on the clouds in the neighbourhood of the field of battle, and it became clearer.

The principal column now advanced out of the wood but before the Prussians could make their appearance, the boughs of the trees were cut by the bullets, and fell on them, and the heavy fire of the cannon was kept up carrying destruction with it; the Prussians continued to advance steadily through the smoke of the firing but found the field of battle covered with the dead and dying; the body of grenadiers with whom they had hoped to unite for victory destroyed, the army of General Ziethen in the distance, and the enemy in security behind their batteries. The Prussian artillery endeavoured to bring up their cannon but this was attended with great difficulty, especially for the heavy artillery, in consequence of the barricades and the advance of the infantry; the horses and drivers were killed, and many of the cannon destroyed.

In the meantime the infantry formed, and made a fresh attack, and the Austrians, who had advanced after the defeat of the grenadiers, were now driven back, and in spite of the heavy fire of musketry from the imperialists, the Prussians continued to gain ground, took several batteries and gained the heights.

But the scene was soon changed, for the Prussian cavalry not having come up, and their cannon being useless from remaining in the wood, the infantry were not supported, so that Daun taking advantage of this and bringing up fresh troops, they made a bloody charge on the Prussians, and drove them back into the wood; their cavalry now came up to their assistance, but being thrown into disorder they were driven back. A fresh attack was however made by them in which the *cuirassier* regiment, led on by Colonel Dalwig, displayed great courage, broke the line of the enemy's cavalry and falling upon the infantry, drove them back and made a number of prisoners. The whole line of the Austrians was in danger, but a large body of their cavalry coming up the Prussians were forced to give way, and although Frederic led on himself a fresh attack with the infantry, it was not attended with any success, and night coming on, the men worn out with fatigue, and the king wounded, the battle was to all appearance lost for him. Daun sent off messengers with the news of the victory which was received in Vienna with the greatest demonstrations of joy.

But Theresa was not fated to gain this victory, for Ziethen had not remained inactive during this time; he had changed his plan of operations in consequence of the occurrences in the king's division of the army, and in spite of having General Lascy's army of 20,000 men opposed to him, he was at last enabled to get the better of all difficulties, and advance to the assistance of the king. General Saldern saw that every thing depended on gaining possession of the heights of Siptitz, and never losing sight of this object advanced on the village which was in flames; Colonel Möllendorf supported this movement by marching through the village, storming the heights of which the Prussians soon became masters and being followed by other troops, who dragged up their cannon under cover of the cavalry, they commenced a cannonade from the heights, which threw the Austrians into great disorder.

Some of the Prussians of the left wing approached at this time, and that their victorious companions in arms might not mistake them in the dark the drummers struck up the Prussian march; they were led on by General Hulsen, who having had all his horses killed, and not being able to walk from age and his wounds, got upon a gun, and was thus taken into the midst of the battle. Lascy who was always the most unfortunate general of his time, endeavoured twice to regain possession of the heights, but the Prussians having driven him back with great slaughter, were enabled to keep the advantages they had gained and this decided the battle which had lasted until near ten at night; the Austrians now only thought of retreating over the Elb by three bridges of boats which had been thrown over this river and the rushing of the stream guided them in which direction to go; as the night was so dark that it was not possible to see.

The Prussians had not this advantage and this caused several bodies of their troops to fire on others of their own men before the mistake could be discovered, and it also frequently occurred that Austrian officers fell into the hands of the enemy and other troops coming up immediately after released them. Even to the king this occurred and he together with his escort fell in with a body of Austrians. To the customary question "Who goes there?" the answer was, "Austrians;" Frederic's escort rushed forwards, and took a whole battalion of Croats prisoners. The darkness was such that it was impossible to bring the troops into anything like order and the men remained during the night dispersed in different parts of the field of battle.

The long winter's night was dreadfully cold, and but a few of the troops were able to get wood to make fires, the others being obliged to keep in motion to warm themselves they constantly stumbled over the dead bodies of the fallen. The ground was soaked with the heavy rain, but in spite of this many lay down to obtain rest, with their limbs stiffened by their wet clothes; many had eaten nothing since morning, and those who found bread in their knapsacks knew not where to get a drop of water. Worn out with fatigue, cold, hunger and thirst, they all looked forward anxiously for daylight.

The position of the wounded was dreadful for only those who could drag themselves from the field of battle reached the village; hundreds of others were stripped of their clothes by marauders, their cries for mercy being in vain and numbers who were only wounded in the legs and not mortally, died from the effects of exposure and the cold of a November night. This night was also remarkable from the manner in which it was passed by the soldiers of both armies who appeared to have decided upon a cessation of hostilities, and congregated together round the numerous fires in the forest of Torgau, where they patiently awaited the return of day, as neither party was aware of the result, and each had determined to give themselves up as prisoners of war to those who were victorious.

The king had gone to the village of Elsnig in the neighbourhood of the field of battle, Where he found every place filled with those of the wounded who had been able either by their own exertions or the help of others to reach this place, and who were now under the hands of the surgeons; Frederic would not allow any of them to be disturbed, but had the church opened, and in it had his wound dressed; from this place he issued orders, and despatched a courier with the news of the battle, in which he considered himself the victor; although not knowing of the retreat of the enemy he expected that it would be renewed in the morning, having already given the necessary orders, and also that the infantry should not fire, but charge with fixed bayonets. But day had hardly began to dawn, when Frederic became aware that he had no enemy to oppose him, and being in possession of the field of battle the victory was most decisive. He was now master of Saxony, for the Austrians crossed the Elb, and retreated upon Dresden along the banks of this river. The Prussians now retired into winter quarters.

Daun who had been severely wounded in this battle had withdrawn from the army, and given up the command to General Buccow, but as this general was shot in the arm as soon as he had been named as leader his place was taken by General O'Donnel, who immediately hastened to cover Dresden, and to take up the strong position at Plauen, and was followed and harassed in his retreat by General Ziethen and the Prince of Würtemberg who took many prisoners. The battle had been very bloody on both sides, for the Austrians lost 12,000 killed and wounded besides 8000 prisoners fifty cannon twenty seven stand of colours and twenty pontoons, and the loss of the Prussians was 10,000 killed and wounded and 4000 prisoners.

Many faults had been committed both before and during the battle by Daun; but in spite of this he had defended himself bravely and the Austrians had shown great courage; so that, notwithstanding the melancholy news of the battle, Theresa was not dissatisfied with her general, who wounded, was hastening to Vienna; she was so noble hearted as to meet him some miles on his way towards the imperial city, and to say to him:

I wished to have the pleasure of being the first, not only to welcome you, but to congratulate you. on your success during this campaign, and at the same time to assure myself of the state of your health, which has caused me so much anxiety.

This queen was accustomed to encourage her troops and would generally be present when any of them passed through Vienna, speaking in the kindest manner to the soldiers calling them, "her children," and laughing when the word, "mother," ran through the ranks, never allowing them to depart without a present.

The consequences of this victory were most important, as all Saxony, with the exception of Dresden, fell into the hands of the Prussians, who could now remain in safety in their winter quarters, and Frederic saw himself in a position to send troops to Silesia, Brandenburg and Pomerania, to clear these provinces of the enemy and also to send a detachment of 8000 men to join Duke Ferdinand. Mecklenburg was again taken possession of, the Swedes were driven to Stralsund by General Werner and the Russians had retired into winter quarters in Poland.

Chapter 10: Opening of the Campaign of 1760 by the French

The plans for the operations of the war, which had been formed by the council in Vienna, were all based upon the false principle of directing the combined forces as much as possible towards the conquest of Silesia, instead of using every possible means for the recovery of Saxony; it was from this that arose much of the inactivity and want of determination on the part of the Austrian generals, and experience taught them that Silesia could only be conquered by means of Saxony.

As the giant Antaeus in wrestling with Hercules always arose from the earth with renewed vigour, so Frederic, in his struggles in Saxony, was never defeated without recruiting his strength by fresh power; for it was from this province that after the defeat of Kollin and the retreat from Bohemia that he gained the necessary forces to conquer at Rossbach and Leuthen, and it was from it that he procured means by which he got the better of the misfortunes of Hochkirch, drove the enemy before him as if they had been defeated, and was enabled to hasten to the relief of Neisse. The consequences of the battles of Kai and of Kunersdorf lost all their terrors so soon as Frederic regained possession of Saxony, and it was from this that the loss of a whole army at Maxen had remained without evil consequences, not even causing a change in the position of the Prussians. The unfortunate engagement at Landshut, the loss of Glatz, the raising the siege of Dresden, and the taking of Berlin lost their importance, for after the battle of Torgau he was enabled to assemble such forces from this country, that he came into the field more powerful than ever.

Those countries which had remained at peace during this time of war had derived great advantage from the prosperous state of their commerce, especially Holland; advantages which consoled this republic for the raillery of the different powers engaged in the war. The French had seized a Dutch post carriage which was on its way to Hamburg and contained 100,000 florins in specie belonging to Dutch subjects; it was in vain that the states general complained of this robbery, which had occurred on their own territory; for the court of Versailles refused all reparation, as they thought they had noticed a partiality on the .part of the Dutch towards the English, and were also anxious to annoy the inhabitants of Hamburg.

The ill will of the French government towards this town had many causes. It was natural that not only the senate but also the inhabitants should be more inclined to be favourable to the arms of their countrymen in the neighbouring provinces than to support those of the enemy; but in spite of this, they had preserved a strict neutrality, that the prosperity of their commerce might not suffer; as this city had been so fortunate as not only to be spared the horrors of warfare, but also to derive advantage from it at a time that all the rest of Germany was more or less devastated. It was here that so many of the contractors got their supplies, that so many speculations were entered into and that such large sums of money were brought from the different powers at war, and especially from England; but this town, so rich and so fortunate in many points of view, was not fated to remain entirely in quiet during these unhappy times.

The French, like all powerful nations accustomed to laugh at the neutrality of smaller states, looked upon all who were not for them during this war as against them; and they who had levied supplies in so many provinces, the allies of the Austrians, without paying for them; and who had taken possession of Frankfort and Bremen, would willingly have made an attempt upon Hamburg had their arms been more successful. But Duke Ferdinand of Brunswick, and not the King of Danemark, was then the protector of Hamburg, and as they could not injure the inhabitants with their arms, they interfered with their commerce.

They soon found an excuse for this purpose; a Hanoverian officer of artillery called on his friend Wuppermann, who was a merchant in Hamburg, and asked him where he could purchase a number of tin pipes ready made; Wuppermann told him, the contract was made, and he became security for the payment. The French minister in Hamburg, Chambeaux, who was of a troublesome disposition, and had already caused much unhappiness in Mecklenburg by his bad advice, heard of this and thought it a good opportunity to display his authority and his zeal for his country. He wrote a memorial, in which he placed the crime of the merchant in the blackest colours as that of being in communication with the enemies of France, threatening him in every possible way, so that the government of the town, alarmed at his threats, immediately took steps to search the house and warehouses of the merchant, but without finding any traces of his having furnished supplies, or preparations for doing so in future.

Notwithstanding this, Chambeaux threatened them with the loss of their commerce with France, and even with sending out privateers against their merchantmen. Wuppermann was now confined a prisoner in his house, there to remain until the court of Versailles should declare his innocence; but as new causes of displeasure arose against Hamburg, from the French not being satisfied that the Prussians and their allies should draw supplies from this city, Louis XV., on the 24th of May 1760, did away with the treaty of commerce which had been granted to the city in the year 1716.

A cessation of hostilities had been agreed to between Laudon and Goltz in Silesia, to continue until the 21st of May 1761, with the understanding that it would not be done away with but by giving four days notice. The Prussian general, the Prince of Bernburg, went into the neighbourhood of Glatz, under faith of this treaty and enlisted soldiers; but Laudon, hearing of this in Vienna, hurried back and required that the men should be given up. The Prince of Bernburg wished to justify himself on the ground that it was the territory of his king, and that he was therefore at liberty to levy men in it; Laudon's answer was decisive, as he fell on the unprepared Prussian garrison of Frankenberg, and took prisoners a whole battalion of infantry and a squadron of hussars; a loss, which was but ill supplied by the possession of a few hundred raw recruits. The cessation of hostilities was now at an end, and the skirmishes which were constant and very bloody without being at all decisive again began.

Frederic had taken up his winter quarters in Leipsic after the Battle of Torgau, and the inhabitants of this city had now to pay for the wish they had expressed of having the troops of the Empire quartered there for the winter. For this they were to be punished, and fresh and heavy contributions were raised on them, not. only in money but also in supplies of the produce of the country; it was in vain that the magistrates stated their poverty, and referred to the written promise of the king that bounds should be set to these demands, and which had now been passed. As there was still some delay in the payments, they were threatened with fire and the cry was: "money or the town will be set fire to." But as the inhabitants had good grounds for supposing that the king would not allow such threats to be put in execution, and soon found that they were only used by the subalterns, they lost their effect and men laughed instead of trembling at them.

Other means were now had recourse to and the highest authorities and the richest merchants were thrown into prison and treated as felons; they were placed in dungeons to lay upon straw, without any of the conveniences of life. At first one hundred and twenty shared this fate, but after ten days, this was reduced to seventeen of the highest personages who remained four months in prison. They suffered every hardship and the customary greeting of the tax-gatherer was: "Now you dogs! will you pay or not;" had they been separated from one another they might have given way, but together they encouraged one another, and it was not until they were threatened to be driven to Magdeburg on foot, with knapsacks on their backs, and preparations were made for carrying this into effect, that their courage gave way and they agreed to comply with every demand as far as they were able.

The position in which Frederic found himself from his provinces being in part devastated and in part in possession of the enemy, and from the necessity of carrying on a tedious and expensive war against the principal powers of Europe, forced him to have recourse to unusual means, and amongst others to that of altering the value of the currency, both in Prussia and Saxony, and that to an unheard of extent. The right of coining was leased to a Jew of Berlin of the name of Ephraim, who issued an immense quantity of gold and silver coins of every denomination and the sum paid for the privilege was every year raised, until it amounted to seven million dollars. At first only gold and silver pieces of Saxony were coined, and in order to remove all suspicion, they were marked with the year 1753; afterwards it was extended to the coinage of Prussia, Mecklenburg and later to that of Bernburg, permission having been purchased from the prince for that purpose.

Every year the coinage became more base, and at last the intrinsic value of the August or Frederic D'or was not more than one third of its nominal value, from being mostly copper with a very small portion of gold; whilst the old coin of the same denomination was worth four times its nominal value in the current coins of the day, which in derision were called Ephraimites; with this base money, the Prussian soldiers were paid, and it was used in payment for all the necessaries of the army, as well as for the salaries of all officials, and the carrying on of commerce. This line of conduct in deteriorating the currency soon found many imitators, and several German princes, the governors of small states who had never availed themselves of the right of coining now took this opportunity of issuing base money with which they paid their expenses, and gave in exchange for the old silver coinage.

Other princes of more extended dominions who were mixed up in the war, were forced to do the same; but Hanover did not follow their example and her money retained its value. Foreign powers entered into this speculation, for the Swedes who were the most in want of money of all the powers engaged in this war, were the first to employ this means for filling their exhausted treasury, and in conjunction with some merchants of Hamburg established a mint at Stralsund; this was also done in secret in the English manufacturing town of Birmingham and many hundred pounds weight of this coin were sent to Holland.

The issuing of so much of this money assisted commerce and trade in the first instance in an extraordinary manner, which caused the want of intrinsic value to be overlooked until many millions had been dispersed in circulation. Hamburg alone was not deceived, as by a wise regulation every thing was reckoned for its value in pure silver, and as soon as remittances were sent in the new coinage it was assayed, and its intrinsic value ascertained; this assay, which immediately became public, might be compared to the famous measure of the Nile in Egypt, for it was a scale by which all Europe could measure the value of this base money.

The whole of the north of Germany was inundated with this coinage, which without changing its form, its size, or its impressure, was ever becoming less in value, and deceiving its possessor with the idea of imaginary riches. Even the Dutch who had large quantities of it, thought that after the end of the war they would be able to purchase Prussian wood and corn with it at a low rate, but everything, and more especially merchandise rose in price in proportion to the deterioration of the currency; and it was only the most necessary articles of consumption that were not dearer, as otherwise the soldier could not have supported himself.

The dreadful effects of this financial system first became apparent by the ruin of many rich persons who had lived in tranquillity, without having otherwise suffered from the war; by the bankruptcy of merchants of high standing, and the reduction of innumerable families to beggary; so that it caused even more universal misery than the war itself.

Maria Theresa made use of other means to supply her necessities at this time, by making her subjects pay a property tax of ten *per cent*, which with the consent of the pope was extended, as long as the war should last, to the religious foundations; but as this was not sufficient, other means were had recourse to. All officers on the staff, from the majors to the field marshals, received their pay, during the latter years of the war, not in money but in paper, which was not like banknotes, or having a definite period to run; but consisted in state bonds, and those who could not wait until the end of the war for their payment, had to sell their paper at a considerable loss to a bank, which had been established for the purpose by the Emperor Francis, who managed it as court banker, and in which he employed his own particular capital. Most of the supplies for the army were paid for with this paper.

Many sacrifices were made from patriotic feelings to assist these resources, and Prince Wenzel of Lichtenstein, the richest subject of the Austrian dominions, afforded a noble example of this patriotism. As commander of the Austrian artillery he not only placed it in excellent condition at his own expense, but also kept up a part of it from his private income, for which the empress caused a statue to be raised to him and placed in the arsenal at Vienna during the war. Rich merchants also came forward and showed their love for their country in many ways, and the ladies of the court of Vienna, even to the empress herself, were occupied in making lint for the wounded. It was now the fashion, and it spread like an epidemic through the whole city, for the women of the working classes sacrificed their linen and that of their husbands, that they might not be merely inactive spectators of the war; the quantities of lint that were sent were so great that it at last became necessary to put a stop to this good work.

The time which had been spent during the last five years in fruitless operations for the conquest of Silesia had not diminished the wish in the imperial city, of becoming again possessed of it, and the taking of Glatz encouraged the hopes which the mighty confederation were ready to support by an equal anxiety for its fulfilment. As they looked on the great victory gained by the King of Prussia at Torgau as being for him equal to a defeat, in consequence of his great loss on that occasion, they determined to adhere, more strictly than ever, to the principal of not exchanging prisoners; but he did not want for soldiers, for the land of his dominions having been laid waste, thousands of country people exchanged the plough for the musket. It is true that the standard of height was not strictly enforced, as it was men who were wanted, and these men were speedily to he changed into soldiers; as soon as they were enlisted, and even before they left their homes, they were drilled from morning to night, without intermission so that by the time they joined their regiments they were ready for duty.

The number of old soldiers was now very small in all the contending armies, in consequence of the number of battles; but with the Prussians military enthusiasm supplied the place of long service. So many officers had been killed and the king not wishing to replace them by any but the upper classes, young men, far removed from manhood were taken from the cadet corps in Berlin, and sent to the army; and although they were wanting in bodily strength they were equal in other respects to experienced officers in other armies.

******

The author was only fourteen when he was sent in 1758, with thirty nine other cadets, to the king's head quarters at Breslau where Frederic himself distributed them among the different regiments.

******

Notwithstanding their high birth, they were accustomed to carry the musket, to hard fare, to mount guard in all weathers, and well acquainted with every part of the service, they were filled with high feelings of military honour. They were not infrequently employed, immediately after joining, on important duties which they performed with the zeal, activity and knowledge of old officers; and often in battle they stimulated old soldiers by their words, and gave courage by their example. The Austrians finding such young men among their prisoners, and only considering their age, looked upon this as a proof of the scarcity of men for replacing Frederic's army who they thought was now forced to have recourse to supply his losses by placing boys in the ranks.

The hatred which naturally exists between contending nations had gradually increased to a very great degree; this was displayed in the feelings of the Prussians and Austrians towards each other, and the examples of it are numerous in the history of this time; and the latter people, at that time so far behind the former in education, and so devoid of general information, distinguished themselves especially in this national hatred. According to their political ideas, the war which Frederic carried on was an insurrection against the power of the Emperor and the Empire, and deserving of punishment; whilst on the other hand, from their religions feeling, they themselves waged war against heretics whose extirpation was a praiseworthy act. In consequence of the defeat of Landshut, and the taking of Glatz at the commencement of the campaign, the number of prisoners who had fallen into the hands of the Austrians had been greatly increased; the greater part of them were ill treated, and afterwards hundreds of these unfortunate Prussians were thrown into the prisons at Vienna which had been intended for felons, and induced to enter the Austrian service to escape the ill treatment they had to undergo.

The Prussian officers who had been made prisoners were kept in small towns, in order, it was said, that they might not diffuse the poison of their opinions in politics and religious matters. Acting upon this principle, they were treated with any thing but generosity of feeling, and were often for a considerable time without receiving any pay, being left to the compassion of strangers for their support; for the complaints of the poor subaltern were equally disregarded with those of the general officers who were prisoners.

Fouquet could not remain silent on this subject, although it is true that he had been treated with the greatest consideration and respect; but his heart was too noble to allow his companions in arms to apply to him in vain, because he himself was not equally a sufferer. He complained bitterly and notwithstanding it was considered that he had, as a prisoner, no right to speak so boldly, he took even higher ground, and although he was aware that he was hated at Vienna as being the personal friend of his monarch, his enthusiasm for the Prussian service was so great, that he was led to make his representations with, it may be, too much energy. He made use of expressions respecting the empress and her ministers, which in England alone would have been allowed to pass unpunished; he spoke of meanness, of deceit and of unworthy statesmen who surrounded the throne of Theresa and prevented her hearing the truth.

This mode of expression was new in Austria and was looked on as a crime against offended majesty, which was but mildly punished by sending the sick general from Brugg on the Leutha to Carlstadt in Croatia, separating him from his servants and by imprisoning him in a fortress. Frederic who had many more general officers as prisoners than the Austrians, revenged his friend by shutting up four of their principal officers in the citadel of Magdeburg, who had previously resided in that town under no restraint. This system of reprisals did not stop here; for the Austrians, not to be behind hand placed those Prussian officers of highest rank who were their prisoners in close confinement in Kufstein. On this Frederic placed all the lieutenant generals in the citadel, where they were forced to remain, so much to their dissatisfaction, that it was necessary in one instance to make use of force to induce an officer to give up his apartment in the town for a room in the fortress. All this gave rise to an extraordinary correspondence between the Markgraf Charles of Prussia and General Laudon, in which each party reproached the other bitterly but without mending matters.

The reprisals continued and all the general officers of either side were placed in as strict confinement as if they had been felons until peace was concluded when the Prussian officers were released. Fouquet's sympathy for his brother officers and the interests of his king did not go unrewarded; never was Frederic more grateful than towards this general whom he loaded with presents and who was allowed to pass the remainder of his life, away from his regiment and the cares of office in the town of Brandenburg and retained the friendship of his monarch even to the grave.

The French opened the campaign of 1760 by bringing 130,000 men into the field, of which number 100,000 were to carry on their operations in Westphalia, and the remainder were to remain in the Rhine districts. Broglio hoped by this means to separate the forces of the allies; but the carrying out his intentions was very much cramped by the insubordination of some of the principal generals, who were dissatisfied with some of his demands respecting their duty. The delays thus caused gave time to Duke Ferdinand to form a junction with the reinforcements from England 7000 strong and he now found himself at the head of 90,000 men of which number 20,000 were English soldiers.

The death of the Landgraf of Hesse-Cassel, which occurred in January, caused no alterations in the arrangements of the allies, as his successor confirmed all the engagements of his father and adhered to the same system. The wife of this prince was now regent of the county of Hanau, as guardian to her sons; but in consequence of the government of this place having made this public, without asking permission from the French general in command, the whole of the town council, as well as all the officials of this small government, were thrown into prison and condemned to a fine of 100,000 dollars.

In consequence of the French having made demonstrations of intending an invasion of Hanover, Ferdinand was desirous of attacking them as soon as he had received his reinforcements, and commenced operations for this purpose. The hereditary prince led on the advanced guard, and falling in with a body of the enemy which he thought was only a detached corps, he received their attack with firmness. This detachment was however supported by the main army of the French, and continually received fresh reinforcements, whilst, on the other hand as it was not possible for Duke Ferdinand to come to the assistance of the hereditary prince in time to be of service to him, the latter had no alternative but to retreat, which he did not without disorder.

The French cavalry made several attempts to cut off his retreat, but the prince placed himself at the head of his men and drove the enemy back. In this engagement the allies lost 800 killed, wounded and taken prisoners together with fifteen cannon. The prince himself was wounded, and in spite of his loss gained great credit both from friend and foe for the decision and promptitude of his measures by which he had been enabled to escape a complete defeat; nevertheless he was most anxious to make good his loss, and only seven days after, on the 16th of July, he attacked another body of French at Emsdorf defeated them and took 2700 prisoners, as well as their leader General Glaubitz, together with a number of cannon colours and baggage. At the same time Broglio had very nearly succeeded in cutting off General Spörken with his Hanoverians, but was prevented by his rapid retreat, and the coming up of the allies to his assistance

The troops from Würtemberg, who had been engaged in Saxony, left the French service in the beginning of this campaign, in consequence of the reigning duke not being willing to comply with the wish of the cabinet of Versailles, that he should serve under the orders of Prince Xavier of Saxony; who as brother of the Dauphiness had considerably more influence at that court than the duke. Much disorder was created in the French army by the withdrawal of the discontented Generals, Count St. Germain, Count de Luc and Marquis Voyer who sent in their resignations; of this Ferdinand determined to take advantage and attacked the smaller army of the French 35,000 strong under the command of the Chevalier Muy, near Marburg, falling on them on both flanks in front and in the rear.

The battle was fought on the 31st of July and was undecided until Lord Granby came up with the English cavalry who after having ridden two leagues at speed, fell on the French and put them to flight. Their cavalry were enabled to cross the Dimel but the flying infantry, who endeavoured to follow their example were most of them drowned. The loss of the French was 5000 killed wounded and taken prisoner but the allies only lost 1200 The uncertainty of the fortune of war was however displayed on this day, for Cassel was taken by the French, in consequence of General Kielmannsegg having been forced to retreat on Hanover from the overpowering superiority of the force opposed to him in Hessia. The hereditary prince fell upon a small body of the French near Zierenberg and took 500 prisoners, and about the same time General Bulow surprised the French at Marburg and destroyed their baking apparatus.

In consequence of there being but few fortified places in Lower Saxony, the war was here carried on with great activity; for the engagements were frequent and both towns and districts were constantly changing masters being no sooner conquered by one party than abandoned to the opposite one. At one moment the French, masters of a province, looked on it as their own property, placed it in the hands of their farmer general from Paris that it might be exhausted according to their principles; but hardly had this been determined on, and before their intentions could be carried into effect, not a single village of the province which had been doomed to devastation, remained in their possession.

The conquests of the French became therefore of slight importance, and the only result they produced was the determining the point on which the allies should first make their attack. A striking instance of the uncertainty of their tenure occurred at this period for at the time that the principal body of the allies were advancing in their victorious career, Minden, Cassel, Göttingen, Eimbeck and Ziegenhain were taken by the French and Hameln was threatened with a siege; but all this passed away like a dream, so short a time did they retain their conquests. A few days after Lückner appeared, stopped their progress, drove them back from Hameln and took a number of prisoners. On the other hand the French took 800 prisoners in Ziegenhain, the field hospital fell into their hands and they appeared desirous of making a stand at this place.

Notwithstanding Broglio had an immense superiority of force he dared not venture a battle in consequence of the discontent which prevailed in his army; he therefore preferred to secure himself by entrenchments near Cassel, having fortified Göttingen; thus allowing Ferdinand to cut off many of the supplies of the French Army and destroy their magazines. It had become extremely difficult to get the necessary sustenance for so large an army in these exhausted provinces and the difficulty now increased every day. The French required so much forage for their horses that it was necessary to send out from fifteen to twenty thousand men under large escorts to procure the requisite supply.

At this period the English had become complete masters of the sea and their ships of war dictated to all the fleets of Europe, at the same time that their progress was unimpeded in the other portions of the globe. After having beaten the French at Quebec, the whole of Canada had fallen into their hands and they now aimed at taking possession of the French islands in the West Indies. The English cabinet, guided by Pitt, determined to carry on the war if possible into the very heart of Prance, and with this view, the Hereditary Prince of Brunswick was sent with 15,000 men to Cleves in order to drive the French from that place; and in order to strengthen his army, he took a portion of the garrisons from Münster and Lippstadt. He then crossed the Rhine sent out his light troops to skirmish in the Netherlands took a number of prisoners and invested Wesel.

His operations were much impeded by the continuance of rain which rendered the roads impassable, the rivers swollen and prevented the advance of his heavy artillery; but in spite of this the trenches were opened on the 10th of October, and the siege regularly began. The importance of the place forced Broglio to take the most decisive steps for its relief, and General Castries was sent with a body of 20,000 men which was augmented by 10,000 who joined him at Nuys. He advanced by forced marches, and arriving at Rhineberg, a battle became unavoidable and took place at Kloster Campen on the 16th of October. The hereditary prince, although much inferior in numbers attacked in person the enemy, who were advantageously posted near a wood at Rumpenbroeck, and took a French colonel prisoner, who not aware of the proximity of the enemy was going his rounds in the wood. This officer was no sooner aware of the presence of the prince, whom he did not know, than he hurried up to him and said "you are my prisoner."

"It is not I who am a prisoner but you yourself," answered the prince, "for you are surrounded by my grenadiers."

The battle continued from the morning until the evening and both sides fought with great courage; but in spite of every effort, the allies could not drive the French out of the field. The prince exposed himself to great danger, was wounded and had his horse killed under him; at last the allies withdrew in good order and without being followed although the retreat had to be made over the Rhine by means of a bridge which had been broken by the force of the stream. They made a number of prisoners including a French general officer, Baron Wrangel, and took several cannon; but their own loss was also great as the battle had been bloody and they had 1200 killed, wounded and missing.

The French had lost 2600 but might easily have gained great advantages from the retreat of the allies being impeded by the destruction of the bridge over the Rhine. The prince was aware of the danger of his position and in order to conceal it, drew his men up in order of battle, as if it were his intention to renew the attack; and by this means he gained the necessary time for the passage of the river. The siege of Wesel was now raised and the hereditary prince encamped near Bruynen.

This battle, which has been thrown in the back ground by more important conflicts, and the results of which in a political point of view were not important, has been rendered remarkable by an extraordinary occurrence that will be remembered by posterity when the recollection of these battles and the leaders in them shall have, passed away; for it was the noblest the greatest and most heroic deed of an individual daring the whole war. The Chevalier Assas, a young French officer of the regiment of Auvergne who commanded an outpost was surprised by the allies during the night in the wood already mentioned. It was dark and he was at some distance from his men, when he was surrounded by a body of soldiers; a hundred bayonets pointed at his breast threatened him with instant death if he uttered the slightest cry. The grand Condé has said:

If I were placed in danger without possibility of assistance I should be dismayed.

There was no prospect of help for the chevalier, even could he make his soldiers aware of the presence of the enemy and indeed his death could not insure their safety But Assas, who only thought of his duty cried out, "Auvergne! the enemy are here!" and in a moment was pierced with bayonet wounds. This noble conduct remained unnoticed for seventeen years, and it was only in 1777 that the minister of war, Prince Montbarry informed the king of it, and requested a pension for the family of this hero, which was granted. The whole nation were now anxious to do justice to his great sacrifice and this was even acknowledged in 1790 by the national convention, who ordered that the pension should still be paid as a debt due from the people.

It was now the beginning of November and although winter had set in, the operations of the allies were continued with activity. Broglio on the other hand had contrary to his usual practice remained in a state of inactivity continuing in his strongly entrenched camp at Eimbeck from which he had sent away several detachments; this and his distant position from the army of Soubise rendered Ferdinand anxious to give him battle, and he made use of every means to induce Broglio to leave his encampment. But in vain; and as to attack him in his strong position would have been risking too much Ferdinand was satisfied by making such movements as made it appear he was desirous of cutting off Broglio's communication with Göttingen. He blockaded this town, so important for the French, and which was garrisoned by a body of picked men of 5000 of the *grenadiers de France* under the command of General Vaux, an old soldier who had already been at eighteen sieges and was crippled by the wounds he had received.

This officer made the best arrangements for defending the town; the inhabitants were exhorted to lay in provisions for five months, every house was visited and note taken of the supply of food of whatever kind. As it was now beginning to freeze the smiths were employed in making hooks and axes to break up the ice; he gave orders to close the arch of the small bridge and to open the sluices by which means a great inundation was produced, and on the 12th of November he made a desperate sortie. The advanced period of the season was a great advantage to him; the rivers were swollen; diseases which carried off men and horses broke out among the troops of the allies, and the roads were impeded by the numbers of dead horses.

The allies now gave up all hope of getting possession of this town which was so well provisioned; but Ferdinand had gained his point completely by means of this blockade which had lasted twenty days. The French general retreated and took up his winter quarters in and about Cassel; Soubise went with his army to the lower Rhine, and quartered his men along the banks of the river. The allies, who had now no enemy to oppose them in Westphalia, took up their winter quarters in this province.

Ferdinand now turned his whole attention to the replenishing the magazines which had been destroyed by the French in Westphalia and East-Friesland. The supplies were brought in part from England and Holland, and also from the ports of the Baltic, where large quantities of provisions and corn had been collected, not only for the troops, but for the exhausted provinces; precautions which the ever ready English gold had enabled the authorities to take, and without which the greatest distress would have prevailed in the devastated districts.

Every one now looked on the campaign as ended; but Ferdinand was laying deep plans which he had determined to carry out in the midst of winter. The French, who occupied the Hessian provinces, were in possession of large magazines and their army was so placed that it formed an immense semicircle which reached from Göttingen to Wesel. On the 11th of February 1761 Ferdinand marched forth in four columns and fell on the French quarters from every direction. The French were dismayed and fled without making any resistance; they left in their rear all the strong places which had supported the line of their army and Cassel was garrisoned with 10,000 men and Göttingen 7500, the weaker positions being abandoned one after another.

They destroyed the magazines and took to their heels, but the allies followed so closely that they were enabled to rescue five of the principal ones from destruction. That every advantage might be taken at this moment, the Hanoverian General Spörken approached the Saxon frontiers at the head of a body of men in order to form a junction with a part of the Prussian army. The Saxon troops in conjunction with those of the Empire used every endeavour to prevent it and this led to a bloody engagement on the 15th of February at Langensalza in which the Saxons were defeated and lost 5000 men; the consequences of this victory were, that the French quitted many of the positions they had still held, and deserters came over to the allies in large bodies; but this was but little advantage so long as Cassel remained in the hands of the French.

To besiege this town was a work of great difficulty, as it was well provisioned and had a large garrison commanded by a courageous and ambitious officer, Count Broglio the brother of the French general. He had made preparations for a lengthened defence and had laid in a supply of salted horseflesh in case of extreme need; nothing was omitted for defence, nothing spared from destruction which could in any way impede that defence, not even the beautiful gardens outside the town, which were levelled with the ground, and every effort was made to repel the enemy.

Ferdinand having placed his army in such a manner that he surrounded Marburg and Ziegenhain and protected the besiegers of Cassel from every attack, the trenches were opened on the 1st of March and orders given to direct the fire of the cannon not on the town but only on the fortifications. The besiegers consisted in 15,000 Hanoverians under the command of Count Lippe-Bückeburg the first artillery officer of the day; but from scarcity of the supply of ammunition, caused by the impassable state of the roads, he was unable to make any impression. At the same time Broglio, who was too anxious to retain possession of this town not to venture every thing, drew his troops together, advanced and attacked the hereditary prince near Grünberg.

The nature of the ground was favourable to the French and the great superiority of their numbers decided the fate of the day in their favour; the allies lost, besides a great number of killed, 2000 men who were taken prisoners, a number of cannon and eighteen stand of colours. This misfortune was but the commencement of a succession of others; the investment of Marburg and Ziegenhain had become regular sieges, for in the last place alone 1500 shells had been thrown into the town in eighteen days; the town had been set on fire but was bravely defended by the French. As it now continued to rain incessantly it was found impossible to open the trenches regularly and both sieges were raised. The same result occurred at Cassel, where the siege had continued for four weeks, and all the strong positions which had been taken were now given up. Ferdinand fell back with his army on Paderborn and the French were once more masters of the whole of Hessia with the road open for them into Hanover. Nothing impeded their progress but the scarcity of provisions, the want of which was now of the greatest importance to them, and both parties were forced to remain in their present position.

This constrained state of inactivity continued until the end of June, when Ferdinand was the first to advance, determined to attack the French army under Soubise; but this general avoided a battle and withdrew with such haste to Soest, that he lost eight cannon and four hundred provision waggons. Broglio also left Cassel and fell in with General Spörken and his Hanoverians on the Dimel, who although advantageously posted would not venture a regular battle with so large a force and retreated constantly fighting and losing 800 prisoner, 19 cannon and 170 waggons.

Ferdinand continued to harass the French Army with his light troops, destroyed their newly formed magazines, and intercepted their supplies. These continued annoyances which were severely felt, induced Broglio now that he had formed a junction with Soubise and had a superior force, to determine on giving battle to the allies, and in case of necessity to force them to one as they did not appear at the present moment so inclined. As soon as Ferdinand was aware of this determination, he took up a strong position at Hohenover, where he was attacked by Broglio on the 15th of July. The fighting continued until dark when the French, driven back, withdrew into the thickets on the Satzbach; at break of day the following morning the engagement was renewed and both French armies joined and advanced in order of battle, Broglio commanding the right and Soubise the left wing.

The cannonade as well as the fire of musquetry was kept up without intermission for five hours and the separated bodies of the allies supported one another on the different positions which were sharply contested, with courage and determination; notwithstanding the difficulties which were opposed to. the carrying out the clever dispositions of the German general, but which were nevertheless completed. The French could not gain an inch of ground and at last the allies getting possession of a height threw the enemy into confusion and drove them back, forcing them to leave their wounded and cannon behind, and putting them to flight. A number of prisoners were taken and the left wing of the French who were fighting hand to hand, with the troops of the hereditary prince now gave up the contest and withdrew. The nature of the ground prevented the cavalry from entering on pursuit to complete the victory, but the loss of the French in this battle, which was named after the village of Villingshausen near which it was fought, was 5000 killed wounded and taken prisoner, whilst that of their opponents was 300 killed and 1000 prisoners.

Never was general more grateful to approved valour or more generous in rewarding courage displayed in a cause not his own, than Ferdinand; the most noble prince of his time and one who so well understood the art of conferring favours. Other generals, masters of immense riches, contented themselves with recommending to the notice of the sovereign, those who had distinguished themselves; but Ferdinand, although master of no territory and of limited income, acted on his own judgment being guided by his noble feelings. He waited not for the delayed and uncertain result of a recommendation; he distributed his own money and thought he could not apply to a better purpose that given by the British monarch, than by rewarding those who had done their duty. His presents were always princely and a number of officers received large sums, among others Generals Wulgenau and Gilse who each had 4000 dollars.

A few days after the battle Prince Albert Henry of Brunswick met with the same fate as his great uncle and his brother; he had but shortly before joined the army and was mortally wounded in a skirmish by a musket ball. Soubise sent his two most celebrated surgeons into the camp of the allies; but their science was exerted in vain to save this noble youth. This courteous behaviour on the part of Soubise did not hinder Lückner from seizing the large magazine at Höxter, or the partisan Freytag from burning the storehouses at Witzenhausen, Eschwege and Wanfried, sinking 33 vessels loaded with ammunition and seizing a military chest at Fritzlar with 25,000 dollars.

Notwithstanding all these advantages, and although Ferdinand was victorious in the last battle, he had gained but little; for the great superiority of the enemy and their numerous resources rendered their loss unimportant; and had the French generals been united in their councils they would probably have again attempted to drive the allies from their position. But a deep rooted enmity existed between them, and this defeat, of which neither would bear the blame, added fuel to the flame and caused an open rupture. Broglio blamed Soubise for having been tardy in his attack, and Soubise, on the other hand, averred that Broglio had began the attack before the time agreed on, in order to gain the victory without his help, and that he had given orders to retreat at the moment that the army of Soubise had good hopes of regaining the victory. The dispute ran so high that it became necessary to refer it to the judgment of the Marshals of France.

This want of unanimity caused the separation of the two armies shortly after the battle, each retreating; Broglio on Cassel and Soubise over the Rohr. The former was very near being taken prisoner when reconnoitring the position of the enemy; one of the Prussian black hussars caught him by the collar of his coat as he was crossing a hedge and had not the hussar's horse fallen, Broglio could not have escaped. He did so but ten of his *aides-de-camp* were taken as well as 200 horsemen of his escort. The Hereditary Prince of Brunswick also narrowly escaped being taken by the French a few days previously, as he was watching their movements near Unna; for he was surprised by them and had to cut his way with his escort through their ranks.

A curious occurrence took place at this time; there was a heavy fog and the armies of both parties were marching at a short distance from one another. In consequence the obscurity a French dragoon found himself in the midst of the columns of the allies, and discovered his mistake when nothing but quickness and determination could save him. He formed his plans in a moment, and seizing an English officer, who was riding carelessly by his side, held his pistol to his head, cried out, "submit or you die." The astonished officer surrendered thinking that, misled by the fog he had strayed into the midst of the French Army. This mistake lasted but a few moments, and he then asked the dragoon how he could think of taking him in his present position. The trooper answered:

I know the danger I am placed in, and will do my best to escape; if I can succeed in getting away from your columns you will remain my prisoner, if not I shall be yours.

It was in vain that the English officer, who looked upon being made prisoner in this manner as a disgrace, offered his watch and his purse to induce the dragoon to set him at liberty; the soldier was immovable, and as he was fortunate enough to escape detection he joined his own corps along with his prisoner.

The positions taken up in this campaign by the two armies were the same as those which the Romans and the ancient Germans had occupied in their wars eighteen centuries previous. In the neighbourhood of Detmold was the old Teutoburg, as has been ascertained by the numbers of Roman arms and coins which have been there dug up; and in the districts of the Lippe, Ravensberg Osnabrück and Münster have been found the tumuli of the conquerors of the world who had been sent forth to conquer Germania but who here found the northern limit of their progress.

The armies of both parties often passed through the Teutoburg wood, which has its name at the present time from the fame of its position, and in the neighbourhood of which the Germans led on by Herrman (Arminius) routed Varus and the Roman legions, the terror of the whole world, and obtained possession of the eagles so rarely the booty of the enemies of Rome. Half naked and almost in the state of barbarians they had fought for their hearths; and inflamed by the love of liberty had conquered the approved and well armed warriors of Rome who fought for the conquest of the world.

Ferdinand now found himself under the necessity of dividing his army in order to watch the movements of both his enemies who were once more on the advance. It was Broglio's object to advance as far as possible into Hanover, and Soubise threatened to besiege Münster which he had already isolated; but he had a watchful enemy to contend with in the hereditary prince. Under his command the allies took the town of Dorsten on the Lippe by storm; a town which had been fortified by the French and in which the preparations for the siege of Münster were being made. The commissariat of Prince Soubise was stationed here and a large supply of provisions and forage were destroyed; the garrison were made prisoners and Soubise was forced to withdraw over the Lippe.

Broglio's army was too powerful to allow of his being prevented from penetrating into Hanover, and Ferdinand therefore endeavoured to bring him to battle in a disadvantageous position, remaining constantly near him. But the French general did not allow himself to be induced to give battle, and as Ferdinand could not check his advance by force he had recourse to artifice, and hurrying into Hessia he cut off the supplies of the French army from that quarter; this plan succeeded and Broglio returned into Hessia. Ferdinand now marched on Paderborn to watch the French in case they should renew their projects on Hanover; and the hereditary prince who was in no apprehension for Münster joined the main army and destroyed on his march the magazines of the French which he found in unfortified places.

In the meantime Soubise again crossed the Lippe and sent out detachments which overran Westphalia and devastated this province. Broglio also sent out skirmishing parties into the Harz who raised heavy contributions, and Prince Xavier of Saxony besieged Wolfenbüttel which surrendered after a bombardment of five days. The town had to pay a contribution of 200,000 dollars, to make a present of 28,000 to the general and a compensation of 14,000 dollars in consideration of their retaining the bells of the different towers. The greater part of this was paid in hard dollars, but the remainder in merchandise and letters of credit, for the payment of which, hostages were taken. The reigning Duke of Brunswick unwilling to be a spectator of the misery of his people retired with his family to Zelle.

Xavier now advanced on the town of Brunswick which he invested; but the same night that the bombardment was to have been commenced the young Prince Frederic came to the assistance of his native city, formed a junction with General Lückner and fell upon the enemy who expected no such attack. They were defeated, after some hard fighting, with the loss of more than a thousand men and several cannon, and not only raised the siege but abandoned Wolfenbüttel.

One of Soubise's detachments seized on Osnabrück, and as the inhabitants did not consent immediately to pay a heavy contribution, treated them with great barbarity. Another body of men appeared before Emden which was garrisoned by only two companies of English invalids who were induced, by the entreaties of the inhabitants and the promises of the French, to give up the town; but these promises were little heeded and contributions were demanded throughout East-Friesland to the amount of a million of dollars. A portion of this was paid, but the greatness of the sum required and the cruel manner in which it was extorted rendered the people desperate. The peasants assembled together, armed themselves as well as they could and falling upon their inhuman enemies drove them out of the country. But shortly after many of these brave peasants had to pay dearly for their self-defence in consequence of the arrival of a fresh body of the troops of the enemy.

The French had never lost sight of the free town of Bremen and its advantageous position on the Weser; its size and its riches together with its proximity to the sea, were inducements to renew those endeavours to become possessed of it, which had been rendered futile by their opponents. This place was also important from its containing the stores of the allies which its position rendered easy of renewal by sea and from its communication with Stade.

The French had already shown in Frankfort on the Main that they could treat the free cities as enemies, and knew that complaints of their conduct to the government of the German Empire would be unavailing; they had therefore determined on taking possession and if possible of keeping Bremen. But the reports of their cruelties, the daily examples of which had been seen in the neighbouring states, caused the inhabitants to determine that it would be better to defend themselves to the last, than to give up the town to such an enemy. The French were driven back with loss, and Ferdinand strengthened the garrison by some English battalions to prevent the recurrence of such an attempt.

If the French had displayed less activity in this campaign they had nevertheless occupied themselves in precautionary measures, and in making fresh preparations. A portion of the walls and ramparts of Duderstadt were to be destroyed and to do this eight hundred peasants were brought from the Harz, for whom the citizens had to find food and drink; even women were not allowed to be idle, for three hundred were employed to carry a number of cannon balls in baskets from the iron works at Lautenberg to Göttingen. Large quantities of linen were required from the principality of Göttingen, but the chief care of the French was to fill their magazines, and to do this, they levied contributions from friend and foe. The circle of Franconia sent in a complaint on this subject on the 10th of November 1761 to the emperor, from which it appeared that the supplies which had been sent in and the loss sustained by the war amounted to twenty three millions of florins; and they begged the emperor to intercede with the King of France that the circle might be exempted for the future, as otherwise the circle must withdraw from its allegiance to the Empire. But the complaint was not listened to, supplies were ordered and sent in, and the threat of the circle was not fulfilled.

An extraordinary document which Anton Ulrich Duke of Saxe-Meiningen addressed, shortly after these oppressive levies, to the states general of the circle of Franconia, displays the character of this oppression in a marked manner. In it he says:

> All the nations of Europe, with the exception of Portugal, had either devastated these provinces or oppressed them by the passage of their armies. None of these refused to the states general the consideration due to them; it was left to our enlightened age that France should treat this assembly, composed of reigning princes and nobility who were their allies, with disrespect, and use coercive measures which they would have hesitated to carry out against the Chambre des Requetes in Grenoble. *In the kings name* and for his service, are the all-powerful *justifications* for every oppression and levy.

This complaint from a German prince was looked upon as a crime and the duke was forced to withdraw it in consequence of threats. But despotism did not stop here: in France it was then necessary to have a *lit de justice* in order to do away with the decisions of the courts of law by the will of the king. This was a brilliant spectacle by means of which the laws were rendered of no avail and the people dazzled and silenced. But in Germany the French court did not think it necessary to use such ceremony; a messenger brought the orders of Louis XV. to the states general of Franconia at Nürnberg to erase from their archives the complaint of the Duke of Meiningen and also the resolutions they had adopted in consequence of it. These orders were immediately obeyed, as they were accompanied by threats in case of non-compliance, to which the proximity of the French army gave due weight.

The French were enabled by these stringent measures to supply all their wants; and their demands extended even to requiring a number of cats from Hanover to destroy the immense quantity of mice in the granaries of the French. As the cats could not bear the confinement, requisitions were sent for hedgehogs and foxes. The example Frederic had given in Saxony was now followed in Hanover, and a number of recruits were raised from the ages of fourteen to forty, to fight against their country, and in case of desertion they were punished with death. In the town of Göttingen the French took upon themselves the duties of the police and the shoemakers whose work was badly done were flogged on the market place in presence of the guild of their trade.

The constant changes and disturbances in this town caused the greater part of the students and professors to go to Clausthal; but the fate of Hessia was worse even than that of Hanover. Recruits were raised and if the soldier, forced to tight against his country and all that was dear to him, endeavoured to escape from his detested colours, he was hanged without mercy. All the men capable of bearing arms were impressed and emigration was to be punished by the galleys. The French soldiers were constantly exercised, as they were trying to introduce the Prussian exercise into their army by means of the deserters who came over to them.

Chapter 11: Campaign of 1761

All the nations engaged in this war were most anxious for peace; not so their rulers, with the exception of Frederic, who alone was willing to make sacrifices to obtain it. At this period Theresa herself would not have been satisfied with regaining possession of all Silesia, if she had failed in her principal object of degrading Frederic from his position of king to that of ruler of a small principality. Elizabeth had satisfied her feelings of revenge, and would not have been disinclined to discontinue a war which was to her a heavy harden, had it not been that she looked upon the kingdom of Prussia as a Russian province of which she could only retain possession during the war, and which she could not make up her mind to resign.

The court of Stockholm and the whole of the Swedish nation were from the first averse to the war with the King of Prussia, but the direction of affairs was in the hands of the council of the kingdom who blindly obeyed the orders of the court of Versailles. The French looked anxiously forward to the termination of a war which drained their country of men and money, and, which having been engaged in, not for the advantage of the nation but from caprice, had been continued for the private advantage of the minister and the mistress of the king, and was now prolonged with acrimony, and without cause after having brought more disgrace on the French arms than any war on record; and yet, in case of a successful termination it offered no prospect of advantage to the state.

Louis XV. thought of nothing but pleasure and cared little for the success or misfortunes of his people. Choiseul, inexhaustible in his resources as a minister, from his knowledge of state policy was now at the head of affairs; he had formed the alliance with Austria, was fond of war and disliked the King of Prussia. His feelings of hatred had been increased by the reading a letter in verse written by Frederic to Voltaire, who was then residing in France, and who, from fear of the Bastille, had communicated it to the minister. Choiseul who had been very roughly handled in this letter, which was not intended for publication, forgot himself so far as to answer it by writing a letter in which he made use of expressions worthy of the *poissardes* of Paris; and from this time his hatred and desire of revenge knew no bounds. He formed numerous plans, and used every endeavour to induce Spain, with whom he had just concluded the famous Bourbon alliance, to join in the war; and that he might gain time to re-equip the navy of France, sought to restrain England in the midst of her victorious career by means of negotiations.

He also determined to send an army in 6000 flat bottomed boats to make good a landing on the coast of England in order to change the face of affairs of the war in America which had hitherto been so unfavourable to France. Count Bussy was sent to London to offer a cessation of hostilities which was not agreed to, although Mr. Stanley was sent as ambassador to France; for the French negotiations were merely dictated by diplomatic intrigue and therefore produced no results. Theresa also thought she might derive advantage by the same means, and expressing her desire for peace, proposed Augsburg as the place of meeting; but in consequence of Frederic's refusing to allow any ambassador from the Emperor to be present, the preliminaries were delayed from day to day.

The court of Madrid, faithful to the secret alliance with France, endeavoured to force her mediation on England. As this was refused, the Spanish ambassador in London made use of some threats towards Pitt who replied to them by saying:

You have heard my determination; I shall not depart from it, until the Tower of London is taken sword in hand.

As the principal point of dispute in all attempts at making peace, with the confederates, was the compensation for the loss of the Electorate of Saxony, Frederic thought to settle this question by an exchange of territory and offered to give up the kingdom of Prussia and his Westphalian provinces in return for the retaining possession of Saxony, and also proposed that the family of Augustus should hold the title of king as hereditary; on the other hand he wished to have that of King of the Vandals. The income of either territory was about the same and the vicinity of the new kingdom to Poland promised great facilities to the continued possession of this crown. The offer was however instantly rejected as Augustus looked on it as an affront and would consent to no terms which referred to his giving up his beloved country; but had it not been for the great changes which took place in Russia during the following years, this project would have been realized and the conqueror would have dictated terms, which must have been accepted *willingly or unwillingly*, and would have retained possession of Saxony.

The enemies of Frederic were under no apprehension that their expectation should be deceived as to the continuation of the zeal of the different courts in the carrying on of the war, or any fear that Spain would fail to add her strength to their powerful coalition; and as there appeared in Vienna, Versailles and St. Petersburg as well as in Warsaw and Stockholm fresh cause for hopes of success, all thoughts of peace were abandoned.

In the mean while Frederic sustained a severe loss by the death of George the Second, King of England who died in October 1760. With him expired the zeal which had characterized all the operations of the English in Germany, or to use the expression of Pitt, the desire to conquer America by means of Germany. The whole people were now convinced of the utility of carrying on a war by land and were anxious for its continuance; but Pitt who was still at the head of affairs had no longer the same power in the council. From the moment of the king's accession he was forced to share his influence with Lord Bute, a minister without any talent in administration and who only knew how to make himself necessary to his monarch, and whose vacillating measures could only, tend to the downfall of a powerful nation.

This was in fact the moment of the decline of the power of Great Britain; a power which had reached its highest point in 1761. Lord Bute, who was aware of his utter incapability to govern, and yet was anxious to be at the head of affairs, thought that he would meet with less difficulties during a time of peace, and that he could then better carry out his projects for extending the power of the king. He was therefore anxious for peace; but as all the other ministers, the parliament and the people were of a different opinion he dared not express his wish, and contented himself by working underhand to reach his object.

The effects of this soon showed themselves, for the treaty with Prussia was not renewed, and Frederic received no more subsidies, although George the Third had promised in his first speech to the parliament to fulfil the engagements made with Prussia against the confederates. The parliament had likewise, in an address to the king, expressed its intentions to the same effect and made use of the following expressions, so honourable to Frederic as coming from the senate of a foreign, nation.

> We cannot sufficiently admire the immovable firmness and the inexhaustible resources of the mind of the King of Prussia, our ally.—We most willingly and without delay grant the supplies for his assistance.

Bute would not hear of this; in the first instance he sought for every means of evasion, and at last the payment of the subsidies was refused, as Bute hoped by this means to force the King of Prussia to come to terms for peace according to his wishes.

In the midst of the turmoil of war Frederic did not neglect science and literature; and especially when in winter quarters he devoted a considerable portion of his time to study and to the arts. Colonel Quintus Icilius, whose family name was Guichard, was daily with him; he possessed great knowledge of ancient and modern literature and had made the art of war of the Greeks and Romans his particular study, which induced Frederic to give him the name of a Roman centurion, and which he retained the whole of his life time.

As Frederic passed the winter for the first time in Leipsic after the Battle of Torgau, Quintus induced him to converse with the professors of this university; but the prejudice of Frederic against German writers was unbounded and he read no books in his mother tongue from the impression that German literature in 1760 was in the same position as it had been in 1730, when he as a prince was a martyr to German pedants, and the court fool Gundling was president of the academy of science at Berlin. But in the midst of devastation and indescribable misery, this literature so much despised by Frederic was breaking forth in its dawn and giving good promise for the future.

The Germans had long been famous as being a most learned people: they studied deeply in science, and by their unbounded application and the acquisition of the languages of other nations became their instructors in many branches of knowledge. But they still remained only men of accumulated learning which in them got the better of genius; and these men who in imagination lived more in Athens and Rome than in Germany, often knew nothing of the principles of good taste. In addition to this their language was not formed, and the beauties the richness and strength it possessed, were unknown until brought into life by the genius of its immortal poets. It was now making rapid progress, but this advancement could not be appreciated by other nations from their want of knowledge of the language. The change occurred during the period of this extraordinary war in which so much genius had been engaged to be brought to light in so astonishing a manner.

Never did the development of the genius of a people occur more rapidly or display itself hi a more extraordinary manner, and never did the greatness of human nature appear under such different aspects as during this period. Whilst the German heroes, Frederic and Ferdinand, were teaching the rest of Europe the art of war in the midst of the roar of the cannon, Winkelman got the better of the errors of antiquity to bring order into the place of the former confusion in science; Euler pointed out the path of the planets and Mengs became the Raphael of the eighteenth century. Artists of all kinds increased in number throughout Germany and displayed their talents in statuary, medals and engravings. The German muse aroused the talent and science of her country in the midst of the turmoil of war and the lyre of the poet and the works of the artists were crowned with their newly planted laurels.

This advancement extended on all sides, and at a time when the science of war was attaining perfection, the German theologians abandoned their incomprehensible doctrinal disputes to teach pure morality. The art of criticism, which in Germany had as yet remained in its infancy, now began to enter upon a more extended career. The learned in the law gave up their barbaric language; physicians no longer showed their learning in Greek to their patients and now began to speak and to write, so as to be intelligible. The German natural historians, although they had no painter of nature equal to Buffon, continued to instruct all the nations of Europe, even the French and the English, by means of their new discoveries, their indefatigable research, and their powers of application.

But in poetry the Germans shone the most; Haller, Hagedorn, Bodmer, Uz and Gellert had already wasted their exertions upon an uneducated people. But a more favourable time had now arrived in which so many events and such passions had awakened the most impenetrable men throughout Germany, if not to activity, at any rate to sympathy; and Wieland, Klopstock and Lessing now came forth; three men destined not only to secure the fame of Germany, during their own existence, but even in futurity, and to be placed by the side of the greatest men of other nations; a destiny towards which they now as young men set forth with slow but certain steps. In addition to these Kleist sang the beauties of nature, Gleim was the Anacreon of Germany, Ramler the Horace and Gessner the Theocritus.

This brilliant commencement of national fame in literature was however not appreciated by Frederic, and he retained the prejudices which the impartiality of his learned friends could not get the better of. At this time there were two staunch defenders of the new German literature about the person of the king; these were the English Ambassador Mitchel, and the French Marquis D'Argens, the friend of Frederic, who both tried to impress on the mind of the monarch the progress of genius in Germany. But as he could not endure the characters of German printing the representations of these learned men were in vain, and Gottsched who was by many looked on as a remarkable man, was unable to get the better of this prejudice when he had the honour of a conversation with the royal poet.

The contracted nature of the powers of this learned man, and his entire want of taste and wit rather tended to strengthen the opinions formed by the king and affirmed his decision on this point for the rest of his life time. Latterly Frederic requested Quintus to introduce Professor Gellert to him and was astonished at the profundity of his knowledge, his good taste and his manner of delivery, which, drew forth such praises as put the modest Gellert to the blush; even the freedom with which he represented to the monarch his too great partiality to the French, and his depreciation of German literature, did not cause displeasure. (The king on this occasion made use of the expression "*C'est le plus raisonnable de tous les savants allemands.*"). He however only had one interview notwithstanding the king begged him to come often; for Gellert as he stated in a letter to Rabener followed the advice, "urge not thy presence on a king."

The unexpected withdrawal of the English subsidies had no doubt some effect in the determination of Frederic to act during the next campaign on the defensive. His caution, to which the Austrians were not accustomed, was looked upon by them as a feint in order to carry his point with the more certainty, and they therefore did not act on the offensive but contented themselves with watching his movements. The principal object of the Austrians and Russians was still the gaining possession of Silesia; to prevent which the king advanced in the spring of the year (1761) into this province, leaving Prince Henry at the head of an army in Saxony, where Daun had remained with his principal force, having sent Laudon to try his fortune against the king.

This latter general, who had hitherto only commanded detached bodies, now led on for the first time a large army and invaded Silesia; but restricted by the orders from his court, he contrary to his custom carefully avoided a general engagement. He remained for two months in the strong position of Braunau trusting, as Daun had ever done, to the protection of the hills for his safety. At last he commenced operations in order to form a junction with the Russians which, as in the previous year, was to be the principal object of the campaign. General Goltz was posted near Glogau with 12,000 men as a corps of observation on the Russians, and the king strengthened his force with 9000 men ordering him at the same time to attack the different detachments of the Russians as they advanced. But Goltz died suddenly and the command was given to Ziethen, who advanced into Poland, but was forced to give up this plan in consequence of the concentration of the whole of the Russian forces.

They now invaded Silesia and endeavoured to form a junction with Laudon who was posted on the opposite bank of the Oder; but the king was enabled to get the start of them by extraordinary forced marches and advanced with the whole of his army on the 4th of August into Silesia, and by means of his rapid movements he rendered it impossible for some time for the Russians to cross the Oder. They had acted with indecision in their operations, and to occupy their time had bombarded Breslau from seven batteries; so that it was not until the 12th of August that the junction was formed at Striegau which should have been completed, according to their plans, in the beginning of July and which had been already determined on four year previously. As there was already a scarcity of provisions in the Russian camp, Laudon sent to Jauer four days afterwards, 400,000 rations of bread for them. A few weeks anterior to this two waggon loads of medals had arrived at the Russian headquarters as rewards for services at the Battle of Kunersdorf, and which were distributed to the soldiers.

Butturlin was the commander in chief of the Russian Army which consisted of upwards of 60,000 men; the strength of the Austrians was 72,000 men and to oppose these Frederic had only an army of 52,000 men with which he occupied a camp at Bunzelwitz near Schweidnitz and defended by that fortress. The army of the enemy were formed in a semicircle round this position leaving the rear of it unopposed. Never had Frederic as king and general, and especially as the latter, been so critically situated; for to give battle, in other cases his best resource, would now have been folly, opposed as he was to such a superior force; for even a victory, dearly as it must have been purchased, would have availed but little against so numerous an enemy, and the result of a defeat would have been most fearful for the king.

But what had so often assisted the Prussians and made up for their deficiency of number was: "Cesar and his good fortune." Frederic took but little time for consideration, and determined for the first time in his life, carefully to avoid a battle. In his main army the flower of his troops there had never been a thought of having entrenchments, especially when the king was at the head of his soldiers; they had been in the habit in his camp of throwing up slight works for the defence of the outposts, and batteries for the heavy cannon; but now the whole camp was to be fortified. In this, as in all the operations of Frederic, the manner of its execution and its rapidity were extraordinary and without example in modern warfare.

The central point of the camp was about two leagues from Schweidnitz and the whole circumference in which the infantry were encamped formed one continuous line. The entrenchments consisted of ditches, sixteen feet deep, and of the same width, and connected together by twenty four heavy batteries; before the lines palisades were planted and *chevaux-de-frise,* and in advance of these rows of false ditches six feet deep. Intervals had been left for the cavalry to pass through and by which the infantry could, according to circumstances, fall upon the flanks or rear of attacking parties. On some points the camp was protected by morasses, on some by the Striegau waters, and on others by the a wood called the Nonnenbusch in which barricadoes were made and sharpshooters posted.

Four fortified mounds inside the camp formed bastions and the hill called Würbenerberg appeared on the left wing like a citadel. Nothing was to be seen but batteries and each of these had mines in them, or in advance of them covered ditches filled with powder and combustibles which could be sprung in a moment, from communication by trains with the interior of the batteries. The king had taken a number of heavy cannon from Schweidnitz to strengthen the batteries which were now mounted with 460 pieces of artillery, and had 182 mines and were placed upon heights, the advance to which was already rendered difficult from the nature of the ground, the small rivulets, and the marshy meadows.

Such was the camp at Bunzelwitz, equal in strength to a fortress and from its uniting the principles of military tactics with those of field fortification was looked on as a model and offered to the enemy insurmountable obstacles in the attack. From the elevated position of the Prussian camp the enemy could not derive the slightest advantage from their cannon, and even still less from the musquetry which were useless against palisades and entrenchments; and from their cavalry nothing could be expected, exposed as it would be to the Prussian artillery in all its movements. But if the nature of the works were admirable how much more so was the rapidity with which they were completed, for this was done in three days and nights; one half of the army worked whilst the others rested and so it went on until every thing was completed. On the plain at the termination of the entrenchments on the left wing were posted ninety squadrons of Prussian cavalry, who were anxious to display the manoeuvres taught them by Seidlitz on ground so favourable to their evolutions.

Laudon had full powers from the empress to give battle or not as he might judge right; he wished to choose the former alternative and in the first instance it was his as well as the Russian general's intention to attack the king. But to carry this into effect it required to form a plan which could not be determined on and carried into effect in a day on account of many different causes, both military and political as affecting the Russians and Austrians, many customs of warfare, doubts, and wants to be supplied. Frederic made use of this invaluable time and when the enemy had settled their doubts and determined on the attack, instead of finding the Prussian camp they saw opposed to them a continued line of strong fortifications which appeared to have arisen out of the earth as by magic.

The way in which these were to be attacked, or rather to be stormed, required fresh plans and raised fresh difficulties, so that in a council of war, at which Laudon was present in the Russian camp, Butturlin expressly declared that he would risk nothing with his army, but that should the Austrians and the Prussians come to an engagement, he would send a body of men to reinforce them. In fact an attack upon the Prussian camp was madness and nothing but dreadful slaughter could be expected, even before they could come hand to hand with the enemy in their place of strength; and the bravest soldiers shuddered at the thoughts of this enterprise which was to he more decisive than any battle in the whole war and would certainly have been the most dreadful contest of the century.

It was nevertheless Laudon's most ardent wish to venture such an attempt, and he was the more desirous of so doing, as however great his loss might be, a victory would decide the fate of the war, and even should he be defeated the retreat of the Austrians and the Russians was secured by their position. But he himself did not think an unfavourable result as probable, at the least he did not allow the Russian general to think that the fortunate result of the attack could be doubtful; nevertheless the latter although jealous of Laudon, as the actual conqueror at Kunersdorf, would not give way and remained firm to his purpose of venturing nothing.

An important consideration however completely decided the question; Laudon was anxious in this battle, the result of which was to procure the possession of Silesia to his mistress, to undertake the most difficult and principal part of. the attack, thinking that by this means he would secure the concurrence of the Russians, who were always complaining that all the fatigues of the war were thrown upon them. But this plan had the disadvantage of making the Russians play a secondary part and of forcing their general, Count Butturlin, although superior in rank and dignity to await the orders of Laudon and in case of a fortunate result to be only an auxiliary to the victorious Austrians; and in case of defeat to be looked on as the sole cause of such an event.

Frederic was during this time ever prepared for battle; by day, when all the operations of the enemy could be watched his soldiers reposed, but as soon as the twilight of evening began to close in, the tents were struck and the whole baggage of the army sent under the cover of the cannon of Schweidnitz; all the regiments remained in the entrenchments under arms, and the whole of the infantry, cavalry and artillery were placed during the night in order of battle. The king generally remained in one of the principal batteries, where a small tent was pitched for him; his baggage was also sent away every night and brought back in the morning. It was only at sunrise that the troops fell out of the ranks and again pitched their tents; the heat was excessive and with the exception of bread, there was a scarcity of provisions, there being no cattle or vegetables.

The soldiers had nothing to cook and were weary of their bread and water; in addition to this they suffered from want of sleep which became every day more distressing, as there was no prospect of their being able to procure more rest; the number of the sick increased amazingly, and these were sent in large bodies to Schweidnitz. The discontent throughout the army was general and many would have deserted their colours had not the entrenchments prevented their doing it by day, and the remaining under arms rendered it impossible during the night. All the precautions which had been taken augmented the indetermination of the generals of the enemy and also their uncertainty as to the strength or weakness of the different portions of the camp.

The junction of the Austrians and Russians which had been so much feared by the king was now a fortunate circumstance for him, for the greater part of the campaign had been occupied with marches to gain this object. Had it not taken place, only the Russian Army would have remained in a state of inactivity, and Laudon would have been left at liberty to act as he pleased with a vastly superior force and advantages; as Frederic in order to watch the operations of the Russians, would have been necessitated to divide his army, which he had now been able to unite under his own command.

The principal dependence of the king was placed upon gaining time and upon starving the enemy, as he himself was free from anxiety on this head, from Schweidnitz being at least well provisioned with bread and forage; and the scarcity of these most necessary of all requisites could not fail to occur in so numerous an army as that of his enemies, confined as it was in a small space between hills where it was difficult to obtain supplies. The price of corn was already enormous and the scarcity which soon became unbearable to the Russians was increased by the operations of Frederic, who sent General Platen with 7000 men in the rear of the Russians. This officer penetrated into Poland, and fell upon a large number of waggons loaded with corn which had been entrenched near Gostin and was defended by 4000 Russians. He gave orders to charge them with fixed bayonets and the Prussians rushed into the entrenchments and made themselves masters of the whole of the waggons.

The 4000 men were driven back, near 2000 made prisoners and three large magazines destroyed; this detachment also threatened the principal magazine in Posen, and the Russians now thought it high time to retreat. After having for twenty days made fresh plans and always given them up and after the united armies had twice advanced to the attack and been recalled without making the attempt, all their projects were abandoned and the dispositions for the battle which had already been made were countermanded. It was however apparent in the midst of this confusion and indetermination that it had been Laudon's plan to make use of the oblique mode of attack which had been so advantageously employed by Frederic.

On the 13th of September Butturlin crossed the Oder with his army having left 20,000 men under the command of Czernichef with the Austrians, and then withdrew into Poland; which country was in fact a Pandora's Box to the Prussian states, as not only did the devastating hordes of Russians pour out from it but also such swarms of locusts came from these districts as to darken the air and overrun upwards of sixty square German miles near Züllichau.

The news of the retreat of the Russians was a source of rejoicing throughout the camp of the Prussians, and they celebrated it as if they had gained a victory; for although Laudon's army with the body of Russians was nearly double in numbers to that of the king, the extreme measures of precaution for defence ceased immediately. The tents remained standing, the baggage was not removed, and tbe men no longer remained under arms during the night; the cannon which had been brought from Schweidnitz was sent back to this fortress, the combustibles were taken out of the mines, the *chevaux-de-frise* burnt, and a great portion of the entrenchments thrown down; in consequence of which the communication with the surrounding country was thrown open and the Prussian camp was now well supplied with every necessary.

Frederic only remained fourteen days in this position after the departure of the Russians; he looked on the campaign as not yet concluded, and was anxious to render it remarkable by his actions. Laudon who was encamped in a strong position showed no disposition to engage in a battle; but the king hoped to induce him to change this by his movements and drive him into Bohemia, or else find a favourable opportunity to attack him. The provisions in Schweidnitz were nearly exhausted by the continued draught on them, and on the other hand there was a plentiful supply in Neisse. All these considerations induced Frederic to break up his camp and to advance to Münsterberg two days march from Schweidnitz.

This fortified place was, as usual with the fortresses of the Prussians, not strongly garrisoned and added to this a great portion of those to whom the defence was entrusted were not to be depended on, from consisting of deserters. The place itself, although often, besieged and celebrated from its position, was anything but a strong fortress; but the commandant General Zastrow appeared by his experience and knowledge able to get the better of all disadvantages. At the same time, from the king being in the immediate neighbourhood there was no prospect of a siege and nothing was farther from Laudon's mind than such an enterprise. However he took the most effectual measures for surprising the place and Czernichef offered all his forces to assist him; but of these Laudon only took 800 Russian grenadiers, which with twenty battalions he placed under the command of General Amade. The secrecy of the preparations and the knowledge of the mode of life of the leader of the expedition, who was much addicted to the pleasures of the table, both tended to favour the surprisal of this weak garrison.

The defence of fortified places in these times depended much upon the artillery and the serving the guns; and it is true that in the fortress there were 240 pieces of cannon, but there were only 191 artillery men. An Austrian officer of the name of Roca who had been taken prisoner and who enjoyed Zastrow's favour, was allowed to range in every part of the place and supplied the Austrians with information on every point. The *commandant* thought not uf danger and was so careless of ail precautions that he never sent out parties to watch the enemy nor threw up lights to examine the country at night, neglecting even to give orders to his officers how to act in case of emergency. Laudon by these means was enabled to arrange every thing without being observed, and even to advance as far as the palisades. He had addressed his troops and given them strict orders not to pillage the town, to compensate for which they were promised 100,000 florins The Walloon grenadiers in reply cried out: "Lead us on to gain glory, we do not want money!"

Laudon surrounded the place with light troops and ordered a feint to be made by a party of Croats, during which the attacking party advanced in four columns with scaling ladders and fascines and without being remarked, reached the outworks on four different points at three o'clock on the morning. They did not wait long, for without firing a shot, they rushed into the covered way, charged the garrison with fixed bayonets drove them back or cut them to pieces, and having made themselves masters of the outworks turned the Prussian cannon against the fortifications, and stormed the ramparts.

It had been thought right, perhaps unknown to the general, to stimulate the courage of the storming party by means of brandy; from this they cared not for danger, especially the Russians, who rushed forward in disorderly masses like madmen. In the midst of the darkness they came to a chasm in the works which stopped their progress; the draw bridges were raised and no impediment had been expected at this point; the foremost ranks halted and called out for scaling ladders and fascines, but the Russian officers thinking this would detain them too long, and that the ditch might as well be filled with men as with fascines, forced those in the rear to advance. The unfortunate soldiers who were in advance were precipitated into the chasm and those who followed marched over the bodies of their companions. The Russians cut down everyone who came before them. At one part of the works, of which they were on the point of making themselves masters, quarter was asked, but the furious Russians cried out: "No quarter!"

A Prussian gunner was determined not to die unrevenged for he blew up a powder magazine which destroyed him with a number of his fellow soldiers and 300 of the enemy. Three bastions were now in their hands and the last attack was made by the leader of Laudon's own regiment Count Wallis upon a strong point, which was bravely defended by the Prussians. The Austrians were twice driven back but Wallis cried out to them:

> We must gain possession of the fortress, or I will never return alive; this I have sworn to our general whose name our regiment bears. Let us conquer or die!

These words did wonders; the officers carried the ladders themselves and the walls were scaled. The Austrian prisoners in the fortress to the number of 250 broke open the doors of the casemates in which they were confined and opened the gates to their countrymen. The Austrians had not required any cannon during the storming the works until they gained possession of that of the Prussians, having only used the bayonet and the sabre. Their loss in killed and wounded was 1600 men.

The storming had lasted three hours and at break of day on the 1st of October the fortress of Schweidnitz was in possession of the enemy together with the garrison of 3700 men, the arsenal, and the magazines. The promise of 100,000 florins instead of other booty was the cause of restraining the disorderly conduct of the soldiery to a certain extent, but the pillage lasted four hours. In this place as in Cüstrin and Dresden many of the inhabitants of the surrounding neighbourhood had deposited their valuables for safety against the depredations of the Cossacks. These fell a prey to the soldiery whose rapacity was continuing to increase until the humane exertions of the Prince of Lichtenstein and Count Kinsky who rode into the town with the cavalry, put an effectual stop to their licentiousness. But in these excesses the Russian grenadiers took no part and gave an unexpected and praiseworthy example; they remained quietly on the ramparts and never even piled their arms. Zastrow, who in spite of his being encompassed with enemies had given a ball on this very night was clever enough to justify himself to his king and to refer to the brave defence he had made. Frederic answered that the whole affair was a mystery to him and that he would delay giving his opinion on it. Most probably he had his own reasons for not bringing this general to a court martial after the end of the war for he contented himself with dispensing with his services.

Laudon had gained a most important advantage for the Austrian arms by the taking of Schweidnitz, as the imperialists were now for the first time enabled to take up winter quarters in Silesia, and which their six bloody campaigns had not as yet enabled them to do. But the reward of this general was in no way equal to the service he had rendered. Ingratitude was what he met with and he would have been punished if the Emperor Francis and the old Prince Wenzel of Lichtenstein, whom the empress respected as her father, had not protected him with all their influence. Count Kaunitz was also favourable to him and in a letter of congratulation which he wrote to the empress on this occasion he wrote:

God preserve the Joshua of Your Majesty!

These powerful favourites anxious for the honour of their court went even further; for they induced the empress not only to write a gracious letter to Laudon but also to send him presents; and this they did that the miserable intrigues of the court might not render it a mark of derision to the rest of Europe. But it is very evident from Laudon's having no important command during the next campaign, the little consideration he enjoyed at court during the remainder of Theresa's life time as well as his not receiving the staff of field-marshal until seven years after, that in spite of the brilliancy of his act he was not forgiven. His crime consisted in having taken so important a town without asking or gaining the permission of the council of war at Vienna and therefore without the consent of the empress; he had neglected taking this precaution as most probably the delay it would have caused would have upset his plans, and rendered them of no avail. The enemies of this great general went so far as to call this brilliant and fortunate enterprise a skirmish of Croats.

The rapid advancement of Laudon, who was a foreigner without birth, fortune, or recommendations, to the highest rank in the army merely from his own merit and not from court-favour was the more extraordinary in a country like Austria, and as yet unexampled in this century. Laudon, a major of Croats who in the year 1756, was modestly awaiting the preparation of the imperial orders from the secretaries of the Austrian government and had to suit their convenience, was in the year 1761 looked on by the whole of Europe as the great support of the throne of Theresia; which in fact he was. It was he who had planned the attack at Hochkirch and it was he who had saved Olmütz in Moravia by the destruction of the immense train of provision waggons; and he it was who had defeated the army of Fouquet and taken that great general prisoner. He had taken Goltz and he, and not Soltikow, had beaten the king at Kunersdorf. The Austrians had to thank him for many other successes and he had now taken Schweidnitz.

The great capabilities of this leader appear to have been originally available for the advantage of Frederic. Previous to the war Laudon had been in Berlin and was anxious to have been made captain in the Prussian service; the king refused his request and this man, who was to have so much influence upon the whole of the war quitted the territory of Prussia. Had Laudon not been in the army of Theresa it would not have been necessary to fight through seven campaigns and the enterprises of Frederic and their consequences would have been far different. Laudon had imparted to the emperor the project for surprising Schweidnitz at the same time explaining to him the difficulties which lengthened formalities would entail on such an undertaking, and telling him that nothing but rapidity of action could ensure its success.

The movements of the king were very uncertain, and the slightest discovery would have rendered the attempt quite impossible; in this state of affairs the emperor took on himself to act for the empress and it was he who carried to her the first intelligence of the success which was indeed worth more than a victory. Theresa unaccustomed to receive information of the operations of the war through such a medium, and extremely jealous of his interference, expressed no pleasure on hearing the news. She was displeased and the council of war at court who were thus thrown in the back ground added fuel to the fire of her rage; reason was not listened to, and had it not been for the noble conduct of Francis, Lichtenstein and Kaunitz, Laudon would have been sacrificed.

Circumstances had occurred twice during this century in Austria having an extraordinary resemblance and which for their similarity even in detail appear to have been meant for the instruction of mankind. For the support of this great Empire at two dangerous periods in her history it became necessary that she should possess in each, a hero endowed with remarkable talents, not the production of every year or to be found in every country. These great men had in fact not been met with in the imperial dominions, but the good fortune of Austria led them each to her assistance at the proper time, and the names of Eugene and Laudon will ever shine in the annals of that Empire.

The fate and the deeds of each had actually a great similarity, for both were foreigners, the talents of each were neglected in their own country and despised by their sovereigns who were destined to feel deeply their power. Louis XIV., who had laughed at the talents of Eugene in warfare when a youth, trembled at his much feared name when a man and a general; and what feelings must the name of Laudon have raised in the breast of Frederic the Great! He heard almost daily of the restless genius of this general, who by his activity so often compensated for the slowness and want of decision of the other generals. It was seldom that the Prussian monarch received good tidings coupled with the name of Laudon; often bad news or distressing intelligence, which as king he bore in silence but as a man with grief.

For seven years Frederic had to contend with the genius and good fortune of Laudon, even as Prince Eugene had rendered futile all the plans of Louis during thirteen years. Those powerful feelings, ambition and revenge, stimulated both these generals to use every effort of their minds to make those feel their value, who had previously despised them. Both were anxious to engage in battle and more calculated by their talents to shine in the attack than in defence; they each were impeded in the midst of their career by the council of war of the court; and in their day each had been the terror of the Turks and planted on the walls of Belgrade the standard of Austria. Both were men of inflexible but noble character, and adored by their soldiers; they died at an advanced age and just at a period when the monarchy was on the point of entering the field against a powerful nation.

The unexpected news of the loss of Schweidnitz caused the greatest astonishment in the army of the king, and no occurrence, no misfortune in the whole course of the war had had such an effect upon the spirits of the Prussians; for they had at once lost all the advantage of an honourable and fatiguing campaign, and had good reason to dread the horrors of another winter campaign. At any rate they had to expect a tedious siege and the bad news from Pomerania rendered their prospects clouded for the future. This state of despondency did not however last long, and the firmness of Frederic was imparted to and animated his whole army; he assembled together the principal officers, stated openly to them his misfortunes and his hopes, and left those who might despond at liberty to retire from the service. But none availed themselves of this offer and all now had fresh hopes.

Never had the king and his troops been more anxious for a battle; but Laudon, content with his success, although ever prepared for an engagement gave them no opportunity for one, as he feared a desperate attack on the part of Frederic, which the orders he was aware had been given, rendered probable; and in spite of his great superiority of numbers he had thought it necessary to pass eight nights with his army in the field without pitching their tents. His men were full of ardour, for Theresa in the place of the 100,000 florins which had been promised, had caused thirteen florins to be given to every soldier who had been present at the storming of Schweidnitz There now lay no impediment in the way of the Austrians marching on Breslau; a step which Czernichef had proposed, Frederic feared, but which Laudon would not venture on; and this latter general remained immovable in his camp at Freyburg by which means he commanded the communication between Saxony, Bohemia and Moravia. On the other hand the king placed his troops in quarters and made Strehlen on the Ohlau his own headquarters.

It was here that a great misfortune nearly occurred to the king from the perfidy of Baron Warkotsch. This wretch who was a Silesian nobleman had been in his youth in the service of Austria, but having left that country had resided for many years as a Prussian vassal, living upon his own large fortune. The king had distinguished him by many marks of favour, and indeed to such an extent, but from what cause no one knew, that during the whole of the war he was not required to send in any supplies from his large estates. This exemption of an individual caused many but fruitless remonstrances to be made to the king who nevertheless continued to favour this unworthy man, to receive him constantly in his intimacy at head quarters, and to have him at his table. Warkotsch determined, in the midst of this enjoyment of royal favour, to deliver up the king to his enemies or at any rate to free the world of him by murder.

This black deed was to have been perpetrated some months previous when Frederic passed the night of the 15th of August in Schönbrunn, a village belonging to the traitor. The king here slept in a room with a secret door and staircase through which the Austrians were to convey him during the night. Every thing had been planned and Warkotsch's orders were to secure the king "Dead or Alive;" but chance saved the unsuspecting hero. The troops under General Ziethen had unexpectedly changed their position, came upon Schönbrunn and surrounded the village. The attempt was therefore not made from the fear of the escape of its proposer, and was put off to a more convenient opportunity

Warkotsch, who was in constant correspondence with the Austrians, and was ever thinking of this intended deed, determined to renew the attempt which the carelessness of Frederic with regard to his personal safety rendered feasible. Nothing was easier than to carry him off in the night; his residence was in the village of Woiselwitz, close by the town of Strehlen, his body guard consisted only of a company of grenadiers of which only thirty mounted guard. In the town lay 6000 men of his best troops but their support could not be reckoned on in case of surprise and in the darkness of night time. A wood close to the village would assist in facilitating the attempt and all that was required was a troop of well mounted hussars with a determined leader; and the king, once taken, would soon have been out of the reach of pursuit, as the wood which led to Laudon's position would have put a stop to the efforts of the Prussians to liberate their king.

Warkotsch was aware of all this, and formed a plan which he imparted to Count Wallis who was stationed at Münsterberg in command of Laudon's regiment, and who undertook the execution of it, Warkotsch advised that ten villages in the neighbourhood of Strehlen should be set on fire to draw off the attention of the Prussians. The traitor was to be rewarded by the sum of 100,000 florins; a sum which could be of no importance to so rich a man, had he not thought that by his means the war would be terminated, and had he not considered Theresa as already mistress of Silesia from the accumulation of misfortunes which had befallen Frederic, A clergyman in Siebenhuben of the name of Schmidt was the medium of communication, and all letters passed through his hands; but religious zeal had no part in this crime as Warkotsch was a Lutheran.

The person who carried the letters that were interchanged was a *jäger* whose name was Cappel, the servant and confident of Warkotsch; he was aware of all the circumstances, as he was in the habit of sealing the letters after his master had read them to him, to see if they met with his approbation. As possessor of so important a secret he was in the habit of presuming on the confidence of his master, and only did what service he pleased; it was this that saved the Prussian monarchy.

The night of the 30th of November was fixed on for carrying the plan into execution, and on the 29th Warkotsch had been riding round with the Markgraf Charles and the adjutant general of the king, Krusemark. It was late when he returned to his residence, and Cappel who had accompanied him was tired and in a bad humour; he had eaten nothing the whole day and went to bed grumbling. Warkotsch. accustomed to this conduct took no notice of it but having written a letter to Wallis roused up Cappel and without paying any attention to his curses ordered him to start instantly. The astonished Cappel acted as if he intended to obey and took the letter of which he did not know the contents, not to Schmidt but to the Lutheran clergyman of Warkotsch's village of Schönbrunn.

This man whose name was Gerlach had, from his good character and disposition, won the love and respect not only of his flock but also that of the Catholics of his neighbourhood. Cappel respected him and went to him at this moment of perplexity and perhaps of repentance, woke him up from his sleep, told him all he knew, and gave him the letter which Gerlach opened and read. He was horrified and pointed out to Cappel the pressing necessity of riding immediately to the head quarters of the king; and giving him his best horse bound him by the most sacred oath to deliver the letter into the hands of Frederic himself; thus was the plot discovered.

By this means the king escaped the greatest danger which had ever threatened him. Warkotsch was enabled to escape through the secret staircase as an officer was on the point of seizing him, and his accomplice Schmidt also got away. The property of the traitor was confiscated and he, as well as Schmidt, drawn and quartered in effigy. When the sentence was brought before the king for approval he said in joke:

It may as well be executed; for in all probability the effigy is as worthless as the original.

Gerlach remained unrewarded and died in poverty, but Cappel received an appointment at Oranienburg.

The Prussians had no sooner left the neighbourhood of Strehlen than Warkotsch accompanied by a troop of Austrian hussars visited his residence in the secret rooms and cellars of which was concealed a great quantity of money, silver and valuables, the recovery of which he had considered as very doubtful. To his great joy he found every thing undisturbed, and commenced packing up; but the imperialists were not willing to remain idle spectators of this clearing out, for accustomed to treat every thing in the country of the enemy as booty, they helped themselves. Warkotsch called the officer in command to his assistance to interfere but he replied:

Make haste for we have but little lime, and thank God that you have the assistance of the hussars.

The court of Vienna denied all participation in the formation of this project, and the noble family of the counts of Wallis declared that the colonel of this name, who was the accomplice of the traitor, was not connected with their house. Warkotsch wandered about in Austria not knowing where to hide his disgrace; but at last this miserable wretch took up his residence in Hungary, and the compassionate feelings of Theresa induced her to give him a yearly bounty of 300 florins.

Shortly after this occurrence the king took up winter quarters along the banks of the Oder from Brieg to Glogau making his headquarters at Breslau.

In the mean while the Russians made use of their superiority in numbers in Pomerania. General Tottleben whose fidelity had been doubted in consequence of his mild treatment of the inhabitants of Berlin was placed in arrest and sent a prisoner to St. Petersburg. This general had distinguished himself by his talents as an officer, and what was still more rare by his noble character, his generosity to his prisoners and his consideration for the inhabitants of the unfortunate Prussian provinces, and was beloved by his troops as a father.

Romanzow now received the command with orders to besiege Colberg, which fortress he approached with an army of 27,000 men in the month of August. A Russian fleet of forty sail of the line left Cronstadt under the command of Admiral Mushakow, and was reinforced by a squadron of the Swedish Navy of fourteen ships in order to besiege for the third time with their united strength this place which although not in itself of great importance was such to the Russians; as by its possession they would be enabled to gain firm footing in Pomerania. The Prussian general, the Prince of Würtemberg made every effort to prevent but gaining their object; he entrenched himself with 6000 men under the cannon of and defended by a chain of forts; his position was also strong in itself, having on the right wing the River Persante, on the left a deep morass, and in the rear the fortress. Romanzow determined to open the trenches against this fortified position and to raise batteries; the bombardment of the camp and of the fortifications was carried on with spirit and the defence was most determined. Both the Prince of Würtemberg in the camp, and the brave commandant Heyden in the town fought for every inch of ground that could be contested.

The bombardment was uninterrupted both by land and seaward; in the morning of the 5th of September 236 shells were thrown towards the town of which 62 burst in the town itself and did much mischief. In the beginning of October a storm damaged the fleets and one Russian ship of the line foundered and sank with her crew and all the troops on board; a hospital ship caught fire and was destroyed and after this the fleets left the coast of Pomerania so that the besieged were now enabled to get provisions from Stettin by water; a scarcity of food was beginning to be felt in the fortress in consequence of the Prussian leader having neglected to fulfil the orders of the king on this point.

The Russians had made themselves masters of a bastion which was of the greatest importance to the Prussians and of which they after some hard fighting repossessed themselves; Romanzow was however unwilling to give up the advantage and this led to a bloody contest which lasted three hours and a half, ending to the disadvantage of the Russians who lost 3000 men and were forced to retire.

Winter was now coming on and with it the difficulties of Russians were accumulating. But in spite of this Romanzow continued the siege with activity having received large reinforcements from Butturlin, who after the retreat from Selesia had turned his steps towards Pomerania. About the same time the king sent General Platen who was just returned from his brilliant expedition in Poland, to the support of the Prince of Würtemberg. The troops of the former general were in high spirits; they were well supplied with provisions but were woefully deficient in clothing, and especially in shoes.

Both leaders took their measures so well that in spite of the efforts of the Russians they formed a junction on the 4th of October. General Knobloch had been sent to Treptow with 2000 men to escort the provision waggons which were destined for the supply of Colberg; and General Schenkendorf who was stationed at Glogau with 3800 men received orders to march on Pomerania that he might strengthen the corps under General Platen; these arrangements, inadequate as compared with the force of his powerful enemy were all that Frederic could do under existing circumstances for the safety of this place. The Russians had never displayed so much activity during this war as at the present time; Knobloch was attacked by a body of 8000 men at Treptow a place without wails and not provisioned but in which he defended himself for five days; but at last he was forced to surrender with his men as prisoners of war from their ammunition being expended and their provisions exhausted.

The scarcity in and about Colberg became the more pressing from the supplies by sea being cut off by the return of some of the Russian frigates. The horses suffered severely as they received only half a bundle of straw for their daily food; but what was most distressing in this time of scarcity was the want of wood, for it was now November and excessively cold, and to supply this want some of the houses were pulled down. Platen advised that in spite of the advantageous position of the Russians, and their superiority of numbers, they should be attacked; the Prince of Würtemberg was unwilling to venture this, thinking that the main army was at a great distance and that the siege must soon be raised as the severity of the season and the bad weather were daily adding impediments to the progress of the besiegers.

Romanzow, whose army had gradually increased to 40,000 men however still kept his ground and summoned the Prussian generals repeatedly to surrender. He insisted that as they had no prospect of receiving relief either by land or water it would be more honourable in them to gain good terms than to sacrifice their men, adding that he was determined not to leave the fortress until he had gained his end; his offers were however firmly refused.

The body of men who were encamped under the cannon of Colberg for its protection augmented the scarcity of provisions in the fortress, and from the increased number of the enemy could offer but little protection to the town. There was therefore more probability of their being of service by acting in the field, and both the Prince of Würtemberg and Platen nought for an opportunity of leaving the entrenchments which had become so closely invested on all sides that it was now impossible to bring any provisions into their camp. The withdrawal from it would be attended with insurmountable difficulties from the number of forts and batteries with which it was surrounded; and had they been willing to expose themselves to the fire of these, and attempt to cut their way through the enemy, the latter would to a certainty have fallen on them on all sides and annihilated them.

The Russians had destroyed all the boats to prevent the Prussians from crossing the Rega, and there only remained ten fishing boats under the cannon of Colberg; besides these there were seven small boats in each of which only six men could be carried; nevertheless on the 14th of November with these insufficient means the attempt was made with every precaution, and under the guidance of a peasant who knew a passage which was fordable across the inundated Roberdam. This time the clever and well formed plans of the Prussian generals were crowned with success; a foot bridge was thrown over the mouth of the Camper for the infantry, and the cavalry swam the river, the hussars taking the grenadiers up behind them. Thus was this retreat, which had been looked on as impossible, accomplished without loss and to the astonishment of the Russians, and contrary to the expectation of Frederic; a retreat which may be classed among the most extraordinary which are to be found in history.

It was not until the twenty third week of its occupation that the Prince of Würtemberg left his camp, having by his protracted defence pained the great advantage of preventing the Russians from carrying out any plans and rendering Colberg, which was now sacrificed, of much less value than it would have been had it been taken earlier, when it might have been provisioned from sea and rendered a place of strength.

Every endeavour was made to send supplies to Colberg; as Heyden in spite of the smallness of the garrison cared but little for the numbers of the besiegers and all his wishes tended towards the procuring bread, of which the scarcity had so much increased that the soldiers and armed citizens only received half their usual daily allowance; but in spite of this none would listen to any proposition of surrendering. Heyden, having asked their opinion on Romanzow's renewing his summons to surrender, received the following answer:

We will defend ourselves as long as we have ammunition and bread.

Platen endeavoured to get supplies into the town, but he was attacked, lost the greater part of the provision waggons, and was driven back to Stettin; and what increased this misfortune was the loss of all the horses they had been able to gather together throughout the country. Although the scarcity among the Prussian troops had been diminished since their leaving Colberg, they were but badly supplied in consequence of the deplorable state of the province. It was impossible to procure provisions for six days supply beforehand, or to lay in any supplies of forage for the horses; the soldiers were short of wood and salt, and the snow lay many feet in depth; and the men discouraged by all these ills, left their ranks daily in large bodies.

A curious circumstance occurred on the march of this body of men; the Prussian commissaries had procured a large quantity of French brandy in Stettin which they did not know how to carry away and were not willing to leave for the Russians; each company received a barrel of it the contents of which were divided among the soldiers and filled into their camp flasks. The officers used every means to prevent an immoderate use of this, but these soldiers, worn out with fatigue and cold, had had nothing but bread to eat and this frozen so hard from the intense cold, that it was only at night, when they had fires, that they could eat it after having thawed it, having by day to bear with their hunger. The enjoyment of a favourite beverage under such circumstances was not to be foregone: they swallowed it every drop, many of them falling to the ground never to rise again.

It was now hopeless to endeavour to relieve the fortress by any great undertaking; but in spite of this the Prince of Würtemberg made an attempt to approach the town that he might if necessary venture a battle; the Russians however avoided this, and prevented his advance by the immense superiority of their numbers, although he had made himself master of a redoubt defended by 500 men. The cold was so severe that on this march 102 soldiers perished from it; and the desertion was to such an extent from the Prussian army that in one month 1100 men left the ranks, and the infantry which consisted of thirty battalions did not number more than 5000 men fit for duty.

It was not even possible to throw in small supplies to Colbert, for the Russian, General Berg was posted with a strong body so as to cut off the communication between it and Stettin; the Russians were also masters of a fort which commanded the entrance of the harbour so that no assistance could come seaward. In this time of need however the besieged received a trifling relief; a small merchantman was sailing past the mouth of the harbour and without considering of what nation she was, some boats were manned which forced her to run into harbour under the guns of the Russians. She was Prussian from Königsberg bound for Amsterdam and laden with corn which the inhabitants of Colberg received as a gift from heaven, as it prolonged their means of subsistence for fourteen days.

Werner, who had relieved this fortress the previous year, and who was so accustomed to have every thing his own way in this country, had been so unfortunate as to be taken prisoner in a skirmish with the Russians. He had been sent with a body of men, by the Prince of Würtemberg to take the Russians in the rear, destroy their magazines and to cut off their supplies; Werner, who knew not what fear was, did not take sufficient precautions, dispersed his men too widely, and after defending himself bravely, was made prisoner in consequence of his horse falling wounded under him.

The besieged were now destitute of all hope; but still, having some provision Heyden continued to defend himself; he had the walls watered, so that as the frost continued they were made as slippery as glass. The Russians attempted to take the place by storm but never succeeded in crossing the ramparts being always driven back with great loss; at last on the 13th of December when the town was summoned for the tenth time all the provisions being exhausted, Heyden entered into negotiations; and the town capitulated on the 16th of December after this most remarkable siege had lasted for four months.

This terminated the campaign in Pomerania in which the Prussian generals, in spite of their losses had gained great renown. The Prince of Würtemberg now went into winter quarters in Mecklenburg and Platen withdrew into Saxony as did also Belling who had equally gained laurels in the campaign of this year. This general constantly harassed the Swedes with a small body of men and was nearly always victorious; by his means they were prevented from supporting the Russians, constantly kept in a state of anxiety for the supplies of their army, as their active enemy was ever ready to engage them and every day took prisoners from them, continuing this petty warfare until the winter put an end to his operations.

Prince Henry had made head during the whole of this campaign against the powerful army of the Austrians under Daun and against the troops of the Empire in Saxony, and had gained considerable advantages. Generals Seidlitz and Kleist especially had beaten the enemy on many occasions and rendered futile all the operations of the main army. But notwithstanding this only a portion of this country could be occupied by the Prussians and but little confidence could be reposed in the garrisons of the towns as they consisted for the most part of the worst kind of light troops and of deserters.

Frederic had given permission to a French adventurer of the name of La Badie to raise a regiment which consisted for the most part of Frenchmen and was called *Les Etrangers Prussiens*. This assemblage of soldiers, whose officers were generally vagabonds, had no kind of discipline; at any rate they knew nothing of that of the Prussians. Three companies mutinied as they were marching from Leipsic plundered the military chest which was well filled, the baggage of their officers and other people of rank, shot their major in command dead, took the two cannon belonging to the regiment and hurried to join the troops of the Empire at Altenburg. The ringleaders of this outbreak were Captains Fontaine and Merlin and Lieutenant Estagnolle who were afterwards hanged in effigy at Leipsic for this conduct.

At last the Imperialists under Daun withdrew towards Dresden and Bohemia, and the troops of the Empire towards France, but leaving the most important positions behind them garrisoned; nevertheless the Prussians took up their winter quarters in Saxony but without any hopes of another campaign.

The Russians now went into winter quarters for the first time in Pomerania and New-Mark and the Austrians in Silesia. The loss of both Colberg and Schweidnitz so closely the one after the other became a source of great misfortune to the king as the Russians in Pomerania could now procure all their provisions and necessaries of war by sea, and the Austrians had firm footing in Silesia; to drive the enemy from these two provinces would require much blood, money, time and even more good fortune. It therefore became necessary to have more resources than ever; but where were these to be found? The most experienced generals with the flower of the nobility had fallen in the field of battle, as well as his old soldiers.

The income from the greater part of the Prussian states had not been paid up or at most only in part; the resources in Saxony began to fail, the English subsidies were no longer paid; Dresden with a part of Saxony was in the hands of the Austrians and all the armies of the enemy were well prepared to attack him. Thus the king found himself, without having lost a battle, in a worse position than he ever had been at the end of any other campaign. But what made these misfortunes bearable was the continued courage of his troops together with the undiminished zeal and activity of so many of his generals, a treasury not yet exhausted and a mind fertile in resources. It was much not to have lost all hope.

But if Frederic and his companions in arms did not despair, this was not the case with his allies and his adherents both in and out of Germany; everyone trembled for the fate of the most powerful of the protestant princes of Germany who had hitherto been the fearful rival of Austria and who had ever been as determined to, as capable of defending the rights of the weaker states of the Empire against the extension of the imperial power; and of protecting the protestant religion against the religious zeal of its opponents, as well as keeping the balance between the component parts of the whole of the German empire.

Dreadful as his position was, the King of Prussia was threatened with a misfortune even greater than those already mentioned and of the occurrence of which he could not have the least suspicion. At this time there was in Magdeburg an immense number of prisoners of different nations; Austrians, Russians, French, Saxons, Swedes, and troops of the Empire. It was the principal fortress of the Prussian states, and it was here that was preserved that royal treasure, the mysterious object of enquiry of so many living statesmen and of posterity, and also the state papers of the Prussian monarchy; in this place resided the royal family as well as many of the first nobility; in this city were the principal magazines for the war, and it was the central point of his power, to which an enormous quantity of valuables had been brought from all parts of the Prussian dominions for safety.

Modern history gives no example of the fate of a whole monarchy being dependent on the possession or loss of one single city; but Magdeburg once lost the war would have been at an end and all the laurels gained in the field would have been useless. Nevertheless this fortress was not protected in proportion to its importance, as its garrison consisted in only a few thousand men some of whom were of the country, others foreigners and the rest deserters; but a siege was not to be thought of in consequence of the preparations which would be required, the length of its duration and the army of the Prussians which was in the field. Frederic would no doubt have sacrificed Saxony, Silesia, in fact every thing to save Magdeburg, and however numerous the besiegers might have been, would have attacked them even in their entrenchments; the certainty of such decisive conduct on the part of the king had deterred the enemy from attempting a siege and Frederic was therefore without anxiety for Magdeburg.

But that which could not be effected by open force was feasible through treachery and more than one plan was formed for the purpose. The king had no idea of the possibility of danger at the time that the Austrian captain of horse Baron Trenk who was a prisoner in this place, ill treated, loaded with chains and immured in the most fearful dungeon was seeking for the means of having Magdeburg taken by surprise; and the fall of the monarch, whom the efforts of all the great powers of Europe could not force to give way was near being decided by a man, devoted to destruction, compelled to eat his mouldy bread, seated on the stone destined to cover his grave but who thought of nothing but freedom and revenge. Fortunately for the king his deeply laid plan failed.

The many false statements in the well known history of this man render even the truths which lie has stated doubtful; but the determination, the activity and the clever projects of Trenk for regaining his liberty and which were so often near completion cannot be doubted. It is likewise certain that he was at this time on the point of the fulfilment of his wishes, that there were at this period a great number of prisoners in Magdeburg, that the garrison consisted for the most part of deserters and soldiers forced into the service and also that it was but small in numbers.

The determination formed in Vienna not to exchange prisoners with Frederic was still adhered to. The Notary of the Empire had declared the treaty of Pirna to be null and void in consequence of the King of Prussia being an enemy of the Empire; and the Prussians having taken prisoners a number of officers of the Nassau-Weilburg regiment belonging to the army of the Empire and released them on their promise in writing being given not to serve until released from this engagement; the Austrian minister in Frankfort Count Bergen declared the orders of the emperor that these were no longer required to serve in consequence of their written promise. The king now required these as well as the Austrian officers to give themselves up as prisoners of war in Magdeburg. Some few came and submitted to their fate but the greater part neglecting the laws of honour did not answer to the summons. The Prussian officers who had been taken prisoners were separated from the soldiers in Austria and dispersed through the Tyrol and Steyermark; the soldiers whose numbers amounted in 1760 to 19,400 were distributed in different towns in Austria.

In consequence of all the great powers of Europe having determined on the downfall of Frederic, he finding that he had ever to contend with his enemies at a great disadvantage, and that George the Third, his only powerful ally, looked upon his position with indifference, now turned his attention towards Asia and endeavoured to induce the Sultan and Khan of Tartary by means of negotiations to invade Hungary. The fame of Frederic's deeds had reached every part of the world and his name was spoken with awe from the Black Sea to the great wall of China, and from the Caucasus to the River Ganges. The eastern people, little acquainted with geography were lost in astonishment, at finding that a prince, of whose existence they had never heard, should have been able for a number of years to resist the powerful nations of the west, and not have been overpowered.

The Turks were the most surprised; for they were aware of the power of the German Empress, the strength of the Russian empire and had a high opinion of the warlike prowess of the Swedes; and they could not conceive how these, with the united strength of the French king, had been unable to subdue the sovereign of such a small an extent of territory. The ambassadors of the belligerent powers, who were at Constantinople, when they were asked the reason, threw the whole blame upon fortune; but the mussulmen were not satisfied, and their consideration for the King of Prussia was much increased.

The Ottoman Porte would in all probability have been induced by their own advantage, and the termination of the truce with Austria to form a treaty of alliance with the king, had not the French court, whose influence was so great in the Divan, prevented its completion. Added to this the *grand vizier* an old man unacquainted with the affairs of war was fearful of placing himself at the head of an army. The Porte therefore contented itself with assembling 100,000 men at Belgrade who spread themselves along the frontiers of Hungary; a mode of proceeding which did not alarm the court of Vienna, who was well aware of the determination of the Divan.

The king however received an ambassador from the Khan of Tartary and this envoy, who held the rank of barber to the Tartar prince, a high post in the Crimea, and was his intimate friend, arrived in the Prussian camp a few days after the loss of Schweidnitz. The *khan* promised to send 16,000 auxiliaries in consideration of a certain sum of money; and Frederic who entered into this proposal, loaded the ambassador with presents for himself as well as his prince and sent him back with the preliminaries of a treaty. Goltz, a young officer in the suite of the king, was to accompany him to hurry the completion of this contract and to be the guide of the Tartars who were to invade Hungary.

The Prussian Embassy was increased by a German physician of the name of Frese, who was well able by his knowledge to gain friends and consideration among this wild people. The king had been working for some time at another plan which offered greater difficulties. His political agent in Tartary, Boscamp, had been using all his endeavours to induce the *khan* to make an attack upon the Russians which the Ottoman Porte would have been forced to support, even against their own wishes. It was on such uncertain grounds that Frederic at this time based his hopes.

The Austrians and Russians were now endeavouring to gain firmer fooling in the Prussian provinces which they had conquered, and which until this period they had never been able to occupy as winter quarters. They treated Silesia as their own property; the inhabitants of the subdued districts were offered by the orders of the court, corn for sowing their land and in Schmiedeberg a public corn market was established; a number of the principal merchants from the mountainous districts were also required to assemble at Prague that new regulations with respect to commerce might be made. In the beginning, of this year 1762, steps were taken for the meeting of a congress at Augsburg for peace; the envoys from the imperial court were already named their expenses arranged, a brilliant suite assembled, and houses taken for their residence in that city.

But all these preparations were without result and peace was no more thought of; although in Vienna they had been so certain of it and even without the meeting of the congress, that in December 1761 a great reduction in the imperial forces had been determined on. From each regiment three companies were dismissed and from the whole army 1500 officers; and even the light cavalry regiments were included in these reductions. All the Austrians who were anxious for the advantage of their country exclaimed against this step, which weakened the army by 20,000 men; a measure if not proposed at any rate sanctioned by Daun who was the oracle of Theresa in all affairs concerning the war. The greater number of the generals openly expressed their disapprobation, and the Prince of Lowenstein, said publicly. "Much to be pitied empress! how badly are you advised!" Many hundreds of officers entered the Spanish service as war had just broken out between England and that country.

Pitt had foreseen this war, and having predicted the period of its declaration had proposed the necessary measures; but the British ministry would not listen to him, and this great man, to the distress of the whole nation gave up the management of affairs. His unworthy successor reaped the fruits of his salutary measures and England was therefore in a position not to be disturbed by her new enemy; her victorious fleet sailed for America and there taught the proud Spaniards in the course of a few months how unequal they were to cope with her.

The Spaniards had but one means of saving their rich islands, and that was by attacking Portugal which was by far the most fertile resource of England. They did this, and the English were forced to protect this kingdom by their troops, as the Portuguese were not able to defend themselves in consequence of the ill appointment of their army. An endeavour was however made to bring into the field this force, which although once that of the bravest people was now so degraded and disregardful of all feelings of honour. To do this it was necessary to have a general of high talent placed at their head, and where was one to be found so easily as in Germany this land of great generals?

★★★★★★

The Abbé Raynal in spite of his prejudice for his countrymen acknowledged this superiority of the Germans. He says in his *History of the European Establishments in India*: "All Europe has soldiers, but Germany alone generals."

★★★★★★

The reigning Count of Lippe-Bückeburg who had hitherto commanded the artillery of the allies was chosen for this purpose; he was a man born to command, of eccentric character, highly educated and acknowledged throughout Europe to be one of the first engineer officers. In stature he was like the great Marshal Saxe and his body had been inured from youth to all sorts of hardships. Even when a general officer he fared as a common soldier, and when engaged in a siege, he never took off his clothes, allowed his beard to grow, and passing every night in the trenches, slept on the bare ground. So great was his equanimity in danger and his confidence in the precision of his gunners that on the birth day of Frederic in 1759 he gave a great dinner to his officers in a tent upon which was placed a flag to serve as a mark for the practice of the cannon during the time they were at table.

He was now placed at the head of the Portuguese troops and established an order and discipline amongst them, which if not equal to that of the German Armies was of great advantage to them; a discipline which, although in its infancy, was the cause of their being able to stop the progress of the Spaniards. The King of Portugal rewarded the great services of this general in a remarkable manner; he received the title of Altezza, also several orders, 100,000 *crusados* and eight golden cannon weighing thirty eight pound and mounted on silver carriages.

But even the great talents of this general at the head of this unformed army could not have prevented the Spaniards from completing the conquest of Portugal, had it not been that the English sent a

296

large force to the assistance of the Portuguese.

War was now raging from one end of Europe to the other and all the different people from the Carpathian mountains to the Atlantic ocean were in arms; but even this vast region seemed too contracted for the. fury of so many contending nations, and the most distant lands and seas became the scenes of warfare. In Canada, in the West Indies and even in the Philippine Isles the desolation of war was spread, the country was devastated and men slaughtered one another.

Chapter 12: Opening of the Campaign of 1762

Frederic, who was now without support and almost without hope, awaited his overthrow, which at this time appeared unavoidable. Victories might check the progress of his enemies, but to get back from them the fortresses they had conquered would require long and undisturbed sieges and numerous engagements, and all his efforts seemed in vain. Nothing appeared more likely than that Stettin would shortly be besieged and taken; his keeping open the communication with Berlin indeed the possession of that capital together with that of the whole electorate of Brandenburg depended entirely on the movements of his enemies, who already by a well disposed force of 15,000 Russians had cut him off from Poland, that inexhaustible granary.

Throughout the devastated Prussian provinces there was a scarcity of provisions and the supplies still in the magazines were not sufficient for a single campaign; and in addition to this the king was in want of fresh recruits, horses and many of the necessaries of war. There was no want of ammunition nor of gold; but the difficulties in conveying powder and ball in large quantities were ever on the increase, and even gold, this all-powerful resource, seemed now to have lost its universal power. In spite of the firmness of the monarch, anxiety laid deep hold on his mind, and he now spoke but little, even with his intimates, generally dining alone; he no longer came to parade, never rode out on horseback and laid aside his flute.

The plans of the king formed during this period for the approaching campaign are a secret, as in consequence of a change in the face of affairs they were either abandoned or entirely altered. Fortune had already favoured this great monarch on many occasions, supported his lofty mind and deceived the expectations of his enemies, but her greatest gift was deferred to the moment of despair when this great man, threatened on all sides by the overpowering force of his enemies, was fully conscious of the hard fate which awaited him.

He had no reason to expect generosity at the hands of enemies, who not caring for the fame of their country or the opinion of posterity were straining every nerve to overwhelm him, as he stood alone, by their united might. Nothing else was to he expected but the extinction of the Prussian monarchy; Frederic's powerful mind could not he deceived by vain hopes, and the causes for anxiety often got the better of him. Nevertheless he was prepared for the worst, and had not only taken measures in case he should have been made prisoner, but also constantly carried poison, in order to avoid the worst of misfortunes by being the means of his own death.

At this hopeless period an occurrence took place which changed the whole appearance of the political horizon; Elizabeth the Empress of Russia was no more. She died on the 25th of December 1761; and the death of this sickly woman on the thread of whose life hung the fate of innumerable people of so many different nations, either annihilated or entirely changed the plans of all the confederates. All the hopes of the enemies of Prussia were now swept away as the Russians, the most fearful of Frederic's opponents, had by the will of their new monarch, become his friends. Peter the Third felt as much regard for the King of Prussia as the Empress Elizabeth had hatred, and one of the first steps of the new emperor was to assure Frederic of his friendship.

This assurance which was brought by the favourite of Peter, Colonel Gudowitz, to headquarters at Breslau, w as followed, in spite of all the efforts of the courts of Vienna and Versailles, by a cessation of hostilities and in a little time a peace was concluded with the most generous terms which was followed by a treaty of alliance. The two monarchs afterwards corresponded together and the emperor expressed feelings of the most exalted veneration for the king which were made apparent in many different ways.

Elizabeth had been aware of what would probably follow at her death, and was therefore to the last moment of her existence occupied with making arrangements for the active prosecution of the war. Even on her death bed she had required the promise of the Russian senate not to make peace with Prussia without the sanction of the confederates; but hardly had she closed her eyes when it was concluded. The Russian troops were now preparing to evacuate the kingdom of

Prussia, Pomerania and the New Mark; Colberg was given up and the Russian Army under Czernichef were ordered to withdraw from the Austrian forces; the generosity of Peter went so far as to send as a gift the requisite seed for the whole of the districts of Pomerania, from the Russian storehouses. Peter entreated the former confederates of his empire to make peace; he recommended them to imitate his example in the cession of all the conquests made by the Russians and referred, as his reason for thus acting, to his duty as a monarch by which he was bound to spare the blood of the subjects entrusted to his care, and if possible, to procure tranquillity to his people; this, he said, was the first duty that the Almighty had imposed on the governors of the people.

The French court answered in the tone of those times in which the Nation was a cipher and the will of the king was everything, that, neither the compassion of the king for his people nor the suggestions for their happiness should in the least affect his determination to fulfil punctually the treaties formed with his confederates, and that this was the proper interpretation given by all Christian kings of the first duty of princes.

As in Vienna the consideration of peace would only be admitted, upon terms which could not be accepted, Czernichef received orders to form a junction with the king, with the 20,000 Russians under his command and to obey Frederic's orders implicitly. This came like a thunderbolt upon Theresa who, elated by the late conquests looked upon the war as already ended and had in consequence reduced her army by 20,000 men.

The new English prime minister, Lord Bute, was so incomprehensibly ignorant that he was not aware of the feelings which Peter cherished towards the King of Prussia for so many years and which he now openly expressed. He thought that the new emperor would be anxious to retain the territory which had been conquered and offered the Russian ambassador in London Prince Gallitzin to prevail upon Frederic to give up all the provinces that Russia might wish for, if the emperor would leave his troops with the Austrian Army. This disgraceful perfidy on the part of an ally met with its reward; for Peter gave a contemptuous reply and sent the original of this proposition to the King of Prussia.

Bute, determined to abase the honour of the British nation by his faithless conduct, now turned his efforts to the court of Vienna in order to conclude a treaty of peace between the empress and the King of Prussia, without the knowledge of the latter, but of whose provinces he was very free in the disposal. Kaunitz who was a clever politician and was aware of Frederic's character looked on this proposition, which could have only been suggested to the brain of a Tyro in diplomacy, as the result of intrigues to disunite the courts of Vienna and Versailles, and gave the English minister a humiliating answer. He said, that his mistress the Empress was powerful enough to make good her demands, and in addition to this it would be unworthy of her dignity to conclude a peace through the medium of England.

It appeared, even to the Prussians, like a dream to see those soldiers in their camp who for six years had fought against them with so much acrimony. In the first instance the Austrians would not believe it, and the officers of the imperialists who were prisoners in Breslau and who consequently saw and heard what was passing, could not believe their eyes and ears, but looked on it as a plan to raise the spirits of the soldiers; and when Czernichef, accompanied by his staff, came to visit the king at Breslau they thought that they were Prussian officers dressed up for the nonce. But all doubt was at end when the Russian army formed a junction with the Prussians in June; Theresa having rejected Laudon's plan for preventing by force thin dangerous concentration.

The Swedes tired of the war and fearful of the Russians had concluded a treaty of peace with Prussia which was ratified on the 22nd of May. The queen of Sweden, the much beloved sister of Frederic, was the mediatrix in this treaty, and her brother declared to the senate at Stockholm that it was entirely for her sake that he allowed things to remain on their former footing. In fact it was now entirely in his power to annihilate the army of the Swedes, and to take possession of Swedish Pomerania, of which he could not easily have been deprived. Frederic used often to jest respecting this war and when the proposition for peace was to be discussed, he said:

He was not aware of any war with Sweden. True he had heard of some transactions Belling had had with them, but that this general could easily set all that to rights.

The war put on another aspect, and all the territories of Frederic from Breslau to the extreme Prussian frontiers were clear of the enemy, with no reason to fear any fresh devastating invasion. Once more the countenance of the king brightened up; he joked as usual, sent for his French cook and brought out his flute.

Peter at his own request had received from the king the command of the Syburg infantry regiment and in return had given him the Schuwalow regiment of dragoons which Frederic wished to have. The emperor also wore daily the order of the Black Eagle which he had solicited, and appeared before the Russians in the Prussian uniform, he was also anxious to join the king in person with a large army and every one was prepared to expect great events. With such brilliant hopes did Frederic open the campaign of 1762 in which the Crown Prince Frederic William first commenced his military career. He was but young and followed the example of all the princes of his house who had each gone into the field of battle; he was always by the side of the king and shared his dangers.

At the latter end of the winter Frederic had received another envoy from the Khan of Tartary who brought promises of holding 40,000 men ready in the spring to be placed at the disposition of the king. The Tartars came into the field, not to attack the Russians but to invade Hungary, and General Werner a native of this country was to join them with a small Prussian force. Much was to be expected from this expedition, as it was probable that the oppressed protestants in Hungary would have risen in rebellion. But the Tartars did not advance; they hovered for some time on the frontiers of Poland and then withdrew into their own country.

The king now increased the strength of every portion of his army, but especially the light troops, so that in these he was superior to the Austrians. New battalions of free bands as well as of hussars and dragoons were raised. The *Bosniaks*, a cavalry corps dressed like the Turks, and armed with lances the same as the *Uhlans*, had till now only consisted of one hundred men; they were augmented to the number of a thousand and placed under the command of an experienced officer, Major Lange, who had previously been in the Austrian service, but having been ill-used on account of his being a protestant had now entered the Prussian service. This augmentation in the army was effected with the greatest rapidity and the artillery, which had in this war for the first time proved of such great service, was increased by 3500 men.

In order to facilitate their movements, and to make the most use of this service, Frederic introduced a valuable improvement, which was after many attempts imitated by the Austrians. He mounted some hundred of these artillerymen who, under the name of horse artillery, rode with the light field pieces and when opportunity occurred dismounted to serve the cannon. By this means the cannon instead of remaining in the rear were enabled to be advanced even with the hussars; and the artillery, no longer fatigued by a long march, could do more effectual service in the heat of the action.

Many foreign officers even from the armies of the enemy now entered the Prussian service; amongst these was Colonel Geschray, an officer in the French service, but by birth a Bavarian. Having distinguished himself in the Austrian wars, the king gave him a separate command of 2400 men, which he was to raise. Another officer from the French service, also a Bavarian and intimate friend of Geschray, Lieutenant Colonel Thürriegel, also entered the service of Frederic and was placed at the head of a corps which he raised by his own exertions in a very short time. This extraordinary man, who was endowed by nature with an enterprising spirit and a crafty disposition, had had the management of the spies in the French Army. He selected them, distributed them, and paid them, giving them the necessary information, constantly corresponding with them, and extracting from their different reports the information which he laid before the generals of the army and the court of Versailles.

He made excursions in person through the provinces in the possession of the enemy under different characters, names and dresses, and supplied with passports and letters of recommendation from the ministers and ambassadors of neutral powers. He was thus enabled to go through the whole of the north of Germany penetrating into camps and fortresses; and so perfect was his disguise that he dined unsuspected at the table of the commandant at Magdeburg at the very time that this officer had received a letter from the king warning him, and putting him on his guard respecting a French spy, who had been sent to acquire information respecting the Prussian fortresses. He was ever able to carry out his plans successfully from his courage and his extraordinary craftiness.

The activity and exertions of this officer were of the greatest use to the French and many misfortunes were averted by his means, at the same time that many of his plans were successfully carried out, and this in a country where the French were disliked and Thürriegel could only gain his end by means of money. The Marshal Saxe was the first to discover his capabilities and turned them to account, and the court having sent him to Minorca before the war, the reports and observations made by him were of no little assistance in the conquest of that island. The retirement of this officer from the French service, with which he was discontented, was a severe loss to the French and his entering the service of the Prussians under such circumstances promised them great advantages.

But the love of fame and the malicious conduct of Geschray disappointed these expectations; for jealous of the consideration of his friend and anxious to get him out of the way, he caused the king to suspect that Thürriegel had only entered his service to betray him. In consequence of this, distrust which was apparently without foundation, led the king to have him sent to Magdeburg to reside within the town where he remained to the end of the war. His removal from the army however was revenged on the man who had caused it, for by the carelessness of General Geschray he and a great, part of his body of men were surprised at Nordhausen, and taken prisoners. Some years after Thürriegel emigrated to those wastes of Spain, the Sierra Morena, with a few thousand Germans and by his exertions converted this desert into a fertile country.

With the assistance of Gotzkowsky the Berlin merchant the question of the contributions which had so much distressed Leipsic was now arranged, and the inhabitants enjoyed some tranquillity. But the continuation of the war required fresh supplies and a tax of three millions of dollars was now to be raised; and this sum, which in spite of the diminution of commerce, the loss of credit and the universal poverty was larger than any of the previous demands, was to be enforced by the most stringent measures; the king was at a distance and the charge of levying the sums required was entrusted to hard hearted men. In this state of distress the inhabitants had recourse to Gotzkowsky who immediately started for Breslau to see the king to whom he made the most earnest representations. The answer of the monarch was:

> With so much of my territory in the hands of the enemy where am I to get money to carry on the war?

He was however induced to diminish the sum required to 1,100,000 dollars for which Gotzkowsky gave his own bills, and was alone responsible. Frederic at the same time reminded him not to forget himself in this transaction, but Gotzkowsky, who did not gainsay this, acted as he had ever done without the slightest regard to his own interest, and with every willingness to assist the inhabitants although the town was still in his debt to a large amount for the former war contribution.

The continuation of the system of the court of Vienna not to exchange prisoners gave rise to a fearful occurrence in Cüstrin; a part of one of the suburbs had escaped being burnt by the Russians, and in it the citizens resided and here also Mere quartered the garrison. The other suburbs were already being rebuilt, or awaiting the return of peace, the ruins were being made habitable; and the old inhabitants of the town who were gradually returning, carried on their trade as well as they could. The garrison consisted of only 550 men and this small number were not only to occupy the ramparts of the fortifications, but also to guard 4900 Austrian prisoners; of these 4100 were regular soldiers, but the 800 remaining were Croats, a species of troops which had been so active not only in this, but likewise in all the wars of the Austrians that they merit a more particular description.

The Croats make the best light troops in Europe. The nature of the soil of their country, sandy and not very fruitful, the quantity of wooded land, a chain of mountains, and a rough climate are the causes of inuring the naturally powerful frame of the Croats, of accustoming them to all the hardships and privations of life, and of making them good soldiers. Hunting to which they are forced to have recourse for their support in their native land, makes them careless all danger and they bear hunger and thirst, heat and cold, the most excruciating pain with the greatest equanimity; added to this they have no fear of death. In their love of their country and of their prince they are surpassed by no people, and with them desertion is never heard of; their arms in the use of which they are very expert, are a musket with a bayonet, and a sabre.

The Croats who were prisoners in Cüstrin had been taken at the battle of Prague, and had now in vain for five years looked forward to their release. The state they were in was pitiable; with only tatters of clothes they lay in the casemates with hardly any straw; and as they could not live on their pay they used to work for a trifle by building for the citizens; but at last seeing no prospect of relief to their sufferings they determined to venture every thing to regain their liberty. They laid a plot to surprise the guard, take possession of the fortress, to plunder the citizens, and having supplied themselves with cannon and ammunition to withdraw to Cottbus, where a troop of Austrians was to be sent to meet them. The other troops refused to make common cause with the Croats and left them to carry out alone a plan, of which, in case of a successful issue, they determined nevertheless to avail themselves. The plan, although known to some thousand men, remained a secret to the garrison.

It was at five in the morning, in the month of June, that these Croats began their attempt by making themselves masters of the main guard, as soon as the doors of the casemates were opened; they here got possession of arms and it was now easy for them to master the other guards and in a quarter of an hour they were in possession of the fortress. They now divided into three bodies, one party taking possession of the gates, a second going to the powder magazine for ammunition, and the third occupying themselves with the cannon; which for fear of evil consequences they first discharged from the ramparts, and then by filling them with stones prevented the possibility of their being used without considerable loss of time. The powder magazine proved a great impediment to the Croats for it was locked, the key not to be found, and the building of too strong a nature to be destroyed without the necessary implements; thus they lost much valuable time.

During this time the small garrison which was in the suburb was assembled together by beat of drum, all the gates were occupied by the Croats, but there was a sally-port of which they were not aware and which opened under the rampart. Lieutenant Tscharnitzky took advantage of this circumstance, and with a guard of thirty men, which he strengthened by about twenty men from other posts, and without waiting for orders, went with his fifty Prussians upon the ramparts and posted himself near another powder magazine upon the possession of which the fate of the fortress depended. This point was sharply contested; the attack being firm and continued, and the resistance not less determined. What compensated for the inequality of numbers was the few stand of arms that the Croats were possessed of, and they had no hopes of getting more as the arsenal was outside the fortifications. Their leader was severely wounded at the commencement of the affray but from the many impediments, Tscharnitzky could only receive but slight reinforcements; half his soldiers were killed or wounded, the strength of the others exhausted, and the Croats, of whom fifty lay stretched on the earth showed themselves determined to conquer or to die.

In this state of affairs the fortress was saved by the courage and cleverness of the garrison chaplain, Benecke. Among the Croat prisoners were two priests of that nation, who awaited at a distance the result of the attempt which they could only support by their prayers. These priests sought out the chaplain and impressing upon his mind the necessity of his going to the scene of action, forced him to accompany them; he placed himself between them and arm in arm they hurried to the combatants. At their appearance the firing ceased and the strongest representations were now made; it was pointed out to the Croats the slight chance there was of their being able to join their own army, as the whole country had been raised by means of messengers, and troops were advancing from all sides that if they should succeed in leaving the fortress, a body of Russians, who were now the allies of the Prussians, were ready to stop their progress. To these representations, which were in part without foundation, were added promises of pardon, if they withdrew quietly and without delay. The Croats anxious at the long and continued resistance, were persuaded to lay down their arms and retire to their prison. They confessed the whole plan, and all the measure which had been prepared; five of the ringleaders were executed by Frederic's orders, but of the other Croats the tenth man, by lot, was punished by the infliction of 100 stripes, in the presence of the other 4000 prisoners.

For the opening of the campaign the Austrians, having sent a large body to join the troops of the Empire, advanced with their principal force upon Silesia. They were masters of Glatz, Schweidnitz and the mountainous districts, but notwithstanding this their consternation at the change of affairs with regard to the Russians was extreme, and the officers as well as the common soldiers looked upon the cause of their empress as desperate. In addition to this, Laudon who was adored by them was forced to give up the command to Field-Marshal Daun, and they did not feel inclined to exert themselves to the honour and distinction of his personal enemy. This feeling led to the field hospitals of the Austrians being tilled by many thousands of these soldiers and served the cause of the king, who was now quietly drawing his forces together, threatening Moravia, and having a body of men ready . to invade Hungary should the Tartars advance into that country.

As it was expected that Schweidnitz would he besieged, great preparations were made to increase the security of the town, and eight thousand peasants and soldiers were employed throughout the winter to throw up fortifications on every height in the neighbourhood, so that the hills formed a chain of forts. The same activity was exerted with respect to the fortress itself, the garrison of which now consisted of 12,000 picked troops and was well supplied with provisions, ammunition and all other necessaries. General Guasco an officer remarkable for his courage and experience was placed in command, and he was supported by General Gribauval, one of the first engineer officers in Europe.

Such was the position of Schweidnitz when the king in conjunction with the Russian Army advanced towards it. This junction had only taken place in the beginning, of June, and thus the expedition had been delayed; but the king now sent out a detachment under the command of General Neuwied, who threatened the Austrians and forced them to fall back for the defence of the magazines in their rear, by which means their communication with Schweidnitz was cut off. There were 2000 Cossacks with General Neuwied's detachment, who following up their usual mode of fighting, skirmished to the very gates of Prague; plundering and devastating every town and village they came near. The imperialists were so alarmed at their depredations that General Serbelloni, who commanded in Saxony, was on the point of leaving every thing to hasten to the assistance of Bohemia. The Cossacks however saved him this trouble for they hurried back that they might bring back their booty in safety; they returned to the army in small bodies and many were a considerable time before they reached it, having driven the cattle they had taken, into Poland for sale.

Notwithstanding the great difference in the outward appearance of the Austrian and Prussian cavalry these wild soldiers could not be made aware of it; and in consequence of this, the whole of the Prussian cavalry wore feathers in their caps to distinguish them from the Austrians; an ornament which was now a useful part of the dress, but which was afterwards continued and was adopted at a later period in all European armies.

Frederic's object in endeavouring to get in the rear of the enemy was to induce Daun, to leave his position on the heights near Burkersdorf and Leutmannsdorf; but this general remained immovable, notwithstanding the confusion the Austrians were thrown into by the advance of the Prussians. General Haddick hurried to Braunau and the Prussians invaded Moravia and Austrian Silesia, raising contributions. The king wrote to the Duke of Bevern on the 11th of July:

As the enemy are in the greatest confusion, we must endeavour to put them to the rout piecemeal.

The Prussians returned from Bohemia laden with booty and every preparation was now made for besieging Schweidnitz. But it was not possible to commence operations so long as the Austrians remained masters of the hills which were so strongly fortified; and to drive them thence by force would have been a dangerous attempt the result of which must have been uncertain.

Affairs were in this position when an extraordinary change took place in Russia; Peter had hardly ascended the throne of this empire before he was precipitated from it. He had during the short period of his reign raised up all classes of society against him by his hurried measures ill digested laws, and his want of necessary precautions. The soldiery and the priesthood, so seldom of the same opinion, were now unanimous, and they hated the monarch who wished to deprive one class of their privileges and the other of their beards. The senate was neglected by him, and the Russian nobility as well as the rest of the nation treated with disrespect; the Germans were preferred in every thing, and his body guard was composed of troops of this country; added to this the customs and laws of the empire were set at nought by him and every thing had to give way to his will; so that, however good his intentions might be, his manner of fulfilling them was inefficacious.

The people were anxious, without knowing why, for the continuation of a war which cost them men and money, and the result of which, with regard to conquest, could give but little increase to their enormous extent of territory. The emperor was opposed to this wish of his people; for though equally fond of war he wished to carry it on, not against Prussia, but against her enemies and against Danemark. Added to all these causes of discontent, was his ill-treatment of his wife, who brought up in the school of adversity, had stored her mind developed her talents and won the love of the whole nation. Peter had declared his determination to cast her from him, and to immure her in a convent where she was to pass the rest of her days, and even if her son was to be excluded from the succession to the throne thus did this monarch work to his own downfall, and it only required a word from Catherine to deprive her husband of his crown.

Self-preservation at last forced her to take this step, and in a few hours this mighty emperor, abandoned by every one, and without the spilling of a drop of blood was dethroned and became a hopeless and pitiable captive. Catherine was now called to the throne as Empress of all the Russias, Peter having formally abdicated. Six days after he was no more. This extraordinary occurrence of the dethronement of Peter, which has become so remarkable as the commencement of the most brilliant era of the Russian empire, took place on the 9th of June. As the senate and the people were anxious for the renewal of the war against the Prussians the necessary preparations for this purpose were made; and on the 16th of July an order was issued requiring that all the inhabitants of the Prussian provinces conquered by the Russians should swear allegiance to the empress; and what led the Russians to be so anxious for this war was the general opinion that Frederic was the promoter and adviser of all the changes made by their dethroned monarch. Even Catherine herself did not look upon him as her friend; and although born in Pomerania, and not without affection for her devastated native land she followed in the stream, anxious to complete the overthrow of the most bitter foe to Russia, as Frederic was styled in her manifesto.

This was the opinion of all; the war was determined on, and the requisition for the oath of allegiance already dispatched, when on searching, a few days afterwards, the papers of the deceased emperor, the letters of Frederic found among them caused universal astonishment. Their contents were far different from what had been expected, for they contained good advice with respect to his mode of governing, and the most earnest exhortations to moderate his feelings; all the changes he was introducing were disapproved of, and Catherine had no reason to he offended with the expressions respecting her, as Frederic had entreated her husband to treat her, if not with affection at any rate with respect. The empress on learning this was moved to tears, the senators were silenced and the hatred towards the King of Prussia having ceased, the orders for the war were countermanded and the peace ratified.

By these changes Danemark had no longer cause to fear the loss of Holstein, the conquest of which had been Peter's most earnest desire; a wish which neither the entreaties and the representations of his friends, nor the remonstrances of the Prussian ambassador, Baron Goltz whom he much valued, could do away with, although at the same time opposed by the repeated and friendly advice of Frederic. His demands from Danemark consisted only in requiring certain districts in Holstein and Schleswig; but he actually wanted to become possessed of the whole of these provinces. He insisted upon the possession of the territory of his forefathers, which as he often expressed himself was dearer to him than the half of his empire; and for this conquest, an army of 60,000 Russians were to be sent, and to be reinforced by 6000 Prussians.

This army was to be led by the emperor in person, and the Russian troops in Pomerania and Prussia, under the command of Romanzow were already on the march; large magazines for their supply had been prepared in Greifenberg, Massow, Golnow, and Stettin, and six and thirty Russian ships with sixteen Swedish ships were to support the attack by sea.

In Danemark the greatest consternation had reigned, for the Danes were in no way prepared for war. Their fleet, the best bulwark of an island kingdom, although not without some reputation, and when in proper condition not unequal to compete with the fleets of their enemies, was now badly manned, and not in a state to be able to put to sea in so hurried a manner. But it was more especially their army which was in a miserable condition, consisting of soldiers unused to warfare and badly provided for; leaders who had never been through a campaign, and understood nothing of discipline or the art of war; having no available implements of war, no magazines of powder, no musketry fit for service, no provision magazines, and no money.

This last want was the most pressing, as the famous Marshal Montecuculi was fond of saying, it is the principal and only real want in a war, and it induced the Danes to visit the town of Hamburg; they advanced to the gates of the city and, prepared to use force, they demanded in the name of their monarch a million of *banco* dollars, by way of a loan. The Hamburghers who were frightened and in their consternation did not take into consideration the force of their opponents, their position, and other circumstances, but rather the effect likely to be produced on their commerce and the destruction of their gardens, granted the request, and the Danes departed.

They had now money and in addition to this a leader in the person of the Count St. Germain who had quitted the French service, but who with all his knowledge and science in the art of war, was unacquainted with the country, with the language and with the manners of the people; and having his head filled with French ideas and principles which could not here be available, and with projects which could not be carried out, was likely to prove but a very inefficient general to so badly an equipped army, who hated him from the first and whose confidence he could never gain. His plan was to take up a strong position near Lübeck and here to await the Russians; still the result of the war could not for a moment be matter of doubt even to the Danes themselves; but all these causes of anxiety ceased at once with the dethronement of the emperor.

Frederic was on the point of attacking the Austrians in their entrenchments on the hills when the dreadful news of the abdication of the Emperor Peter reached him; and Czernichef imparted to him the orders of the senate to withdraw his troops from the Prussian Army. This gave rise to a complete change in the plans for the campaign, especially as reports came from Prussia and Pomerania that the Russians were preparing to commence hostilities. The king had only to expect, that from the change of feeling towards him in the Russian court, either this body would form a junction with his enemies or act on the offensive against him themselves. It was in his power to disarm these 20,000 men, but he acted in a far different way, and parted with these troops with every expression of good feeling; and on their retreat all their wants were supplied so long as they traversed the Prussian provinces the same as if they had still continued the auxiliaries of that power. This noble conduct caused the Russian generals to be very unwilling to separate from the Prussian Army, and especially Czernichef who received the most handsome presents from Frederic.

The orders for the march of the Russians remained for some days a secret, not only to these troops themselves but also to the Prussian soldiers; and in the Austrian army there was no idea that they were on the point of departing. It was necessary to make preparations for the supplies and transport of so large a body of men, and as these arrangements required some time the march was not to be began for three days; Frederic made use of this valuable time in a masterly manner. He determined to attack the entrenchments of the Austrians on the heights near Burkersdorf without further delay, taking advantage of the Russians still occupying their position in the field of battle, and of the certainty that if they were attacked they would defend themselves; added to this he was convinced that Daun would send a body of men against them, and by this means weaken his own force.

At the same time he was desirous of giving the Russians, previous to their departure, an example in proof of the courage and capabilities of the Prussian Army. In order to deceive the watchfulness of Daun, and to prevent his being aware of the enemy taking up a position on his right, several small bodies were sent out under the command of the Prince of Würtemberg and of Generals Manteufel, Gablenz and Ramin to threaten him with an attack. After all these measures had been taken the Prussians began, on the 20th of July as soon as it was. dark, to throw up a large battery on the plain in advance of the entrenched hills.

These hills were high and steep and defended with palisades and *barricadoes*, having on the summits bomb-proof redoubts; some of the hills were separated by ravines, but others connected by means of entrenchments; all these posts were under the command of General O'Kelly. During the day there had been no appearance of the Prussian camp not even an advanced post to be seen; but in the plain in the course of the night a line of troops had been formed, which at day break stood in order of battle; a large battery with forty five howitzers and twelve pieces of heavy artillery had been thrown up and appeared to have started from the earth; and another had been erected upon a height with thirty pieces of cannon. At daybreak the Prussians began pouring in a heavy fire, and the Austrian cavalry, who were posted in the ravines, were thrown into great disorder by the balls from the howitzers, and driven far up the valleys; they rode over the infantry, who had been posted near them to reinforce the troops in the fortifications on the hills and who now joined them in their flight. The entrenchments were then attacked with a heavy fire and stormed on each side and in the rear.

Several of the best Prussian regiments were sent on this dangerous service under the command of General Möllendorf, and nothing could resist the impetuosity of their attack. General Möllendorf discovered a path which led to the summit of the heights, and as it was impossible for horses to advance up these steep hills, the soldiers of the regiment of the crown prince dragged one of the cannon up the hill themselves. The enemy now fled in every direction, and these hills which had been fortified with so much care were taken in the course of four hours, 1400 of the enemy killed and 2000 taken prisoners. A number of cannon fell into the hands of the Prussians, and the Austrians were driven hack on the main body of their army, by which means the pass of Leutmannsdorf, so important to the Austrians was also lost by them. Daun had sent General Brentano with reinforcements but they arrived too late, and were put to flight as were also the Austrians who had made a sortie from Schweidnitz.

During these occurrences the whole of the troops, Russians as well as Prussians remained under arms, in order to observe the main army of the Austrians who however remained immovable. But the same evening Daun left his position and withdrew further back among the hills. The principal Russian generals were spectators of this engagement which Frederic had displayed to them as a parting remembrance. He had the satisfaction of knowing that he had made no use of the presence of these allies during the few weeks they had remained with him; for with the exception of the Cossacks, who had accompanied General Neuwied in his march into Bohemia the Russians had remained quietly in camp.

The day following this brilliant engagement the Russians left the Prussian camp; the officers unwillingly as they could not expect to find such another school for military tactics, but the common soldiers with satisfaction as, with the exception of bread which was served out regularly to them, they suffered from the scarcity of provisions. With their small pay they could not buy anything, and as in Silesia they dared not pillage, two pounds of bread daily without other food was a poor allowance for a Russian stomach. When these hungry soldiers met a Prussian officer they shrugged up their shoulders and pointed to their mouths, and many of them went into the camp of the Prussians to procure bread; which if they got it from compassion, they would throw themselves at the feet of their benefactors and then hurry back with their booty.

In consequence of the period for the cessation of hostilities with the Porte being at an end the court of Vienna became extremely anxious as to the course the Turks would pursue; and Baron Peukler, who had already long resided in Constantinople, and was well acquainted with the language, was sent as ambassador to the Sultan with valuable presents. But the king expected that the Turks would advance in September, and this expectation as well as his plans in case of misfortune be had expressed in his private correspondence with the Duke of Bevern. Had his attack on the Austrian entrenchments not been successful he had determined after the departure of the Russians merely to protect Cosel and Neisse until the approach of the Turks. In consequence of this arrangement the Duke of Bevern was to march upon Cosel and General Werner upon Neisse previous to the engagement at Burkersdorf.

Daun was now completely cut off from Schweidnitz and the road to this fortress was open on all sides to Frederic who made every preparation for besieging it. The Duke of Bevern was ordered to join him, although he and General Werner had both gained considerable advantages; for every thing had now to give way to the taking of Schweidnitz. These troops were to escort the heavy cannon from Neisse, the want of which was delaying the siege; Frederic was constantly insisting on the necessity of hurrying the advance, and the duke replied to his requests:

What man and beast can do, shall and must be done!

During the time that the most extensive preparations were being made for the siege, Daun withdrew to the heights of the Eulengebirge and appeared to resign himself to despair; he had had the misfortune to lose the services of General Draskowitz, one of the best Austrian generals, who was taken prisoner not far from Neisse. The siege of Schweidnitz was began on the 8th of August and General Tauenzien, who had been stationed at Breslau, was placed in command of the besiegers who were composed of twenty four battalions of infantry and some regiments of cavalry with a heavy battering train. They were supported by an army headed by the king, and a large body under the command of the Duke of Bevern. This siege was certainly one of the most remarkable during the war, both from the science displayed in the attack and in the defence; from the continuance and many other circumstances attendant upon it.

One fact was perhaps of unheard of occurrence; the engineers both within and without the walls were commanded by Frenchmen, Gribauval and Le Fevre; they were friends and had been companions in arms. The first was still in the French service, but in consequence of his great experience had been sent to the Austrian Army by Louis XV; Le Fevre was in the service of the King of Prussia. They had both written on fortification and having different views on the art of carrying on a siege had expressed and defended their opinions in their writings. They now had an opportunity of proving the truth of their systems in the presence of the whole world, and the materials for such proof were entirely at their disposal; Le Fevre was desirous of taking the place by means of mines and in a very short space of time; he however did not complete his object and was at last forced to follow the old system.

Upon the town being summoned to surrender the commandant replied, that he would endeavour to do justice to the fame of the Austrian arms, and to gain the consideration of his Prussian majesty. The bombardment was now commenced and was continued day and night. The defence of the garrison was very spirited and the cannon were well served; sorties were also made nearly every night but without producing any advantage.

Daun once more took courage and having determined to relieve the town, he only put off for six days the executing his plan, of the success of which he had no doubt. Between the Austrian Army and Schweidnitz, the Prussian body under the Duke of Bevern was posted and was not connected with that of the king; this body was to be attacked on all sides and destroyed before reinforcements could be sent by the king who was at some distance. The Austrians reckoned on their great superiority of numbers, and therefore hoped in this state of affairs to renew the scenes of Maxen. Four bodies under Lascy,

O'Donnel, Beck, and Brentano attacked the Prussians in the front, the rear and on either flank; but the duke defended himself like a great general; the enemy attacked the baggage which was on the point of being lost and some generals were desirous of defending it with their brigades; but the duke would not allow this. He said:

> If we are defeated we shall be unable in our position to save our baggage; but if we are victorious it will not be long before we get it again.

Following up this wise determination, founded on the same principle which had gained the Battle of Soor for Frederic in the year 1745, the Prussians gave up their baggage to be plundered by the enemy and fought without dividing their forces. General Beck had made a spirited attack and gained some advantage, but was badly supported by Lascy and Brentano; the Prussians standing firm in their ranks, relying in full confidence on the activity of the king, and the certainty of his coming to their assistance.

The expectations of the troops were not deceived for on the report of the first cannon being heard, the Duke of Würtemberg had placed himself at the head of the cavalry and advancing at full gallop, fell upon the body under the command of O'Donnel and put them to the rout. The cavalry was immediately followed by the horse artillery of the king's army and shortly after the king himself came up at the head of a hussar regiment; these were to he supported by the advance of some brigades of infantry, but before the latter arrived the enemy had been beaten out of the field with a loss of 1200 killed and wounded and 1500 taken prisoner. The Prussians loss was 1000 killed and wounded, and some hundreds of prisoners; of the baggage which had been in the hands of the enemy they lost but little, the Austrians having abandoned it in their retreat.

Many officers had distinguished themselves on this occasion and the duke was anxious they should be rewarded; but the king would not hear of it and expressed himself thus:

> If distinctions are to be bestowed on every occasion on which an officer does that which his duty requires him to do, these will become too common, and in the end cease to be distinctions.

Daun now marched on Glatz leaving Schweidnitz to its fate. The garrison although they had no hopes of succour from without did not despair; there was no scarcity of provisions within the walls and the soldiers were allowed brandy and wine. In consequence of a private communication from Daun received immediately after the engagement at Reichenbach, the commandant, General Guasco, was desirous of negotiating a capitulation; he demanded that he should be allowed to withdraw his forces but this was flatly refused.

Tauenzien appealed on this occasion to an extraordinary declaration of General Laudon, who in his correspondence in the previous year with the Markgraf Charles of Prussia on the subject of an arrangement, had distinctly stated, that his court did not consider itself bound to fulfil the promise given to the king with respect to the exchange of prisoners, or indeed any other promise. Six days later the commandant renewed his proposals, offering to give up all the cannon, magazines and the military chests, and to bind himself that the troops should not serve against the king for a year. This proposition was hardly listened to and shortly after an Austrian officer eluded the vigilance of the outposts, and conveyed orders to General Guasco not to capitulate without being allowed to withdraw his forces, except in case of the most pressing need.

The siege was continued with much vigour but the efforts of the Prussian miners were counteracted by those of the Austrians, the numbers of their miners being greater than those of the Prussian Army. The bombardment continued day and night, and Frederic who was daily in the trenches began to be dissatisfied with the tediousness of the siege. He made several dispositions which showed that he had no slight knowledge in the art of besieging towns, and he caused a breaching battery to be erected; but the taking of Schweidnitz now appeared very doubtful, and after having expended two months, it was certain that if Schweidnitz were not taken in a very short time the siege must be raised.

This state of affairs had been brought about by the peculiar ambition of Frederic which prevented him from listening to any terms from the enemy. The commandant requested permission to be allowed to send an officer to Daun, that he might he free from responsibility; but this was refused, and by this means three weeks were lost during which time the siege was prolonged at a needless expense of life and money. At last a circumstance occurred which was of great advantage to the besiegers; a shell burst near a powder magazine the door of which was open and which exploded destroying a bastion of Fort Jauernick and killing a great number of men. By this means there was a considerable breach in the fortifications and the following night it was rendered practicable and every preparation was made for storming; but General Guasco did hot await this and surrendered on the 9th of October sixty three days after the opening of the trenches. The garrison of 9000 men were taken as prisoners of war.

The king did justice to the bravery of the *commandant* and invited him to his table, generously forgetting that this Italian had behaved so badly to the garrison at the taking of Dresden, and had broken faith with Schmettau. The terms of this capitulation were strictly fulfilled as had always been the case on the part of the Prussians, whenever they, as victorious, had to dictate. A large quantity of ammunition, shells, and provisions were found in this fortress as well as a great number of cannon. The prisoners both officers and men were sent to Prussia; those, who had money, were allowed to travel by land, but the others were embarked at Stettin at the king's expense. They were overtaken by a dreadful storm and several ships were lost with all on board, others being stranded on the coast; by this means several hundred regained their liberty and were enabled to reach their homes through Poland.

On this occasion everyone in Vienna was much displeased with Daun, and the feeling of dissatisfaction was to such an extent that the wife of the field-marshal was insulted as she went to court, and her carriage pelted with night caps as a symbol of the supineness of her husband. There were not wanting caricatures which displayed as much wit as truth, and which were placed not only on the walls of the residence of Daun, but also on those of the imperial palace.

★★★★★★

One of these represented the siege of Schweidnitz; Guasco was on the ramparts screaming for help; at a distance the army of Daun was drawn up on parade as spectators and the general was seated in an arm chair with a night cap on his head holding up the consecrated sword which he had received from the Pope with both hands as if in the act of blessing the troops. The sword was in the scabbard; on the left stood Laudon, with his hands tied behind him; and on the right Lascy with a roll of parchment in his hand headed "Plan of the campaign of 1763," but the parchment had nothing on it. The remainder of the generals were divided in three groups, the first rubbing their eyes as half asleep, the second gaping and the third laughing at the others in mockery.

★★★★★★

The king now made arrangements to march into Saxony; but, having been taught prudence by adversity and experience, and being not wholly without anxiety for the safety of his Silesian fortresses, he took every precaution to secure them against surprisal, and left the Duke of Bevern in this country with a strong body of men. Previous to marching himself he sent General Neuwied with twenty battalions and forty squadrons into Saxony to strengthen the army under Prince Henry. This leader had been very active in his operations, for having been reinforced by General Belling, who in consequence of the peace concluded with the Swedes at Mecklenburg was enabled to join the prince, the latter had found himself sufficiently strong to advance and for a time prevent the junction of the Austrians with the troops of the Empire. He attacked the Austrian General Serbelloni near Döbeln and put him to flight, with a loss of 2000 men. A few weeks after this Serbelloni attacked the Prussian outposts but was repulsed with severe loss. General Seidlitz also defeated the enemy in some sharp encounters near Auersbach and Töplitz, and General Kleist displayed his customary bravery, and with his usual good fortune beat the enemy under General Zettwitz near Waldheim.

But in the meanwhile the troops of the Empire rejoiced in a victory, for they attacked with the whole of their cavalry a small detachment of Prussians who were forced to give way to the great superiority of numbers. Belling invaded Bohemia and advancing as far as Eger raised contributions on the intermediate districts. The court of Vienna highly dissatisfied with this accumulation of reverses took the command from Serbelloni and placed Haddick at the head of the troops, who displayed much more activity, and forced Prince Henry to change his position more than once.

A battle was now become necessary for the Prussians to retain their ground; Henry had encamped near Freyberg and a large body of Austrians had formed a junction with the troops of the Empire under the command of the Prince of Stolberg. These troops were, as Marshal Saxe used to say like brazen horses, who although the foot be raised never leave the spot they are placed on. The enemy now relied on their great superiority of numbers, and gave the Prussians an advantageous opportunity for a battle which took place at Freyberg on the 29th of October; it only lasted two hours, but was bloody and decisive. The Austrian light troops were put to the rout, and the troops of the Empire were attacked in their entrenchments and forced to retreat over the Mulde. The other Austrians who had a body of Prussians opposed to them did not think themselves sufficiently strong to dispute the victory with the enemy and were driven out of the field, being pursued by the Prussian cavalry under Seidlitz to whom was attributed in a great measure the success of the day. The loss of the Prussians was 1400 killed and wounded but that of the enemy 3000, and 4400 taken prisoners, with 27 cannon, 9 stand of colours, much baggage and a number of ammunition waggons.

A few days after the battle General Neuwied arrived with his body of men; he had intended to make himself master of the heights of Weissig near Dresden and to bombard this city from the side on which the new-town is built; but he was too late, for Daun had sent a detachment from Silesia to Keep the Prussians in check and this body under the command of Prince Albert had already taken possession of these important heights.

The defeated army now withdrew into Bohemia, and Kleist was sent after them with a body of light troops 6000 strong; he destroyed several magazines and levied contributions to the very gates of Prague. This general had received orders from the king to burn several of the villages by way of reprisals for the cruelties the Austrians had exercised throughout the Electorate of Brandenburg; but this noble hearted man fulfilled the order in an exemplary manner, for he had a quantity of straw collected on a high hill and set fire to it, by which means some miserable huts in the neighbourhood were destroyed, but not until the inhabitants had had time to withdraw their property.

The king received the news of the victory of Freyberg when he was on the march to Saxony and it tended to hasten his placing his troops in winter quarters. He now formed a line from Thuringia through Saxony, Lusatia, and Silesia, and agreed on a cessation of hostilities with the Austrians. After all their conquests, these troops, at the end of seven campaigns, were only in possession of the small district about Dresden together with the country of Glatz, and as they found the King of Prussia so powerful, now that he was no longer opposed by the Russians, were anxious to refresh their men and therefore glad of the cessation of hostilities which however only extended to Saxony and Silesia.

The allies of Frederic had opened the campaign with unfavourable expectations as to its results; for although they were promised to be reinforced by the junction of 20,000 Russians and every preparation had been made for the march of these troops, still they came not.

Added to this they appeared on the point of losing the support of England, as the new administration in that country was, as has been before observed, extremely indisposed to assisting in the war in Germany, and did not therefore display any zeal in supporting the efforts of Ferdinand. Nevertheless the prime minister Lord Bute did not think it right to oppose entirely the wishes of the whole nation, and a number of recruits as well as a regiment of Highlanders were sent to Germany in the course of the spring. As the devastated state of the different districts of Westphalia and Lower Saxony did not promise any means of support, the governments of these provinces purchased a quantity of provisions and corn in England and the ports of the Baltic. A fortunate circumstance for the success of the allies now occurred. The Duke of Broglio was sacrificed to his enemies at Versailles, and having been removed from the command of the army, where he was replaced by the Marshal D'Estrées, was sent in disgrace to reside on his own estates.

The winter was not ended when the allies commenced operations for opening the campaign of 1762. The hereditary prince attacked the castle of Arensberg which was in possession of the French, and was important to them by enabling them to keep up their communication with Cassel. The *commandant*, Muret required that he should be allowed to withdraw his forces; this was refused and after the castle had been bombarded for six hours, Muret surrendered unconditionally. Not a single man was killed on either side and only one, an English officer, wounded. The hereditary prince made use of his success, approached the Rhine, raised recruits and levied contributions, bringing away hostages with him. These measures forced the French generals into the field; Soubise and D'Estrées commanding on the upper Rhine and the Prince of Condé on the lower Rhine.

It soon became evident that Broglio was no longer in command; a succession of misfortunes which befell the French Army during this campaign revenged the unmerited disgrace into which this general had fallen with his court. Ferdinand advanced and on the 24th of June at day break crossed the Diemel in seven columns, and surprised the French who were encamped at Wilhelmsthal; he attacked them and drove them under the cannon of Cassel some seeking safety by crossing the Fulda. They lost 4000 killed and taken prisoner and among the latter the greater part of the regiment of grenadiers de France. The French officers who were taken prisoners had lost the greater part of their baggage, but Ferdinand compensated for this loss in a noble manner; he invited them to a great dinner the day after the battle, and as part of the dessert, there were a number of covered dishes. When everyone was on the point of rising from table, the duke pointing to these dishes said to the officers:

"Gentlemen, there is still something for you."

As no one was willing to take off the covers Ferdinand did so himself; and the officers were astonished at finding a number of gold watches, boxes, rings and other valuables of which each took what he pleased.

In order to drive the French from their strong position near Cassel, Ferdinand cut off their communication with Frankfort and General Rochambeau who was posted to keep it open was attacked and put to flight; by which means the magazines at Rothenburg fell into the hands of the allies. Another engagement took place at Lutternberg between Münden and Cassel and the army under Prince Xavier was defeated. Prince Frederic of Brunswick also drove the enemy from Kratzenberg, and took a number of prisoners.

The French had been so much weakened by these disasters that the Prince of Condé hurried to the assistance of the army in Hessia; but the hereditary prince opposed his progress and attacked him on the first of September, at Johannisberg. At first fortune appeared .to favour the allies, but the advantageous position of the French, their superiority and the hereditary prince having received a dangerous wound in the body, decided the battle; however Ferdinand who was in the neighbourhood came up in time to prevent a complete defeat.

The French armies were now able to form a junction, and again beginning to act on the offensive, they besieged the castle of Amöneburg on the Ohm. The bridge over this river as the principal means of passage was protected by a fort and at first was only defended by the allies with 200 men; each army however continued to send up fresh troops to keep up this engagement which lasted for fourteen hours. The French had planted thirty heavy pieces of artillery and the allies as many to defend this post. The first who had defended the fort were the Hanoverians; these were followed by the Highlanders and after them came the English regiments, all having displayed the greatest bravery. Fresh regiments were always coming up to relieve those engaged so that nearly half the infantry were in turn occupied in this ball practice. It was necessary for the French to make themselves masters of this post to enable them to assist Cassel, and it was only night which put an end to the slaughter of this engagement.

This was on the 21st of September. The allies had remained masters of the bridge; but as honour rather than actual advantage had been fought for, and as the French would have been able from their superiority of numbers to keep up the contest longer than their opponents Ferdinand retired from his position, and the following day Amöneburg surrendered.

Winter was now coming on, and although efforts were being made to procure peace its conclusion was by no means certain. Ferdinand was therefore anxious to terminate the campaign by a remarkable effort, and turned his attention on Cassel. The taking of this city which would ensure the deliverance of the whole province from the presence of the enemy was of the greatest importance; and the conducting the siege was entrusted to Prince Frederic of Brunswick, the brother of the hereditary prince, who although young, had shown himself worthy of the fame of his house. General Diesbach was commandant of Cassel in the place of the Count Broglio who had left the service as soon as his brother was no longer in favour at court. The town had been invested for two months, but it was not till the 16th of October that the trenches were opened.

The defence was most courageous, and the garrison 6700 strong made bold but fruitless sorties. The town was but ill prepared for a siege, and there were no hopes of receiving supplies, as every avenue being occupied by Ferdinand's troops it became impossible for the French to relieve the fortress. The inhabitants were in the greatest distress for provisions, and every thing was at an exorbitant price; the garrison from the first had been rationed on salted horseflesh. The scarcity forced the commandant to surrender on the 1st of November, the troops being allowed to leave the town with the honours of war. This siege in which much blood had been spilt on both sides was the last contest in which these enemies were engaged; for two days after, the preliminaries of the treaty were signed which ended the war between France and England.

Ferdinand now dismissed his troops having addressed them previously in a manner which brought tears in the eyes of most of them. He thanked them for the confidence they had reposed in him, and for their obedience; terminating with the assurance that the thought of having fought for his country with such brave soldiers would be remembered to the day of his death. All England rang with the praises of this general and the British parliament having voted him a pension of three thousand a year the house of commons sent him a letter of thanks through the speaker. The English army which from 25,000 men was reduced to 16,000 now commenced its march to Holland in order to be sent thence to England by means of transports.

France was now the most anxious of all the contending powers for peace, in consequence of her treasury being exhausted, her commerce injured, her fleet annihilated and almost all her possessions in Asia and America having fallen into the hands of the English. In addition to these many causes of distress, the whole kingdom was suffering from the great scarcity of specie, the greater part of that of France having either been sent into Germany, or having fallen into the hands of the English privateers. Louis XV., the Princes of the Blood, and the principal nobility of France sent their plate to the mint; but these means were not equal to the exigencies and were merely proofs of the state of need. Voltaire said:

> The alliance of France with Austria for six years has exhausted her more in men and money, than wars with Austria during two hundred years.

In this fearful position her last hope appeared to fail as the King of Spain, the new ally of France had been driven out of the field in a single year by the English. The Havanna, the key of the Spanish possessions in America and the bulwark of their market for gold and silver had fallen into the hands of the English together with the treasures there deposited. Portugal of which the Spaniards had almost possessed themselves was now evacuated; the town of Pondichery was destroyed and the trade of the French on the coast of Africa destroyed; and Canada, as well as the most important islands of the West Indies, was in the hands of the English who were now masters of the sea. All these conquests which had cost so much blood and caused such a heavy national debt to be incurred, were with the exception of Canada restored to the French by the conditions of this extraordinary treaty of peace.

By this treaty, which was concluded by means of Lord Bute, Frederic was given up to his enemies; and as if anxious to throw every impediment in the way of this great man it was stipulated that Hanover, Hessia, Brunswick and the other provinces belonging to the allies should be evacuated and restored by the French to their respective sovereigns; on the other hand those districts of the Prussian territories which were in the hands of the French, Cleves, Geldern and others in Westphalia were only to be evacuated. The previous treaty between

England and Prussia, which in the fourth article distinctly stated that neither party should conclude a treaty of peace or even a cessation of hostilities without the consent of the other was utterly disregarded by the English ministry. The advantage of the state, the honour of the British name and the wishes of the people were entirely lost sight of and the making this peace was any thing but a cause of rejoicing in England.

The Prussian ambassador in London made the strongest representations with respect to this peace so contrary to the faith of former treaties as respected his monarch; but in vain, for on the 10th of February 1763 the ratifications were exchanged. This conduct made a deep impression on the mind of Frederic, and caused a feeling of dislike, not against the court who was the cause of it, but against the whole nation, who had ever been anxious for his deliverance from his enemies, and always rejoiced at his successes. But instead of gratitude for this feeling, which was expressed on every possible occasion, Frederic only felt a dislike to the English which he often displayed and cherished to the day of his death.

The King of Prussia took advantage of the, cessation of hostilities to send a body of 10,000 men into the states of the Empire in order to force them to remain neutral; and this command was entrusted to General Kleist who fulfilled his orders with decision and intelligence. He advanced into Franconia which was throughout its whole extent in the coalition against Frederic; he took Bamberg and other important towns and after this marched on Nürnberg, a most remarkable city and the Venice of Germany. This imperial free city presented an extraordinary appearance; with the manners and language of Germany, it had the government and political feelings of Venetians; with the management of affairs confined to particular families, little freedom for the citizens, and but few good regulations for the promotion of commerce but having a high opinion of its own importance.

The first magistrate of this city had its gates opened to the Prussian general after having sent him a request for terms couched in the barbarous style of the Imperial writings, and requiring liberty *in saecularibus et ecclesiasticis, in civilibus et militaribus*. This language was new to the general, and he therefore promised to reply to every thing so soon as he should be in the city. The magistrates did not remain long, without an answer but it was couched in a different style to their request, and required a contribution of a million and a half of dollars as well as the destruction of the arsenal. Kleist did not allow his hussars to remain idle during this time, but they spread over the whole neighbourhood raising contributions to the banks of the Danube, and liberated all the different hostages which had been brought from Prussia during the war by the troops of the Empire.

In the southern states of the Empire the Prussians were only known by reports, and people who were in towns defended by walls generally laughed at small bodies of light troops. But these hussars were in the habit of dismounting from their horses and then storming the towns. It was thus that they took the free town of Windsheim; and the free town of Rothenburg on the Tauber opened its gates to twenty five Prussian hussars who had threatened to take it by storm. All the princes of the Empire in southern Germany became alarmed, and the Duke of Würtemberg who had so much to answer for was on the point of seeking safety by flight into Alsace.

The Prussian hussars continued to advance and carried their depredations to within a couple of leagues of Regensburg and the dismay of the states of the Empire became even greater as those princes who had been during the whole war inimical to Frederic at the *Diet* now feared his vengeance. Many made every preparation for flight and the boats on the Danube were loaded with their valuables. The *Diet* appeared at an end, and in the midst of this universal consternation every measure of policy and every feeling was lost sight of for self-preservation; the protection of Baron Plotho the Prussian ambassador, who for seven years had met with nothing but reproaches, was now nought for; and they entreated him to protect the meetings of a *Diet* which had so indefatigably occupied itself to procure the downfall of his monarch. The authorities of Regensburg sent a deputation to him and entreated for the mercy of the king; Plotho who was fully empowered to do so, granted them the protection they asked for, and from this time the Prussian hussars came no more into the vicinity of Regensburg.

The Austrians, thinking themselves bound by the truce, had been quiet spectators of this expedition, but at last orders came from Vienna, and a large body of Austrians advancing by forced marches out of Bohemia formed a junction with the troops of the Empire under the Prince of Stolberg. This army marched into Franconia and Prince Xavier advanced with a strong force of Saxons from Würzburg. Kleist, too weak to run the risk of a battle with so large an army, now retired back into Saxony bringing with him a number of hostages, a great quantity of money, and twelve newly-cast pieces of artillery.

The states of the Empire who had learned with astonishment that the French had determined to retire across the Rhine, and who were aware of the decided advantage Prussia had gained over Austria now expressed their disinclination to continue the war. Bavaria gave the strongest proofs of her desire to abstain from any participation, for the troops of the Electorate occupied, the passes to the Danube and refused to allow the passage of the Austrians; and in fact the troops of Bavaria and of the Palatinate were the first to separate from the army and in spite of the remonstrances of the generals commenced their march to their homes in the middle of January. The Elector of Bavaria now formally requested to make peace and his example was followed by the Elector of Mainz and the Bishops of Würzburg and Bamberg; Mecklenburg had in December made peace with Prussia and paid the sum of 120,000 dollars which had been advanced by the King of Danemark

Frederic, now that his hands were free of so many enemies determined that the next campaign should be decisive, and for this purpose took every precaution and made use of every resource. Leipsic was once more called upon and the king required 400,000 *ducats* from this city; the inhabitants now again applied to Gotzkowski and entreated for his assistance although it was hardly to be expected by them; as, when once the danger had been passed, the feelings of gratitude had grown cold, especially as they had to pay their debts. It had been said that the strong measures used against them would have been given up had they persisted in their resistance, and that they had to thank his mediation as the cause of their being obliged to pay the money.

The expression of these opinions combined with their want of good faith in the payments, induced Gotzkowski who was at Hamburg to refuse to undertake again so unthankful an office and which had entailed such heavy calls on his own coffers. But the entreaties of the magistrates at last prevailed on him generously to forget the past, and the king was induced by his representations to reduce the sum required but for which Gotzkowski became responsible. Many towns in the different districts of Saxony found themselves in great difficulty and having requested the assistance of this merchant he took their debts upon his own responsibility; but from this time all the levying of war taxes was at an end.

******

This man, so worthy of respect in so many different points of view was entirely ruined by the general bankruptcy in Holland in 1764. Not a few widows and other needy persons then learnt for the first time from whom they had received annuities, as they then ceased. He died at Berlin in 1775, not actually in want, but in poverty.

******

Maria Theresa was anxious to see the termination of the war, all hostilities in the states of the Empire having ceased with the brilliant expedition of Kleist; and all hopes of the conquest of Silesia having been abandoned in consequence of the defection of Russia and Sweden, the war was now only continued for the vindication of honour. An effort was however made on the part of Austria to take possession of the territory of the King of Prussia which had been evacuated by the French; an attempt which the latter appeared willing to favour, by delaying their departure until an army of Austrians was assembled at Röremond. But at this time Frederic having strengthened his army by engaging the light troops of the allied army in his pay, as well as the Hessians and Brunswickers, was in no want of men and therefore dispatched a force into Westphalia; by this means the plan was given up and the Prussians took possession of all these places in December 1762.

The king had determined to open the campaign at the head of 200,000 men who were to operate at the same time in Saxony, Silesia and on the Rhine; 25,000 men being reserved to impress upon the states of the Empire still in arms against him, the propriety of making peace. A campaign in the states of the Empire had great charms for the Prussians, from the facility of conquest which it promised as well as the large amount of booty that was expected.

But the desire of continuing the war became every day less in Vienna; for Frederic now in possession of all his territory and even of those portions of his dominions, the kingdom of Prussia and the Westphalian provinces, of which he had been for so long a period deprived appeared as powerful as ever, although without allies or the support of foreign subsidies and having stood the brunt of seven campaigns. Everyone expected to see him in Bohemia at the head of his large army, whilst on the other hand Theresa found herself alone and without allies; for she could not reckon on the assistance of any of the states of the Empire, as the most zealous of her supporters among them, weary of the duration of the war, were gradually recalling their troops, from their fears being excited by the invasion of the Prussians.

The scarcity of money was not so general in Austria as in France, but the finances of the state were exhausted; and the treasury not well filled at the commencement of the war, was now empty in spite of loans, taxation and every means that could be resorted to. Frederic was in no want of money; loans had never been thought of, and what was more remarkable his subjects had no war or other additional taxes to pay.

Germany had suffered fearfully during this war; whole districts were devastated and in others commerce and manufacture were at a stand still, in spite of the immense sums of money which had been brought into Germany from England, France, Russia and Sweden partly as subsidies and partly for the support of the armies. These sums had been calculated to exceed five hundred millions of dollars, which in part had gradually found their way into the treasuries of the different princes where they remained locked up, and in part had gone to the commercial nations in consequence of the increased taste for luxury, but without enriching the Germans.

The whole of one portion of Pomerania and a part of Brandenburg had become literally a desert; other countries were not in a much better position, and in many not a man was to be seen; the women working at the plough and at all kinds of heavy labour in the fields. But in some districts even this was not seen and there were large tracts of country, where the very traces of cultivation had been obliterated and the hitherto highly cultivated fields of Germany on the Oder and the Weser offered to the view the same appearance as the American wastes of the Ohio and the Orinoko. An officer wrote that he had ridden through seven villages in Hessia, and that in all these he had only found a single individual; and he was a clergyman.

This universal desolation was put an end to on the 15th of February; for on this day peace was concluded at Hubertsburg in Saxony, the *Diet* at Regensburg having a few days previous declared its neutrality. A few weeks only were necessary to conclude the negotiations and the most efficient means were taken to shorten all delays as peace was now really wished for. The plenipotentiaries who were employed in forming this treaty were not ministers of state or ambassadors but three men, distinguished more by their activity and experience than by their titles. These were the Austrian privy councillor Kollenbach, the Prussian secretary of legation Hertzberg, afterwards minister of state, and the Saxon privy councillor Fritsch. Having full powers to act, they determined on articles for peace based on the principle that all conquered territory and places were to be evacuated, and ail compensation was to be renounced on either side; these were the terms proposed by Frederic.

The court of Vienna endeavoured to retain possession of Glatz and offered to give money and other territory in exchange for it; but Frederic would not hear of relinquishing this place on any terms. The Austrians were therefore necessitated to give it up which they did with its new fortifications in their actual state; Kollenbach stating that his court had no thought of gaining any advantage by so doing. On the other hand the king gave orders that the Austrians should not be hurried in evacuating the place as there was difficulty in so doing on the appointed day from a scarcity of horses. They left all the cannon and mortars belonging to the fortifications as well as a large quantity of ammunition, shells and cannon balls, to save the expense of carriage; an extraordinary present, as the intention for which they had been here collected on the frontiers of Bohemia could not be doubtful.

Saxony was now evacuated by the Prussians, but previous to this the stringent measures had been more actively employed to procure the payment of the contributions. The Saxon subjects seeing the prospect of peace would not hurry themselves with their payments, and the rich people were in consequence arrested and threats were made, that the young men of the higher families would be placed in the ranks as common soldiers as well as that the towns should be given up to pillage. By these means which the generals were forced to carry out by orders from the king, the end was attained and large sums which were never meant to be paid were obtained.

★★★★★★

General Count Lottum commanded in the district of Zwickau in which the author was quartered. This general was any thing but a hard hearted man, and he entreated, expostulated and represented the consequences of their refusal; but in vain. They could not by words be persuaded to pay the money; and it was not until the angry expressions of the king followed up his orders that General Lottum had recourse to stringent measures.

★★★★★★

The operations of the Prussians in the civil department in Saxony were terminated in an extraordinary manner; in order to replace the deficiency of population in his own dominions Frederic gave orders that the soldiers should be compelled to marry. The generals not wishing to have so large a train of women, as this measure would necessarily cause, and fearing that want of discipline would arise among the troops, were very sparing in their orders to this effect until the king required the list of those who had been married. Orders for matrimony were now issued and the troops marched in whole companies to church to be married. A great number of women accompanied the Prussians when they left Saxony, and many young women followed after them with their families to populate the devastated provinces.

The Prussians had been engaged in sixteen battles during this war without reckoning numerous engagements of importance. Twenty sieges had been carried on by them and their opponents. The expenses of the war had cost Frederic 125 millions of dollars which he had drawn from the revenue of his dominions from Saxony, Mecklenburg, and the other states of his enemies. The disbursements for carrying on the war had fallen so heavily on Theresa that the state was encumbered with a fresh debt of 100 million of dollars: but France had suffered the most, for the cost of the war had been 677 millions of *francs* and this at a time when the whole revenue of France for a year did not exceed 307 millions; and the French had therefore sacrificed more than two years income for a war carried on to benefit a foreign power.

The powers of Europe now found themselves after the seven years of a bloody contest, in exactly the same position from which they had started as regarded their plans for conquest; whilst on the other hand the blood of many hundred thousand men had been spilled and innumerable families rendered miserable; a fact which will serve for the consideration of and may prove a lesson to future generations. All the powers which had taken part in the war with the exception of Prussia, had loaded their people with heavy debts which will burthen them long after this generation has passed away and the names of the heroes who fought so bravely shall have been forgotten. The object of the enemies of Frederic had entirely failed; and the hero whose downfall appeared unavoidable to the whole world and who in the midst of his victories was almost doubtful of his safety, now concluded a peace without losing a single inch of his territory.

It was at this period in the midst of the most fearful war that the refinement and progress of arts took their rise among the Germans; and it would appear that such has been the case among the most celebrated people; for it was thus that under Alexander and Augustus, under the Medici and Louis XIV. that the arts and learning flourished and attained their greatest vigour, in the midst of the warlike deeds of the Greeks, the Romans, of the republican Italians and the French. So

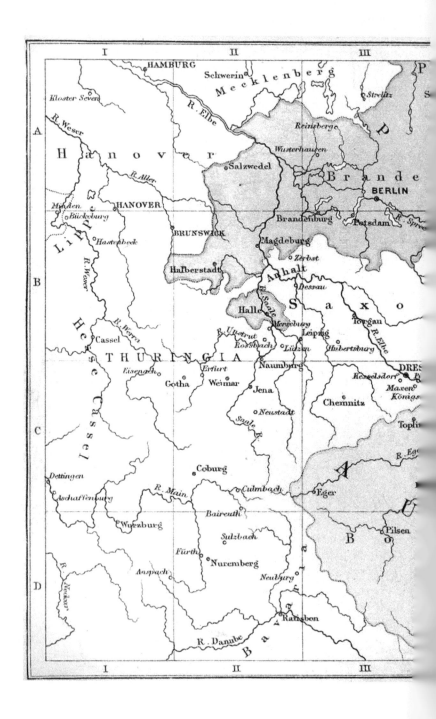

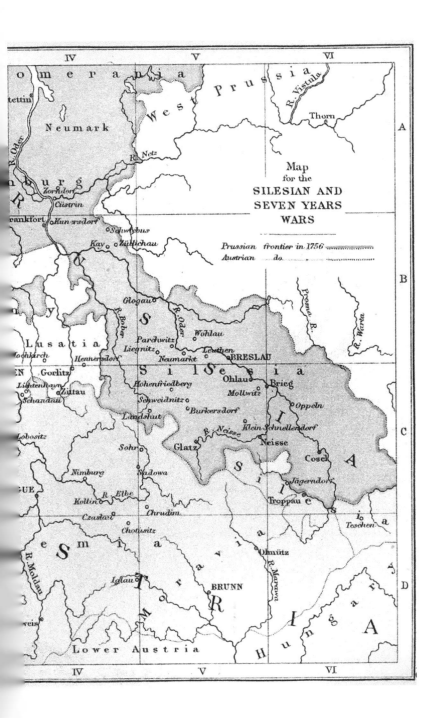

Map
for the
**SILESIAN AND
SEVEN YEARS
WARS**

Prussian frontier in 1756 〜〜〜〜〜
Austrian do. 〜〜〜〜〜

was it in the time of Frederic with the Germans, in spite of the difficulties they had to combat from their language and the opinions of other nations. During the time that all Europe was astonished at their deeds in the field they were gaining laurels in the regions of learning and taking up a position as an educated people that few nations had attained for the last thousand years.

The mind of the Germans once excited by the stimulus of these extraordinary warlike occurrences, the genius of this people now took another direction and spanned the immeasurable field of creation. The muses, who had been scared by the tumult of war so soon after their first appearance in Germania now returned to their peaceful homes to quiet by their softer tones the excited mind of the warrior; and the most brilliant period in Germany was, as in Rome, when her legions celebrating their victories with those of the arts and science, the temple of Janus was closed.

Thus ended the seven years' war comprising one of the most remarkable periods recorded in the annals of history and as astonishing as any in foregone times; a war which deceiving all human expectation is not only so replete with extraordinary occurrences but must also be so instructive to the generals, the statesmen, and philosophers of every state and of every age.

Lightning Source UK Ltd.
Milton Keynes UK
UKHW010012230819
348409UK00001B/160/P